T0237750

Lecture Notes in Computer

Commenced Publication in 1973
Founding and Former Series Editors:
Gerhard Goos, Juris Hartmanis, and Jan van Leeuwen

Christophe Dony   Jørgen Lindskov Knudsen
Alexander Romanovsky   Anand Tripathi (Eds.)

Advanced Topics in Exception Handling Techniques

 Springer

Volume Editors

Christophe Dony
Montpellier-II University and CNRS
LIRMM Laboratory
161 rue Ada, 34392 Montpellier Cedex 05, France
E-mail: dony@lirmm.fr

Jørgen Lindskov Knudsen
University of Aarhus
Department of Computing Science
Aabogade 34, 8200 Aarhus N, Denmark
E-mail: jlk@daimi.au.dk

Alexander Romanovsky
University of Newcastle upon Tyne
Department of Computing Science
Newcastle upon Tyne, NE1 7RU, UK
E-mail: alexander.romanovsky@ncl.ac.uk

Anand Tripathi
University of Minnesota
Department of Computer Science and Engineering
Minneapolis, MN 55455, USA
E-mail: tripathi@cs.umn.edu

Library of Congress Control Number:2006930921

CR Subject Classification (1998): C.2.4, D.1.3, D.2, D.4.5, F.2.1-2, D.3, F.3

LNCS Sublibrary: SL 2 – Programming and Software Engineering

ISSN	0302-9743
ISBN-10	3-540-37443-4 Springer Berlin Heidelberg New York
ISBN-13	978-3-540-37443-5 Springer Berlin Heidelberg New York

Springer is a part of Springer Science+Business Media

springer.com

© Springer-Verlag Berlin Heidelberg 2006
Printed in Germany

Typesetting: Camera-ready by author, data conversion by Scientific Publishing Services, Chennai, India
Printed on acid-free paper   SPIN: 11818502   06/3142   5 4 3 2 1 0

Preface

Exception handling is an essential part of software and system architectures and a crucial element in the tool-set that enables the building of resilient, robust and safe software systems. The term "exception" has been variously defined but most commonly is used to refer to, as explained in the foreword to this book, "predictable but uncommon situations" encountered during the execution of a program. Since the mid-1970s, when John Goodenough, David Parnas and Brian Randell published the first papers to define the research areas of fault-tolerant computing and programmed exception handling, a range of design principles and programming techniques have been developed to cope with such uncommon situations. A 'when others' clause has also been introduced, as it is sometimes clearly impossible to predict all of them.

Having held a fruitful ECOOP workshop in 2000, in 2001 we published the first collection of papers on this topic (*Advances in Exception Handling Techniques*, LNCS 2022), which brought together a range of studies and solutions available at the time in all areas of software engineering where exceptions have to be dealt with: programming languages, software design and modelling, as well as concurrent, distributed, information and workflow systems.

Discussions held and findings presented at the 2000 workshop also clearly showed that exception handling was – and still remains – a vital research area for the following two complementary reasons.

Firstly, while various exception handling mechanisms are supported in languages and design methodologies, there are still very serious problems when applying them in practice. This may be due to a number of factors: the complexity of exception code design and analysis, failing to employ exception handling at appropriate development phases, subtle semantic differences between proposed constructs, lack of methodologies and lack of experimentation. Let us consider such examples as hierarchies of exception classes, exception objects passed to handlers, and context-dependent dynamic scope handlers defined by dedicated "try-catch"-like primitives or via built-in higher-order functions and lexical closures. It is generally agreed that these are state-of-the-art solutions to some of the challenges of exception handling in sequential programs. On a large scale, however, these solutions (whatever their concrete instantiation in a given language) have not yet been used extensively enough, and recent case studies have revealed many unanticipated drawbacks. This indicates that, even in the restricted context of sequential programming, no solution or system for exception handling can yet be regarded as definitively accepted. The situation is clearly exacerbated with regard to concurrent programming, where, despite many sound proposals – largely presented in our 2001 collection – it is difficult to see any standard solution coming; we are obviously still in the exploratory research phase.

Secondly, many new research challenges stem from the unique nature of every emerging application environment or paradigm, such as pervasive computing, ambient computing, grid computing over the Internet, component-based and service-based applications, mobile applications, sensor networks and network transparent distributed systems. These modern systems are growing increasingly more complex, making it imperative for application software to handle errors and other potentially damaging events. It is also necessary to take into account such orthogonal concerns as self-repair, adaptation, openness and reflectivity, which bring complex crosscutting constraints into the equation.

It was in order to address these issues that we organized two ECOOP workshops on exception handling in 2003 and 2005. This book is primarily an outcome of these two events, where a number of original proposals were presented. In a manner similar to the preparation of our first book, several workshop participants as well as a number of other leading researchers in the field were invited to contribute a chapter each. It is only natural that the choice of contributors to this book reflects our personal views on this research area. We hope, however, that reading this volume will prove rewarding to any computer scientist or practitioner who is striving to build a resilient, robust and safe system.

The book is composed of five parts; the first four deal with topics relevant to exception handling in the areas of programming languages, concurrency and operating systems, pervasive computing, and requirements and specifications. The last one focuses on case studies, experimentation and qualitative comparisons. As any other attempt to carve up a complex field into a few neat domains, this one will suffer from numerous exceptions. For example, a number of papers included elsewhere are also directly related to the programming language part. We regard it as more important to foreground concurrency and pervasive computing, which we believe are major research trends in exception handling. It is also worth noting that almost half of the papers deal with asynchronous and concurrent systems, which have become hugely significant in modern computing environments and pose one of today's most important challenges for the exception handling research community.

Our thanks go to all our authors, whose work made this book possible. We would also like to thank Emeritus Prof. Brian Randell for contributing the foreword. We are grateful to Alfred Hofmann, of Springer, for recognizing the importance of the project. Finally, we appreciate the help of William Bail, Michael E. Caspersen, Dickson Chiu, Erik Ernst, Alessandro Garcia, Jörg Kienzle, Devdatta Kulkarni, Ole Lehrmann Madsen, Robert Miller, Christelle Urtado, Sylvain Vauttier and Ian Welch in the reviewing process.

June 2006

Christophe Dony
Jørgen Lindskov Knudsen
Alexander Romanovsky
Anand Tripathi

Foreword

The subject of exception handling, though it has its roots in programming language design, can and I suggest should be viewed in more general terms. It is of course at base just another "divide and conquer" approach to coping with complexity – originally just the complexity of conventional (sequential) programs. Well-designed language constructs allied to sanitary programming languages enable programmers to simplify their task by identifying and dealing separately with various predictable but uncommon situations – typically error situations. Each such situation, described perhaps by a set of logical pre-conditions, can have its own separately coded exception handler associated with it, designed to deal just with these particular pre-conditions, and if possible to achieve the desired post-conditions. The fact that this might not always be possible leads naturally to the idea of having various different sets of post-conditions, one for the normal (assumed to be error-free) situation, the others for various separate pre-defined error states. These other post-conditions can then, if appropriate, lead to exception handling at a higher level.

In a more interesting and more general case one is concerned not with isolated sequential programs, but rather with programs that define interacting asynchronous processes (often running on separate computers). Such interaction can be in order to cooperate in pursuit of some common goal, for example, to search a huge index of web pages efficiently, and/or in order to compete, for example, in making use of some common resource, such as a shared database. In such circumstances exception handling facilities need to concern themselves not just with the structuring of the text of complex programs, but also with the structuring, in time and space, of the complex asynchronous activities that these programs give rise to. Thus the exception handling facilities have to include means of isolating the various error handling processes from each other (that is, means of error confinement) so that the various error handlers can as far possible be designed (and validated) independently of, and operate separately from, each other. Transactions, conversations and coordinated atomic actions are all examples of means for such error confinement.

But when one takes this view of exception (or error) handling it is but a short, and very useful though not always taken, step to regarding exception handling as a means of *system*, not just software, structuring. One consequence, of course, is the idea of employing exception handling as an architectural structuring principle, used at each stage of system design, including before any actual program code is written – ideally a structuring that is retained very explicitly in the final completed system, not just in the original design documentation. But what is to my mind the more fundamental consequence is that an adequately general method of exception handling in asynchronous systems can be used in the design not only of computer systems and their software, but of large systems made up of computers *and* the devices that they monitor and control. (For example, my colleagues and I have investigated the utility of such techniques in several safety-critical factory automation scenarios, in which various machines needed to be operated in a coordinated fashion so as to avoid physical clashes – the method of structuring used greatly aided both the design of the overall control system and the formal proof of its safety.)

Indeed such a general method of exception handling can, I believe, be of great use in what can be termed computer-based systems, i.e., systems made up of computers *and* people. For example, an adequately general exception handing approach can be an aid to deciding which tasks are best allocated to computers, for example, because of their predictability and frequency, and which are best left to human beings who can, one hopes, recognize and act sensibly in awkward, unusual or even unpredicted situations – and then of organizing the interactions that have to occur between the computers and the humans. Achieving an effective such separation of logical concerns is of course not easy, and requires very careful consideration of the placement and design of interfaces, and hence the establishment of protocols for communication between the computers and the humans, both during normal operation and when things start going wrong. Nevertheless, such design if done well can lead to an overall computer-based system that makes effective use of the complementary abilities of computers and humans. But done badly, one can end up with a system that is extremely frustrating to the humans involved, and which is in all probability very unsatisfactory, with respect to overall security and dependability as well as usability.

Incidentally, this more general (in fact recursive) approach to exception handling involves abandoning such simplistic notions as "outermost" transactions that assume that the overall information that has been transmitted to a computer system by a user (or vice versa) has been completely and irrevocably validated. And it involves careful consideration of the likely effectiveness of any planned error confinement strategies, and of what to do when such strategies break down, since maintaining error confinement in the world outside the computer can be problematic.

In summary, exception handling techniques, though by no means a panacea, can be a powerful aid to structuring and hence simplifying very complex situations and the design of systems that have to cope with these situations. Moreover, such simplification is not bought at the cost of ignoring complex realities – the pursuit of simplicity in system design is always commendable, but, to quote Einstein: "Everything should be made as simple as possible, but not simpler." The availability of good exception handling facilities encourages system designers to provide for the possibility of various obscure types of faults occurring, and of multiple coincident faults, in software or hardware or among external devices and humans, rather than risk relying on being able to muddle through somehow and then patch their design when the need arises.

June 2006

Brian Randell
University of Newcastle upon Tyne

Table of Contents

Requirements and Specification

Engineering and Experience

Bound Exceptions in Object-Oriented Programming

Peter A. Buhr and Roy Krischer

Waterloo, Ontario, Canada, N2L 3G1
{pabuhr, rkrische}@plg.uwaterloo.ca
http://plg.uwaterloo.ca/~usystem/uC++.html

Abstract. Many modern object-oriented languages do not incorporate exception handling into the object model. Specifically, no provision is made to involve the object responsible for raising an exception in the catching mechanism. Thus, discrimination among multiple objects raising the same exception is difficult. The notion of a *bound exception* is introduced to associate a *responsible* object with an exception during propagation and allow the catch clause to match on both the responsible object and exception. Multiple strategies for determining the responsible object are presented, along with extending bound exceptions to nonlocal propagation among coroutines/tasks.

1 Introduction

This discussion deals with the control-flow aspect of exception handling, where exceptional control-flow is an extension of the basic call/return mechanism, providing additional efficiency and software-engineering advantages. An *exception handling mechanism* (EHM) specifies program behaviour after an exceptional event is detected and is supposed to make certain programming tasks easier, in particular, writing robust programs. Robustness results because exceptions are an active rather than a passive phenomenon, forcing programmers to think about and react to the exceptions.

The chapter focuses on a deficiency of many EHMs for *object-oriented* programming languages: the EHM is not fully incorporated with the object model. Specifically, the inability to discriminate among different objects raising the same exception complicates control flow and fails to support the object-oriented design model. With the notion of bound exceptions, it is possible to associate a responsible object with an exception during propagation and allow the catch clause to match on both the responsible object and exception.

2 Bound Exceptions

The possibility of exception matching on data as well as an exception type exists in Lisp [1], Smalltalk [2] and Beta [3] through a general mechanisms. The mechanism allows a handler to replace some or all of the propagation matching-algorithm; a handler must then communicate back to the propagation algorithm its next action, *e.g.*, continue, stop here, or possibly return to the raise point.

C. Dony et al. (Eds.):Exception Handling, LNCS 4119, pp. 1–21, 2006.
© Springer-Verlag Berlin Heidelberg 2006

While this approach maximizes generality because the handler can perform an arbitrary computation to determine matching, it makes reasoning about propagation difficult as there is no longer a fixed matching-algorithm. Furthermore, many of these generalized matching schemes rely on coding conventions between the propagation algorithm and the handler for correct behaviour, which complicates the writing of a handler. As a result, this work has not produced a significant effect on main-stream object-oriented programming languages (one exception is the __except language extension in Microsoft C++ [4, pp. 14–16]). While we strongly agree a more precise matching capability is needed, we do not believe a completely general matching approach is required. Instead, we argue a simple extension to the matching algorithm can cover the majority of cases in object-oriented programming where precise matching is needed, allowing a simple, uniform matching algorithm, which simplifies understanding and usage, and can be efficiently implemented. Hence, this discussion focuses on a simple extension to the matching capabilities, first studied in Ada [5] and C [6], but for object-oriented languages, resulting in a significantly more powerful EHM.

2.1   Motivation

Except for a few cases, most languages with an EHM provide a fixed *matching-by-type* algorithm, based solely on exception types to find a matching handler (or the data types of the exception object in languages that do not have a specific exception type, like C++). However, for object-based languages, this approach provides no connection between the exception and the object performing the operation that raises the exception. For example, in Figure 1(a), FileError exceptions can be raised by the write method of objects logFile, dataFile and tmpFile. However, all exceptions are handled by a single unbound handler, regardless of which operation actually causes the error (note, SpecialFileError is derived from FileError). This lack of specificity means it is impossible to know which file raised the exception in a catch clause. In many circumstances, it is unlikely that errors from three different file objects can be uniformly handled by a single handler. When appropriate, it should be possible to easily handle exceptions from each file by a separate handler. Again, our thesis is that matching only by type is insufficient in complex situations, and especially in object-oriented systems. Burns and Wellings [7, §6.2.2] identify the same shortcoming of the matching-by-type strategy in Ada, which could be elegantly solved with bound exceptions.

From an object-oriented standpoint, the conventional matching-by-type is inconsistent, as objects are the main components in object-oriented software design, and their actions determine program behaviour. Hence, an exception situation is (usually) the result of an object's action, suggesting the object responsible may need to be associated with catching. Most object-oriented languages do not support this association, leading to a situation in which an exception is detached from the overall object model.

```
class FileError { ... };                          procedure BoundExceptions is
class SpecialFileError : FileError {...};            generic package FileType is
class FileType {                                        FileError : exception;
    virtual void write() {                              procedure write;
        ... throw FileError(); ...                   end FileType;
    }                                                package body FileType is
};                                                     procedure write is
class SpecialFileType : FileType {                     begin
    virtual void write() {                                 ... raise FileError; ...
        ... throw SpecialFileError(); ...              end write;
    }                                                  end FileType;
};                                                     package dataFile is new FileType;
FileType logFile;                                      package logFile is new FileType;
FileType dataFile;                                     begin
SpecialFileType tmpFile;                                   dataFile.write;
try {                                                      logFile.write;
    ... logFile.write(); ...                           exception
    ... dataFile.write(); ...                              when dataFile.FileError=>... --bound
    ... tmpFile.write(); ...                               when logFile.FileError =>... --bound
} catch( FileError ) {...}  // unbound             end BoundExceptions;
```

(a) C++ : Unbound Exception   (b) Ada : Bound Exception

Fig. 1. Exception Matching

2.2 Ada Approach

Ada [8] generic packages are not classes, but they serve as templates from which specific package instances can be obtained. These instances resemble objects closely enough that they are applicable in this discussion. In Ada, an exception defined in a generic package is bound to the package instances; in effect, each package instantiation creates its own distinct exception type. Thus, the same exception originating from different package instances must be handled individually. In Figure 1(b), the FileError exception is declared *inside* the generic package FileType; procedure write raises the exception. Pseudo-objects dataFile and logFile are created as instances of package FileType. The handler binds the FileError exception with dataFile and logFile using the dot-notation. Matching now uses both the exception type and the package instance raising the exception.

However, Ada precludes having an unbound version of FileError as it is part of the generic package. As well, Ada provides no inheritance support for exception types. This restriction is undesirable as a programmer may want to handle only some cases as instance specific and the rest by one general handler. Hence, the Ada package-specific exception serves more as a data-abstraction mechanism, rather than being truly object-oriented, and is more appropriately classified as data-oriented [5].

```
try {
    ... logFile.write(); ... dataFile.write(); ... tmpFile.write(); ...
} catch( logFile.FileError ) {...}        // bound
  catch( dataFile.FileError ) {...}        // bound
  catch( FileError ) {...}                 // unbound
```

Fig. 2. Abstract Bound Exception

2.3 Ideal Approach

Figure 2 proposes an object-oriented abstraction for matching bound exceptions using C++/C#/Java-like syntax and the dot-operator inspired by Ada. The dot-notation, **catch**(*object . exception-type*), is an extension to the catch parameter and only matches if the raised exception is of type *exception-type* and bound to *object*. Notice that exceptions from logFile and dataFile are handled by specific handlers, while tmpFile is handled by a general handler. Finally, the exception raise has to be extended to transfer an object-exception pair. Initially, it is assumed the object used at the raise remains unchanged during propagation, called *fixed binding* (see Section 6 for an alternate approach).

Can this ideal form of bound exceptions be simulated in existing EHMs, and if not, how difficult is it to extend them with this feature? Both questions are addressed next.

3 Simulating Bound Exceptions

Since few object-oriented languages support bound exceptions, this section examines the possibility of achieving the same functionality through simulation with existing language mechanisms.

3.1 Tight Handling

A simple approach to mimic bound exceptions is to embed each operation in its own try-block [7, p. 136], as in:

```
try {
    ...
    try {
        logFile.write();
    } catch( FileError ) {...}        // bound
    try {
        dataFile.write();
    } catch( FileError ) {...}        // bound
    ...
} catch( FileError ) {...}            // unbound
```

Since every method call has its own try-block, each error condition can be handled individually. However, because the try-block must be *tight* around the call, nonlocal error-handling is impossible. Additionally, this example is not logically

```
class FileType_FileError : public FileError { };
class SpecialFileType_FileError : public FileError { };
class SpecialFileType_SpecialFileError : public SpecialFileType_FileError { };
class FileType {
    virtual void write() { ... throw FileType_FileError(); ... }
};
class SpecialFileType : public FileType {
    virtual void write() { ... throw SpecialFileType_SpecialFileError(); ... }
};
FileType logFile;
FileType dataFile;
SpecialFileType tmpFile;
try {
    ... logFile.write(); ... dataFile.write(); ... tmpFile.write(); ...
} catch( FileType_FileError ) {...}            // bound
  catch( SpecialFileType_FileError ) {...}     // bound
  catch( FileError ) {...}                      // unbound
```

Fig. 3. Class-specific transformation

equivalent to the example in Figure 2. If the first handler catches the exception, the remaining code is still executed, while in Figure 2, execution continues *after* the single block, and hence, does not call **write** for **dataFile**.

3.2   Class-Specific Exception Types

An intermediate approach to mimic bound exceptions is to encode the binding as part of the exception type, and thus, exploit the matching-by-type strategy, while retaining the ability to have unbound handling. Since instances of the same class raise the same exception types, this approach only supports bound exceptions among classes rather than the more general case of objects. A simple ad-hoc transformation is applied to construct the class-specific exceptions. Figure 3 shows the transformation applied to the example from Figure 1(a). Notice two new exception types are created, FileType_FileError and SpecialFileType_FileError, that inherit from FileError, and the raise points are changed to raise the new specific exceptions. The handler can now distinguish between exceptions from objects logFile and dataFile of type FileType and object tmpFile of type SpecialFileType, but other file exceptions can be handled by the general exception FileError because of inheritance.

The advantage of this approach is that it provides discrimination among classes in bound matching while preserving unbound handling. As well, no language extensions are needed, as it relies entirely on the existing EHM. However, there are several major disadvantages. First, there is the number of new classes that must be introduced and managed. In the worst case, the number of classes times the number of exceptions must be created. Second, ensuring a class-specific exception behaves like its general type may require complex multiple-inheritance relationships. Third, it is still only possible to distinguish among classes when

```
class BoundException {
    void *origin; // member storing the object's ID/address
    public:
    BoundException( void *p ) : origin( p ) {} // store origin at construction
};
class FileError : public BoundException { ... };
class SpecialFileError : public FileError { ... };
class FileType {
    virtual void write() { ... throw FileError( this ); ... }
};
class SpecialFileType : public FileType {
    virtual void write() { ... throw SpecialFileError( this ); ... }
};
FileType logFile;
FileType dataFile;
SpecialFileType tmpFile;
try {
    ... logFile.write(); ... dataFile.write(); ... tmpFile.write(); ...
} catch( FileError e ) {
    if (e.origin == &logFile) { ...            // bound
    } else if (e.origin == &dataFile) { ...    // bound
    } else if (e.origin == &tmpFile) { ...     // bound
    } else throw;                              // reraise
}
```

Fig. 4. Catch-and-reraise

matching handlers, not objects. To overcome this restriction, if the number of instances of a class is known at compile-time, it is conceivable to create that many
different *object*-specific exception types and associate them with the individual
objects at runtime. However, this solution results in an even larger increase in
the number of new classes created, and often the number of objects in a program
is unknown at compile-time. Finally, in languages that do not support inheritance of exception types (*e.g.*, Ada, Modula-3 [9]), the new exception types can
still be created, but the ability to have unbound handlers is lost because there
is no polymorphism in matching handlers. A similar problem exists with the
elementary data types in C++, which can be used as exception types, but cannot be inherited from.

3.3   Catch-and-Reraise

The most advanced approach to mimic bound exceptions is through the catch-
and-reraise approach from [10, §6.4]. The parameter mechanism is used to pass
the "bound value" from the raise to the catch, such as the object's id (*e.g.*, its
address), and this association can be interpreted as a binding relationship. In
C++, the latter can be done by introducing a member into the exception class
(see Figure 4). After catching the exception, the passed value is compared to the
desired binding; if equal, the exception can be handled, otherwise it is reraised.

```
try {
        ... logFile.write(); ... dataFile.write(); ... tmpFile.write(); ...
} catch( SpecialFileError e ) {
        if ( e.origin == &tmpFile ) { ...
        } else throw;                               // reraise
} catch( FileError e ) {
        if (e.origin == &logFile) { ...            // bound
        } else if (e.origin == &dataFile) { ...    // bound
        } else if (e.origin == &tmpFile) { ...     // bound
        else throw;                                // reraise
}
```

Fig. 5. Reraise anomaly

start:

- *start with the first catch clause of the current try-block;*
- **repeat**
  - *check the type of the current catch clause;*
  - **if** *a "related" bound catch-clause has been found already in this try-block:*
    - *∗ move current clause and following clauses into new (wrapping) try-block;*
    - *∗ **goto** start;*
  - *continue to next catch clause (if possible);*
  - **until** *there are no catch clauses in the try-block*

Fig. 6. Try-blocking splitting algorithm

This solution is now able to differentiate between exceptions raised by **logFile** and those raised by **dataFile**, which is a major advance over class-specific exception types. On the other hand, this approach increases the program's complexity by adding additional data and code to the exception handling process. In particular, it requires the programmer to follow the strict convention of manually checking the binding information after catching the exception and reraising it if there is no handler for that binding. Following such a convention is always unreliable and error-prone.

However, Figure 5 shows a situation in which the catch-and-reraise approach fails. In the example, a **SpecialFileError** bound to **tmpFile** is to be handled, or a **FileError** bound to **logFile**, **dataFile**, or **tmpFile** (note **SpecialFileError** inherits from **FileError**). If **tmpFile** raises a **SpecialFileError** exception, the first catch matches and the handler is executed correctly. If one of **logFile** or **dataFile** raises a **SpecialFile Error** exception, the first catch also matches but the binding fails, and therefore, the exception is reraised. However, because a catch clause has already been matched for the guarded block, the reraise cannot perform further matching on the lexically following catch clauses of the same try-block. Thus, the catch-and-reraise strategy cannot reach the second catch clause, which would otherwise

```
                                          try {
           try {                             try {
             ...                               ...
           } catch( Type₁ ) {...}            } catch( Type₁ ) {...}
             catch( Type₂ ) {...}              catch( Type₂ ) {...}
             ...                               ...
             catch( Typeₖ ) {...}              catch( Typeₖ ) {...}
             catch( Typeₖ₊₁ ) {...}         } catch( Typeₖ₊₁ ) {...}
             catch( Typeₖ₊₂ ) {...}           catch( Typeₖ₊₂ ) {...}
             ...                               ...
             catch( Typeₙ ) {...}             catch( Typeₙ ) {...}
```

Fig. 7. Quasi-equivalent try-blocks

match and handle the exception. This behaviour is counter-intuitive, does not match the usual semantics of exception handling, and results in control flow that is difficult to predict. This anomaly is also discussed in [10, §6.4].

3.4   Enhanced Catch-and-Reraise

The solution to the reraise anomaly is to not let a catch clause lexically follow a related bound clause in the same try-block, where catch clauses are "related" if there exists an exception type all can match [11]. A typical example of related catch-clauses are those handling both derived and base exception types in the same try-block. For multiple inheritance, the derived type can be caught by catch clauses for its base types. Hence, these base-type catch-clauses are related to their derived types *and* with each other even if they have no common ancestor.

   To prevent the anomaly, related catch clauses must be separated into different (nested) try-blocks, but since the order of catch clauses is important, the catch clauses lexically following a related one must also go into the containing try-block. Figure 6 is the algorithm for try-block splitting.

Theory of Try-Block Splitting. The try-block splitting algorithm works because the two constructs in Figure 7 are logically equivalent if raises inside the handlers are ignored. The propagation mechanism sequentially checks all handlers, regardless of the number of nested try-blocks. Should one handler match, execution continues at the end of the outermost try-block as there is no code between the two try-blocks. By induction, it is possible to show that this quasi-equivalence holds for an arbitrary number of splittings ($< n$) and resulting try-blocks ($\leq n$).

   If the equivalence were perfect, this approach would be useless since it just changes the code but not the way it works. Now, consider raises inside handlers. In the catch-and-reraise approach, the problem is that an exception that is caught but rejected, and hence reraised, is not matched against following

```
class Beatles { };
class John : public Beatles { };
class Paul : public Beatles { };
class George : public Beatles { };
class Ringo : public Beatles { };

// binding objects
AlbumClass white, pepper;

try {
    ...
} catch( Paul ) {
    // A
    throw;   // original reraise
} catch(pepper.Beatles &e){
    // B
} catch( white.Ringo e ) {
    // C
} catch( John ) {
    // D
} catch( white.Beatles ) {
    // E
} catch( George ) {
    // F
} // try
```

(a) before

```
{
  bool OrigThrow = false;
  try {
    try {
      try {
        try {
          ...
        } catch( Paul ) {
          // A
// user-defined reraise, set flag
          OrigThrow = true;
          throw;  // original reraise
        } catch( Beatles &e ) {
          if ( e.origin == &pepper ) {
            // B
          } else
            throw; // inserted reraise
        } // try
      } catch( Ringo e ) {
        if ( e.origin == &white ) {
// if binding matches, handle exception
          // C
        } else
          throw; // if not reraise
      } catch( John ) {
        // D
      } // try
    } catch( Beatles UniqueIdent ) {
// catch exception, give it a name
// check flag in every subsequent eligible handler
      if ( OrigThrow )
        throw; // accidentally caught exception
      if ( UniqueIdent.origin == &white ) {
        // E
      } else
        throw;
    } // try
  } catch( George ) {
    // F
  } // try
}
```

(b) after

Fig. 8. Try-block splitting conversion

handlers. If there is a second try-block enclosing the first one, the handlers of
that second try-block can now catch the exception that would otherwise not be
checked, fixing the catch-and-reraise anomaly.

Problems Creating New Try-Blocks. However, preexisting raises inside handlers, *i.e.*, raises not part of the try-block splitting, now cause a problem. If preexisting raises or reraises appear inside one of the handlers, the correctness of the code fails as a raised exception might be handled by a handler in one of the enclosing try-blocks created as part of try-block splitting. To deal with this problem, preexisting raises and those of the catch-and-reraise mechanism are distinguished. The distinction is accomplished by defining a boolean variable in a new block before the beginning of the original try-block. This variable is used to indicate if the current exception is preexisting. Subsequent handlers check this variable and ignore the exception (*i.e.*, reraise it) if they accidentally catch it. After handling the exception, the variable is destroyed by automatic storage management when the block terminates. Note, the requirement to initialize a boolean variable incurs a run-time cost even in the absence of raises, which is generally considered undesirable [12, §16.2].

Try-Block Splitting Example. Figure 8(a) shows a bound exception example using the proposed syntax from Section 2.3 and Figure 8(b) shows its conversion following the enhanced catch-and-reraise approach. In Figure 8(b), handlers A and B stay in the same try-block, as the catch clause for Paul is unbound (even though the handlers are related). Handler C is separated into a new try-block, as handler B is in a bound catch clause of type Beatles, which is related to C's type Ringo. Handlers C and D remain in the same try-block, as types Ringo and John are unrelated. Handler E is separated into a new try-block, as its type Beatles is related to Ringo in C's catch clause. Finally, F is separated into a new try-block, as its type George is related to E's type Beatles. Variable OrigThrow is set to indicate the currently propagated exception is the result of a preexisting raise (for more complex cases, setting OrigThrow can be more complicated). It is checked in all subsequent handlers that can catch the reraised Paul exception, *e.g.*, in E since E handles Beatles exceptions that can catch a reraised Paul exception. This check is unnecessary in B's catch clause as it is in the same try block as the reraise, and hence, cannot catch it.

While the enhanced catch-and reraise approach can mimic bound exceptions with conventional exception handling, the conversion is complicated, can produce large amounts of additional code, and introduces a runtime-cost in the absence of raises. It is unreasonable for a programmer to write this much extra code to replace a missing language feature. Additionally, enforcing such a programming convention – especially if it is as complicated as in this case – cannot be a reliable practice. Therefore, if bound exceptions are a desirable feature, it is necessary to implement them as part of the language.

4   Designing Bound Exceptions

This section examines the issues of inserting bound exceptions into C++ and μC++ [13]: where and how bound exceptions can be declared, as well as when and how the binding occurs and to which object an exception is bound.

4.1   Bound Exceptions Declaration

There are multiple options for declaring a bound exception.

Class Member. Due to the way generic packages work in Ada, every bound exception is part of the instance it is bound to. Looking for an analogy in C++, defining bound exceptions as members of a class would make them part of the objects they are bound to, *e.g.*:

```
class FileError {...};
class FileType {
    FileError err;      // bound exception
    ...
};
```

However, for C++, this design is unreasonable for various reasons. First, for every (containing) object instance, an exception instance is created, even if the exception is never thrown. Creating these exception instances is a potential waste of storage since even empty objects must have a unique address, and hence, require some storage.

Second, this approach forces the exception to be constructed before any possible raise point. Hence, the exception's constructor cannot be used to pass local arguments at the raise into the exception instance, and thus, to the handler. Instead, additional methods must be defined in order to pass information into the exception object, which is clumsy at best.

Class Scope. C++ also offers the possibility to declare the exception type inside the scope of a class. So instead of making the bound exception a member of the class, it is possible to declare its type inside the class and then access it with the :: operator, *e.g.*:

```
class FileType {
    class FileError {...};  // declaration in class-scope
    void write() {
        ... throw FileType::FileError( "Disk full" ); ...
    }
};
```

Exception types declared outside classes remain unbound. The advantage of the class-scope approach is the lexical association between the exception and the bound object through declaring the exception inside the object's class. Also, class-scope exception types do not take up space or require construction when the enclosing class is instantiated.

The disadvantage of the class-scope approach is the requirement to add exception classes into existing classes of legacy programs (ones that were not intended to use bound exceptions). This requirement precludes using class-scope exceptions with legacy code containing unbound exceptions, *i.e.*, it would be convenient if binding capabilities could be added to existing code just by (or even without) recompiling it. Of course, this code could not use (*i.e.*, catch) bound exceptions as it is unaware of this capability (or the concept), but it could be made to raise them by including a binding object in the propagation. Note, these legacy issues also apply to bound exceptions defined as class members.

Therefore, declaring exceptions as a class member or using class scope is undesirable for bound exceptions. Furthermore, the location in which an exception is declared should not affect its binding character. A programmer should decide to declare exceptions inside classes due to the program design, not due to syntactic requirements of the EHM.

Qualifier. Since the declaration location is dismissed for defining the binding characteristic, a binding *qualifier* is examined, which can be specified as part of the exception type, the handler, or the raise.

Exception type: The binding characteristic can be specified as part of the exception type, *e.g.*:

```
class Overflow  { ... };          // unbound
bound class FileError { ... };    // bound
```

The bound qualifier makes instances of FileError bound, while instances of Overflow are unbound. However, this solution is unsuitable for reasons similar to the ones for the class-scope approach. Again, a class which is not planned to be used as a bound exception could never become one because of legacy issues with syntax and semantics. Additionally, the classification of some exception classes as bound and others as unbound is inconsistent with the C++ approach of allowing any object to be used in any exception context. It is better to give every exception class the potential to be unbound or bound.

Handler: The binding characteristic can be specified as part of the handler. Using the proposed syntax from Section 2.3, it is possible to write **catch**(obj.FileError) to handle a FileError bound to obj. It is also possible to write **catch**(FileError) to handle an unbound version of FileError. In fact, it makes sense for the second catch clause to also deal with the bound versions of FileError since those are just special cases of FileError (see also the discussion in Section 2.2).

Raise: The binding characteristic can be specified as part of the raise. An example would be **throw** FileError() to raise an unbound FileError exception and **boundthrow** FileError() to raise a bound FileError exception.

Given that associating the binding character as part of the exception type is rejected, Table 1 summarizes the four possible combinations of unbound/bound catching/raising and the resulting handling (it is assumed that the exception types match in all cases). In case 1) the catch and raise are unbound, which is conventional exception handling with unbound handler matching. In case 2) the catch is unbound and the raise bound, so the handler is not object-specific. The unbound catch-clause can handle *all* exceptions of that type, both unbound

Table 1. Unbound/bound catching/raising options

	unbound raise	bound raise
unbound catch	1) unbound	2) unbound
bound catch	3) not handled	4) bound

and bound. Hence, the bound exception is handled by an unbound handler. In case 3) the catch is bound and the raise unbound, but the bound catch-clause cannot handle this exception because it is unbound. Case 4) is a bound catch and a bound raise (to the same object), so the catch clause is able to provide an object-specific handler and the exception is handled as a bound exception.

It is possible to simplify the table, with only minor loss in functionality, by defining all raises to be bound, *i.e.*, always associate the object raising the exception with the exception. In this design, no functionality is lost between Case 1) and Case 2), as both perform an unbound catch. However, the functionality of Case 3) is eliminated as there is always a binding at the raise. In general, it seems questionable to prematurely restrict an exception to unbound handling at the raise since a bound handler should be as well suited (or probably better) to handle it as an unbound handler. Nevertheless, this questionable functionality is still achievable through a mechanism presented in Section 4.2 (null binding value). Hence, making all raises bound eliminates the left column, so *all* raises, and hence, *all* exceptions become bound. Now the binding decision is made solely in the catch clause.

A positive consequence of this design decision is that legacy code continues to work with existing exceptions, while gaining the ability to implicitly raise bound exceptions (possibly by recompiling). That is, the binding information is an additional option that can be used or is completely transparent if it is not used. A negative consequence is that all raises now require additional memory for the binding information and time to store the binding information, regardless of whether the binding information is used. However, the additional space is marginal compared to the memory usually allocated for normal (unbound) exception handling purposes in current implementations. Also, a raise only occurs in exceptional situations and the performance during exceptional situations is usually slower than during normal situations. Therefore, the space and time overhead is not considered to be a problem when offset by the simplification in the design.

4.2 Object Binding

It has already been argued that the object responsible for raising the exception should be designated the bound object. The reason is that an object's actions take place in its member functions, which suggests this is also where exceptions are raised. Hence, if an exception is raised inside an object's member function, it should naturally be bound to that object (since all exceptions can be logically bound). Thus, the bound-to object is defined as the one whose member function contains the raise. For non-member functions (*i.e.*, global functions) as well as static class-members, there is no object. Therefore, exceptions raised inside these functions have an empty (null) binding. Hence, if a programmer does not want an exception raised inside an object's member to have a direct binding, it is possible to define a static member routine for the sole purpose of raising that exception.

A consequence of this design is that it is impossible to raise an exception bound to a *different* object (*e.g.*, **throw** logFile.FileError). Such a possibility weakens the object-oriented design of a program and is therefore rejected. To achieve the same functionality, it is possible to define a member function inside FileType for the sole purpose of raising a FileType exception (*e.g.*, logFile.raiseFileErrorException();).

5 μC++ Design

μC++ is a dialect of C++, providing high-level object extensions, such as coroutines, monitors and tasks, as well as advanced exception-handling features such as resumption and nonlocal exceptions. When trying to extend the design of bound exceptions to μC++, it is necessary to consider these advanced exception handling features.

5.1 Resumption

In addition to termination, μC++ provides a resumption handing model, in which the handler returns and execution continues after the raise. Interestingly, extending the concept of bound exceptions to resumption is straight-forward since there are no differences during propagation with bound matching between termination and resumption exceptions (other small differences may exist).

5.2 Nonlocal Exceptions

For both termination and resumption exceptions, μC++ provides the concept of nonlocal propagation. Through this feature, it is possible to raise (send) either kind of exception from a source to a faulting execution. More precisely, it is possible to raise exceptions between coroutines during synchronous execution, and between tasks during asynchronous execution.

The issue with nonlocal exceptions is the object binding. The binding rule in Section 4.2 is inappropriate for nonlocal exceptions because the object raising the nonlocal exception in the source execution may not be meaningful or even known in the faulting execution. Even if the faulting execution "knows" the object, it does not mean it knows any of the circumstances leading to the exception, as these circumstances occurred in the source execution. In the worst case, the programmer must prepare bound handlers in the faulting execution for all possible objects generating nonlocal exceptions, because the faulting execution does not know what code the source execution is executing. For concurrent exceptions, nonlocal exceptions can essentially happen anytime, anywhere [1].

A better solution is to bind the exception to the source execution, so it appears to the faulting execution that the nonlocal exception emanates from the source

---

[1] There are clearly defined times when exceptions are delivered, but some of them cannot be anticipated by an execution.

execution. For example, concurrent exceptions can provide a special form of inter-task communication, and it is helpful to control delivery of exceptions by senders, *i.e.*, provide different handlers for the same exceptions sent by different tasks. For the case where a coroutine or task does not care about the specific tasks sending it nonlocal exceptions, *e.g.*, clients communicating with a server, it is possible to process the exceptions using unbound handlers.

6   Transient Binding

This section introduces *transient binding*, a new kind of binding strategy, which has advantages over fixed binding.

6.1   Fixed Binding Problems

The problem with fixed binding is that the object raising the exception may be a local variable of a block. Therefore, once the exceptions is propagated outside of the declaring block, the binding object is deallocated, and therefore, useless as it references a nonexistent object. Alternatively, an object can be passed as an argument and it can raise an exception when used. However, the argument object may not be visible to the user of an object referencing the argument object. These cases are illustrated in Figure 9.

```
class Database {
    FileType f;   // or alternatively: FileType &f
    public:       // for initialization through constructor
      void commit() {
          try {
              ... f.write(); ...   // raises FileError
          } catch( f.FileError ) {...} // OK
      }
};
void DB_Manager::flush( Database &db ) {
      try {
          db.commit();
      } catch( f.FileError ) {...}    // syntax error
        catch( db.FileError ) {...}  // OK, but never matched
}
Database db(...);
class Driver {
    public:
      static void run() {
          DB_Manager dbman;
          dbman.flush( db );
      }
};
```

Fig. 9. Fixed binding problems

The global declaration of db can pass a file for initializing variable Database::f or Database::f can be a local variable. In either case, routine DB_Manager::flush does not know about this file object (especially if these components are separately compiled). Now the catch clause inside commit is within the scope of f, so it can catch any exceptions raised by f. However, the attempted catches in flush are syntactically or semantically incorrect, but logically correct. The first catch is syntactically incorrect since f is invisible inside the scope of flush (unless coincidentally there is an f variable in the current scope, which would result in a difficult to locate error). The second catch is semantically incorrect since db does not raise the bound exception FileError, so this catch is never matched. While these catch clauses are wrong, logically the user is trying to do the correct thing. That is, catch the specific FileError exception associated with its operation (flush), but not catch FileError exceptions associated with other operations, which might be handled at a higher level of abstraction. In fact, the catch clause catch(db.FileError) is probably what a user really wants to write, as db exists in the current scope and (from a logical point of view) is responsible for raising the exception. Thus, there are reasonable situations in which fixed binding is inadequate for nonlocal error handling.

It is conceivable for Database to provide some kind of direct or indirect mechanism to reveal f, *e.g.*:

```
catch( (db.f).FileError ) {...}          // direct
catch( db.access_f().FileError )         // indirect
```

However, neither mechanism is appealing, safe or good software engineering. Furthermore, these negative properties are exacerbated by an explosion in access methods because methods must be supplied for every internal object raising exceptions, and recursively for every object that these objects use.

6.2 Principle of Transient Binding

Most fixed-binding problems could be solved if the exception changed its binding during propagation at each object it traverses through, *e.g.*, from f to db in Figure 9 when moving from commit into flush. Then db can be used as the binding in the catch clause of flush to catch the FileError exception. It is now sufficient to know that Database can raise (or rather propagate) a FileError exception. Thus, all the fixed-binding issues are eliminated once the bound-to object is re-associated from f to db. Most importantly, this solution matches the common-sense expectation that if an exception is raised as a result of a call to db.commit(), then db is actually the object responsible for the raise, and hence, is the one to which the exception should be bound. Similarly, Driver::run, which calls flush, expects an exception to be bound to dbman and not to db, as ideally, it knows nothing about the implementation of flush or how db is used inside it. The formal rule for transient binding is: in any given try-block, the exception is bound to the object associated with the member call in that block responsible for raising the exception.

```
class Database {
    FileType f;
  public:
    void commit() {
        try {
            ... f.write(); ...  // raises FileError
        } catch( FileError e ) {... throw e; ...} // change bound object
    }                                             // by catch and reraise
};
void DB_Manager::flush( Database &db ) {
    try {
        db.commit();
    } catch( db.FileError ) {...}          // handle
      catch( FileError e ) { throw e; }    // or catch and reraise
}
... same as Figure 9 ...
```

Fig. 10. Simulating transient binding – catch-and-reraise

6.3   Implementations

Catch and Reraise. Given fixed binding, it is possible to simulate transient binding by explicitly catching and reraising all bound exceptions in all methods callable from different objects, as in Figure 10. In the example, the FileError exception inside commit changes binding to db when it is explicitly reraised, so catch(db.FileError) can be matched. Through this convention, an exception is always bound to the last object reraising it, as the binding follows the call stack during unwinding.

However, as discussed in Section 3.3, requiring programmers to follow conventions is always unreliable and error-prone. Additionally, this convention requires every method call to have at least one try-block and one handler; depending upon the implementation of the EHM, this could cause a substantial increase is space and/or time for both normal and exception code.

Integrated. The best solution is to integrate transient binding into the propagation mechanism and *automatically* change the binding during stack unwinding. Figure 11 shows the algorithm for this binding approach. Notice, when only one level of stack unwinding occurs, fixed and transient binding are equivalent.

Rule 2 (b) in the algorithm requires explanation because there is an alternative approach. The alternative is to change the binding to null indicating there is no

1. Initial binding is the current object or null.
2. For every stack frame during propagation:
   (a) if a current object in the previous stack frame, change binding to that object
   (b) if no current object in the previous stack frame, do not change binding

Fig. 11. Transient binding algorithm

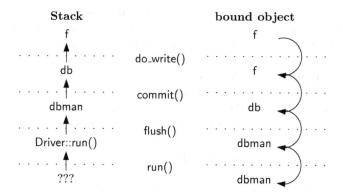

Fig. 12. Change of binding information

binding (exception becomes unbound). This solution is appealing because it is consistent with the fixed-binding algorithm when raising exceptions in non-member functions and static class-members. However, this design violates the principle of modularity, which requires no difference between executing a piece of code in-line or wrapping it into a function and calling that function. For example, the programmer could decide to move a section of the code into a general function. In this case, bound exceptions passing through that function during propagation might not be handled anymore since they become essentially unbound with the null binding, where before they were bound to some object. If the binding information stays the same, the catching code continues to work because nothing changes for the exception.

Using the program in Figure 9 with transient binding, Figure 12 illustrates the changing of binding information if a FileError exception is raised in write. Inside f.write(), the binding is to f since it is the initial binding (rule 1). After one level of unwinding, at db.commit()'s stack frame, the binding is still f because the previous stack frame had f as its current object (rule 2 (a)). Note, up to this point, transient and fixed binding behave identically. At the next level of unwinding the binding changes, so inside dbman.flush(), the bound-to object is db according to rule 2 (a) (using fixed binding, the binding would remain at f). In Driver::run the binding is changed to dbman since that is the object of the previous stack frame (rule 2 (a)). This change makes sense because at this level Driver may know nothing about exceptions from db. Finally, from Driver::run to its caller, the binding remains unchanged because Driver::run happens to be a static member, and hence, there is no current object in that frame (rule 2 (b)).

6.4   Transient Binding Problems

During unwinding, the exception type does not change, whereas the binding object does change for transient binding. This can lead to a situation in which an exception is (transiently) bound to an object that at first glance does not have much to do with the exception. In Figure 12, a FileError exception can be bound to dbman, without an obvious association between these two. This situation can be especially confusing if a programmer is used to bound exceptions being declared inside the scope of the bound-to object's class (as in Ada's generic packages). We argue this problem is best addressed by using an exception hierarchy to differentiate between low-level and high-level exception issues: the further away (on the call-stack) the catch clause is located from the potential raise point, the less specific the exception type of the catch clause should be.

6.5 Transient Versus Fixed Binding

Even with the advantages of transient binding, fixed binding is still useful. There are situations in which knowing the first bound object is useful, *i.e.*, the one

```
void Transaction::do_transaction( Database &db, UserLog &ul ) {
    FileType dataFile;
    FileType logFile;
    try {
        ul.log_events( logFile );
        db.begin_transaction( dataFile, logFile );
    } catch( db.FileError ) {...}        // assume transient binding
      catch( logFile.FileError ) {...}   // assume fixed binding
}
void UserLog::log_events( FileType &f ) {
    ... f.write(); ...        // raises FileError
}
void Database::begin_transaction( FileType &d, FileType &l ) {
    ... d.write(); ...        // raises FileError
    ... l.write(); ...        // raises FileError
}
```

Fig. 13. Transaction example

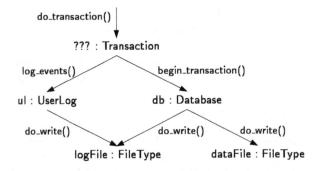

Fig. 14. Call/object chain for Transaction

used by fixed binding. Consider the example in Figure 13, which produces the object/call chain in Figure 14.

Assume logFile's write member raises a FileError exception in begin_transaction that is caught in do_transaction. Fixed binding states the logFile object is responsible, while transient binding states the db object is responsible. In this case, transient binding is needed to know if the exception is from the ui or db object. Now, assume the identical scenario of logFile's write raising a FileError exception. Fixed binding states the logFile object is responsible, while transient binding states the db object is responsible. In this case, fixed binding is needed to know if the exception is from the logFile or dataFile object.

In general, fixed binding is required when an intermediate object accesses multiple sub-objects and the user of the intermediate object(s) needs to know precisely which low-level sub-object raises the exception. In general, transient binding is necessary when an object accesses multiple intermediate objects and the user needs to know which intermediate object the exception propagates through. In theory, a user might want to know the bindings of all intermediate-level objects, but this would result in a complex mechanism and implementation. Therefore, only fixed and transient binding are suggested, and by using a good exception-handling design (*i.e.*, an appropriate placement of try-blocks and catch clauses), it is possible to cover all the cases in between. Finally, there is no semantic problem with the coexistence of fixed and transient binding, and only a small amount of additional syntax is needed to allow a catch clause to indicate the kind of binding for matching. An implementation only requires an additional field during propagation to maintain both the fixed and transient information. Therefore, there is good reason for an EHM to support both fixed and transient binding.

7   Conclusion

The ability to associate exceptions with objects strengthens the relationship between an exception and the object responsible for its raise. This feature, while keeping code-complexity low, creates more powerful exception handling capabilities, contributing to building more robust software. This work shows a complete simulation of bound exception is extremely difficult, making it impractical as a coding convention; therefore, bound exceptions need to be part of the programming language. While prior work has examined the association of exceptions with instances of data, this work extends the approach by implicitly associating a responsible object with an exception, and thus, truly incorporates exception handling into the object-oriented domain. Transient binding, as a novel contribution, improves the connection between an object's actions and their resulting exceptions, providing a new dimension in the object-oriented design process with exceptions. Finally, identifying that both fixed and transient bound-exceptions can coexist and that each provides distinct capabilities to allow a user precise control in matching exceptions is an additional contribution.

While this work presents a design for bound exceptions in C++/μC++, much of the results are applicable to EHMs in other object-oriented languages. The implementation of fixed-bound exceptions in μC++ provides a platform for evaluating some of these features under practical circumstances. With resumption, nonlocal and concurrent exceptions, μC++ supports basically all exception models in use today. Therefore, it can serve as a test platform for researchers to evaluate the usefulness of bound exceptions and if further extensions are needed.

Acknowledgments

We would like to thank Ashif Harji and Richard Bilson for their comments.

References

1. Pitman, K.M.: Condition handling in the lisp language family. In: Exception Handling. Volume 2022 of LNCS., Springer-Verlag (2001) 39–59
2. Dony, C.: A fully object-oriented exception handling system: Rationale and smalltalk implementation. In: Exception Handling. Volume 2022 of LNCS., Springer-Verlag (2001) 18–38
3. Knudsen, J.L.: Fault tolerance and exception handling in BETA. In: Exception Handling. Volume 2022 of LNCS., Springer-Verlag (2001) 1–17
4. Microsoft Corporation: Microsoft Visual C++ .NET Language Reference. (2002) Microsoft Press, Redmond, Washington, U.S.A.
5. Cui, Q., Gannon, J.: Data-oriented exception handling. IEEE Transactions on Software Engineering 18 (1992) 393–401
6. Buhr, P.A., Macdonald, H.I., Zarnke, C.R.: Synchronous and asynchronous handling of abnormal events in the μSystem. Software—Practice and Experience 22 (1992) 735–776
7. Burns, A., Wellings, A.: Real-Time Systems and Programming Languages. second edn. Addison-Wesley (1997)
8. Intermetrics, Inc.: Ada Reference Manual. International standard ISO/IEC 8652:1995(E) with COR.1:2000 edn. (1995) Language and Standards Libraries.
9. Nelson, G., ed.: Systems Programming with Modula-3. Prentice Hall Series in Innovative Technology. Prentice-Hall, Inc. (1991)
10. Buhr, P.A., Harji, A., Mok, W.Y.R.: Exception handling. In Zelkowitz, M.V., ed.: Advances in COMPUTERS. Volume 56. Academic Press (2002) 245–303
11. Krischer, R.: Bound exceptions in object-oriented programming languages. Diplomarbeit, Universität Mannheim, Mannheim, Deutschland (2002) ftp://plg.uwaterloo.ca/pub/theses/KrischerThesis.ps.gz.
12. Stroustrup, B.: The Design and Evolution of C++. Addison-Wesley (1994)
13. Buhr, P.A.: μC++ annotated reference manual, version 5.3.0. Technical report, School of Computer Science, University of Waterloo, Waterloo, Ontario, Canada, N2L 3G1 (2006) ftp://plg.uwaterloo.ca/pub/uSystem/uC++.ps.gz.

Exception-Handling Bugs in Java and a Language Extension to Avoid Them

Westley Weimer

University of Virginia, Charlottesville, Virginia, USA, 22904
weimer@virginia.edu

Abstract. It is difficult to write programs that behave correctly in the presence of exceptions. We describe a dataflow analysis for finding a certain class of mistakes made while programs handle exceptions. These mistakes involve resource leaks and failures to restore program-specific invariants. Using this analysis we have found over 1,200 bugs in 4 million lines of Java. We give some evidence of the importance of the bugs we found and use them to highlight some limitations of destructors and finalizers. We propose and evaluate a new language feature, the compensation stack, to make it easier to write solid code in the presence of exceptions. These compensation stacks track obligations and invariants at run-time. Two case studies demonstrate that they can yield more natural source code and more consistent behavior in long-running programs.

1 Introduction

It is easier to fix software defects if they are found before the software is deployed. It is difficult to use testing to evaluate program behavior in exceptional situations, and thus difficult to use it to find exception-handling bugs. This chapter presents an analysis for finding a class of program mistakes related to such exceptional situations. It also describes a new language feature, the compensation stack, to make it easier to fix such mistakes.

In this context an *exceptional situation* is one in which something external to the program behaves in an uncommon but legitimate manner. For example, a request to write a file may fail because the disk is full or the underlying operating system is out of file handles. Similarly, a request to send a packet reliably may fail because of a network breakdown. Such examples represent actions that typically succeed but may fail through no fault of the main program.

Testing a program's behavior in exceptional situations is difficult because such situations, often called *faults* or *run-time errors*, must be artificially introduced while the program is executing. Since a program cannot perform correctly if all of its actions fail, a special *fault model* governs which faults may occur and when they may occur. Once the fault model has been established the faults must still be *injected* during testing. Both physical techniques [1] and special program analyses and compiler instrumentation approaches [2] have been used to inject faults. These approaches are still based on testing, however, and require indicative workloads and test cases.

C. Dony et al. (Eds.):Exception Handling, LNCS 4119, pp. 22–41, 2006.

Languages like Java, C++ and C# use language-level *exceptions* to signal and handle exceptional situations. The most common semantic framework for exceptions is the *replacement model* [3]. Complicated exception handling is difficult to reason about and to code correctly. It can become a source of software defects related to reliability. In particular, our experiments show that programs make mistakes when attempting to handle multiple cascading exceptions or multiple resources in the presence of a single exception.

In this chapter we use a fault model linking some run-time errors with certain language-level exceptions [1,4]. The model requires programs to behave correctly in the presence of common environmental conditions, like network congestion or database contention. It does not require that we consider memory-safety faults (e.g., array bounds-check failures). The model allows multiple "back-to-back" faults and is good at finding error-handling bugs. Our notion of correct behavior in the presence of exceptions is restricted to a few simple *specifications* for proper resource and API usage. We believe that programs should adhere to these specifications even in the presence of run-time errors.

We present a static dataflow analysis to find bugs in a program with respect to a given specification and a given fault model. An error report from the analysis includes a program path, one or more run-time errors and one or more resources governed by the specification. Such an error report claims that if the run-time errors occur at the given points along the program path, the program will misuse the given resources. The analysis is path-sensitive, intraprocedural and context-insensitive. It precisely models control flow, especially that related to exceptions. It abstracts away data values and only tracks the resources mentioned in the specification. Given a few simple filtering rules, the analysis reported no false positives in our experiments, but it can miss real errors. The analysis is quite successful at finding a certain class of mistakes: it found over 1,200 bugs in four million lines of code. In the few cases where we were able to make such measurements, 44-45% of the reported bugs were fixed by developers.

Based on that work finding bugs we propose the *compensation stack*, a language feature for ensuring that simple resources and API rules are handled correctly even in the presence of run-time errors. We draw on the concepts of compensating transactions, linear sagas, and linear types to create a model in which important obligations are recorded at run-time and are guaranteed to be executed along all paths. By enforcing a certain ordering and moving some book-keeping from compile-time to run-time we provide more flexibility and ease-of-use than standard language approaches to adding linear types or transactions. We provide a static semantics for compensation stacks to highlight their differences from pure linear type systems and we present case studies using our implementation to show that they can be used to improve software reliability.

The rest of this chapter is organized as follows. We describe of the state of the art in handling exceptional situations at the language level in Section 2. We present a static data-flow analysis that finds exception-handling mistakes in Section 3. In Section 4 we present the results of our analysis, including experiments in Section 4.1 to measure the importance of the bugs found. We discuss finalizers and destructors in Section 5 and highlight some of their weaknesses in this context. In Section 6 we propose the compensation stack as a language feature. We describe our implementation in Section 7 and our type system in Section 8. In Section 9 we report on experiments in which we apply compensation stacks to error-handling in real programs in order to improve reliability.

2   Handling Exceptional Situations in Practice

The goal of an exception handler is program- and situation-specific. For example, a networked program may handle a transmission exception by attempting to resend a packet. A file-writing program may handle a storage exception by asking the user to specify an alternate destination for the data. We will not consider such high-level policy notions, instead focusing on generic, low-level notions of correctness related to resource handling and correct API usage.

```
01: Connection cn; PreparedStatement ps; ResultSet rs;
02: try {
03:    cn = ConnectionFactory.getConnection(/* ... */);
04:    StringBuffer qry = ...; // do some work
05:    ps = cn.prepareStatement(qry.toString());
06:    rs = ps.executeQuery();
07:    ... // do I/O-related work with rs
08:    rs.close();
09:    ps.close();
10: } finally {
11:    try { cn.close(); } catch (Exception e1) { }
12: }
```

Fig. 1. Ohioedge CRM Exception Handling Code *(with bug)*

We begin with an example showing how error-handling mistakes can occur in practice. The code in Figure 1 was taken from Ohioedge CRM, the largest open-source customer relations management project. It uses language features to facilitate exception handling (i.e., nested **try** blocks and **finally** clauses), but many problems remain. **Connections**, **PreparedStatements** and **ResultSets** are important global resources associated with an external database. Our specification of correct behavior requires that the program eventually **close** each one.

In some situations the exception handling in Figure 1 works correctly. If a run-time error occurs on line 4, the runtime system will signal an exception, and the program will close the open **Connection** on line 11. However, if a run-time error occurs on line 6 (or 7 or 8), the resources of **ps** and **rs** may not be freed.

One common solution is to move the **close** calls from lines 8 and 9 into the **finally** block (e.g., before **cn.close** on line 11). This approach is insufficient for at least two reasons. First, the **close** method itself can raise exceptions (as indicated by the fact that it is surrounded by a **try-catch** and by its type signature), so a failure while closing the first resource might leave the last one dangling. Second, such code may also attempt to `close` an object that has never been created. If an error occurs on line 4 after `cn` has been created but before `rs` has been created, control will jump to line 10 and then invoke `rs.close` on line 11. Since `rs` has not yet been allocated, this will signal an error and control will jump to line 13 without invoking `close` on `cn`.

Using standard language features there are two common ways to address the situation. The first involves using nested `try-finally` blocks. One block is required for each resource handled simultaneously. This approach is rarely used correctly in practice, as methods commonly use three to five resources simultaneously. The second approach is to use special sentinel values or run-time checks to ensure proper resource handling. This approach has the advantage that one `try-finally` statement can handle any number of simultaneous resources. Unfortunately, it is difficult for humans to write such bookkeeping code correctly. If the guarded code contains any control-flow (e.g., allocating a list of `ResultSet`s), that flow must be duplicated in the `finally` clause.

The Ohioedge CRM code highlights a number of observations. First, programmers are aware of the safety policies: `close` is common. Second, programmers are aware of possibility of run-time errors: language-level exception handling (e.g. `try` and `finally`) is used prominently. Third, there are many paths where exception handling is poor and resources may not be dealt with correctly. Finally, fixing the problem typically has software engineering disadvantages: the distance between any resource acquisition and its associated release increases, and extra control flow used only for exception-handling must be included. In addition, if another procedure wishes to make use of `Connection`s, it must duplicate all of this exception handling code. Duplication is frequent in practice: the Ohioedge source file containing our example also contains two similar procedures with the same mistakes. Developers have cited this required repetition to explain why exception handling is sometimes ignored [5]. In general, correctly dealing with N resources requires N nested `try-finally` statements or a number of run-time checks. Such problems are error-prone in practice.

3   Bug-Finding Dataflow Analysis

We now present an analysis to find error-handling bugs. The analysis yields paths through methods on which mistakes may occur and can be used to direct changes to the source code to improve exception handling. The analysis may mistakenly report correct code as buggy and may fail to report real errors. We chose to take a fully static approach to avoid the problem of test case generation.

The analysis uses standard finite state machine specifications [6,7,8,9] to describe proper resource and API usage. We use a Java-specific fault model [4] to construct a control-flow graph where method invocations can raise declared `checked` exceptions. We chose Java because experiments show that its exceptions and run-time errors are correlated [1] and because method signatures include exception information. The analysis itself is language-independent. It is path-sensitive because we want to consider control flow and because the abstract state of a resource (e.g., "opened" or "closed") depends on control flow. It is intraprocedural for scalability. This leads to false positives, which we eliminate via heuristics that may mask real errors. The analysis abstracts data values, keeping sets of outstanding resource states as per-path dataflow facts. This abstraction can lead to false positives and false negatives, but stylized usage patterns allow us to eliminate the false positives in practice. At join points we keep dataflow facts separate if they have distinct sets of resources. We report a violation when a path leaves a method with a resource that is not in an accepting policy state.

3.1   Analysis Details

Our analysis sybmolically executes all code paths in each method body, abstracting data values but tracking control flow, exceptions and the specification.

Given the control-flow graph, our flow-sensitive, intraprocedural dataflow analysis [6,7,10] finds paths where programs violate the specification (typically by forgetting to discharge obligations) in the presence of run-time errors. We retain as dataflow facts paths through the program and a multiset of resource safety policy states for each path. That is, rather than tracking which variables hold resources we track a set of acquired resource states. We begin the analysis of each method body with an empty path and no obligations.

The analysis is given with respect to a safety policy specification $\langle \Sigma, S, s_0, \delta, F \rangle$. Given such a policy we must determine what state information to propagate on the CFG by giving flow and grouping functions. Each path-sensitive dataflow fact f is a pair $\langle \mathcal{T}, L \rangle$. The first component $\mathcal{T}$ is a multiset of specification states. So for each $s \in \mathcal{T}$ we have $s \in S$. We use a multiset because it is possible to have many obligations for a single resource type (e.g., to have two open Sockets). The second component L is a *path*, used when reporting violations, that lists program points between the start of the method and the current CFG edge.

3.2   Flow Functions

The analysis is defined in terms of the flow functions given in Figure 2. The four types of control flow nodes are branches, method invocations, other statements and join points. Because our analysis is path-sensitive and does not always merge dataflow facts at join points, each flow function formally takes a single incoming dataflow fact and yields a set of outgoing facts.

We handle normal and conditional control flow by abstracting away data values: control can flow from an if to both the then and the else branch (assuming that the guard does not raise an exception) and our dataflow fact propagates from the incoming edge to both outgoing edges. We write $\text{extend}(f, L)$ to mean the singleton set containing fact f with location L appended to its path.

A method invocation may terminate normally, represented by the f_n edge in Figure 2. If the method is not covered by the policy (i.e., meth $\notin \Sigma$) then we propagate the symbolic state f directly. If the method is in the policy and the incoming dataflow fact f contains a state s that could transition on that method we apply that transition δ and then append the path label L. This is similar to the way tracked resources are handled in the Vault type system [11].

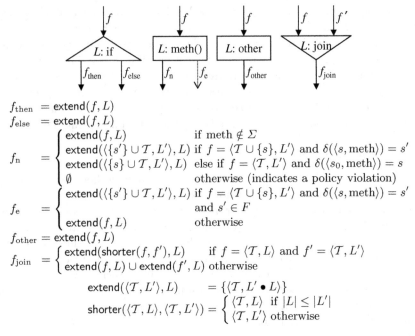

$$f_{\text{then}} = \text{extend}(f, L)$$
$$f_{\text{else}} = \text{extend}(f, L)$$

$$f_{\text{n}} = \begin{cases} \text{extend}(f, L) & \text{if meth} \notin \Sigma \\ \text{extend}(\langle\{s'\} \cup \mathcal{T}, L'\rangle, L) & \text{if } f = \langle \mathcal{T} \cup \{s\}, L'\rangle \text{ and } \delta(\langle s, \text{meth}\rangle) = s' \\ \text{extend}(\langle\{s\} \cup \mathcal{T}, L'\rangle, L) & \text{else if } f = \langle \mathcal{T}, L'\rangle \text{ and } \delta(\langle s_0, \text{meth}\rangle) = s \\ \emptyset & \text{otherwise (indicates a policy violation)} \end{cases}$$

$$f_{\text{e}} = \begin{cases} \text{extend}(\langle\{s'\} \cup \mathcal{T}, L'\rangle, L) & \text{if } f = \langle \mathcal{T} \cup \{s\}, L'\rangle \text{ and } \delta(\langle s, \text{meth}\rangle) = s' \\ & \text{and } s' \in F \\ \text{extend}(f, L) & \text{otherwise} \end{cases}$$

$$f_{\text{other}} = \text{extend}(f, L)$$

$$f_{\text{join}} = \begin{cases} \text{extend}(\text{shorter}(f, f'), L) & \text{if } f = \langle \mathcal{T}, L\rangle \text{ and } f' = \langle \mathcal{T}, L'\rangle \\ \text{extend}(f, L) \cup \text{extend}(f', L) & \text{otherwise} \end{cases}$$

$$\text{extend}(\langle \mathcal{T}, L'\rangle, L) = \{\langle \mathcal{T}, L' \bullet L\rangle\}$$
$$\text{shorter}(\langle \mathcal{T}, L\rangle, \langle \mathcal{T}, L'\rangle) = \begin{cases} \langle \mathcal{T}, L\rangle & \text{if } |L| \leq |L'| \\ \langle \mathcal{T}, L'\rangle & \text{otherwise} \end{cases}$$

Fig. 2. Analysis flow functions

A method may also create a new policy resource. For example, the first time new Socket occurs in a path we create a new instance of the policy state machine to model the use of that Socket object.

The final case for a successful method invocation indicates a potential program error. In this case we have an event covered by the specification but the analysis is not tracking any resource that is in a state for which that event is valid. For the common two-state, two-event, open-close safety policies these violations correspond to "double closes". With more complicated policies they can also represent invoking important methods at the wrong time (e.g., trying to write to a closed File or trying to accept on an un-bound Socket). We report such potential violations and stop processing along that path (i.e., the outgoing fact is the empty set) to avoid cascading error reports.

A method invocation may also raise a declared exception, represented by the f_e edge in Figure 2. Our fault model is any method can either terminate normally or raise any of its declared checked exceptions. It is this assumption that allows us to simulate faults and find error-handling mistakes. Unlike the successful invocation case, we do not update the specification state in the outgoing dataflow fact. This is because the method did not terminate successfully and thus presumably did not perform the operation to transform the resource's state. However, as a special case we allow an attempt to "discharge an obligation" or move a resource into an accepting state to succeed even if the method invocation fails. Thus we do not require that programs loop around close functions and invoke them until they succeed — that would create unnecessary spurious error reports.

The check $s' \in F$ requires that the result of applying this method would put the object in an accepting state.

The grouping (or join) function tracks separate paths through the same program point provided that they have distinct multisets of specification states. Our join function uses the *property simulation* approach [7] to grouping sets of symbolic states. We merge facts with identical obligations by retaining only the shorter path for error reporting purposes (modeled here as shorter(s_1, s_2)). We may visit the same location many times to analyze paths with different sets T.

To ensure termination we stop the analysis and flag an error when a program point occurs twice in a single path with different obligation sets (e.g., if a program acquires obligations inside a loop). In our experiments that never occurred. We did encounter multiple programs that allocated and freed resources inside loops, but the (lack of) error handling was always such that an exception would escape the loop. The analysis is exponential in the worst case but quite efficient in practice. Analyzing the 57,000-line `hibernate` program, including parsing, typechecking and printing out the resulting violations, took 104 seconds and 46 MB of memory on a 1.6 GHz machine.

The analysis goal is to find a path to the end of a method where a safety policy resource does not end in an accepting state. That is, for each $f = \langle T, L \rangle$ that enters the end node of the CFG, if $\exists s \in T. \ s \notin F$ the analysis reports a candidate violation along path L.

It is desirable to use heuristics in a post-processing step to filter candidate violations [4,12]. In this case three simple filters eliminate *all* false positives we encountered but could cause this analysis to miss real errors. Based on a random sample of two of our benchmarks, applying these three filters causes our analysis to miss 10 real bugs for every 100 real bugs it reports. We discuss the analysis results in the next section.

4   Poor Handling Abounds

In this section we apply the analysis from Section 3 and common specifications to show that many programs make mistakes in handling exceptional situations. We consider a diverse body of twenty-seven Java programs totaling four million lines of code. The programs include databases, business software, networking applications and software development tools.

Figure 3 shows results from this analysis. The "Bugs" columns show the number of methods that violate at least one policy. We applied four library-resource policies (i.e., `Sockets`, `Streams`, file handles and JDBC database connections) to all programs. In addition, a total of 69 program-specific policies (found via specification mining [13]) were also used where applicable.

All of the reported methods were then manually inspected to verify that they contained at least one error along a reported path. Simple heuristics eliminated all false positive reports for these programs.

All paths in Figure 3 arose in the presence of exceptions the program did not handle correctly. More than half of these paths featured some exception

Program		Lines of Code	Bugs	Program		Lines of Code	Bugs
javad	2000	4k	1	hibernate	2.0b4	57k	106
javacc	3.0	13k	4	jaxme	1.54	58k	6
jtar	1.21	17k	5	axion	1.0m2	65k	60
jatlite	3.5.97	18k	6	hsqldb	1.7.1	71k	53
toba	1.1c	19k	6	cayenne	1.0b4	86k	25
osage	1.0p10	20k	3	sablecc	2.17.4	99k	3
jcc	0.02	26k	0	jboss	3.0.6	107k	134
quartz	1.0.6	27k	17	mckoi-sql	1.0.2	118k	106
infinity	1.28	28k	21	portal	1.8.0	162k	39
ejbca	2.0b2	33k	31	pcgen	4.3.5	178k	17
ohioedge	1.3.1	40k	15	compiere	2.4.4	230k	322
jogg	1.1.3	47k	7	aspectj	1.1	319k	27
staf	2.4.5	55k	12	ptolemy2	3.0.2	362k	99
				eclipse	5.25.03	1.6M	126

Fig. 3. 1251 Error handling mistakes in 3.9 million lines of code. The "Bugs" columns indicate the number of distinct *methods* that contain violations of various policies.

handling (i.e., the exception was caught), but the resource was still leaked. This result demonstrates that existing exception handlers contain mistakes.

4.1   The Importance of the Detected Bugs

Beyond raw numbers, the utility of the bugs found also matters. Even if a bug represents a violation of the policy, it may not be worth the developer's time to fix. Commercial software ships with known bugs. Bugs that are viewed as unlikely to affect real users go unfixed at many points in the development cycle.

Our analysis finds bugs that show up in the presence of exceptional situations by reporting resource leaks along paths that contain one or more run-time errors. We must show that these bugs are a serious problem "in the real world". A thorough evaluation of the importance of a bug is situation-specific and beyond the scope of this chapter. Aspects such as the performance or security impact of a bug or the cost of fixing it are difficult to measure quantitatively. We present some evidence to suggest that the bugs we report are important.

One of the authors of `ptolemy2` was willing to rank bugs we found on his own five point scale. For that program, 11% of the bugs we reported were in tutorials or third-party, and thus unimportant, code, 44% of them rated a 3 out of 5 for taking place in "little used, experimental code", 19% of them rated a 4 out of 5 and were "definitely a bug in code that is used more often", and 26% of them rated a 5 out of 5 and were "definitely a bug in code that is used often." The 45% of the bugs that rated a 4 or 5 were fixed immediately. The author claimed that for his long-running servers resource leaks were a problem that forced them to reboot every day as a last-ditch effort to reclaim resources. We cannot claim that this breakdown generalizes, but it does provide one concrete example.

The direct experiment of finding bugs, reporting them to developers and then counting how many are fixed is difficult to perform, especially in the open-source community. We thus performed a *time travel* experiment to determine whether the bugs found by our analysis were important enough to fix.

We used version control systems to obtain a snapshot of `eclipse 2.0.0` from July 2002 as well as one of `eclipse 3.0.1` from September 2004. We analyzed `eclipse 2.0.0` and noted the first 100 bugs reported. Without reporting any bugs to developers we looked for those bugs in `eclipse 3.0.1` to see if they had been fixed by the natural course of `eclipse` development. In our case 43% of the bugs found by our analysis in `eclipse 2.0.0` had been fixed by `eclipse 3.0.1`. Given our stated goal of improving software quality by finding and fixing bugs before a product is released, this number is important and helps to validate our analysis. Combined with our zero effective false positive rate it suggests that using our analysis is worthwhile because almost half of the bugs it reports would have to be fixed later anyway.

This section presents a static dataflow analysis that can locate software errors in a program's exception handling with respect to specification of correct behavior. The analysis examines each method in turn and tracks resources governed by the specification along all paths. Implementation details of the analysis presented here were previously discussed in earlier works [4,13].

5   An Attempt to Use Existing Language Features

Based on the mistakes found by our analysis, we claim that `try-finally` blocks are ill-suited for handling certain classes of resources during run-time errors. In essence, exceptions create hidden control-flow paths that are difficult for programmers to reason about. Before proposing a new language feature to simplify resource reclamation in exceptional situations, we must consider the advantages of two existing features: destructors and finalizers.

A *destructor* is a special method associated with a class. Destructors are used in C++ as well as other languages like C#. When a stack-allocated instance of that class goes out of scope, either because of normal control flow or because an exception was raised, the destructor is invoked automatically. Destructors are tied to the dynamic call stack of a program in the same way that local variables are. Destructors provide guaranteed cleanup actions for stack-allocated objects, even in the presence of exceptions. However, for heap-allocated objects the programmer must remember to explicitly delete the object along all paths. We would like to generalize the notion of destructors: rather than one implicit stack tied to the call stack, programmers should be allowed to manipulate first-class collections of obligations.

In addition, we believe that programmers should have guarantees about managing objects and actions that do not have their lifetimes bound to the call stack (such objects are common in practice — see e.g., Gay and Aiken [14]). In many domains, multiple stacks are a more natural fit with the application. For example, a web server might store one such stack for each concurrent request. If the normal request encounters an error and must abort and release its resources, there is generally no reason that another request cannot continue. A destructor can be invoked early, but would typically have to use a flag to ensure that actions are not redone when it is called again. We want such bookkeeping to be automatic. Destructors are tied to objects and there are many cases where a program would want to change the state of the object, rather than destroying it. We shall return to that consideration in Section 7.

A *finalizer* is another special method associated with a class. Finalizers are available in Java as well as other languages like C#. A finalizer is invoked on an instance of a class when that instance is reclaimed by the garbage collector. The collector is not guaranteed to find any particular object and need not find garbage in any order or time-frame. Compared to pure finalizers, most programmer-specified error handling must be more immediate and more deterministic. Finalizers are arguably well-suited to resources like file descriptors that must be collected but need not be collected right away. Even that apparently-innocuous use of finalizers is often discouraged because programs have a limited number of file descriptors and can "race" with the collector to exhaust them [15]. In contrast, resources like JDBC database connections should be released as quickly as possible, making finalizers an awkward fit for performance reasons. For example, the Oracle9i documentation specifically states that finalizers are not used and that cleanup must be done explicitly. We want a mechanism that is well-suited to being invoked early. Like destructors, finalizers can be invoked early but doing so typically requires additional bookkeeping.

More importantly, finalizers in Java come with no order guarantees. For example, a `Stream` built on (and referencing) a `Socket` might be finalized after that `Socket` if they are reclaimed in the same collection pass. We desire an error handling mechanism that can strictly enforce dependencies and provide a more intuitive ordering for cleanup actions. In addition, finalizers must be asynchronous, which complicates how they can be written.

Finally, it is worth noting that Java programmers do not make even a sparing use of finalizers to address these problems. Some Java implementations do not implement finalizers correctly [16], finalizers are often viewed as unpredictable or dangerous, and the delay between finishing with the resource and having the finalizer called may be too great. In all of the code surveyed in Section 4, there were only 13 user-defined finalizers. Standard libraries might make good use of finalizers, but this is not always the case. The GNU Classpath 0.05 implementation of the Java standard library does not use finalizers for any of the resources we considered in Section 4. Sun's JDK 1.3.1_07 does use them, but only in some situations (e.g., for database connections but not for sockets). While other or newer standard libraries may well use finalizers for all such important resources, one cannot currently portably rely on the library to do so. We want to make something like a finalizer more useful to Java programmers by making it easier to use and giving it destructor-like properties.

The results in Section 4 argue that language support is necessary: merely making a better `Socket` library will not help if `Socket`s, databases, and user-defined resources must be dealt with together. Using exception handling to deal with important resources is difficult. In the next section, we describe a language mechanism that makes it easy to do the right thing: all of the bugs presented here could have been avoided using our proposed language extension.

6   Compensation Stacks

Based on existing mistakes and coding practices, we propose a language extension where program actions and interfaces are annotated with *compensations*, which are closures containing arbitrary code. At run-time, these compensations are stored in first-class stacks. *Compensation stacks* can be thought of as generalized destructors, but we emphasize that they can be used to execute arbitrary code and not just call functions upon object destruction.

Our compensation stacks are an adaptation of the database notions of *compensating transactions* [17] and *linear sagas* [18]. A compensating transaction semantically undoes the effect of another transaction after that transaction has committed. A saga is a long-lived transaction seen as a sequence of atomic actions $a_1...a_n$ with compensating transactions $c_1...c_n$. This system guarantees that either $a_1...a_n$ executes or $a_1...a_k c_k...c_1$ executes. The compensations are applied in reverse order. This model is a good fit for run-time resource error handling. Many program actions require that multiple resources be handled in sequence.

Our system allows programmers to link actions with compensations, and guarantees that if an action is taken, the associated compensation will be also executed.[1] Compensation stacks are first-class objects that store closures. They may be passed to methods or stored in object fields. The Java language syntax is extended to allow arbitrary closures to be pushed onto compensation stacks. These closures are later executed in a last-in, first-out order. Closures may be run "early" by the programmer, but are usually run when a stack-allocated compensation stack goes out of scope or when a heap-allocated compensation stack is finalized. If a compensating action raises an exception while executing, the exception is logged but compensation execution continues.[2] When a compensation terminates (either normally or exceptionally), it is removed from the compensation stack.

Compensation stacks normally behave like generalized destructors, deallocating resources based on lexical scoping, but they are also first-class collections that can be put in the heap and that make use of finalizers to ensure that their

---

[1] We do not model abnormal program termination. Whether functions like `exit(1)` cause pending compensations to be executed or not is implementation-specific.

[2] Neither Java finalizers nor POSIX cleanup handlers propagate such exceptions. Lisp's `unwind-protect` may not execute all cleanup actions if one raises an exception. In analogous situations, C++ aborts the program. Since our goal is to keep the program running and restore invariants, we log such exceptions. Ideally, error-prone compensations would contain their own internal compensation stacks for error handling. A second option would be to have the type system verify that a compensation cannot raise an exception. This option is not desirable for Java programs. First, it would require checking *unchecked* exceptions, which is non-intuitive to most Java programmers. Second, most compensations can, in fact, raise exceptions (e.g., `close` can raise an `IOException`).

contents are eventually executed. They are as convenient as destructors when lexical and lifetime scoping coincide and are flexible enough to handle resources when they do not. The ability to execute some compensations early is important and allows the common programming idiom where critical shared resources are freed as early as possible along each path. In addition, the program can explicitly discharge an obligation without executing its code (based on outside knowledge not directly encoded in the safety policy). This flexibility allows compensations that truly undo effects to be avoided on successful executions, and it requires that the programmer annotate a small number of success paths rather than every possible error path. Additional compensation stacks may be declared to create a "nested transaction" effect. Finally, the analysis in Section 3 can be easily modified (based on the type system described later in Section 8) to show that programs that make use of compensation stacks do not forget obligations.

7   Compensation Stack Pragmatics

We implemented compensation stacks via a source-level transformation for Java programs. We defined a CompensationStack class, added support for closures [19], and added syntactic sugar for lexically-scoped compensation stacks.

Consider again the client code from Figure 1. Our first step is to annotate the interfaces of methods that acquire important resources. For example, we associate with the action getConnection the compensation close at the interface level so that all uses of Connections are affected. Consider this definition:

```
public Connection getConnection() throws SQLException {
  /* ... do work ... */
}
```

We would change it so that a CompensationStack argument is required. The new syntax compensate { a } with { c } using (S) corresponds to executing the action a and then pushing the compensation code c on the stack S if a completed normally. The modified definition follows:

```
public Connection getConnection(CompensationStack S) throws SQLException{
  compensate {
    /* ... do work ... */
  } with {
    this.close();
  } using (S);
}
```

As in Section 5, this mechanism has the advantages of early release and proper ordering over just using finalizers. Not all actions and compensations must be associated at the function-call level; arbitrary code can be placed in compensations. After annotating the database interface with compensation information, the client code might look like this:

```
01: Connection cn; PreparedStatement ps; ResultSet rs;
03: CompensationStack S = new CompensationStack();
04: try {
05:    cn = ConnectionFactory.getConnection(S, /* ... */);
06:    StringBuffer qry = ...; // do some work
07:    ps = cn.prepareStatement(S, qry.toString());
08:    rs = ps.executeQuery(S);
09:    ... // do I/O-related work with rs
10: } finally {
11:    S.run();  // execute all accrued compensations
12: }
```

As the program executes, closures containing compensation code are pushed onto the `CompensationStack S`. Compensations are recorded at run-time, so resources can be acquired in loops or other procedures. Before a compensation stack becomes inaccessible, all of its associated compensations must be executed. A particularly common use involves lexically scoped compensation stacks that essentially mimic the behavior of destructors. We add syntactic sugar allowing a keyword (e.g., `methodScopedStack`) to stand for a compensation stack that is allocated at the beginning of the enclosing scope and `finally` executed at the end of it. In addition, we optionally allow that special stack to be used for omitted compensation stack parameters. We thus arrive at a simple version of the original client code:

```
01: Connection cn; PreparedStatement ps; ResultSet rs;
02: cn = ConnectionFactory.getConnection(/* ... */);
03: StringBuffer qry = ...; // do some work
04: ps = cn.prepareStatement(qry.toString());
05: rs = ps.executeQuery();
06: ... // do I/O-related work with rs
```

All of the release actions are handled automatically, even in the presence of run-time errors. An implicit `CompensationStack` based on the method scope is being used and the resource-acquiring methods have been annotated to use such stacks. Note that annotating interfaces with compensating actions does not force a choice between lexically-scoped and heap-oriented resource management: when an object is first created using an interface its associated obligations can be put on any compensation stack.

Compensations can contain arbitrary code, not just method calls. For example, consider this code fragment adapted from [5]:

```
01: try {
02:    StartDate = new Date();
03:    try {
04:       StartLSN = log.getLastLSN();
05:       ... // do work 1
06:       try {
07:          DB.getWriteLock();
08:          ... // do work 2
```

```
09:     } finally {
10:        DB.releaseWriteLock();
11:        ... // do work 3
12:     }
13:   } finally { StartLSN = -1; }
14: } finally { StartDate = null; }
```

We might rewrite it as follows, using explicit `CompensationStacks`:

```
01: CompensationStack S = new CompensationStack();
02: try {
03:    compensate { StartDate = new Date(); }
04:    with        { StartDate = null; } using (S);
05:    compensate { StartLSN = log.getLastLSN(); }
06:    with        { StartLSN = -1; } using (S);
07:    ... // do work 1
08:    compensate { DB.getWriteLock(); }
09:    with        { DB.releaseWriteLock();
10:                  ... /* do work 3 */ }
11:    ... // do work 2
12: } finally { S.run(); }
```

Resource finalization and state changes are handled by the same mechanism and benefit from the same ordering. Assignments to `StartLSN` and `StartDate` as well as "`work 3`" are examples of state changes that are not simply method invocations. This rewrite also has the advantage that "undo" code is close to its "do" counterpart.

Traditional destructors are tied to objects, and there are many cases where a program would want to change the state of the object rather than destroying it. Destructors could be used here by creating "artificial objects" that are stack-allocated and perform the appropriate state changes on the enclosing object. However, such a solution would not be natural. For example, the program from which the last example was taken had 17 unique compensations (i.e., error-handling code that was site-specific and never duplicated) with an average length of 8 lines and a maximum length of 34 lines. Creating a new object for each unique bit of error-handling logic would be burdensome, especially since many of the compensations had more than one free variable (which would generally have to become extra arguments to a helper constructor). Nested `try-finally` blocks could also be used but are error-prone (see Section 2 and Section 4).

Previous approaches to similar problems can be vast and restrictive departures from standard semantics (e.g., linear types [11] or transactions [20]) or lack support for common idioms (e.g., running or discharging obligations early). We designed this mechanism to integrate easily with new and existing programs, and we needed all of its features for our case studies. With this feature, we found it easy to avoid the mistakes that were reported hundreds of times in Section 4. In the common case of a lexically-scoped linear saga of resources, the error handling logic needs to be written only once with an interface, rather than every time a resource is acquired. In more complicated cases (e.g., storing compensations in heap variables and associating them with long-lived objects) extra flexibility is available when it is needed.

8   Compensation Stack Static Semantics

We provide a simple static type system for the correct use of explicitly-declared compensation stacks. This allows us to highlight the differences between our system and a full linear type system for tracking resources. It also provides a framework in which to describe the ordering guarantees provided by our system.

$e ::=$ skip	no-op
$\mid\quad e_1 ; e_2$	sequencing
$\mid\quad$ if $*$ then e_1 else e_2	non-deterministic choice
$\mid\quad$ while $*$ do e	non-deterministic looping
$\mid\quad$ let $c_i =$ new CompStack() in e	compensation stack creation
$\mid\quad$ compensate a_j with b_j using c_i	compensation stack use
$\mid\quad$ store c_i	store a stack in memory (address not modeled)
$\mid\quad$ let $c_i =$ load in e	load a stack from memory (address not modeled)
$\mid\quad$ run c_i	discharge all of a stack's obligations
$\mid\quad$ runEarly a_j from c_i	discharge one obligation early

Fig. 4. A simple expression language with compensation stacks

Figure 4 shows a simple expression language involving compensation stacks. Normal program variables (e.g., integers) and objects (e.g., Sockets) are abstracted away. The join points after the non-deterministic conditional and loop model arbitrary control flow. This draconian simplification is sufficient for modeling compensating actions along all paths: gotos, while loops and exceptions merely provide additional control-flow branches and join points. Exceptions are tricky for programmers to deal with because they introduce control-flow that is invisible to human eyes. Such control flow paths are examined by our analysis (see Section 3); the type system presented here works similarly.

The compensation expressions are as described in Section 7. Each static let $c_i =$ new CompStack() in e in the program is annotated with a fresh i for bookkeeping purposes. The store c_i expression represents storing a compensation stack in a global variable and setting a finalizer to run its compensations. Perhaps the most important detail is that run c_i and runEarly a_j from c_i remove compensations from stacks after executing them at run-time. Compensations are removed from stacks even if those stacks are stored in memory or global variables. There is no danger of a "double-free" in calling run c_i multiple times.

Each compensation stack in this system is similar to a tracked resource in a linear type system [11]. Whenever a compensation stack is in scope, we know statically at what location i it was allocated (or loaded). The typing rules for compensation stacks are orthogonal to the typing rules for normal program objects. This type system rejects programs in which it cannot be guaranteed that all compensations will be executed.

A compensation stack, which might store un-executed compensations, may only go out of scope if it is stored in a global or if we can prove statically that

$$\frac{}{C,D \vdash \mathsf{skip} : C,D} \; skip \qquad \frac{C_1,D_1 \vdash e_1 : C_2,D_2 \quad C_2,D_2 \vdash e_2 : C_3,D_3}{C_1,D_1 \vdash e_1 \; ; \; e_2 : C_3,D_3} \; seq$$

$$\frac{C_1,D_1 \vdash e_1 : C_2,D_2 \quad C_1,D_1 \vdash e_2 : C_3,D_3 \quad C_2 \cup D_2 = C_3 \cup D_3}{C_1,D_1 \vdash \mathsf{if} * \mathsf{then} \; e_1 \; \mathsf{else} \; e_2 : (C_2 \cup C_3),(D_2 \cap D_3)} \; if$$

$$\frac{C_1,D_1 \vdash e : C_2,D_2 \quad C_1 \cup D_1 = C_2 \cup D_2}{C_1,D_1 \vdash \mathsf{while} * \mathsf{do} \; e : C_1 \cup C_2, D_1 \cap D_2} \; while$$

$$\frac{C_1,D_1 \cup \{i\} \vdash e : C_2,D_2 \quad i \in D_2 \quad D_3 = D_2 \setminus \{i\}}{C_1,D_1 \vdash \mathsf{let} \; c_i = \; \mathsf{new} \; \mathsf{CompStack}() \; \mathsf{in} \; e : C_2,D_3} \; let$$

$$\frac{i \in C}{C,D \vdash \mathsf{compensate} \; a_j \; \mathsf{with} \; b_j \; \mathsf{using} \; c_i : C,D} \; compC$$

$$\frac{D_2 = D_1 \setminus \{i\} \quad i \in D_1}{C,D_1 \vdash \mathsf{compensate} \; a_j \; \mathsf{with} \; b_j \; \mathsf{using} \; c_i : C \cup \{i\},D_2} \; compD$$

$$\frac{C_2 = C_1 \setminus \{i\} \quad i \in C_1}{C_1,D \vdash \mathsf{store} \; c_i : C_2, D \cup \{i\}} \; storeC \qquad \frac{i \in D}{C,D \vdash \mathsf{store} \; c_i : C,D} \; storeD$$

$$\frac{C_1 \cup \{i\},D_1 \vdash e : C_2,D_2 \quad C_3 = C_2 \setminus \{i\} \quad i \in C_2 \quad D_3 = D_2 \setminus \{i\} \quad i \in D_2}{C_1,D_1 \vdash \mathsf{let} \; c_i = \; \mathsf{load} \; \mathsf{in} \; e : C_3,D_3} \; load$$

$$\frac{C_2 = C_1 \setminus \{i\} \quad i \in C_1}{C_1,D_1 \vdash \mathsf{run} \; c_i : C_2, D \cup \{i\}} \; runC \qquad \frac{i \in D}{C,D \vdash \mathsf{run} \; c_i : C,D} \; runD$$

$$\frac{i \in C \cup D}{C,D \vdash \mathsf{runEarly} \; a_j \; \mathsf{from} \; c_i : C,D} \; early$$

Fig. 5. Expression language static semantics

all of its compensations have been executed. We approximate this by requiring that run c_i or store c_i occur after the last compensate a_j with b_j using c_i before c_i goes out of scope. Our typing judgment maintains two *disjoint* sets: C, a set of "live" compensation stacks that may have un-executed compensations, and D, a set of "dead" compensation stacks on which all compensations have been executed or stored in memory. Adding a compensation to a dead stack makes it live. Thus we propose an effect type system for compensation stacks.

The form of our typing judgment is $C,D \vdash e : C',D'$. This judgment says that expression e typechecks in the context of live compensation stacks C and unused stacks D and that after executing the expression the set of live stacks will be C' and the set of unused stacks will be D'.

Figure 5 shows the typing rules for the language in Figure 4. The *seq* rule shows that this is a flow-sensitive type system for compensation stacks. The conservative *if* rule describes the effects of a conditional. Recalling the invariant $C \cap D = \emptyset$, at the conditional join point the resulting live set C_3 contains all stacks that might be live after either branch and the dead set D_3 contains all stacks that are dead after both branches. The $C_2 \cup D_2 = C_3 \cup D_3$ requirement prevents programs from creating a new compensation stack on one branch of the conditional. This is impossible in our example language where newly-created compensation stacks have local scope, but is possible in our Java implementation.

The *while* rule is also conservative. If the loop body can make a stack live, we assume that it does. If body might make a stack dead, we assume that it does not (a program must execute those stacks again later).

The *let* rule makes a new compensation stack and requires that it be dead as it goes out of scope. The *comp* rules are relatively simple since stack management happens at run-time. Adding a compensation to a dead stack makes it live and compensations can only be added to valid, in-scope stacks.

The *store* rules simulate storing a compensation stack in a global variable and consigning ultimate care of it to a finalizer. When it is finalized the run-time system will execute any remaining compensations associated with it. There is rarely a reason to store a stack with no outstanding obligations; the *storeD* is provided for completeness. The *load* rule is similar to the *let* rule but the stack need not be locally dead as it goes out of scope since it is still live in memory.

The *run* rules execute all remaining compensations in the given stack and ensure that it is dead. The *run* and *store* rules are the only way to move a stack from the live set C to the dead set D, so every stack must pass through a *run* or *store* rule at least once just before going out of scope.

The *early* rule models our syntax for allowing the user to execute certain compensations early. If the particular compensation has already been executed or is otherwise no longer on the appropriate stack, nothing happens at run-time. Regardless, the *early* rule cannot make a stack dead.

We say that a program e typechecks if $\emptyset, \emptyset \vdash e : \emptyset, \emptyset$. Our system can be viewed as a linear type system for *sets of resources* rather than a linear type system for individual resources. A program containing a loop that allocates resources and puts obligations to deallocate them on a stack c_i can be statically type-checked provided that run c_i occurs after any compensations are added to c_i on all paths containing c_i before it goes out of scope. Similarly, programs in which only one branch of a conditional adds an obligation to a compensation stack are handled naturally. We also expect that it will be easier to avoid aliasing compensation stacks than it is to avoid aliasing individual resources (e.g., in the same way that it is easier to manually allocate and destroy regions of objects then it is to manually use `malloc` and `free` for individual objects).

This formal model does not track whether individual elements in a compensation stack have been executed. In practice, especially for lexically-scoped compensation stacks that do not escape their scope, a static analysis similar to the one in Section 3 can often determine exactly what the elements of such a stack might be. In such cases the implementation can optimize away the dynamic compensation stack object and insert the compensation code directly (effectively writing correct nested `finally-close` blocks for the programmer). We do not model such performance optimizations here.

We do not discuss method calls and returns here. An annotation system similar to the one described in Vault [11] suffices: each function type also specifies its requirements for compensation stacks and how it transforms them. The type system is also amenable to the standard extension for handling exceptions. For example, "try A B C catch D", where B may raise an exception, can be modeled as if $*$ then A ; B ; C else A ; B ; D. Type checking can be done by dataflow analysis (as in Section 3) without such code transformations.

9   Case Studies

We hand-annotated two programs to show that: (1) the run-time overhead is low; (2) it is easy to modify existing programs to use compensation stacks; and (3) it would not be difficult to write a new program from scratch using them. Guided by the dataflow analysis in Section 3, the programs' error handling was modified to use compensation stacks; no truly new error handling was added and the behavior was otherwise unchanged. This commonly amounted to removing a `close` call (and its guarding `finally`) and using a `CompensationStack` instead (possibly with a method that had been annotated to take a compensation stack parameter). The overhead of maintaining the stack was dwarfed by the I/O latency in our case studies. As a micro-benchmark example, a program that creates hundreds of `Socket`s and connects each to a website is 0.7% slower if a compensation stack tracks obligations to close the `Socket`s.

The first case study, Aaron Brown's undo-able email store [5], is a mail proxy that uses database-like logging. The original version was 35,412 lines of Java code. Annotating the program took about four hours and involved updating 128 sites to use compensations as well as annotating the interfaces for some library methods (e.g., `sockets` and databases). The resulting program was 225 lines shorter (about 1%) because redundant error-handling code and control-flow were removed. The program contains non-trivial error handling, including one five-step saga of actions and compensations and one three-step saga. Compensating actions ranged from simple `close` calls to 34-line code blocks with internal exception handling and synchronization. The annotated program's performance was almost identical to the original on fifty micro-benchmarks and one example workload (all provided by the original author). Performance was measured to be within one standard deviation of the original, and was generally within one half of a standard deviation; the overhead of tracking obligations at run-time was dwarfed by I/O and other processing times. Compensations were used to handle every request answered by the program. Finally, by injecting a run-time error in the same cleanup code in both versions of the program, we were able to cause the unmodified version to drop all SMTP requests. The version using compensations handled that cleanup failure correctly and proceeded normally. While targeted fault injection is hardly representative, it does show that the errors addressed with compensations can have an impact on reliability.

The second case study, Sun's `Pet Store 1.3.2` [21], is a web-based, database-backed retailing program. The original version was 34,608 lines of Java code. Annotations to 123 sites took about two hours. The resulting program was 168 lines smaller (about 0.5%). Most error handling annotations centered around database `Connection`s. Using an independent workload [1,22], the original version raises 150 exceptions from the `PurchaseOrderHelper`'s `processInvoice` method over the course of 3,900 requests. The exceptions signal run-time errors related to

RelationSets being held too long (e.g., because they are not cleared along with their connections on some paths) and are caught by a middleware layer which restarts the application.[3] The annotated version of the program raises no such exceptions: compensation stacks ensure that the database objects are handled correctly. The average response times for the original program (over multiple runs) is 52.06 milliseconds (ms), with a standard deviation of 100 ms. The average response time for the annotated program is 43.44 ms with a standard deviation of 77 ms. The annotated program is both more consistent, because less middleware intervention was necessary, and also 17% faster.

Together, these case studies suggest that compensation stacks are a natural and efficient model for this sort of run-time error handling. The decrease in code size argues that common idioms are captured by this formalism and that there is a software engineering benefit to associating error handling with interfaces. The unchanging or improved performance indicates that leaving some checks to run time is reasonable. Finally, the checks ensure that cleanup code is invoked correctly along all paths through the program.

10   Conclusion

Software reliability remains an important and expensive issue. This chapter presents an approach for addressing a certain class of software reliability problems. We focus on exceptional situations, an aspect of software reliability that remains under-investigated.

First, we presented a static dataflow analysis for finding bugs in how programs deal with important resources in the presence of exceptional situations. The flow-sensitive, context-insensitive analysis scales well to large programs. The analysis found over 1,200 methods with mistakes in almost 4 million lines of Java code.

Second, based on those exception-handling bugs we designed a language feature to make it easier to fix such mistakes. We characterized why existing language features were insufficient. We proposed that programmers keep track of important obligations at run-time in special compensation stacks We provide a static semantics for compensation stacks to highlight their differences from previous approaches like pure linear type systems. In two case studies we showed that it is easy to apply compensation stacks to existing Java programs and that they can be used to make programs simpler and, in some cases, more reliable.

We find this work to be a successful step toward making software more reliable in the presence of exceptional situations. Using our analysis we can analyze programs to find error-handling mistakes. Once mistakes have been located we provide programmers with an easy-to-use tool for fixing them. All of this can be done cheaply, before the program is deployed. We hope that this approach, or approaches like it, will be more frequently adopted in the future.

---

[3] While updating a purchase order to reflect items shipped, the processInvoice method creates an Iterator from a RelationSet Collection that deals with persistent data in a database. Unfortunately, the transaction associated with the RelationSet has already been completed.

References

1. Candea, G., Delgado, M., Chen, M., Fox, A.: Automatic failure-path inference: A generic introspection technique for internet applications. In: IEEE Workshop on Internet Applications, San Jose, California (2003)
2. Fu, C., Ryder, B., Milanova, A., Wannacott, D.: Testing of java web services for robustness. In: International Symposium on Software Testing and Analysis. (2004)
3. Goodenough, J.B.: Exception handling: issues and a proposed notation. Communications of the ACM **18** (1975) 683–696
4. Weimer, W., Necula, G.C.: Finding and preventing run-time error handling mistakes. In: Object-oriented programming, systems, languages, and applications. (2004) 419–431
5. Brown, A., Patterson, D.: Undo for operators: Building an undoable e-mail store. In: USENIX Annual Technical Conference. (2003)
6. Engler, D., Chelf, B., Chou, A., Hallem, S.: Checking system rules using system-specific, programmer-written compiler extensions. In: Operating Systems Design and Implementation. (2000)
7. Das, M., Lerner, S., Seigle, M.: ESP: path-sensitive program verification in polynomial time. SIGPLAN Notices **37** (2002) 57–68
8. Ball, T., Rajamani, S.K.: Automatically validating temporal safety properties of interfaces. In: SPIN 2001, Workshop on Model Checking of Software. Volume 2057 of Lecture Notes in Computer Science. (2001) 103–122
9. Chen, H., Dean, D., Wagner, D.: Model checking one million lines of C code. In: Network and Distributed System Security Symposium, San Diego, CA (2004)
10. Kildall, G.A.: A unified approach to global program optimization. In: Principles of Programming Languages, ACM Press (1973) 194–206
11. DeLine, R., Fähndrich, M.: Enforcing high-level protocols in low-level software. In: Programming Language Design and Implementation. (2001) 59–69
12. Kremenek, T., Ashcraft, K., Yang, J., Engler, D.: Correlation exploitation in error ranking. In: Foundations of software engineering. (2004) 83–93
13. Weimer, W., Necula, G.C.: Mining temporal specifications for error detection. Volume 3440 of Lecture Notes in Computer Science. (2005) 461–476
14. Gay, D., Aiken, A.: Memory management with explicit regions. In: Programming Language Design and Implementation. (1998) 313–323
15. O'Hanley, J.: Always close streams. In: http://www.javapractices.com/. (2005)
16. Boehm, H.J.: Destructors, finalizers and synchronization. In: Principles of Programming Languages, ACM (2003)
17. Korth, H.F., Levy, E., Silberschatz, A.: A formal approach to recovery by compensating transactions. In: The VLDB Journal. (1990) 95–106
18. Alonso, G., Kamath, M., Agrawal, D., Abbadi, A.E., Gunthor, R., Mohan, C.: Failure handling in large-scale workflow management systems. Technical Report RJ9913, IBM Almaden Research Center, San Jose, CA (1994)
19. Odersky, M., Wadler, P.: Pizza into Java: Translating theory into practice. In: Principles of Programming Languages. (1997) 146–159
20. Alonso, G., Hagen, C., Agrawal, D., Abbadi, A.E., Mohan, C.: Enhancing the fault tolerance of workflow management systems. IEEE Concurrency **8** (2000) 74–81
21. Sun Microsystems: Java pet store 1.1.2 blueprint application. In: http://java.sun.com/blueprints/code/. (2001)
22. Chen, M.Y., Kiciman, E., Fratkin, E., Fox, A., Brewer, E.: Pinpoint: Problem determination in large, dynamic Internet services. In: International Conference on Dependable Systems and Networks, IEEE Computer Society (2002) 595–604

Exception Handling in the Choices Operating System

Francis M. David, Jeffrey C. Carlyle, Ellick M. Chan,
David K. Raila, and Roy H. Campbell

University of Illinois at Urbana-Champaign, Urbana IL 61820, USA
{fdavid, jcarlyle, emchan, raila, rhc}@uiuc.edu
http://choices.cs.uiuc.edu/

Abstract. Exception handling is a powerful abstraction that can be
used to help manage errors and support the construction of reliable operating systems. Using exceptions to notify system components about
exceptional conditions also reduces coupling of error handling code and
increases the modularity of the system. We explore the benefits of incorporating exception handling into the Choices operating system in order
to improve reliability. We extend the set of exceptional error conditions
in the kernel to include critical kernel errors such as invalid memory access and undefined instructions by wrapping them with language-based
software exceptions. This allows developers to handle both hardware and
software exceptions in a simple and unified manner through the use of
an exception hierarchy. We also describe a catch-rethrow approach for
exception propagation across protection domains. When an exception
is caught by the system, generic recovery techniques like policy-driven
micro-reboots and restartable processes are applied, thus increasing the
reliability of the system.

1   Introduction

Improving operating system reliability has always been a hot research topic
[1,2,3,4]. In today's world, this goal is more important than ever before because
the need for better networking, security, performance and features has resulted
in increasingly complex systems. Resilience to faults, in both hardware and software, is an important factor affecting reliability [5]. There are many serious
errors that can occur inside an operating system [6]. Deadlocks, race conditions, and buffer overflows are some software errors that can cause operating
system failure. Hardware errors, such as memory access errors, can also occur
in a running system. Most operating systems will terminate user processes that
encounter hardware errors; however, the operating systems themselves usually
crash if they encounter such errors when executing critical kernel code [7].

On detecting critical errors in kernel code, Linux, Mac OS and several other
UNIX-like operating systems call a panic function which brings the system to
a halt. Microsoft Windows displays a kernel stop error message in a blue background [8]. Some of these signaled failures [9] might be avoidable through techniques like micro-rebooting [10], automatic data structure repair [11] or device

C. Dony et al. (Eds.):Exception Handling, LNCS 4119, pp. 42–61, 2006.
© Springer-Verlag Berlin Heidelberg 2006

driver recovery [12]. These techniques can be deployed more effectively when a framework for detecting and communicating errors within the operating system kernel is available.

Exceptions are currently widely used in user-space code to handle software error conditions. We were motivated to explore the benefits of incorporating exception handling support in an operating system in order to build a more robust and reliable kernel that can detect and recover from errors in both hardware and software. Creating software exceptions upon encountering hardware errors and allowing them to be handled by operating system code in the same manner as explicitly thrown software exceptions results in a flexible and unified approach for conveying both hardware and software errors.

In this paper, we explore the feasibility and limitations of using exception handling in an operating system. In particular, we describe our experiences using C++ exception handling support in the object oriented Choices operating system [13]. Exceptions can be thrown for any detected error that can be attributed to a process. This paper specifically addresses errors signaled by the processor. Processor exceptions generated by errant code or faulty hardware are converted to software exceptions and are thrown using C++ language semantics. This is accomplished with no modifications to the compiler or the run time library.

Choices has support for switching memory protection domains within the kernel in order to isolate parts of the kernel from each other. This support is similar to the work done in the Nooks project [4]. To allow exceptions to work across protection boundaries, they are caught at the entry point of the callee domain and are re-thrown in the caller domain.

Exceptions present a strong framework for building recovery solutions in the operating system. Exception handlers are used to enhance Choices with support for automatically restartable processes and a simple form of micro-rebooting. Policies are used along with these recovery mechanisms and provide more flexibility in controlling and managing them. In addition to these generic recovery mechanisms provided by Choices, exceptions also allow kernel developers to write custom localized error handlers.

Once the exception handling framework was implemented, less than 100 lines of code in the Choices kernel were required to implement automatically restartable processes and micro-reboots. Without the use of exceptions, implementing these recovery mechanisms would involve the design of complex asynchronous signaling schemes to send and receive error notifications. The semantics of such a scheme might be unfamiliar to new developers. Exception handling abstracts away complexity and presents a clean and widely accepted means to manage errors.

Our exception framework exploits the polymorphism provided by C++ and is easily portable and maintainable. Machine and processor independent code in Choices only work with abstract exception objects. This results in more maintainable code when newer exception objects are added to a particular architecture. The code is also portable because machine and processor independent code need not change when exception support is added to newer architectures.

An important advantage of using C++ exceptions to clean up after a serious operating system kernel error is the automatic language-supported garbage collection during stack unwinding. The C++ exception handling framework automatically calls destructors for objects associated with a stack frame when unwinding the stack. This provides some benefits by reducing memory leaks when a kernel process is terminated by an exception.

There is a trade-off between space and performance when switching between different C++ compiler implementations of exceptions. The performance overhead when using exception handling is negligible if the compiler implementation of exceptions uses tables [14] instead of time consuming context saves and restores [15]. We evaluate this trade-off in more detail in section 5.

Researchers have worked on including exception handling support in the Linux kernel [16]; however, unlike our work, they have not incorporated support for generating C++ exceptions from hardware errors. We compare and contrast our work with other related research in more detail in section 6.

Our contributions in this paper include:

1. A unified framework for handling both hardware and software generated errors in kernel space code using exceptions.
2. A design for handling exceptions across virtual memory protection domains within the Choices kernel.
3. A description of initial experiences with operating system recovery mechanisms, namely automatically restartable processes and micro-reboots, that can be deployed using exceptions.
4. An evaluation of the space and performance overhead associated with the use of exception handling in an operating system kernel.

The remainder of this paper is organized as follows. Section 2 presents a brief introduction to exceptions and the Choices operating system. It also describes the terminology used in this paper. In section 3, we discuss our design and implementation of the exception handling framework within Choices. Section 4 illustrates some applications and usage of the exception framework. We then present results of some experimental evaluations in section 5, explore related work in section 6 and conclude in section 7.

2   Background

2.1   Exceptions

Exceptions are events that disrupt the normal execution flow of a program. Languages like Java and C++ provide constructs for programmers to write code to both generate exceptions and handle them. In C++, an exception is generated using the **throw** keyword. The **catch** keyword is used to define a code block that handles exceptions.

Exceptions have several advantages [17] over traditional mechanisms for conveying errors. The use of exception handling allows software developers to avoid return value overloading and clearly separate error handling code from regular code. Using error codes to signal error conditions either requires ugly global variables or requires propagating them down the call stack, sometimes through methods that do not care about them. Exceptions, on the other hand, are directly dispatched to methods that have handler code. Yet another benefit of using exceptions is apparent in the object-oriented world. When exceptions are expressed using objects, class hierarchies can be used to classify and group error conditions.

2.2   The Choices Operating System

Choices is a full featured object-oriented operating system developed at the University of Illinois at Urbana-Champaign. The Choices kernel is implemented as a dynamic collection of interacting objects. System resources, policies and mechanisms are represented by objects organized in class hierarchies. The system architecture consists of a number of subsystem design frameworks [18] that implement generalized designs, constraints, and a skeletal structure for customizations. Key classes within the frameworks can be subclassed to achieve portability, customizations and optimizations without sacrificing performance [19]. The design frameworks are inherited and customized by each hardware specific implementation of the system providing a high degree of reuse and consistency between implementations.

Choices has been ported to and runs on the SPARC [20], Intel x86 [21] and ARM platforms. Similar to User Mode Linux [22], a virtual machine port called Virtual Choices [23] which runs on Solaris and Linux has also been developed. Choices is currently being used as a learning tool in operating systems courses at the University of Illinois at Urbana-Champaign. It is also being used as an experimental platform for research in operating systems for mobile devices and multi-core processors.

2.3   Terminology

Since there is varied usage of the terms used in this paper, we clearly define the terms we use. The terms fault, error and failure are used as defined in [9].

As shown in figure 1, processor interrupts can arise from both hardware and software sources. Peripheral devices can use hardware interrupts to communicate asynchronous events to the processor. For instance, a serial port may interrupt the processor to indicate it has received data.

In addition to hardware sources of interrupts, the software running on a processor may also directly cause an interrupt. Software sources of interrupts can be classified into two categories. Processors generally provide a means for invoking an interrupt via the instruction set. The x86 architecture provides the INT instruction, and the ARM architecture provides the SWI instruction. This mechanism is used to implement system calls. The other category is processor exceptions. A processor exception indicates that some sort of "exceptional" event has occurred during execution. There are many causes of processor exceptions,

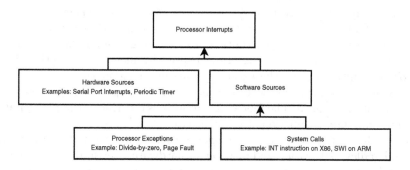

Fig. 1. Terminology

and possible processor exceptions vary between architectures. Example processor exceptions include division by zero, execution of an undefined instruction, and page faults. It is important to note that not all processor exceptions indicate errors. For instance, page faults are usually handled by the operating system and only result in an error if the faulting process has no valid mapping for the requested page.

In the following sections, words that are in italics, like *Process*, are Choices classes.

3   Exception Handling in Choices

Our kernel-level exception handling support has been implemented in the ARM port of Choices. The Choices ARM port currently runs on hardware development platforms based on the Texas Instruments OMAP [24] architecture. Choices also runs under the QEMU [25] ARM system emulator which emulates the hardware found in the Integrator family [26] of development boards. Since most of our exceptions code is processor and machine independent, porting it to another platform is not a difficult task. Also, a large portion of work described in this paper is OS independent and not tightly coupled with Choices. Several ideas and techniques presented in this paper are directly applicable to other operating systems as well. This is discussed in more detail in section 7.

3.1   Creating C++ Exceptions from Processor Exceptions

The first implementation of Choices predates the introduction of exceptions into the C++ language. Therefore, C++ exceptions were not used in the code. We added support for C++ language exceptions to Choices by porting Choices to compile under the GNU g++ compiler which automatically includes all of its exception management libraries.

When using exception handling in an operating system, the use of language exceptions to represent error conditions resulting from processor exceptions is a natural next step. This results in a seamless and uniform framework for working with operating system error conditions. C++ "catch" statements would then be able to handle serious processor exceptions like invalid instructions which might be caused by memory corruption or other programming faults. There is, however, a caveat when handling errors caused by memory corruption. If the memory corruption affects the exception handling code or support data itself, recovery may be difficult. Other than this scenario, exceptions are a useful error management mechanism. The following paragraphs describe our implementation of exception handling functionality in Choices.

Choices has a per processor *InterruptManager*. It manages all of the initialization, handler registration and dispatch of hardware interrupts, software interrupts and processor exceptions in a unified manner. All processor interrupts are first delivered to the *InterruptManager*. The *InterruptManager* then dispatches the interrupt to a pre-registered handler. The *InterruptManager* is a machine independent abstract C++ class. It only includes code for handler registration and dispatch, and it delegates hardware initialization and interrupt number lookup to machine specific subclasses.

Choices registers special handlers with the *InterruptManager* for all processor exceptions like invalid instructions or memory access errors that require the generation of language exceptions. When the processor is handling an interrupt, the context of the interrupted process is available in a *Context* object associated with the *Process*. If the interrupt is due to a processor exception that signals an error, the registered special handler is invoked. The handler creates an appropriate *Exception* object and associates it with the *Process* object representing the currently running process. The *Exception* object includes a saved copy of the current context and a stack backtrace. This information is useful for debugging. The handler then updates the program counter (PC) in the *Context* of the interrupted process to point to the throwException function (see listing in figure 2). The special processor exception handler now returns, and the context of the interrupted process (with the modified PC) is restored to the processor. This causes the process to immediately jump to throwException.

The code in throwException extracts the saved exception object from the *Process* object and throws it. Thus, it appears as if the process called a function throwing a C++ exception at the exact instruction address where it encountered a processor exception. This implementation allows for precise identification of the instruction that encountered the error and allows for a smooth translation of processor exceptions to C++ exceptions. Figure 3 illustrates the flow of control in the interrupt handler for a processor exception.

```
void throwException() {
  // Throw saved exception object
  throw thisProcess()->getException();
}
```

Fig. 2. Code for the function that throws the exception

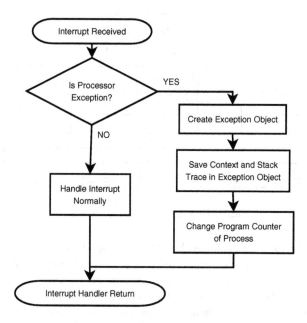

Fig. 3. Processor exception control flow

Another implementation option that was considered was directly modifying the processor exception causing instruction and replacing it with a call to `throwException`. The idea was to execute the calling instruction on returning from the interrupt handler. On processors with separate instruction and data caches, this technique would require a cache flush in order to ensure that the modified instruction is correctly fetched when execution is resumed. But this design is not safe when there are multiple processes that share the same code. This implementation was therefore discarded in favor of the PC modifying technique.

Since processor exceptions may occur anywhere in the code, the stack unwinding libraries must be prepared to handle exceptions within any context. This functionality is enabled by a special GNU g++ compiler flag, "-fnon-call-exceptions". Without the use of this flag, only explicitly thrown exceptions are handled. This option is typically used from user-space code that attempts to throw exceptions from signal handlers. In the kernel, this allows an exception to be correctly dispatched even in the absence of an explicit throw call.

Unlike the x86 architecture, which detects a large set of processor exceptions such as divide-by-zero, protection faults, device unavailable, invalid opcode, alignment checks and so on, the ARM processor only classifies exceptions into three types. The C++ exception class hierarchy in Choices for the ARM processor is modeled in figure 4. *ARMDataAccessException* is thrown when the processor encounters an error while trying to fetch data. This is the result of a page fault when virtual memory is enabled. *ARMInstructionAccessException* is thrown when the processor encounters an error while trying to fetch an instruction. This is also called a prefetch abort. *ARMUndefinedInstructionException* is

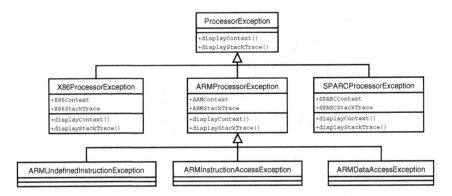

Fig. 4. Processor exception classes

thrown when the instruction is invalid. This is equivalent to the Invalid OpCode exception for x86. All processor exceptions are derived from an abstract super-class called *ProcessorException. ProcessorException* exports abstract methods implemented by subclasses to access the context and stack trace of processor-specific exceptions. This classification allows processor-specific code to respond differently to different types of exceptions. The use of the abstract superclass allows machine and processor independent code to catch all processor exceptions independent of the architecture and handle them using generic mechanisms.

3.2   Cross Domain Exceptions

Choices supports a simple form of virtual memory based protection domains within kernel code in order to detect errors because of invalid accesses to memory. This was designed to isolate code within the kernel similar to the Nooks project [4] and run device drivers in untrusted isolated domains. Protection is possible for I/O regions, kernel text sections and other defined sensitive code or data regions. For example, the serial port driver is the only object in the system that is allowed to access the serial port I/O addresses. Wrapper objects are used to switch the domain associated with a process when calling a method on an object associated with a different domain. When the method call is completed, the wrapper switches the process back to its original domain. The stack and the heap of the process are also switched when switching to an untrusted domain. They are switched back when returning to the caller. But, the normal method call return is not the only possible return path. Switching back to the calling domain is also necessary when an exception is thrown. In order to correctly switch back to the calling domain in the presence of exceptions, the wrapper catches all exceptions thrown in the called domain and rethrows them in the calling domain after switching back domains. Objects allocated in the callee domain are also visible in the calling domain. There is therefore no need for copying of exception objects between the domains.

The implementation uses user-mode privileges for untrusted domains. A protection domain in Choices only protects against errors in software code like invalid accesses to memory. We have not yet considered deliberately malicious code. We are in the process of refactoring more device drivers to isolate them into untrusted domains.

Unlike other systems that support cross domain exceptions, like Java, there is no need for serialization or deserialization of the exception objects. This is because the protection domains in Choices are virtual memory based and exception objects are visible in the calling domain. There exist no network or language representation issues that force the need for a serialized representation of objects.

4   Applications

4.1   Stack Garbage Collection

An important advantage when using exceptions to recover after a serious error is the automatic language supported garbage collection of stack objects during unwinding. The C++ exception handling framework automatically cleans up objects associated with a stack frame when unwinding the stack. This prevents some memory leaks and is useful in user processes. Using language exceptions in kernel processes brings these benefits to the operating system. For example, when a *HashTable* object is created on the stack by a kernel process, it requests heap memory to store internal data structures. This heap memory is reclaimed only when the destructor of the object is called. If exception handling is not used, and the fault is handled by just terminating the process, the stack is discarded and the heap allocated memory cannot be reclaimed. Exception handling does not eliminate all possible memory leaks during stack unwinding. Memory leaks can still occur when some objects allocated on the heap are not reclaimed because references to them were not stored into stack objects before the exception was thrown.

This issue does not arise in user-space because the entire process memory is reclaimed when the process is terminated. Microkernel operating systems are also less prone to this problem because system processes are treated like user processes and have access to their own private heap memory. In this case, terminating a kernel process correctly reclaims all associated memory. The Choices kernel, like most other monolithic operating system kernels, is susceptible to such memory leaks because it shares the same heap allocator for the trusted kernel domain across all kernel processes. Using exception handling reduces these memory leaks, which would otherwise persist until a reboot and result in poor memory utilization.

4.2   Restartable Kernel Processes

Transient memory errors due to cosmic radiation or buggy hardware can cause an operating system process to crash. Restarting processes afresh after they crash is usually an effective recovery technique. Microsoft Windows, for example, allows user-space services to be configured so that they are automatically restarted when they crash. The same principle can also be applied to kernel processes in Choices. With the exception handling framework in place, it is easy to write a wrapper for processes to be automatically restarted if an unhandled exception unwinds to the first stack frame.

A *RestartableProcess* class encapsulates the entry point of a restartable process and wraps a C++ try catch block around the initial start call to the process. The try catch block is enclosed in an infinite loop. This results in the ability to create infinitely restartable kernel processes within Choices. The process is terminated only when it explicitly calls the `die()` function. This implementation of restarts differs from a normal terminate and re-create because it does not destroy the *Process* object. The same object is reused and continues to represent the restarted process. Restart time is only governed by the time taken to run the exception handling routines. Thus, restarts through exceptions could be faster than restarts through terminating and re-creating processes if the stack does not contain many objects that need to be destroyed.

Exception handling also helps reduce memory leaks during restarts as described in 4.1. Without exceptions, repeated restarts that leak memory would eventually result in a full kernel heap, rendering the system unusable.

4.3   Micro-reboots

A simple form of micro-rebooting [10] is also easily implemented using exception support. We implement micro-reboots as function call level retries with an optional reboot (reconstruction) of the callee object. This is different from the process level restarts described in the previous section.

When calling into exclusively owned objects that might cause an exception, a *MicroReboot* wrapper is used. The wrapper is implemented as a preprocessor macro. It is designed to retry the request if it encounters an exception. Some errors however, will occur again on a simple retry if the state of the object is corrupted. It is possible that checking and repairing object state could fix the fault and prevent it from occurring again. Objects can export a method called `sanitize` that cleans up internal state. If an exception is raised within an object that exports this method, the wrapper runs the state sanitizer and retries the request. If state sanitization isn't supported, the object is micro-rebooted, that is, destroyed and reconstructed. The current implementation places the burden of writing a state sanitizer on the developer, but this does not preclude the possibility of including an automatic state cleanup mechanism like automatic data structure repair [11] or environment modifying mechanisms like RX [27].

Our implementation of micro-reboots only applies to objects that are restored to correct state when destroyed and reconstructed. This requirement, however, applies to all micro-rebootable systems [10].

4.4   Policy-Driven Restarts

The implementation of infinitely restartable processes described in 4.2 does not provide much flexibility in control or management. In order to provide developers

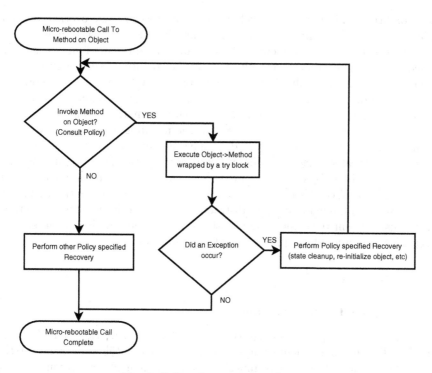

Fig. 5. Policy-driven micro-reboots

more control over restartable processes, this implementation has been extended with support for specification of simple policies that govern restarts. For example, a policy can specify a limit on the number of times a process is restarted. A similar policy specification is also available for controlling micro-reboots. The flow of control for policy-driven micro-reboots is shown in figure 5. Policy specification requires process-specific semantic information and is therefore entrusted to kernel developers. Our current implementation stores policy information in integers which are used as arguments to the *RestartableProcess* object or the micro-reboot macro.

Policies can be made more expressive when encapsulated in an object. Exceptions can interact with these policies and provide helpful feedback for recovery. For example, this allows a stack overflow exception to be handled by increasing the size of the stack before the restart. This is somewhat similar to the effect achieved in the RX work [27] which improves recoverability by changing environment parameters and restarting. Policy objects are not yet implemented in Choices.

4.5   Improved Error Reporting

The use of exception handling is attractive to many kernel developers because it provides a simple mechanism for providing detailed information about an error condition and allows the developer to avoid return value overloading. For instance, consider the `kmalloc` function in the Linux kernel. `kmalloc` is used to allocate kernel addressable memory. The return value of this function is overloaded. If the return value is non-null, the value is a pointer to the newly allocated memory. A null return value indicates that an error was encountered; however, there is no indication as to why the call failed. Using exceptions, it is easy to create and throw an *Exception* object with rich information about the cause of the error and there is no reason to overload the meaning of the return value.

This method of reporting errors does have its drawbacks. It conflicts with some object oriented design paradigms [28] because implementation information may be exposed to objects earlier in the call chain that were interacting with an abstract interface. Using a class hierarchy for exceptions is useful in this case because components at high abstraction levels can interact with abstract exceptions. System developers should also carefully design their code so that exceptions are handled at appropriate abstraction levels.

5   Evaluation

5.1   Compiler Implementations

The GNU g++ compiler supports two different implementations for C++ exceptions. The first implementation is extremely portable [15] and is based on the `setjmp`/`longjmp` (SJLJ) pair of functions. This implements exceptions using a `setjmp` call to save context at C++ try blocks and in all functions with local objects that need to be destroyed when an exception unwinds stack frames. The `longjmp` call is used to restore saved contexts during stack unwinding. Since the context saves are performed irrespective of whether an exception is eventually raised or not, this implementation suffers a performance penalty. For example, this penalty is observed when the **new** operator is used to allocate memory from the heap. The standard library version of **new** is designed to throw a "bad_alloc" exception if the allocation fails. This design results in a context save at the beginning of every memory allocation request. Using SJLJ exceptions in an operating system also requires special precautions because the implementation uses state variables that need to be updated when switching contexts.

The DWARF2 [29] debugging information format specification allows for a table driven alternative implementation of exceptions that only executes extra code when an exception is actually thrown. There is no performance overhead during normal execution. This approach uses a static compiler-generated table which defines actions that need to be performed when an exception is thrown. Table 1 compares these two implementations. The trade-off in this approach is size for performance. Modern compilers implement exceptions using the table driven approach for better performance.

We have studied the size and performance impacts of our exception handling framework under both SJLJ and table-driven implementations. To test SJLJ exceptions, we build an ARM compiler from the published GNU g++ source code and enable SJLJ exceptions as part of the build process. For table driven

Table 1. Comparing SJLJ and Table-Driven implementations of exceptions

Characteristic	**SJLJ**	**Table-Driven**
Portability	Portable	Not portable
Normal execution performance	Affected because of frequent context saves	Not affected because tables are computed at compile time
Exception handling performance	Fast because context restore is cheap	Slower because of table based unwinding
Space overhead	Code to save contexts	Table entries for unwinding

exceptions, we use a version of the GNU g++ compiler published by Codesourcery [30] that implements table driven exceptions and also conforms to the ARM Exception Handling ABI [31]. We use the same version (4.1.0) of both these compilers.

5.2   Space Overhead

Adding exception handling support results in a larger operating system kernel. Researchers have reported kernel size increases of about 10% when adding exception handling to the Linux kernel [16]. Similar numbers for Choices are unavailable because the GNU g++ compiler does not allow disabling of exception handling support for C++ code. In this section we compare Choices kernels using SJLJ exceptions with kernels using table-driven exceptions. For each of these implementations, we build two versions of the kernel. One version only supports normal explicitly thrown exceptions. The other version includes support for mapping processor exceptions to language exceptions by using the "-fnon-call-exceptions" compiler flag.

All kernels were compiled to the ELF format with g++ optimization level 2. We measure the size of the .text section which holds program instructions, the .data section which holds program data, the .bss section which holds uninitialized data and the size of the sections holding exception handling data, such as tables and indices. Table 2 shows the results of our measurements. The sizes are also displayed in graphical form in figure 6.

The figure shows that the use of SJLJ exceptions increases the size of the program text area compared to table-driven exceptions. This is because of the extra

Table 2. Section sizes (in bytes) for different exception handling implementations

Choices	**SJLJ**		**Table-Driven**	
ELF section	Normal	Processor Exceptions	Normal	Processor Exceptions
.text	1,252,980	1,296,176	1,063,600	1,066,484
.data	29,056	29,056	28,500	28,500
.bss	297,984	297,984	297,740	297,740
exception data	9,476	10,980	117,364	131,284
everything else	275,868	288,152	272,044	274,512
Total	1,865,364	1,922,348	1,779,248	1,798,520

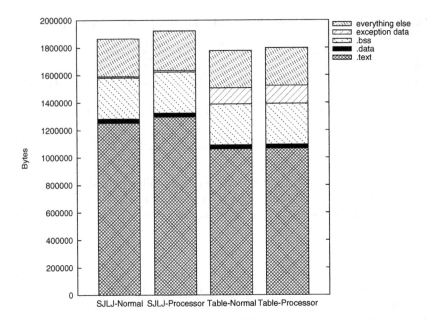

Fig. 6. Size comparison of Choices using different exception handling mechanisms

instructions for saving and restoring context that are inserted into all functions that define local objects. A small portion of the kernel (0.5%) is reserved for data that is used during exception handling. Adding support for mapping processor exceptions results in just a 3% increase in the size of the kernel. This increase is due to some extra exception handling code and data.

The kernel compiled with table-driven exceptions is about 4% smaller in size. There is a significant reduction in the size of the program text compared to SJLJ exceptions due to the elimination of extra instructions for saving context. But this reduction in size is offset by the large number of exception table entries. It is possible to reduce this overhead using table compression [14]. When processor exceptions support is added, the size of the kernel only increases by 1%.

5.3   Performance

In this section, we present the results of several performance tests of our kernel extensions. All experiments were conducted on the Texas Instruments OMAP 1610 H2 hardware development kit which is based on an ARM926EJ-S processor core. The processor clock frequency is set to 96MHz.

The overhead of using a single try block in a function was measured to be 14 nanoseconds for table-driven exceptions. This is less than the time taken to run two hardware instructions on the processor. Thus, table-driven exceptions have no noticeable impact on performance. For SJLJ exceptions, this overhead was measured to be 833 nanoseconds. This reflects the significant number of extra instructions that are executed by this implementation to support exception

Table 3. Time (in microseconds) for creating and restarting processes

Operation	SJLJ Exceptions	Table-Driven Exceptions
Create *Process*	6529	6330
Create *RestartableProcess*	6543	6347
Restart *Process*	6345	6200
Restart *RestartableProcess*	4320	4515

handling. But this overhead is still small compared to the time taken for most high-level kernel operations in Choices. For example, creating processes takes thousands of microseconds.

Table 3 shows the performance impact of using SJLJ exceptions versus table-driven exceptions for restartable processes. The overhead involved in creating a restartable process compared to a normal process is negligible for both cases. The table also shows the performance of restarts implemented through exceptions and the performance of restarts implemented through a terminate and re-create approach. These measurements are for a process that encounters an error when the call stack is one level deep and there are no objects on the stack. For both SJLJ and table-driven exceptions, the *RestartableProcess* performs slightly better because of the extra overhead involved in re-creating a normal process when it dies. It is possible that the stack unwinding for a *RestartableProcess* might take longer than re-creating the *Process* object if the call stack is deep or if a large number of objects need to be destroyed. SJLJ exceptions performs better for a restart of a *RestartableProcess* because exception propagation using longjmp is faster than unwinding the stack using tables.

Micro-reboot is implemented as a pre-processor macro and uses a single try block. The overhead associated with a micro-rebootable function call is essentially the overhead associated with the single try block. The overhead for domain crossings is similar to that of micro-reboot calls. These overheads are negligible when using table-driven exceptions.

5.4   Recovery Effectiveness

The automatic restart and micro-reboot wrappers have been extensively tested with test processes and manually injected faults. These wrappers were very effective at recovering from errors in the test cases. Initial results when converting some Choices kernel processes like the dispatcher to automatically restartable processes are encouraging. The dispatcher is what picks up ready processes from the scheduler and runs them. It is a critical Choices process that cannot afford to crash. In the original implementation, any error in the dispatcher resulted in the process being killed, rendering the system unusable. This behavior was changed by converting the dispatcher to an infinitely restartable process. In a QEMU based fault-injection experiment that was performed 1000 times, we randomly insert transient memory abort errors (both instruction and data) into the dispatcher. We found that the process was restarted and Choices was able to continue running other processes 78.9% of the time. We counted a restart as successful if Choices was able to load and run a program without errors after the restart. The failure to recover in some cases was due to locks that were held by the dispatcher when it crashed. Releasing acquired resources before restarting the process would increase the possibility of successful recovery.

We are in the process of gathering data to evaluate the effectiveness of the micro-reboot wrapper in recovering from errors within Choices. We expect our data to further support the findings in previous work [32,10] discussing the effectiveness of this technique in enhancing reliability.

6 Related Work

Motivated by the desire to use language frameworks for handling exceptions, researchers in Reykjavik University have added C++ style exception handling to the Linux kernel [16]. But their implementation is for the procedural C language based Linux environment. This unfortunately means that they cannot take advantage of rich exception objects and object oriented exception hierarchies. They have also not yet designed a mechanism to map processor errors to C++ exceptions. They have, however, optimized the exception handling code in order to increase performance. This and other techniques on enhancing exception handling performance [33,34,14,35] are complementary to our work and can be used to improve the performance of our system as well.

In UNIX-like systems, application programs are notified of issues like memory errors or divide by zero errors through signals instead of exceptions. Though it is possible to use compiler support to write signal handlers that throw exceptions, this behavior is deemed to be implementation defined in the ISO C++ standard [36]. Choices does not use signals, and exceptions are thrown from a function that is run by the errant *Process*. The SPIN operating system [37] written in Modula-3 also uses exception handling within the kernel, but processor errors are not mapped to language exceptions and instead cause the running process to be terminated.

Systems like CORBA [38] and Java also include support for cross-domain exceptions. These are implemented over heavyweight mechanisms like remote procedure call (RPC) and require serialization and deserialization of exception objects. Our implementation makes use of zero-copy transfer of exception objects between domains.

Most run-time systems choose to terminate a thread or the entire process if there is an unhandled exception. Microsoft's .NET framework [39] allows users to define global handlers for unhandled exception events. This avoids writing code to catch generic exception objects throughout the application. Java also allows for the specification of a handler which is called when a thread abruptly terminates due to an uncaught exception. Instead of terminating the thread, our design allows for the thread to automatically restart by resuming execution from its entry point. This design can also be easily implemented in other systems. Policy-driven exception handling has also been studied in other systems. Researchers have proposed a generic framework to design policy-driven fault management in distributed systems [40]. Recently, there has also been some work in designing policy-driven exception handling for composite web services [41].

There is a plethora of related work in fault tolerance. Researchers have been working on fault tolerance for decades. A NASA funded technical report [42] classifies existing techniques into single version techniques and multi-version techniques. Exception handling as described in this paper uses a single version of the software to try and recover from faults. Jim Gray described various techniques used to increase the mean time between failures for computer systems and concluded that transactions in addition to persistent process-pairs result in fault-tolerant execution [43]. Micro-rebooting [10] and automatic data structure recovery [11] are also single version techniques. Shadow device drivers [12] swap a faulty driver with a shadow driver for recovery. Ignoring errors for failure oblivious computing has also been explored [44]. Hypervisor based fault tolerance [45] runs OS replicas in sync with each other using a hypervisor. A reactive approach [46] builds self-healing software by detecting faults in an emulator and preventing that fault from occurring again. Error isolation and containment by using virtual memory protection has also been studied for device drivers [4]. Multi-version techniques include recovery blocks [47] and N-version software [48].

7   Conclusions and Future Work

Many of the ideas described in this paper are generic and are applicable to systems other than Choices. Creation of language exceptions from processor exceptions is possible in most operating systems that support only explicit exceptions. In particular, adding processor exception handling support to the exception enhanced Linux kernel can be accomplished by a technique similar to the PC-modifying method described in this paper. This would allow similar designs for restartable processes and micro-reboots to be used in Linux. Our designs for restartable processes and micro-reboots can also be used in user level application processes for some classes of exceptions. We are investigating the creation of a framework library that provides these mechanisms to application software.

Some exceptions are not recoverable through mechanisms described in this paper. Undefined instructions, for example could be encountered if there is corruption in memory. In this case, recovery may entail reloading the appropriate page of the executable from disk. Further research is needed in this area. We have also not considered exceptions that might be triggered in destructors during stack unwinding or in the exception handlers themselves. This is a limitation of our work and needs further investigation. Exceptions, while providing a unified framework for communicating faults, do not ensure that the operating system is in a safe state. Fail-stop operation of the kernel might avoid corruption of data, but could also lead to loss of data. Research is needed to explore the safety of the operating system in the presence of exceptions and recovery mechanisms.

The implementation of micro-reboots described in this paper relies only on exception handling for recovery. It is possible that the object causing the crash might have corrupted external state. Recent research [49] has shown that there is a good likelihood that operating systems can be recovered to a correct state if checkpoints are used. If micro-reboots are combined with checkpoints, external state corruption can be reduced. This is an avenue for future research.

We have described a unified framework that allows the use of exceptions in an operating system to manage errors caused by both hardware and software. We have also explored exceptions based extensions to Choices that support recovery through policy-driven automatic process restarts and micro-reboots and shown that they exhibit acceptable performance. These results indicate that exception handling presents a strong foundation for building reliable operating systems.

Acknowledgments

We would like to thank Gabriel Maajid for helpful discussions during the writing of this paper. We are also grateful for the detailed comments provided by the anonymous reviewers which helped shape the final version of this paper. Part of this research was made possible by a grant from DoCoMo Labs USA and generous support from Texas Instruments and Virtio.

References

1. Randell, B.: Operating Systems: The Problems of Performance and Reliability. In: Proceedings of IFIP Congress 71 Volume 1. (1971) 281–290
2. Denning, P.J.: Fault Tolerant Operating Systems. ACM Comput. Surv. 8(4) (1976) 359–389
3. Lee, I., Iyer, R.K.: Faults, Symptoms, and Software Fault Tolerance in the Tandem GUARDIAN90 Operating System. In: FTCS. (1993) 20–29
4. Swift, M.M., Bershad, B.N., Levy, H.M.: Improving the Reliability of Commodity Operating Systems. In: Proceedings of the nineteenth ACM Symposium on Operating Systems Principles, New York, NY, USA, ACM Press (2003) 207–222
5. Patterson, D., Brown, A., Broadwell, P., Candea, G., Chen, M., Cutler, J., Enriquez, P., Fox, A., Kiciman, E., Merzbacher, M., Oppenheimer, D., Sastry, N., Tetzlaff, W., Traupman, J., Treuhaft, N.: Recovery Oriented Computing (ROC): Motivation, Definition, Techniques, and Case Studies. Technical report, Berkeley, CA, USA (2002)
6. Chou, A., Yang, J., Chelf, B., Hallem, S., Engler, D.R.: An Empirical Study of Operating System Errors. In: Symposium on Operating Systems Principles. (2001) 73–88
7. Ganapathi, A.: Why Does Windows Crash? Technical Report UCB/CSD-05-1393, EECS Department, University of California, Berkeley (2005)
8. Blue Screen. (http://support.microsoft.com/kb/q129845/)
9. Avizienis, A., Laprie, J.C., Randell, B., Landwehr, C.E.: Basic Concepts and Taxonomy of Dependable and Secure Computing. IEEE Transactions on Dependable and Secure Computing 1(1) (2004) 11–33
10. Candea, G., Kawamoto, S., Fujiki, Y., Friedman, G., Fox, A.: Microreboot – A Technique for Cheap Recovery. In: Symposium on Operating Systems Design and Implementation, San Francisco, CA (2004)

11. Demsky, B., Rinard, M.: Automatic Data Structure Repair for Self-Healing Systems. In: Proceedings of the First Workshop on Algorithms and Architectures for Self-Managed Systems, San Diego, California (2003)

12. Swift, M.M., Annamalai, M., Bershad, B.N., Levy, H.M.: Recovering Device Drivers. In: Symposium on Operating Systems Design and Implementation. (2004) 1–16

13. Campbell, R.H., Johnston, G.M., Russo, V.: "Choices (Class Hierarchical Open Interface for Custom Embedded Systems)". ACM Operating Systems Review **21**(3) (1987) 9–17

14. de Dinechin, C.: C++ Exception Handling. IEEE Concurrency **8**(4) (2000) 72–79

15. Cameron, D., Faust, P., Lenkov, D., Mehta, M.: A Portable Implementation of C++ Exception Handling. In: USENIX C++ Conference, USENIX (1992) 225–243

16. Glyfason, H.I., Hjalmtysson, G.: Exceptional Kernel: Using C++ Exceptions in the Linux Kernel. (2004)

17. Advantages of Exceptions. (http://java.sun.com/docs/books/tutorial/essential/exceptions/advantages.html)

18. Campbell, R.H., Islam, N., Johnson, R., Kougiouris, P., Madany, P.: *Choices, Frameworks and Refinement.* In Luis-Felipe Cabrera and Vincent Russo, and Marc Shapiro, ed.: Object-Orientation in Operating Systems, Palo Alto, CA, IEEE Computer Society Press (1991) 9–15

19. Russo, V.F., Madany, P.W., Campbell, R.H.: C++ and Operating Systems Performance: a Case Study. In: USENIX C++ Conference, San Francisco, CA (1990) 103–114

20. Raila, D.: The Choices Object-oriented Operating System on the Sparc Architecture. Technical report, The University of Illinois at Urbana-Champaign (1992)

21. Lee, L.: PC-Choices Object-oriented Operating System. Technical report, The University of Illinois at Urbana-Champaign (1992)

22. Dike, J.: A user-mode port of the Linux kernel. In: Proceedings of the 4th Annual Linux Showcase and Conference, Atlanta, Georgia (2000)

23. Tan, S., Raila, D., Liao, W., Campbell, R.: Virtual Hardware for Operating System Development. Technical report, University of Illinois at Urbana- Champaign (1995)

24. Texas Instruments OMAP Platform. (http://focus.ti.com/omap/docs/omaphomepage.tsp)

25. Bellard, F.: QEMU, a Fast and Portable Dynamic Translator. In: USENIX Annual Technical Conference, FREENIX Track. (2005)

26. ARM Integrator Family. (http://www.arm.com/miscPDFs/8877.pdf)

27. Qin, F., Tucek, J., Sundaresan, J., Zhou, Y.: Rx: Treating Bugs as Allergies - A Safe Method to Survive Software Failures. In: Symposium on Operating Systems Principles. (2005) 235–248

28. Miller, R., Tripathi, A.: Issues with Exception Handling in Object-Oriented Systems. In: European Conference in Object-Oriented Computing. (1997)

29. Tools Interface Standards: DWARF Debugging Information Format. (http://www.arm.com/pdfs/TIS-DWARF2.pdf)

30. Codesourcery. (http://www.codesourcery.com)

31. Exception Handling ABI for the ARM^{TM}architecture. (http://www.arm.com/miscPDFs/8034.pdf)

32. Candea, G., Fox, A.: Recursive Restartability: Turning the Reboot Sledgehammer into a Scalpel. In: Proceedings of the Eighth Workshop on Hot Topics in Operating Systems, Washington, DC, USA, IEEE Computer Society (2001) 125

33. Drew, S., Gouph, K., Ledermann, J.: Implementing zero overhead exception handling. Technical report, Queensland University of Technology (1995)
34. Schilling, J.L.: Optimizing away C++ exception handling. SIGPLAN Not. **33**(8) (1998) 40–47
35. Thekkath, C.A., Levy, H.M.: Hardware and software support for efficient exception handling. In: Proceedings of the Sixth International Conference on Architectural Support for Programming Languages and Operating Systems, San Jose, California (1994) 110–119
36. ISO 14882: C++ Programming Language. (http://www.iso.ch/)
37. Bershad, B.N., Savage, S., Pardyak, P., Sirer, E.G., Fiuczynski, M., Becker, D., Eggers, S., Chambers, C.: Extensibility, Safety and Performance in the SPIN Operating System. In: 15th Symposium on Operating Systems Principles, Copper Mountain, Colorado (1995) 267–284
38. Vinoski, S.: Distributed Object Computing with Corba. C++ Report Magazine (1993)
39. Microsoft .NET. (http://www.microsoft.com/net/)
40. Katchabaw, M.J., Lutfiyya, H.L., Marshall, A.D., Bauer, M.A.: Policy-driven fault management in distributed systems. In: Proceedings of the The Seventh International Symposium on Software Reliability Engineering, Washington, DC, USA, IEEE Computer Society (1996) 236
41. Zeng, L., Lei, H., Jeng, J.J., Chung, J.Y., Benatallah, B.: Policy-Driven Exception-Management for Composite Web Services. In: Proceedings of the 7th IEEE International Conference on E-Commerce Technology. (2005) 355–363
42. Torres-Pomales, W.: Software Fault Tolerance: A Tutorial. Technical Report NASA/TM-2000-210616, NASA Langley Research Center (2000)
43. Gray, J.: Why do computers stop and what can be done about it? In: Proceedings of the 5th Symposium on Reliability in Distributed Software and Database Systems. (1986) 3–12
44. Rinard, M., Cadar, C., Dumitran, D., Roy, D.M., Leu, T., William S. Beebee, J.: Enhancing Server Availability and Security Through Failure-Oblivious Computing. In: Symposium on Operating Systems Design and Implementation. (2004) 303–316
45. Bressoud, T.C., Schneider, F.B.: Hypervisor-based fault tolerance. ACM Trans. Comput. Syst. **14**(1) (1996) 80–107
46. Sidiroglou, S., Locasto, M.E., Boyd, S.W., Keromytis, A.D.: Building a Reactive Immune System for Software Services. In: USENIX 2005 Annual Technical Conference. (2005)
47. Randell, B.: System structure for software fault tolerance. In: Proceedings of the International Conference on Reliable Software. (1975) 437–449
48. Avizienis, A.: The N-Version Approach to Fault - Tolerant Systems. In: IEEE Transactions on Software Engineering. (1985) 1491–1501
49. Chandra, S., Chen, P.M.: The Impact of Recovery Mechanisms on the Likelihood of Saving Corrupted State. In: ISSRE. (2002) 91–101

Handling Multiple Concurrent Exceptions in C++ Using Futures

Matti Rintala

Tampere University of Technology
matti.rintala@tut.fi

Abstract. Exception handling is a well-established mechanism in sequential programming. Concurrency and asynchronous calls introduce a possibility for multiple simultaneous exceptions. This complicates exception handling, especially in languages whose support for exceptions has not originally been designed for concurrency. Futures are a mechanism for handling return values in asynchronous calls. They are affected by concurrent exception handling as well, since exceptions and return values are mutually exclusive in functions. This paper discusses these problems and presents a concurrent exception handling mechanism for future-based asynchronous C++ programs.

1 Introduction

During the last decade exception handling has become more and more common as a means of handling abnormal situations. Most commonly used programming languages now support exceptions. However, basic ideas behind exception handling are far older [1]. Exceptions are now considered as a standard way of signalling about exceptional situations and they have widely replaced the use of specially coded return values, additional boolean state flags, etc.

At the same time concurrency has become increasingly important in programming. Reasons for this trend include the need for more processing power, asynchronous calls in distributed systems, as well as improving program structure in reactive systems.

Basically exception handling is about separating exception handling code from "normal" code. This improves readability by structuring the code logically. Exception handling also introduces its own control flow to the program, so that normal code does not have to explicitly prepare for every abnormal situation and divert the program execution to an appropriate handler.

Because exception handling is also about control flow, concurrency cannot be added to a programming language without affecting exceptions. Concurrency introduces several (usually independent) threads of execution, each of which has its own control flow. This causes several problems to exception handling, some of which are analysed in [2]. Asynchronous calls and futures (delayed return values) [3] complicate the problem even further. Combination of exception handling and concurrency have also been discussed in [4,5,6].

C. Dony et al. (Eds.):Exception Handling, LNCS 4119, pp. 62–80, 2006.

There are several ways to combine exception handling and concurrency in an object-oriented language, all of which have their benefits and drawbacks [7]. However, when adding concurrency to an originally sequential programming language like C++, the exception handling mechanism has already been fixed, and added concurrency features should be designed to be compatible with the existing mechanisms. This unavoidably means that some compromises have to be made.

This paper shows how support for multiple concurrent exceptions can be added to a concurrent variant of C++. The solution is library-based and does not extend the normal C++ syntax. The mechanisms described in this paper are compatible with normal C++ exception handling practises, and allow programmers to choose the exception handling strategy best suited for their programs. The solution described in this paper is part of KC++ [8], a concurrent C++ system based on active objects. Source code for the current test version of KC++ can be obtained from the author.

2 Issues Caused by Asynchrony and Exceptions

Introducing asynchronous calls (and thus concurrency) also affects exception handling, and this has to be taken into account when designing exception handling mechanisms. This section describes issues caused by asynchrony.

If exceptions are propagated from an asynchronous call back to the caller, it is not self-evident where those exceptions should be handled. The caller has already continued after calling the function, and may in fact have terminated its execution. Exception handling mechanisms in most languages bind exception handlers to specific parts of the code (try blocks etc.), and the caller may have left these by the time the exception is raised.

The mechanisms in this paper use the KC++ concurrency model, which is similar to its predecessor, UC++ [9]. Concurrency in KC++ is based on active objects with their own thread of execution, asynchronous method calls, and futures [3] for delayed return value passing. A class is marked active by deriving it from a special base class. All methods of an active object are called asynchronously, and their return values are handled with futures.

However, the described exception handling mechanisms do not depend on the active object model and could also be used in other systems using asynchronous calls and futures.

2.1 General Exception Handling Issues

Even without concurrency, most programming languages have to deal with multiple exceptions in certain situations. In the simplest case, another exception can be thrown in an exception handler. Most languages allow this "stacking" of exceptions, as long as exceptions thrown in the handler are handled to completion during the execution of the same handler. If an exception thrown in a handler escapes the handler, it causes the original exception to be discarded in most systems (C++, Java, and Ada, for example). As a result, in these situations the two exceptions do not compete with each other.

Some languages allow code to be executed after an exception has been thrown, but before it has been caught in a handler. In C++ this is possible with destructors of local objects, in Java with "finally" blocks. If this code throws an exception and does not handle it locally, two competing exceptions exist. C++ reacts to the problem by terminating the execution of the program. Java in turn discards the original exception. This situation is quite similar to a case where two concurrently thrown exceptions occur.

Finally, many systems allow asynchronous signals which can be raised at any time. These signals are usually associated with signal handlers, whose execution interrupts the normal execution of the program. It is possible that another signal is raised while a signal handler is being executed. In POSIX signals [10, Chap. 10], this is handled by associating each signal handler with a signal mask describing the signals that are allowed to interrupt the handler. The signal masks provide a simple priority scheme for signals. However, even such a scheme does not easily allow handling based on the occurrence of more than one signal.

2.2 Exceptions and Asynchrony

Asynchronous calls allow the calling thread to continue its execution before the return value of the call is available. Mechanisms like futures (explained in Sect. 3) make it possible to refer to an asynchronous return value "in advance", but exceptions thrown from an asynchronous call are more problematic.

In C++, exception handlers (catch clauses) are only "active" while the thread of execution is in the respective try block. Therefore, catch clauses can only catch exceptions from asynchronous calls, if the calling thread waits for the call to complete *before* leaving the try block. It should be noted that leaving a try block may be caused by normal program execution or by another thrown exception.

Several asynchronously executing threads also introduce the possibility of several exceptions being raised concurrently. If exceptions are sent to other threads (using mechanisms described in [11] or similar), this can result in more than one exception being propagated into a *single* thread.

The way return values from asynchronous calls are handled also affects exception handling. In a sense, an exception is an alternative to a return value. In synchronous calls, return values and exceptions are mutually exclusive. If an exception is thrown from a call, a return value is not created, and vice versa. However, mechanisms like futures act as a placeholder for the return value, and they are created *before* the call completes. This means that the placeholder exists and can be accessed even if the call terminates with an exception.

Futures can usually be copied or even sent to other threads before the call completes. This possibility has to be taken into account, if an exception is thrown from an asynchronous call. Exceptions should work consistently in this situation as well. The situation becomes especially interesting if there is more than one thread waiting. Normal sequential exceptions are not usually thrown more than once (unless they are explicitly re-thrown), but propagating an exception to several threads would lead to throwing a copy of the same exception multiple times, once in each thread.

2.3   Special Issues in C++ Exception Handling

Exception handling features in the C++ language resemble exceptions in the Ada language, after which parts of the C++ exception handling were modelled. Likewise, Java took most of its exception handling features from C++. The roots of exception handling are of course much deeper (an overview of its history can be found in [12]). However, there are some unique features and limitations in C++ exception handling that have to be taken into account when concurrency is introduced to the language and which limit available options for concurrent exception handling.

The C++ standard divides the lifetime of an exception to three parts [13, 15.1/7]: An exception is *thrown* when a throw statement is executed. The actual thrown exception object is a *copy* of the object used in the throw statement. An exception becomes *handled* when an appropriate catch clause is found and entered. Finally, an exception is *finished* when the execution exits the catch clause, causing the exception object to be destroyed. This paper uses the terms *thrown exception* and *handled exception* as defined by the C++ standard.

One distinguishing feature in C++ is the fact that local objects must have their destructors executed while searching for the appropriate exception handler. This language feature is called *stack unwinding*. It complicates issues because user code is executed while searching for the exception handler. However, the destruction mechanism allows additional handling code to be executed after an exception is thrown, but before it is handled, or before the execution of a program otherwise leaves a try block.

Because C++ destructors make it possible to execute user code while searching for an exception handler, destructors can throw additional exceptions (a similar situation occurs if copying the exception object throws an exception). Therefore, the C++ language has to consider several thrown exceptions even without concurrency.

Standard C++ allows several thrown exceptions to exist simultaneously as long as they are on different levels and do not compete for the same handlers. When stack unwinding causes a destructor of a local object to be executed, the destructor may throw additional exceptions. C++ requires that these exceptions must be handled in the destructor and may not leak out of it [13, 15.2/3]. The C++ standard dictates that violating this rule is considered a fatal error and such a program is terminated [13, 15.5.1].

Thrown C++ exceptions can be nested or "stacked" on top of each other during stack unwinding, but the latest exception is always handled completely before earlier exception handling continues. When concurrency is introduced, multiple exceptions on the same level have to be handled in a special way because the language itself makes it hard to throw them normally.

In many ways exceptions and return values can be regarded as similar methods for returning from a function. However, one feature that C++ inherits from the C language is that the caller of a function may ignore and discard the return value. In this respect exceptions are different from return values, since they cannot be silently ignored. This distinction becomes important with asynchronous calls and futures, because if a future is a placeholder for both the return value and the possible exception, it becomes possible to ignore exceptions also.

In many languages all exception classes are required to be derived from a common base class representing all exceptions. C++ makes no such requirements, although it supports inheritance hierarchies in exception handling. However, the lack of a common base class makes it difficult to handle exceptions in a uniform way, since in C++, a common base class is the only way to treat objects poly-morphically at run-time. For this reason the mechanism presented in this paper requires that all asynchronous exceptions are derived from a common KC++ exception base class. This base class also provides necessary code for serialisation. (KC++ provides a way to map non-KC++ exceptions to suitable counterparts derived from the proper base class. This mechanism is described in [11].)

3   Asynchronous Calls and Futures

Futures are a mechanism to return a value to the caller from an asynchronous function call. They were originally introduced in Multilisp [3], but have since been used under different names in many other languages, like wait-by-necessities in C++// [15] or IOUs in the Threads.h++ library [16]. The current Java 5 (often called Java 1.5.0) also provides futures in its library [17, Future].

3.1   Futures and Future Sources

Futures are placeholders for the eventual return value from an asynchronous call. In C++, futures can be implemented as a template class parametrised with the return value type. When an asynchronous call is performed, the caller immediately gets an "empty" future object representing the return value, while the call itself continues to execute concurrently. When the call completes, its return value is automatically transferred to the future, where the caller can access it. If the value of the future is requested before the call completes, the future suspends the execution of the requesting thread until the value becomes available.

Figure 1 shows a simple KC++ code example with asynchronous calls.[1] Class Server is an "active" class, which executes its methods asynchronously. Func-tions caller1 and caller2 are meant to be executed from different threads. Figure 2 shows a UML sequence diagram of one possible execution sequence. Continuous arrows denote method calls. A filled arrowhead marks a synchronous call, a stick arrowhead an asynchronous call. Where necessary, dashed arrows de-note return values.

---

[1] Details of KC++ can be found in [8], but are not necessary to understand the example.

```
class Server : public Active
{
  FutureSrc<int> fs;
public:
  Future<int> asyncCall1() { return 1; } // 4.
  Future<int> asyncCall2() { return fs.getFuture(); } // 6.-8.
  void setValue(int i) { fs.bind(i); } // 13.-14.
};

void caller1(Server& server) { // Executed in thread #1
  Future<int> f1, f2; // 1.-2.
  f1 = server.asyncCall1(); // 3.
  f2 = server.asyncCall2(); // 5.
  cout << f1.value(); // 9.-10.
  cout << f2.value(); // 11. & 15.
} // 16.-17.

void caller2(Server& server) { // Executed in thread #2
  server.setValue(2); // 12.
}
```

Fig. 1. Asynchronous calls using futures (numbers in comments are references to Fig. 2)

With message 3, `caller1` calls a method asynchronously, which continues its execution concurrently with the server. When the server completes the request, it sends the return value to the future `f1` (message 4), from which the client later retrieves it (msgs 9–10).

Normally, a future gets its value automatically when an asynchronous call completes, but this is restrictive in some cases. Sometimes it is practical to delay the future even further, and leave the return value future empty when the call completes. The value for the future is provided later by another call (likely called by a different thread), which binds the future to a value and thus releases the thread waiting for the future. This possibility makes futures even more useful for explicit synchronisation and signalling. Futures are well suited for such a use, because they also allow data to be passed between threads.

To allow explicit synchronisation, KC++ provides *future sources* in addition to futures. A future source is an object, from which the program can create an indefinite number of "empty" futures. These futures may then be returned as return values, and the future source keeps track of them. Later the program can *bind* the future source, giving it a value. The act of binding sends the given value to all futures generated from the future source. This allows manual and explicit synchronisation while the caller can still use normal futures as placeholders.

In Figs. 1 and 2, messages 5–8 and 11–15 show an example of future sources. Method `asyncCall2` gets its return value future from the future source `fs`. Initially this future source contains no value, and futures generated from it are empty. Thus future `f2` stays pending after the asynchronous call completes. (msgs 6–8). Later a thread running `caller2` calls a method which binds the

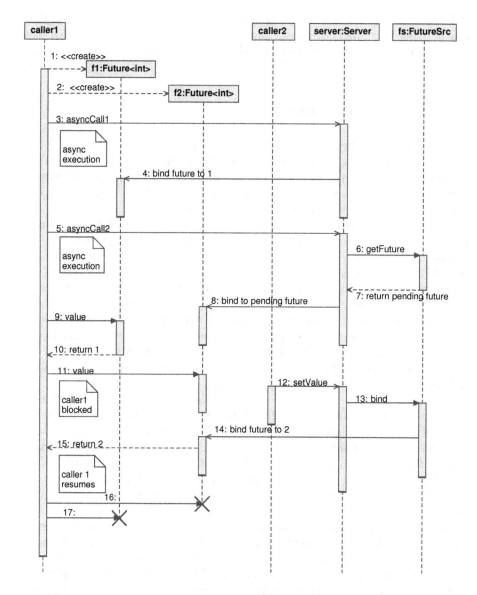

Fig. 2. Sequence diagram of Fig. 1

future source to a value. This value is automatically propagated to f2, and caller1 waiting for its value is released (msgs 12–15).

Future sources combined with futures are somewhat similar to *barriers* [18, Ch. 4]. However, synchronisation with futures sources can be triggered at any time, whereas barriers usually require a predetermined number of participants. In addition to this, future sources allow data to be passed from the synchroniser to released threads.

Futures in KC++ can also be copied without waiting for their value, and they can be passed to other threads or processes. When the call is completed, the return value is automatically propagated to all futures copied from the original future.

3.2 Exceptions and Futures

If an exception is thrown during the execution of an asynchronous call and is not handled locally, it must be propagated to the caller. Since the call is asynchronous, in KC++ the only way for an exception to propagate further is through futures. As well, in a concurrent environment there may be several waiting threads, if futures have been copied to other threads.

When an exception is thrown from an asynchronous call, the KC++ library code responsible for handling the call catches the exception. It serialises the exception object and embeds the data in the call's reply message which is sent back to the caller using mechanisms described in [11]. In the caller, a copy of the exception object is created from the message data and a pointer to this exception object is stored inside the future. This exception object, which is not yet thrown, is called a *pending exception* in this paper. If the future is copied to another thread, the future's serialisation code also serialises the pending exception object. If a future is still empty when it is copied, the KC++ library keeps track of the future. Later, when the future receives its value or an exception, the result is automatically propagated to all copied futures.

Whenever the value of a future is needed, the future checks whether it contains an exception instead of a value. If this is the case, the future throws the pending exception, which is then handled using normal C++ exception handling mechanisms. If the value of the future is accessed another time, the future throws the same exception again. It should be noted that copying the future object itself, assigning it to other futures or passing it as a parameter does not throw the exception. The exception is thrown only when the value of the future is accessed.

Exceptions thrown in asynchronous calls must be propagated to *all* affected futures, which implies copying the exception object. Fortunately, this is not in contradiction with normal C++, since the language gives compilers the right to copy exception objects when necessary [13, 15.1/3]. However, it means that a copy of the same exception may be thrown in several places and may be handled several times in multiple exception handlers when futures are copied and passed to other execution threads. Although this behaviour is logical and practically the only option, programmers must consider its implications in the program logic.

Exceptions should also affect the semantics of future sources. A future source does not represent a return point from a call. However, if a valid value cannot be bound to a future source, it must be possible to bind an exception in place of the value. The bound exception object is then sent to all generated futures. For this reason future sources provide a way to send pending exception objects to generated futures (without first throwing the exception).

In KC++, future sources get their value using the `bind` method. In addition to this, future sources contain a method called `bindThrow`, which takes a KC++ exception object as its parameter. The method copies and stores the exception object inside the future source and sends it to generated futures. The same applies also to all futures that are generated from the future source after `bindThrow` has been called. This manual exception propagation is consistent with the manual value binding, making it straightforward to use.

Since each future source can only contain one value or exception, an attempt to bind the same future source twice results in an exception (thrown only to the binder). Similarly it is an error to destroy a future source without binding it. If this happens, a predefined exception `FutureSrcNotBound` is sent to all generated futures, preventing deadlocks.

4   Concurrent Exceptions

Asynchronous calls make it possible to end up in a situation where several exceptions are raised concurrently. If the caller continues its execution while an asynchronous call is active, both the client and server threads may end up throwing an exception, and both of these exceptions should be propagated into the client thread. The C++ language cannot handle more than one thrown exception in the same level, and this exception cannot be changed before it is caught. This forces some compromises to be made in KC++.

4.1   Problems Caused by Multiple Exceptions

The C++ exception handling model makes it impossible to resume the execution of a try block after an exception is handled (reasons for not using an alternative resumption model in C++ can be found in [19]). When the C++ exception handling mechanism searches for a correct exception handler, it permanently exits from try blocks, destroying their local variables. This includes the try block which contains the chosen handler. After the exception is finished, program execution continues from the point after the try-catch-compound containing the chosen exception handler.

If several concurrent exceptions end up in one thread, only one of them can be handled at a time. However, handling the first exception means leaving try blocks (and their respective catch-handlers). This would make it impossible to search for handlers for the rest of the exceptions, since all handlers are no longer available (the program execution has already left try blocks). This kind of behaviour would be necessary in situations where there are several independent exceptions, and the caller wants to react accordingly to more than one of these before letting the exception handling proceed further.

Another problem with handling concurrent exceptions one at a time would be to choose the order in which the exceptions should be handled. Exceptions may be thrown from several (mutually independent) locations, so deciding the correct handling order would either require a global priority scheme for exceptions, or mean that there would have to be a mechanism for informing the relative priority of a thrown exception (and maybe change it during exception handling when the exception is propagated to other parts of the program). Unfortunately this kind of simple priority scheme is not enough for all programs.

The third and maybe the most important aspect in concurrent exception handling is the fact that several concurrently thrown exceptions may in fact be caused by the same abnormal situation. If thrown exception objects have the same cause and contain the same data, they could be reduced to a single exception. However, sometimes the nature of the actual abnormal situation may only be understood by analysing *all* of the exceptions it causes, in which case it is important that the exception handling mechanism can cope with several pending exceptions. Sometimes it would also be beneficial to be able to *replace* a set of exceptions (caused by the same abnormal situation) with a new exception representing the whole exceptional situation. For example, several timeout exceptions from processes running on a remote machine could be mapped to an exception representing connection failure to the whole machine.

Writing exception handling becomes easier if these exception reductions can be performed *before* an exception handler is chosen. An exception handler can then catch a single exception whose type represents the whole situation. It is often impossible to give a global rule for reducing multiple exceptions to one, since this reduction may depend on the context where exceptions occur. It is important that the program can provide its own algorithms for reduction.

Figure 3 shows the structure of KC++ exception handling mechanism. It is based on futures and future sources, as well as *future groups* for collective synchronisation, *compound exceptions* for handling multiple exceptions, and *reduction functions* for exception analysis and reduction. These mechanisms have been influenced by earlier works on exception reduction, resolution and concertation, for example [4,6,20]. The behaviour of KC++ exception reduction is described in the following sections.

4.2   Compound Exceptions

The C++ language can only propagate one exception at a time. Another exception may be raised during stack unwinding triggered by the first exception, but these additional exceptions must be handled to conclusion before stack unwinding proceeds further. In a concurrent program this limitation is problematic, because several exceptions may need to be propagated from asynchronous calls to a single try block.

KC++ provides a *compound exception* class to represent a set of exceptions. It is a normal KC++ exception class, but its instances may contain an unlimited number of other KC++ exceptions. As compound exceptions are KC++ exceptions, they can be passed among execution threads. Usually compound exceptions are created by future groups, which collect exceptions from several futures to a compound exception. Compound exceptions are then passed to reduction functions for analysis and manipulation.

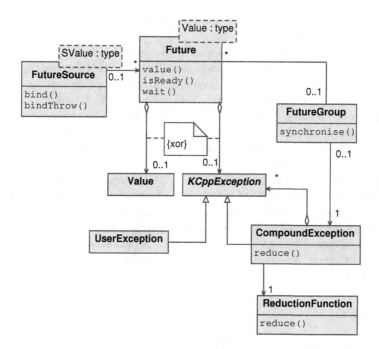

Fig. 3. Structure of KC++ exception handling

The interface of the compound exception class allows addition of new exceptions and removal of existing ones. In addition, all exceptions may be moved from one compound exception to another, making it possible to combine compound exceptions in reduction functions or exception handlers. Compound exceptions also provides iterators to iterate through all exceptions of a certain type.

Exception reduction is performed when future groups are asked to synchronise with all their futures. During reduction, it is often useful to replace a compound exception with a selected top-priority exception. However, it may still be useful to keep the "secondary" lower-priority exceptions, in case they are useful later. In KC++, *all* KC++ exception objects may contain an optional compound exception object to which secondary exceptions may be stored for later handling. This approach is somewhat similar to Java's chained exceptions, where each exception object may also contain a reference to its *cause*, which is a single exception object [17, Throwable].

4.3   Future Groups

Sometimes "delayed" exceptions caused by asynchronous calls and futures are what the programmer wants, but in many cases a try block needs to contain multiple asynchronous calls, and the programmer wants to know if any of them ends with an exception before leaving the try block. Checking each future separately would be awkward and not even straightforward in the case of multiple exceptions. For these reasons KC++ offers *future groups* to help with synchronised exception handling.

Future groups are objects to which futures may be registered. They have an operation `synchronise`, which waits for all the group's futures to receive a value (or a pending exception). In this respect future groups are similar to barrier synchronisation [18, Chap. 4] and future sets in ES-Kit [21]. If pending exceptions are found in the futures during synchronisation, the future group collects these exceptions in a compound exception. The exceptions in the compound exception are then reduced using reduction functions (Sect. 5), and an exception suitable for the situation is thrown.

When the program asks for a value of a future belonging to a future group, the future first waits for its asynchronous call to complete. Then, if the call ended with an exception, the future asks its future group to perform synchronisation. This makes sure that all exceptions in the group are available before exception handling is started. Finally, exception reduction is performed and an appropriate exception is thrown. The code in Fig. 4 demonstrates the use of a future group in a try block.

```
Future<int> f1;
try {
  FutureGroup group(&reductionFunction);
  f1 = aobj.call1(); // An asynchronous call
  group.add(f1);     // Register f1 to the group
  group.add(aobj.call2());   // Register without storing the future
  int i = f1.value(); // Synchronises with group first
} // Destruction of group synchronises with all futures
catch (const Exception& e1)
// ...
```

Fig. 4. Using future groups to synchronise several futures

If the future receives a normal return value instead of an exception, it directly returns this value without synchronising the future group, since no exception reduction is needed yet. An alternative strategy would be to perform synchronisation in this case also. However, forcing synchronisation in every case would seriously limit the amount of asynchrony in the program. However, a future group can be asked to perform explicit synchronisation at any point, if needed.

If a future group is destroyed before its synchronisation method is called, the destructor of the group performs synchronisation automatically. This makes future groups very close to the Resource Acquisition Is Initialisation (RAII) idiom [14, Sect. 14.4], which is very common in C++ for exception-safe resource management. In RAII each resource is wrapped inside an object whose destructor releases the resource, preventing the possibility of resource leaks even in case of exceptions. Future groups represent a responsibility to synchronise with one or more futures (asynchronous calls), and their destructor makes sure this responsibility is fulfilled.

5   Exception Reduction

As mentioned previously, several futures in a try block may receive pending exceptions. In that case it would be beneficial if these exceptions could be reduced to a single exception object representing the complete situation. Even if the exceptions are not the result of the same cause, finding "the most important" of the exceptions depends often on program context.

Because there is no single all-purpose way to reduce a set of exceptions to a single exception or a smaller set of exceptions, KC++ does not force programs to any predefined behaviour. Rather it allows programs to register *reduction functions* to future groups. Reduction functions can analyse the current set of pending exceptions, alter it, and select an appropriate exception to be thrown.

5.1   Reduction Functions

Reduction functions are user-defined functions (or function objects) that can be added to a future group to perform exception reduction. After a future group synchronises with its futures, it collects pending exceptions from the futures into a compound exception object. Then it asks its reduction function to perform exception reduction.

The reduction function receives as parameters a pointer to the compound exception object, an already-thrown exception object (if exception handling is already active and a new exception cannot be thrown), and an optional pointer to an external exception store for storing exception objects.

Reduction functions may use these parameters to decide how to simplify or modify the given set of exceptions. They may add and remove exceptions or transfer them from one parameter to another. It should be remembered that every KC++ exception object may contain an additional compound exception object, so exceptions can also be added to and removed from the already-thrown KC++ exception object, if any. For example, a reduction function might decide to embed all exceptions from the future group's compound exception as "sub-exceptions" in an already-thrown KC++ exception.

After analysis, the reduction function may return an exception which it regards as the "most important" of the exceptions. Alternatively, it may return a completely new exception object representing the most appropriate exceptional situation.

KC++ tries not to force programmers into a specific way of exception handling. In many programs, choosing one exception object or throwing a compound exception is enough, but sometimes it is useful to collect exceptions from (at least some) future groups into an external exception store to be handled later.

For this purpose each future group can be given an additional compound exception object, which is passed to reduction functions as an external exception store. Reduction functions may use this compound exception as a store for exceptions that are not thrown or embedded in other exceptions.

One limitation caused by the C++ language is that when an exception has been thrown, it cannot be replaced by another exception until it has been caught in a catch-clause. This means that reduction functions cannot change the type of a thrown but not handled exception, even if a more important exception is found, or if the nature of the thrown exception changes during reduction. However, since KC++ futures automatically perform synchronisation and reduction, reduction is usually performed *before* exceptions have been thrown.

It is possible that an exception is thrown from another source than a future, in which case reduction cannot be performed in advance. One solution to this potential problem is to catch the thrown exception and perform reduction in the catch clause. This is not difficult to do, but KC++ also offers ready-made macros for this purpose. These macros can be placed after a try block in place of a normal catch-clause, and they perform reduction on the thrown exception.

Exceptions not derived from the KC++ exception base class cannot be handled by KC++. They cannot be propagated among threads, embedded in futures or handled by reduction functions. Use of non-KC++ exceptions should be minimised in KC++ programs, especially in places where futures and reduction functions are used. The KC++ library provides a wrapper template for creating KC++ counterparts of such exception classes [11].

5.2   Example of Reduction

Figure 5 shows a simple example using a future group and a reduction function. In the example, `Server` (whose implementation is not shown) is responsible for concurrently acquiring and summing up integers. If all necessary numbers cannot be acquired, server throws a `MissingNumber` exception, which contains a list of missing numbers (the exception is a struct to make the example shorter). The template inheritance used to derive new exception classes in KC++ is described in [11], and is not important for the example.

The example uses a reduction function `reductionFunc` to resolve exceptions. This simple reduction does not need all the data provided to it, so it ignores all its parameters but the first, which is a compound exception to which exceptions from futures have been collected by the future group. The reduction function uses exception iterators to iterate through all exceptions of type `MissingNumber`. It creates a new exception object and copies all missing numbers into it. This exception object is then returned as the actual exception to throw. If no `MissingNumber` exceptions are found, the original compound exception is returned.

Function `client` creates a future group, makes two asynchronous calls and adds their futures to the future group. If either of those calls ends with an exception, the future group synchronises with both futures and calls the reduction function. The reduction functions reduces `MissingNumber` exceptions to a single exception, which is then thrown and caught by the catch clause. In this example, all exceptions except `MissingNumber` are considered secondary, and are ignored by the reduction function unless no missing numbers are found.

```
struct MissingNumber : public Exception<MissingNumber>
{ vector<int> nums; }; // A simple exception class

ExceptBase* reductionFunc(CompoundExcp* groupCE, // Rest of args not
            needed bool, ExceptBase*, CompoundExcp*) {
  ExceptIter<MissingNumber> it = groupCE->begin();
  if (it != groupCE->end()) { // MissingNumbers found in compound
    MissingNumber* mn = new MissingNumber; // Final exception
    while (it != groupCE->end()) { // Iterate, add numbers to mn
      mn->nums.insert(mn->nums.end(), it->nums.begin(), it->nums.end());
      it = groupCE->erase(it); // Remove exception, get next
    }
    return mn; // Return the list of all missing numbers
  } else { // Otherwise the whole compound exception is returned
    return groupCE;
  }
}

int client(Server& s1, Server& s2) {
  try {
    FutureGroup fg(&reductionFunc);
    Future<int> n1 = s1.sumNums(); fg.add(n1);
    Future<int> n2 = s2.sumNums(); fg.add(n2);
    return n1.value()+n2.value();
  }
  catch (const MissingNumber& mn) {
    cerr << "Missing numbers:";
    for (unsigned int i=0; i<mn.nums.size(); ++i)
    { cerr << " " << mn.nums[i]; }
    abort();
  }
}
```

Fig. 5. Example of future groups and reduction functions

6   Related Work

Problems with asynchrony described in this paper have been solved differently in different programming languages. This section lists some languages and how the combination of exception handling and concurrency has been implemented in these languages.

The strategy used in the Ada language [22] is quite common in other languages, too. In Ada, new tasks (threads) can be created, and the new tasks start executing asynchronously with their creator. Problems with multiple asynchronous exceptions have been avoided by declaring that if an exception tries to leave the task body (i.e. if the task does not handle the exception locally), the exception is not propagated further and the task in question is simply terminated. Communication among tasks happens using the *rendez-vous* mechanism, in which one tasks calls a service on another task, which explicitly accepts the call. If an exception occurs during the rendez-vous, the exception is propagated from the accepting task to the calling task (as well as propagated within the called task). However, this causes no problems in the calling task because normally rendez-vous is a synchronous operation, so the calling task is waiting for the call to complete.

Ada-95 also defines an *asynchronous* accept statement. However, this is not an asynchronous call, but rather a way to execute a sequence of statements while waiting for an event to occur, like a rendez-vous call, time expiration, or external signal. When the event happens, normal execution of the statements is immediately aborted. This mechanism does not suffer from the exception problems of asynchronous calls, but introduces its own problems, for example because the abortion mentioned can occur in the middle of exception handling.

Ada-95 provides also *asynchronous remote procedure calls*. Since remote calls are procedure calls, they cannot have return values. If an asynchronous remote procedure call results in an exception after the caller has continued its execution, the exception is simply ignored.

The Java language [23] has also built-in concurrency. The exception handling strategy in the language is very close to the Ada approach. All exceptions are handled locally inside a thread, and they are lost if the thread does not contain an appropriate exception handler. All Java inter-thread communication happens either through shared objects or synchronous method calls (like Remote Method Invocation (RMI)). Java 5 has also classes `FutureTask` and `Future` to perform asynchronous computation. The future mechanism is similar to the KC++ approach, except for future sources. Grouping and reduction of exceptions are not supported.

Although the exception mechanism in Java is close to Ada, different concurrency features affect exception handling in both languages. These differences (as well as differences in other concurrency features) are analysed in [24].

Even though Java does not provide asynchronous method calls by default, there are several extensions to the language for this purpose. One of these is Java Asynchronous Remote Method Invocation (ARMI) [25], which is built on normal synchronous Java RMI. ARMI uses futures to represent results of asynchronous calls. For exception handling, ARMI provides two alternative methods. The Delayed Delivery Mechanisms (DDM) embeds the possible exceptions inside futures. The exceptions are thrown from the future when the return value of the asynchronous call is requested. The second choice called the Callback Mechanism (CM) allows the programmer to attach special exception handlers to a future. Each exception handler is capable of handling a specific type of exception. If that exception occurs, ARMI automatically calls the appropriate exception handler.

Another asynchronous extension to Java is JR [26]. JR implements asynchronous calls via *send* and *forward* statements. Exceptions are handled by requiring that each *send* and *forward* statement also specifies a *handler object*. Handler objects must implement the `Handler` interface and provide a method for each possible exception type, with the exception object as a parameter. When an exception occurs in an asynchronous call, an appropriate method in the handler object is called. The handler methods cannot throw any additional exceptions and they have to be able to completely handle the exceptional situation. The JR compiler statically checks that the handler object is able to handle all possible exceptions the call may throw. [5]

In addition to Ada and Java, there are many other concurrent object-oriented languages like pSather which resolve asynchronous exception problems by defining that exceptions must always be handled locally inside each thread of execution. This solution is easy but forces the programmer to rely on older, more primitive exception signalling methods like special return values and status flags.

A general analysis of concurrent exception handling in object-oriented systems can be found in [7]. Ideas for dealing with multiple concurrent exceptions in a distributed system have been developed in [6]. This work also introduces the idea of exception resolution. The idea of adding exception resolution to Ada and Java has been analysed in [4].

The Argus language implements asynchronous calls using *call-streams* and uses a very future-like construct called a *promise* to handle return values from asynchronous calls [27]. In Argus promises are strongly typed and represent the result of the asynchronous computation including possible exceptions. The type of the promise identifies the type of the return value and lists all possible exceptions which the promise may contain. Every asynchronous call returns a promise, which the caller can either poll periodically or start waiting for the call to complete ("*claim*" the promise). Waiting for the result of a promise either returns the normal return value of the call, or raises the exception the call has raised. If the same promise is claimed again, it re-returns the return value or re-raises the exception.

In the programming language Arche [28], asynchrony and synchronisation have been implemented quite differently. Every object in the language has its own thread of control, and every method call is synchronous. However, concurrent objects can communicate and co-operate asynchronously using *multimethods* (invocation of a method in a group of objects). Exception handling problems are solved by attaching to each multimethod a *coordinator*, which controls the overall action. The coordinator may have a *resolution function* which receives exceptions from all participants and computes a *concerted exception* representing the resulting "total" exception [20]. The initial idea of the resolution trees has been developed in [29].

7   Conclusion and Future Work

Concurrency and exception handling affect each other and are complicated to implement together in any programming language. Handling of multiple concurrent exceptions is especially challenging. The underlying programming language and its limitations force additional compromises to concurrent exception handling.

This paper has shown how support for multiple exceptions in asynchronous concurrent calls can be added to C++. This capability is achieved with futures and future sources for asynchronous return value handling, future groups for mutual synchronisation, and compound exceptions combined with reduction functions for exception resolution and selection. All this has been achieved using a library-based approach, without changing the C++ syntax or the compiler.

The mechanisms described in this paper have been implemented in KC++, a concurrent active object based system implemented on top of C++. Optimisations and performance measurements of reduction function based exception handling are still in progress.

Future improvents on KC++ and its exception handling are also in progress. For example, currently reduction functions are associated to future groups. However, separation of concerns would be better if future groups would be only responsible for synchronisation. For this reason, in the future reduction functions will probably be moved to another class called a *reduction context*. This would also allow better support for repeated reduction, as future groups are usually local variables in a try block and will be destroyed when exception handling begins.

References

1. Goodenough, J.B.: Exception handling: issues and a proposed notation. Communications of the ACM **18**(12) (1975) 683–696
2. Buhr, P.A., Mok, W.Y.R.: Advanced exception handling mechanisms. IEEE Transactions on Software Engineering **26**(9) (2000) 820–836
3. Halstead, R.H.: Multilisp: A language for concurrent symbolic computation. ACM Transactions on Programming Languages and Systems **7**(4) (1985) 501–538
4. Romanovsky, A.: Extending conventional languages by distributed/concurrent exception resolution. Journal of Systems Architecture **46**(1) (2000) 79–95
5. Keen, A.W., Olsson, R.A.: Exception handling during asynchronous method invocation. In: Euro-Par 2002: Parallel Processing. Volume 2400 of LNCS (Lecture Notes in Computer Science)., Springer-Verlag (2002) 656–660
6. Xu, J., A.Romanovsky, Randell, B.: Concurrent exception handling and resolution in distributed object systems. IEEE Transactions on Parallel and Distributed Systems **11**(10) (2000) 1019–1032
7. Romanovsky, A., Kienzle, J.: Action-oriented exception handling in cooperative and competitive object-oriented systems. [31] 147–164
8. Rintala, M.: KC++ — a concurrent C++ programming system. Licentiate thesis, Tampere University of Technology, Tampere, Finland (2000)
9. Winder, R., Roberts, G., McEwan, A., Poole, J., Dzwig, P.: UC++. [30] 629–670
10. Stevens, W.R.: Advanced Programming in the UNIX(R) Environment. Addison-Wesley (1992)
11. Rintala, M.: Exceptions in remote procedure calls using C++ template metaprogramming. Software – Practice and Experience (?) DOI: 10.1002/spe.754. Accepted April 8th 2006. To appear.
12. Ryder, B.G., Soffa, M.L.: Influences on the design of exception handling ACM SIGSOFT project on the impact of software engineering research on programming language design. SIGSOFT Software Engineering Notes **28**(4) (2003) 29–35
13. ISO/IEC: International Standard 14882 – Programming Languages – C++, Second Edition. (2003)

14. Stroustrup, B.: The C++ Programming Language (Special Edition). Addison-Wesley, Reading, Massachusetts (2000)
15. Caromel, D., Belloncle, F., Roudier, Y.: C++//. [30] 257–296
16. Thompson, P.: IOUs: A future implementation. C++ Report (1998) 29–32
17. Sun Microsystems, Inc.: Java^TM 2 platform standard edition 5.0 API specification. http://java.sun.com/j2se/1.5.0/docs/api/ (2004)
18. Andrews, G.R.: Concurrent Programming — Principles and Practice. Addison-Wesley, Reading, Massachusetts (1991)
19. Stroustrup, B.: The Design and Evolution of C++. Addison-Wesley, Reading, Massachusetts (1994)
20. Issarny, V.: Concurrent exception handling. [31] 111–127
21. Chatterjee, A.: Futures: a mechanism for concurrency among objects. In: Proceedings of the 1989 ACM/IEEE conference on Supercomputing, ACM/IEEE, ACM Press (1989) 562–567
22. Intermetrics, Inc.: Ada 95 Reference Manual. (1995)
23. Arnold, K., Gosling, J.: The Java Programming Language. Addison-Wesley, Reading, Massachusetts (1998)
24. Brosgol, B.M.: A comparison of the concurrency features of Ada 95 and Java. In: Proceedings of the 1998 annual ACM SIGAda international conference on Ada, Washington, D.C., United States, ACM Press (1998) 175–192
25. Raje, R.R., Williams, J., Boyles, M.: An asynchronous remote method invocation (ARMI) mechanism for Java. Concurrency: Practice and Experience 9(11) (1997) 1207–1211
26. Keen, A.W., Ge, T., Maris, J.T., Olsson, R.A.: JR: flexible distributed programming in an extended Java. In: Proceedings of the 21st IEEE International Conference on Distributed Computing Systems, IEEE (2001) 575–584
27. Liskov, B., Shrira, L.: Promises: Linguistic support for efficient asynchronous procedure calls in distributed systems. In: Proceedings of the SIGPLAN'88 Conference on Programming Language Design and Implementation. (1988) 260–267
28. Benveniste, M., Issarny, V.: Concurrent programming notations in the object-oriented language Arche. Research Report 1822, INRIA, Rennes, France (1992)
29. Campbell, R.H., Randell, B.: Error recovery in asynchronous systems. IEEE Transactions on Software Engineering 12(8) (1986) 811–826
30. Wilson, G., Lu, P., eds.: Parallel Programming Using C++. MIT Press, Cambridge (MA), USA (1996)
31. Romanovsky, A., Dony, C., Knudsen, J.L., Tripathi, A., eds.: Advances in Exception Handling Techniques. 2022 of LNCS (Lecture Notes in Computer Science). Springer-Verlag (2001)

Exception Handling and Asynchronous Active Objects: Issues and Proposal

Christophe Dony[1], Christelle Urtado[2], and Sylvain Vauttier[2]

[1] LIRMM - CNRS and Montpellier II University - 161 rue Ada
34 392 Montpellier - France
dony@lirmm.fr

[2] LGI2P - Ecole des Mines d'Alès - Parc scientifique G. Besse - 30 035 Nîmes - France
{Christelle.Urtado, Sylvain.Vauttier}@site-eerie.ema.fr

Abstract. Asynchronous Active Objects (AAOs), primarily exemplified by actors [1], nowadays exist in many forms (various kinds of actors, agents and components) and are more and more used because they fit well the dynamic and asynchronous nature of interactions in many distributed systems. They raise various new issues regarding exception handling for which few operational solutions exist. More precisely, a need exists for a generic, simple and expressive, programmer level, exception handling system that appropriately handles the following main exception handling issues or requirements in the context of AAOs: encapsulation, object autonomy, coordination of concurrent collaborative entities [2], "caller contextualization" [3], asynchronous signaling and handler execution, resolution of concurrent exceptions [4,5], exception criticality [6] and object reactivity.

This paper presents the specification of an evolution of the SaGE exception handling system [7], which provides solutions to those issues in the context of systems developed with active objects using one way asynchronous communications and interacting via the request / response protocol. Such a context, in which synchronizations constraints are, when needed, handled at the application level, allows for a very generic view of what could be done regarding exception handling in all systems that use active objects. The SaGE solution is original and provides a good compromise between expressive-power and simplicity.

Keywords: active objects, agents, distributed components, message driven components, exception handling, reliability, asynchronous message-based communication.

1   Introduction

Active objects are *"objects having their own computing resources i.e. their own private activity"* [8], or, said differently, objects *"decoupling method execution from method invocation"* [9]. *Asynchronous Active Objects* (AAOs) come in many forms (actors, agents or components), with various interaction schemes (request / response or publish / subscribe [10]) and various forms of asynchronous

C. Dony et al. (Eds.):Exception Handling, LNCS 4119, pp. 81–100, 2006.

communication (one-way or two-ways). They are more and more used as, for example, in multi-agents systems [11], in some distributed components architectures such as J2EE's with *Message Driven Beans*, in programming languages dedicated to grid applications (e.g. [12]) or to wireless devices on top of mobile networks as in [13]. AAOs, particularly in these new contexts, raise numerous issues regarding exception handling that have only been partially studied.

While the masterpieces of a generally accepted solution for exception handling in sequential programs are known, this is not yet the case for concurrent systems [14], even if some agreements exist. When systems with asynchronous communications are concerned, research works are still much more scattered. Initial actor languages included basic proposals to cope with exceptions [15] in which handlers were some dedicated actors, ancestors of today's exception supervisors, that had the same lacks, regarding handler contextualization (see Sect. 3.3), as Smalltalk or Ada initial lexical-scope handlers. Asynchrony has more recently motivated many research works in various contexts [16,17,18,19,20,21,22,23]but they only partially address AAO needs. Actually, agent systems are the AAO context in which exception handling proposals are the most achieved. However the supervisor model described in [24,25] does not properly handle the contextualization issue. Guardian [26,27] is a general and powerful solution which nonetheless proves to be complex to master and use. As explained in [26], *"Often exception handling in a program is the most complex [...] part of the system [...] and has to be either simplified or taken out of the hand of the average programmer"* and a solution for this is to *"separate global level exception handling from the application agents"*.

We have imagined an alternative solution consisting in analyzing and designing a language-level exception handling system dedicated to AAOs that:

- integrates what we consider to be the major research results from studies in sequential, concurrent or asynchronous contexts, and is expressive enough to address standard exception handling situations,
- reflects and takes into account the way AAOs and their execution are structured[1],
- is simple enough to be universally used by standard programmers.

The key requirements of the system are: to enforce encapsulation, to provide a representation for collaborative concurrent activities [14] so that they can be coordinated and controlled [2], to achieve caller contextualization [28,3] for handler definition and execution, to handle concurrent exceptions with resolution functions [4,29], to support asynchronous signaling and handler search and thus maintain object reactivity and to cope with broadcast messages, widely used in the request / response protocol.

The paper is organized in four sections. Section 2 recalls some basic vocabulary and introduces an example. Section 3 presents the rationale of our main

---

[1] We have considered active objects in their less constrained form i.e. as autonomous entities that provide inter and intra-object concurrency, interact via a request / response protocol and use one-way asynchronous communications.

conceptual choices. Section 4 describes the system specification. It focuses on the description of the asynchronous handler search policy and explains its utility. Section 5 compares our proposal with related works.

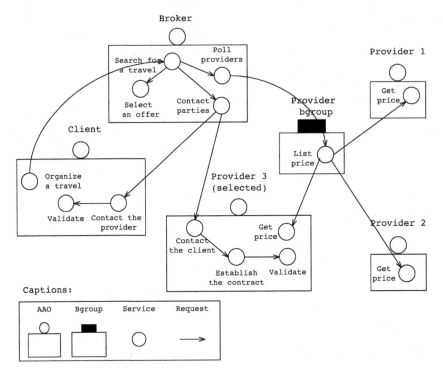

Fig. 1. Execution resulting from a request to a travel agency

2   Definition, Terminology and Example

All objects in our discussion will be AAOs. The following object characteristics define the context of this study. Objects communicate by exchanging messages that carry information [10]. Messages are queued in the object's message box. Each object owns a thread dedicated to managing its message-box: its scans and interprets the received messages to trigger corresponding actions. The program unit executed when a recipient accepts a request carried in such a message is called a **service**. Objects can own several services that can be executed concurrently in dedicated threads (intra-object concurrency). The request / response interaction protocol generally comes along with a contract-based approach of software development, which states that whenever an object accepts a request, it must provide a response, either standard or exceptional. Our objects use one-way communications[2] which means that responses to requests are not carried

---

[2] Two-ways asynchronous communications generally use *future* objects [16] which are more restrictive because the order in which they are read imposes synchronization constraints.

```
( 1)   public class Broker implements AsyncActiveObject
( 2)     {
( 3)     ...
( 4)
( 5)     public void handle (GlobalNetworkException exc)
( 6)     // handler associated to the Broker asynchronous active object
( 7)        { ... }
(10)
(11)     class PollProviders implements Service
(12)        {
(13)        ...
(14)        public void body ()
(15)           { ... }
(16)        public void handle (BadParameterException exc)
(17)        // handler associated to the PollProviders service
(18)           { signal (new NoAirportInDestinationException (...); }
(19)        public void handle (NoProviderException exc)
(20)        // handler associated to the PollProviders service
(21)           { ... }
(22)        }
(23)
(24)     class ContactParties implements Service
(25)        {
(26)        public void body ()
(27)           {
(28)           ...
(29)           sendMessage (new RequestMessage (aClient,
(30)                           "ContactSelectedProvider")
(31)                           {
(32)                           public void handle (OffLineException exc)
(33)                           // handler associated to a request
(34)                              {
(35)                              wait(120);
(36)                              retry();
(37)                              }
(38)                           });
(39)           ...
(40)           }
(41)        }
(42)     ...
(43)     }
```

Fig. 2. Service and handler definitions in SaGE

back away in the same communication channel that has carried the request, but by sending new separated messages back to callers [10]. Objects are autonomous: they can independently decide to start any activity or to handle any received message in whatever order. A collaborative activity is an activity that involves several objects or several services of an object in achieving a common goal.

As an illustration, we use the canonical *Travel Agency* example in which a *Client* can send a *Broker* a reservation message to request a bid for a travel. The contacted broker then sends a bid request to several travel providers and waits for their responses. Then, the *Broker* selects the best offer and requests the *Client* and the selected *Provider* to establish a contract (cf. Fig. 1). Our code examples use a Java-like syntax. Figure 2 thus shows examples of service definitions: lines 11–22 define the *Poll providers* service and lines 24–41 the *Contact Parties* one. We call **complex services**, services the code of which contain other messages and *atomic services* the others. In the example, *Get price*, that returns a *Provider*'s bid, is an atomic service (cf. Fig. 1) and *Organize a travel*, which handles a *Client*'s initial request, is a complex one. Broadcast message that contain collective requests, are frequently used in AAO applications and are generally delivered via entities that represent groups of objects as, for example, *roles* in MadKIT or *topics* in J2EE MDBs. We take this kind of requests into account and use entities that we call **bgroup**s (for *broadcast groups*) to denote such groups of objects. A *bgroup* possesses an (implicit) complex service that broadcasts the requests it receives to all objects in its collection.

This simple example brings to the fore many pertinent issues: how to control and interpret an exception asynchronously raised by one of the travel providers? Where is the best place to interpret it? Should all providers be notified when one of them fails? Should the broker be able to cancel all requests to travel providers for a given reason? Where and how to associate a handler for the collaborative activity that consists in requesting several travel providers concurrently? When should it be invoked and in which context?

3   Rationale for the SaGE Exception Handling System

Each of the following sub-sections discusses the rationale of some of our choices.

3.1   Coordination of Concurrent Activities

As shown in our previous works [7,30], efficiently handling exceptions in concurrent systems using asynchronous communications requires *cooperative concurrency* to be supported, as for other concurrent systems [2,14].This amounts to provide a representation of collective activities and a way to define handlers at all places in a program where several concurrent participants are working together to the achievement of a global task. In the example, such a handler should be defined somewhere at the level of the requesting *Broker* object it should be invoked whenever one or more travel providers signal an exception, and it should be able to access the *Broker* context.

3.2   Encapsulation

A well-known consequence of the introduction of exception handling primitives in a language is that it gives programmers constructs to break encapsulation

[31]. If it seems unavoidable to pass arguments from signalers to handlers, it is possible to act on another concern with encapsulation which occurs each time handlers are executed in a context where the data they need is not accessible. This can globally be the case in object languages with all kinds of supervisor-based models for exception handling [15,32,24] or, more marginally, in procedural languages with handlers associated to shared data, as initially suggested by [33].

Supervisors are objects dedicated to exception handling, which can be considered themselves as handlers or to which handlers are attached. The actor proposal for exception handling [15] is based on that idea. The issue with this approach is that supervisors are not encapsulated within the objects that experience the failure and therefore cannot access their internal state without breaking encapsulation. Our solution to prevent this, experimented in [3,7] is to define and encapsulate handlers within the object or activity they control.

3.3   Contextualization

"Contextualization" refers to two connected issues: the scope of handlers and the context in which they are executed. The scope of a handler determines the way and the order in which they are searched for. It directly impacts the signaling algorithm. The way handlers are defined and executed determines their context. Two main approaches can globally be distinguished. In the static approach, handlers have a lexical scope and are executed in an environment that lexically contains the signaling one. Its main advantages are its simplicity and the fact that it requires no additional language construct. Conversely, its main drawback is that it fails to achieve fault tolerant encapsulations [3]. In the dynamic approach, handlers have a dynamic scope: the portion of the program they control is execution dependent .

"Caller contextualization" is a variant of the latter approach in which handlers have a dynamic scope and are executed in the lexical context of the caller of the faulty routine where they are defined. A simple example of the interest of caller contextualization is the *DivideByZero* exception. It is easy to verify that, whatever the reason *DivideByZero* has been raised, only the caller of the *divide* operation can give a semantically founded interpretation of the reason why the divisor equals zero and can take an appropriate decision, in its context. This policy has been globally accepted as the best one for achieving fault-tolerant encapsulations in contract-based request / response interactions in all sequential languages (from PL/I, Clu, Mesa, Lisp, Flavors, Clos, C++, ANSI Smalltalk, to Java).

As far as AAOs are concerned, a choice has to be made among various alternatives. Original actor languages proposed dynamic scope handlers. It was proposed in [15] to associate an exceptional continuation actor to each message sending. However, such an actor is unable to access the calling context and therefore to give context-dependent answers to exceptions. The exception handling systems based on supervisors [24] and those that do not propagate exceptions outside of the thread in which they are signaled (as J2EE MDBs) suffer from the same lack. Some languages propose both static and dynamic scope handlers to respectively achieve fault tolerance and exception handling. It is the case of Beta

[34] and Smalltalk in its original blue book version[3]. They propose two kinds of exceptions and two means to signal them. The issue for a programmer with such a system is to know which kind of exceptions to signal.

In fact, caller contextualization is equally well adapted to both sequential and concurrent contexts. It has been made available to AAO systems by recent research proposals [7,27]. It has to be noted that applying it to its whole extent excludes solutions in which an exception in a participant of a collaborative task is signaled to its brother participants. In our example, this means that an exception in a single *Travel provider* would be signaled to all the other providers working on the same request. Although of effective potential interest [35], we reject this solution because of its intrinsic complexity for programmers. In our example, it could lead to very complex and intricate situations as soon as several travel providers signal exceptions concurrently.

3.4   Resolution, Criticality

Entities that represent a set of collaborating objects are a natural place where to enable programmers to specify policies to deal with the multiple exceptions they may concurrently signal. Some resolution mechanism to "concert" or "resolve" such exceptions have been proposed in [4,17,36]. A resolution function is a user defined function that can be attached to entities that represent collaborative activities (complex services or bgroups). It is invoked to concert the set of exceptions that have been signaled to the entity in which it is defined. It receives the exception object as an argument. Its role is to analyze the situation, to block and monitor under-critical exceptions [6] or to let pass through critical (concerted) ones. A concerted exception globally reflects the incorrect behavior of the collective activity. In the example, when a *Provider-Bgroup* sends n requests to n providers, a resolution function attached to the bgroup can determine that the failure of one of them is not critical for the collective activity and simply has to be monitored and that the failure of 90 percent of them should entail the signaling of a concerted one. In an asynchronous communication world, we propose to improve these ideas by calling the resolution function (1) as soon as an exception is signaled in a thread of a collective activity and (2) each time an exception is signaled, without waiting for the termination of all the services that constitute the collective activity. The signaling algorithm will be responsible for achieving these requirements.

4   Specification of SaGE

Our specification classically comes in four steps indicating: to which program units to attach exception handlers, how to signal exceptions, what can be written within handlers to put the system back into a coherent state and in which order handlers are searched for.

---

[3] In the original Smalltalk, lexical scope handlers are standard methods and dynamic scope handlers are lexical closures passed as arguments (e.g.: `aCollection find: anObject ifAbsent: [...]`).

4.1   Data Structures for Coordination and Contextualization

Coordination and contextualization require that some dedicated internal data structures be defined. Caller contextualization first requires that a doubly-linked tree of service execution contexts be monitored. In such a tree, a node represents a **complex service** execution context and a leaf the one of an **atomic service**. Callee to caller links are used to look for handlers. Caller to callee are used, for example, to kill the sub-services of a terminating complex service. Figure 1 shows the execution context tree that results from the services executed in the travel agency example. Complex services execution contexts are also used to collect and monitor the results of the execution of their sub-services, either they be standard results or exceptions.

4.2   Defining Handlers

The standard Fipa request / response interaction pattern is divided in four main steps:

- **Request and acknowledgment:** A *sender object* sends a *request* to a *receiver object*[4], which can be an individual object or a *bgroup*.
- **Acceptation:** The receiver indicates whether he accepts the request or not. Acceptation is a commitment to provide a response, either normal or exceptional.
- **Execution:** The receiver executes a service.
- **Response:** The service execution is finished and the receiver either sends back a normal response or signals an exception.

These steps highlight the role of four key entities in this interaction pattern: the request, the service, the active object, the *bgroup*. They are the four program units to which exception handlers could be attached:

- Handlers attached to **requests** allow, for example, to specify two different reactions to the occurrences of two exceptions raised by two invocations of the same service. Figure 2 (lines 29–38) shows how a handler can be attached to a specific request.
- Handlers attached to **services** allow to treat exceptions that are raised, directly or indirectly, by their execution. If the service is complex, the handler has to be able to deal with concurrent exceptions, to compose with partial results or to ignore partial failures. Figure 2 (lines 16–22) shows an example in which two handlers are attached to a service.
- Handlers attached to **bgroups** amount to attach them to their implicit service (see Sect. 2).

---

[4] The complete protocol includes an acknowledgment step to check that the message has not been lost. For the sake of simplicity, we will always consider here that sent requests arrive to their destination and that it is the transport layer (middleware) responsibility to guarantee this.

- Finally, handlers attached to **objects** (see Fig. 2, lines 5–7) are those handlers common to all services, designed, for example, to maintain in an uniform way the coherence of the object private data.

These capabilities are powerful enough to encompass most cases and simple enough to be easy to learn and use. Other systems are either more complex or less expressive but the comparison requires that the signaling algorithm be presented. All handlers have a dynamic scope. Resolution functions will be considered later.

4.3 Signaling

Signaling is done by the means of a classical *signal* primitive (cf. Fig. 3). Signaling is possible anywhere in the code and of course within handlers.

```
signal(new SaGEException("select\_error",getownerQueue()));
```

Fig. 3. The *signal* primitive

4.4 Defining Handlers

Exception handlers are classically [37] defined by the set of exception types they should catch and by their body (as illustrated by Fig. 2, lines 32–37, for example):

- A handler can simply restore whatever should be, to put back data into a coherent state, and can **return** a value that becomes the value of the expression the handler is associated to. In case of a message sending expression (standard or broadcast), the value returned by the handler is the value of the expression. In case of a handler attached to a service, the value becomes the value of the service execution. In case of a handler attached to an object, the value becomes the value of the service execution that raised the exception.
- A handler can also classically **signal** a new exception (generally of a higher conceptual level) or **re-signal** the original one. This behavior is illustrated on Fig. 2 line 18. Of course, handlers cannot protect themselves against the exceptions they signal.
- A handler can finally **retry** the execution of the program unit it is attached to. To retry [38,39] amounts to entirely re-execute the program unit it is attached to, generally after having modified the local environment, but in the same historical context. This possibility is illustrated on Fig. 2, lines 32–37. In case of handlers attached to objects, retrying means re-executing the service that signaled the exception.

4.5 Handler Search

Let S_n be the service in which an exception E is raised i.e. that contains the signaling point (the "*call-site*"). When E is raised, the execution of S_n is suspended (cf. Algo. 1) and the handler search is done using the thread of S_n. If S_n

is complex, it continues to monitor responses and other exceptions coming from its sub-services, the execution of which is not interrupted yet. If a concurrent sub-service signals another exception E_2 during handler search for E, it will be either ignored or considered later if no handler is executed for E. It may happen that no handler be executed for E when a resolution function considers that E is not critical.

Algorithm 1. The signal primitive

Require: Exception exc // raised exception object
    Service sce ← service in which the signal primitive is called
    if sce's state is "suspended" // exc is signaled during a handler execution **then**

        if the handler that is being executed is attached to a request **then**
            execute LocalSearch (exc, sce)
        else
            call CallerSearch (exc, calling-service)
            terminate sce
        end if
    else
        // exc is signaled from outside a handler
        sce 's state ← "suspended"
        execute LocalSearch (exc, sce)
    end if

Then, a handler for E is searched for locally:

- first, in the list of handlers associated to S_n ,
- then, in the list of handlers associated to the owner object of S_n.

If a suitable handler H is found there, it is executed and its execution terminates the execution of S_n. Along with the execution of H all pending sub-services of S_n, if any, are terminated. The caller service of S_n (and all of its other sub-services) remain unaffected and normally pursue their execution concurrently with H's.

If no handler is found locally, the search process proceeds in the calling context (service S_{n-1}), in order to guarantee caller contextualization (cf. Sect. 3.3). First S_{n-1} is suspended and the search for a handler initiated. The search in S_{n-1} is done concurrently with the termination of S_n. This original capability guarantees that all activities that have become useless because of a failure are terminated as soon as possible. This preserves system resource. The process carries on as follows:

- first, it searches the list of handlers associated to the request which initiated S_n. There, the resolution function associated to S_{n-1} is executed. If it lets the exception pass through, the search process continues. If not, the search process stops and no handler will be executed (cf. Sect. 4.6).
- then, it searches the list of handlers associated to S_{n-1}
- finally, it searches the list of handlers associated to the owner of S_{n-1}.

Algorithm 2. Handler Search - LocalSearch (Exception exc, Service sce)

Require: Exception exc of type T, Service sce // raised exception object and current service

if a handler H_T exists attached to sce **then**
  execute H_T
else
  if a handler H_T exists attached to the AAO to which sce belongs **then**
    execute H_T
  else
    if a calling service exists **then**
      call CallerSearch (exc, calling-service)
    else
      execute default handler // top-level has been reached
    end if
  end if
end if
terminate sce // terminates the service and (if it is a complex one) recursively all its sub-services

---

Algorithm 3. Handler Search - CallerSearch (Exception exc, Service sce)

Require: Exception exc of type T, Service sce // raised exception object and current service

if a handler H_T exists attached to the request sent by sce **then**
  execute H_T
else
  log exc into sce's exception log
  execute sce's resolution function[5]
  if the resolution function returns a concerted exception **then**
    sce 's state ← "suspended"
    execute LocalSearch (exc, sce)
  end if
end if

If no handler is found, the same three steps are repeated once again into the caller's caller context (S_{n-2}). This process iterates until either an adequate handler is found and executed or the root of the service tree is reached. In the latter case, a default top-level handler is executed.

Algorithm 1 describes the signaling of an exception. Algorithms 2 and 3 describe the local and the caller's context part of the handler search process. To ease the writing of these algorithms, let us note H_T an exception handler defined to treat exceptions of type T. Let us also define two primitives to call sub-procedures: *execute*, to denote a sequential call and *call*, to denote an asynchronous concurrent call. When a procedure is called through the *execute* primitive, it executes in the same thread as its caller. When a procedure is called

---

[5] This is also valid in the case of a Bgroup because the resolution function is *in fine* attached to the (default) broadcasting service.

```
public SaGEException concert (Vector subServicesInfo)
{
    int failed = 0;

    // count the number of exceptions raised in subservices and
    // the number of subservices that are still running
    for (int i=0; j<subServicesInfo.size(); i++)
        {
        if ((ServiceInfo) (subServicesInfo.elementAt(i)).getRaised
           Exception()
           != null)
           failed++;
        }

    // if more than 30% failed, there are too many bad providers
    if (failed > (0.3*subServicesInfo.size()))
        return new SaGEException("too_many_bad_providers",getAddress());

    // computing still running - no critical situation
    return null;
}
```

Fig. 4. Java-like code of an exception resolution function associated to the Provider Bgroup

through the *call* primitive, it executes in a thread different from its caller's. The remaining instructions in its caller's context are then executed concurrently with the called procedure.

4.6   Concerted Exception Support

SaGE provides an exception resolution support (cf. Sect. 3.4) that is integrated to the handler search. It enables resolution functions to be defined at places where concurrent activities are launched and have to be co-ordinated i.e. at the complex service level. There is no need for a resolution function either at the request level, because requests are atomic, or at the AAO level because all semantically sound activities of objects, that need to be co-ordinated, are accessible via services. *Bgroups* own resolution functions that are attached to the implicit complex service they execute. The *bgroup* acts first as a request broadcaster and then as a response collector in order to send back a single (composite) response to the client AAO. The default behavior of the resolution function associated to a bgroup service is, once all recipients have replied, to aggregate all the exceptions that occured into a concerted one. Of course, a programmer can define his own exception resolution function as in the example of Fig. 4.

   In our model, a resolution function is executed each time an exception handler is searched for in the caller's context (cf. Algorithm 3). Whatever is done in the function, three cases are finally possible:

- the exception is critical for the service. The resolution function returns the exception object and the handler search process carries on.
- the resolution function evaluates that the exception is under-critical and that nothing more should be done yet. The exception is logged, the resolution function returns null and the handler search process stops. The collective activity is not affected. The only service that is terminated is the defective sub-service.
- the resolution function evaluates that the exception is under-critical but that there is a need to signal something, for example because too many under-critical exceptions have been logged. The resolution function returns a special exception that reflects the situation and the handler search carries on.

Such a use of resolution for concerted exception differs from the original one [40,29] in that it is adapted to a context in which there are no synchronization points. A mechanism to calculate the time when the resolution function should be executed has been proposed in [6]. Our solution consists in tightly integrating the execution of the resolution function to our handler search mechanism. Our resolution function is executed each time the handler search process goes back from a context to its caller. At each step, it can stop the process or let it continue (with either the original exception or a new, concerted one). This characteristic makes our system more reactive, because our resolution function evaluates the situation each time an exception is signaled.

5   Related Works

Concurrent programming systems fall into three main categories when exception handling is considered. These categories correspond to the kind of concurrency that is supported [14]. This directly determines how AAOs can interact, and, as part of their interactions, how exceptions can be signaled between them.

5.1   Isolated Concurrency

Isolated concurrency is provided by standard programming languages such as Java. Its goal is to allow several AAOs (threads) to execute concurrently in a shared context (the address space of a virtual machine) as if each of them was the only existing AAO. To achieve this, the system enforces that the activity of an AAO does not interfere with another one. For example, locks are managed on shared resources in order to transparently serialize concurrent accesses to them. In the same way, no standard means is provided to send information from a thread to another. When an exception is raised in an AAO, it is signaled along its own execution stack (in its separated execution thread). When the exception is not caught and reaches the top level of the execution stack, the AAO is destroyed by the system (the thread is discarded by the thread manager). The other AAOs are not warned of the failure in order to maintain their isolation.

5.2   Cooperative Concurrency and Exception Handling

Isolated concurrency is only suitable when strictly parallel computations are to be managed,for example when handling requests from different clients. But when a set of entities are intended to participate together to the achievement of a global activity, means to handle their cooperation are then required. More specifically, in such forms of cooperative concurrency, there is a crucial need to manage how the individual failure of an AAO impacts the global activity and, as a consequence, should impact the activity of other entities.

Monitors. A first technique is to provide specific entities which role is to monitor other entities and to implement how errors are to be handled when the global context of the monitored entities is considered. Java proposes that a thread can belong to a *ThreadGroup*. When an exception is raised and uncaught in a thread T , it is then signaled to the thread group to which T belongs. A unique handler, that catches all the signaled exceptions, can be associated with the thread group. This allows basic actions to be carried out, such as to kill threads that are still running in the thread group, in order to terminate the whole activity of the group. Some SMAs provide such a mechanism in the form of supervisor agents. Supervisors are agents that monitors other agents in the system and to which exceptions are signaled.They are used, for example, to react to the death of an agent (killed by an uncaught exception) and warn other agents that it cannot be reached any more. In Erlang [22], supervisor processes can be tied to other ones to be informed of their termination. In Oz [20], asynchronous exception related to distribution are handled thanks to dedicated monitors. Monitors enable a good separation of concerns, because they keep behaviors dealing with errors well separated from behaviors dealing with normal activities. However, they raise encapsulation and contextualization issues. When used for AAOs, monitors can only perform external, platform-level, generic actions such as to suspend, restart or destroy an AAO. Monitors are finally somehow restricted to the handling of generic exceptions because they have no access (unless breaking encapsulation) to objects' internal state and, generally, to any contextual information about the cause of the exception. This drastically limits the applicability of monitors when specific errors, regarding the specific coordinated activity of a set of entities, are to be handled.

CA Actions. A common solution, in systems that tackle this contextualization issue, is that collective activities of coordinated concurrent entities must become explicit, in order to structure the global execution contexts and provide a support to handle exceptions. A CA Action [14] allows the representation of a collective activity to which different entities, called participants, contribute concurrently. Different variants of this concept, along with different EHSs, have been proposed. In [41], a CA Action is defined as a sort of contract that ties together all the participant entities. As a part of the contract, these participants must provide support for the handling of a common set of exceptions. When an exception is raised by one of the participants, it is signaled to the others. This way, all the participants to a CA Action suspend their individual activity (and thus suspend the execution of the whole global activity). The system then enforces a synchronization point between all the participants. When multiple, concurrent exceptions are signaled, this policy ensures that a same set of exceptions is finally signaled to each participant. Each participant resolves this exception set thanks to an exception resolution tree provided by the CA Action (and thus common to all the participants): this entails that each participant finally handles the same resolved exception. However, the handlers that are eventually triggered are specific to each participant and are cohesive parts of their behavior. This model addresses the contextualization issue stressed above. Exceptions pertaining to a global activity are handled by having its participants contribute collectively to their treatment, as a result of the coordinated execution of their own handlers. One concern with such a model is the cost of the coordination between the participants. Indeed, it implies the exchange of numerous messages in order to inform the other participants of exceptions and of execution suspensions. Moreover, it entails a strong coupling between the participants as it requires a common set of exception types and a common exception resolution tree to be used. This model is therefore not perfectly suited for highly distributed and open systems.

Guardians. Among other things, various improvements have been introduced to the above model in [26,42,27]. A CA Action is monitored by a special participant, called a "guardian". Participants signal to the guardian exceptions that are global to the CA Action. The guardian then suspends the execution of all the participants, while collecting concurrent exceptions. The set of exceptions collected by the guardian is then resolved thanks to a first set of rules that determines what unique global exception is to be handled. Next, a second set of rules is used to transform the global exception into the specific exceptions that will finally be signaled to each participant. This way, only one participant, the guardian, needs to track the exceptions and the status of other participants. Moreover, the cooperation of the participants, when handling global exceptions, is defined by the set of rules of the guardian. Rules are tailored to adapt to the specific behavior of each participant, so that no predefined requirement is to be imposed to the participants. Providing a complex and powerful solution, Guardian is especially relevant to deal with exceptions related to shared environments where all participants can effectively cooperate to restore a consistent state. This kind of exceptions encompasses system-level exceptions that warn of the faulty state of some shared resource (disk, memory, network, ...). SaGE provides a simpler solution when handling exceptions related to collaborating pairs of objects such as clients and servers.

5.3   Collaborative Concurrency and Exception Handling

Models discussed in the previous section indeed share the idea that when an exception occurs in the context of a collective activity, handlers are sought and executed in all its participants. Besides, in situations in which couples of entities collaborate together, for example when a server informs its client that it has

failed to achieve some requested service, signaled exceptions are to be handled
in the context of the caller. Exceptions are therefore much more efficiently handled as responses sent by the server than as broadcasted information. To deal
with such responses, many systems for asynchronous programming use "future"
objects [16,43,20]. Futures are response holders that are immediately returned
to client entities when they asynchronously request a service to a server AAO.
When a client needs to use the value of a response, it tries to access the value of
the corresponding future. If no value is yet bound, the client AAO can perform
a blocking wait. When an exception is bound to a future instead of a standard
value, it is signaled to a client when the future is read. The client then usually handles it with some classical built-in *try-catch* like constructs. The main
advantages of such a solution are its simplicity and its ability to be seamlessly
integrated to existing programming languages. Its drawback is that it does not
cope with complex situations. For example, when requests are sent concurrently
to different servers, it is difficult to foresee the best order in which futures should
be read in order not to wait for an unbound response while others are yet available and could be treated. This is one of the reasons why we think that reactive
AAO models are more interesting for exception handling. With futures, exceptions cannot be treated as soon as possible and can sometimes be simply lost
when some futures are not read. In a reactive system, like the one in which we
have specified our system, exceptions are signaled asynchronously by sending
messages and can therefore be treated as soon as they occur. The implementation of SaGE in a future-based context has not been done yet but the resulting
system would be more limited than today's one.

Erlang [22] has a sophisticated EHS to deal with exceptions within concurrent
processes and also proposes an asynchronous message sending based solution to
signal process termination exceptions from one process to another. In Erlang,
messages that contain exceptions cannot be distinguished from others and, as a
consequence, the handling of asynchronous exceptions can only be *ad hoc*. On
the contrary, SaGE carry exceptions with messages that, when received, trigger
a full-fledged EHS. Finally, to cope with concurrent exceptions, [44] also suggests the introduction of future groups in order to gather the exception of a set
of futures and apply a resolution function to them. But this solution requires
the writing of a lot of code to explicitly deal with future groups. With SaGE,
the support for exception resolution is directly integrated in the EHS. Provided
that corresponding resolution functions are defined, concurrent exception management does not require any extra programming.

6   Conclusion and Future Work

In this paper, we have proposed a specification of an exception handling system
adapted to asynchronous active objects. We have especially focused on service-
oriented systems and on the request / response interaction scheme. Our system
aims at combining simplicity, usability at the language level by standard programmers, integration and adaptation of known key-solutions for sequential and

concurrent exception handling and full integration of active objects. Our solution conforms to all the key requirements identified in Sect. 1: encapsulation and reactivity enforcement, ability to write context-dependent handlers, ability to coordinate and control group of active objects collaborating to a common task, ability to configure the exception propagation policy by defining *exception resolution functions*, ability to immediately handle exceptions that are critical or to only log under-critical ones until their conjunction enables a diagnosis to be established. We propose dynamic scope handlers associated to requests, services and objects. Resolution functions can be defined at the service level, which is the place where collaborative tasks can be coordinated. They come together with a signaling primitive, a handler search algorithm and a handler invocation mechanism that take into account the execution history and, when possible, work asynchronously to improve object reactivity. So this model is especially suited for applications that need few synchronization and a high level of concurrency and reactivity.

We implemented and successfully experimented this model both with MadKIT, to handle exceptions in multi-agents systems, and with the open-source JONAS J2EE implementation, to provide a fault-tolerant support to the execution of asynchronous message driven beans (MDBs). We think the set of design choices that make SaGE a good compromise between expressive-power and simplicity can be adapted to various kinds of active objects, to various forms of asynchronous communications (e.g. future-based) and to different interaction protocols (e.g. publish/subscribe). We also think it is general enough to be used as a base level for the implementation of systems offering higher-level control structures for fault tolerance, such as conversations [45] or transactional systems [46,47].These all are future works objectives as is the introduction of the *resumption* model of exception handling in our system. Indeed, we do think that the *restart* construct and protocol introduced in the Flavor system [37,48] are of primary importance in a dynamic world of interacting objects.

Acknowledgments. The authors wish to thank Jacques Ferber for many fruitful discussions on SMAs and for having given Madkit to the community as an experimentation tool, Anand Tripathi for his helpful comments on the preliminary version of this paper, and Frédéric Souchon who has implemented SaGE both in MadKIT and JONAS.

References

1. Carl Hewitt, Peter Bishop, R.S.: A universal modular actor formalism for artificial intelligence. In: Proceedings of the International Joint Conference on Artificial Intelligence. (1973) 235–246
2. Randell, B., Romanovsky, A., Rubira-Calsavara, C., Stroud, R., Wu, Z., Xu, J.: From recovery blocks to concurrent atomic actions. In: Predictably Dependable Computing Systems. ESPRIT Basic Research Series (1995) 87–101
3. Dony, C.: Exception handling and object-oriented programming : towards a synthesis. ACM SIGPLAN Notices **25**(10) (1990) 322–330 *OOPSLA ECOOP '90 Proceedings*, N. Meyrowitz (editor).

4. Issarny, V.: An exception handling model for parallel programming and its verification. In: Proceedings of the ACM SIGSOFT'91 Conference on Software for Critical Systems, New Orleans, Louisianna, USA (1991) 92–100

5. Romanovsky, A.: Practical exception handling and resolution in concurrent programs. Computer Languages **23**(1) (1997) 43–58

6. Lacourte, S.: Exceptions in Guide, an object-oriented language for distributed applications. In Springer-Verlag, ed.: Proceedings of ECOOP 91. Number 5-90 in LNCS, Grenoble (France) (1990) 268–287

7. Souchon, F., Dony, C., Urtado, C., Vauttier, S.: Improving exception handling in multi-agent systems. In de Lucena, C.J.P., Garcia, A.F., Romanovsky, A.B., Castro, J., Alencar, P.S.C., eds.: Software engineering for multi-agent systems II, Research issues and practical applications. Volume 2940 of Lecture Notes in Computer Science. Springer (2004) 167–188

8. Briot, J.P., Guerraoui, R.: A classification of various approaches for object-based parallel and distributed programming. In Padget, J.A., ed.: Collaboration between Human and Artificial Societies. Number 1624 in Lecture Notes in Artificial Intelligence. Springer-Verlag (1999) 3–29 Invited conference.

9. Lavender, R.G., Schmidt, D.C.: Active object: An object behavioral pattern for concurrent programming. In Coplien, Vlissides, Kerth, eds.: Pattern Languages of Program Design. Addison-Wesley Reading (1996)

10. FIPA: Foundation For Intelligent Physical Agents : Request Interaction Protocol Specification. (2002)

11. Ferber, J.: Multi-Agent Systems: An Introduction to Distributed Artificial Intelligence. Addison-Wesley Pub Co; 1st edition (February 25, 1999) (2005)

12. Clement Jonquet, S.A.C.: The strobe model: Dynamic service generation on the grid. Applied Artificial Intelligence Journal Special issue on Learning Grid Services **19**(9-10) (2005) 967–1013

13. Dedecker, J., Cutsem, T.V., Mostinckx, S., D'Hondt, T., Meuter, W.D.: Ambient-oriented programming in ambienttalk. In: Proceedings ECOOP'06 (European Conference on Object-Oriented Programming), Springer-Verlag (2006) To appear.

14. Romanovsky, A.B., Kienzle, J.: Action-oriented exception handling in cooperative and competitive concurrent object-oriented systems. In: Advances in Exception Handling Techniques. (2000) 147–164

15. Theriault, D.: A primer for the Act-1 language. Technical Report AI Memo 672, MIT Artificial Intelligence Laboratory (1982)

16. Halstead, R., Loaiza, J.: Exception handling in multilisp. In: 1985 Int'l. Conf. on Parallel Processing. (1985) 822–830

17. Campbell, R., Randell, B.: Error recovery in asynchronous systems. IEEE Transactions on Software Engineering (SE) **SE-12 number 8**(8) (1986) 811–826

18. Gärtner, F.C.: Fundamentals of fault tolerant distributed computing in asynchronous environments. ACMCS **31**(1) (1999) 1–26

19. Keen, A.W., Olsson, R.A.: Exception handling during asynchronous method invocation. In Monien, B., Feldmann, R., eds.: Proceedings of Euro-Par 2002 Parallel Processing. Lecture Notes in Computer Science. Springer-Verlag (2002) 656–660

20. Van Roy, P.: On the separation of concerns in distributed programming: Application to distribution structure and fault tolerance in Mozart. In: Fourth International Workshop on Parallel and Distributed Computing for Symbolic and Irregular Applications (PDSIA 99), Tohoku University, Sendai, Japan, World Scientific (1999)

21. Campéas, A., Dony, C., Urtado, C., Vauttier, S.: Distributed exception handling : ideas, lessons and issues with recent exception handling systems. In: Proceedings of RISE'04 : First International Workshop on Rapid Integration of Software Engineering techniques, Luxembourg (2004) 82–92

22. Carlsson, R., Gustavsson, B., Nyblom, P.: Erlang: Exception handling revisited. In: Proceedings of the Third ACM SIGPLAN Erlang Workshop. (2004)

23. Iliasov, A., Romanovsky, A.: Exception handling in coordination-based mobile environments. In: Proceedings of 29th IEEE International Computer Software and Applications Conference (COMPSAC 2005), 25-28 July, Edinburgh, Scotland, UK. (2005) 341–350

24. Klein, M., Dellarocas, C.: Exception handling in agent systems. In Etzioni, O., Müller, J.P., Bradshaw, J.M., eds.: Proceedings of the Third Annual Conference on Autonomous Agents (AGENTS-99), New York, ACM Press (1999) 62–68

25. Klein, M., Dellarocas, C.: Towards a systematic repository of knowledge about managing multi-agent system exceptions, ases working paper ases-wp-2000-01 (2000)

26. Tripathi, A., Miller, R.: Exception handling in agent oriented systems. In: Advances in Exception Handling Techniques. LNCS (Lecture Notes in Computer Science) 2022. Springer-Verlag (2001) 128–146

27. Miller, R., Tripathi, A.: The guardian model and primitives for exception handling in distributed systems. IEEE Trans. Software Eng. 30(12) (2004) 1008–1022

28. Dony, C.: An object-oriented exception handling system for an object-oriented language. In: Proceedings of ECOOP'88. (1988) 146–161

29. Issarny, V.: An exception handling mechanism for parallel object-oriented programming: Towards the design of reusable, and robust distributed software. Journal of Object-Oriented Programming 6(6) (1993) 29–39

30. Souchon, F., Urtado, C., Vauttier, S., Dony, C.: Exception handling in component-based systems : a first study. In Romanovsky, A., Dony, C., Knudsen, J., Tripathi, A., eds.: Technical Report TR 03-028. Proceedings of the Exception Handling in Object-Oriented Systems workshop at ECOOP 2003. Department of computer science, University of Minnesota, Minneapolis, Darmstadt, Germany (2003) 84–91

31. Miller, R., Tripathi, A.R.: Issues with exception handling in object-oriented systems. In: Proceedings of ECOOP'97. (1997) 85–103

32. Dellarocas, C.: Toward exception handling infrastructures for component-based software. In: Proceedings of the International Workshop on Component-based Software Engineering, 20th International Conference on Software Engineering (ICSE), Kyoto, Japan, April 25-26, 1998. (1998)

33. Levin, R.: Program structures for exceptional condition handling. Phd dissertation, Dept. Comput. Sci., Carnegie-Mellon University Pittsburg (1977)

34. Knudsen, J.L.: Fault tolerance and exception handling in beta. In: Advances in Exception Handling Techniques. LNCS (Lecture Notes in Computer Science) 2022, Springer-Verlag (2001)

35. Burns, A., Randell, B., Romanovsky, A., Stroud, R., Wellings, A., Xu, J.: Temporal constraints and exception handling in object-oriented distributed systems. Design for Validation (DeVa) - Third Year Report, Esprit LTR Project 20072 - DeVa (1998)

36. Tartanoglu, F., Issarny, V., Levy, N., Romanovsky, A.: Dependability in the web service architecture (2002)

37. K.Pitman: Error/condition handling. Technical report, Contribution to WG16. Revision 18.Propositions for ISO-LISP. AFNOR, ISO/IEC JTC1/SC 22/WG 16N15 (April 1988)

38. Goodenough, J.B.: Exception handling: Issues and a proposed notation. Commun. ACM **18**(12) (1975) 683–696
39. Meyer, B.: Disciplined exceptions. Technical report tr-ei-22/ex, Interactive Software Engineering, Goleta, CA (1988)
40. Issarny, V.: Concurrent exception handling. In: Advances in Exception Handling Techniques. LNCS (Lecture Notes in Computer Science) 2022. Springer-Verlag (2001) 111–127
41. Randell, B., Romanovsky, A., Stroud, R.J., Xu, J., Zorzo, A.F.: Coordinated Atomic Actions: from Concept to Implementation. Technical Report 595, Department of Computing Science, University of Newcastle upon Tyne (1997)
42. Miller, R., Tripathi, A.: Primitives and mechanisms of the guardian model for exception handling in distributed systems. In: Exception Handling in Object Oriented Systems: towards Emerging Application Areas and New Programming Paradigms Workshop (at ECOOP'03 international conference) proceedings. (2003)
43. Caromel, D., Henrio, L., Serpette, B.: Asynchronous and deterministic objects. In: Proceedings of the 31st ACM Symposium on Principles of Programming Languages, ACM Press (2004) To appear.
44. Rintala, M.: Handling multiple concurrent exceptions in C++ using futures, kokoelmassa romanovsky. In: Developing Systems that Handle Exceptions, Proceedings of ECOOP 2005 Workshop on Exception Handling in Object Oriented Systems, ACM Press (2005)
45. Romanovsky, A.B.: Conversations of objects. Computer Languages **21**(3/4) (1995) 147–163
46. Kienzle, J.: Open Multithreaded Transactions - A Transaction Model for Concurrent Object-Oriented Programming. Kluwer Academic Publishers (2003)
47. Guelfi, N., Razavi, R., Romanovsky, A., Vandenbergh, S.: Drip catalyst: An MDE/MDA method for fault-tolerant distributed software families development. In: Proceedings of the OOPSLA and GPCE Workshop on Best Practices for Model Driven Software Development. (2004)
48. Pitman, K.M.: Condition handling in the lisp language family. In: Advances in Exception Handling Techniques. LNCS (Lecture Notes in Computer Science) 2022. Springer-Verlag (2001) 39–59

Exception Management Within Web Applications Implementing Business Processes

Marco Brambilla, Sara Comai, and Christina Tziviskou

Politecnico di Milano, Dipartimento di Elettronica e Informazione
Via Ponzio 34/5, 20133 Milano, Italy
{mbrambil, comai, tzivisko}@elet.polimi.it

Abstract. Web applications are more and more used nowadays to implement business processes that have to be executed on the Web. These applications support the modeling, execution, and monitoring of B2B interactions, as well as the management and publishing of content data, value-added services, and so on. The integration of these different technologies raises new problems that may occur during the process execution on the Web. Exceptional situations may be caused by the improper user navigation through Web pages, by system failures that interrupt the B2B interaction, or by events semantically related to the business process. We present a classification of exceptions, the capturing and notification mechanisms, and the recovery policies that may be applied on the business process in order to solve the exception. We also show how the proposed approach can be applied to WebML, a high-level modeling language for Web applications, and compare it with existing standards.

1 Introduction

In recent years, the Web is more and more being used as the implementation platform for B2B applications, aiming at supporting business processes, content management, document approval flows, value-added services, and so on. This leads to the integration of several technologies, which go far beyond the simple implementation of Web applications composed of Web interfaces for content publishing. This is confirmed by current efforts towards the modeling of process-oriented Web applications [5].

In this context, Web applications assume a mission-critical role within the enterprise and the need arises of solid approaches to users' behavior modeling, to fault management, and to exception handling.

Contributions from software engineering and other fields can partially address these issues as shown in [1], [2], [10], [11], [12], [14], [17], although the Web context introduces new and original problems, due to the powerful interaction options provided by browser-based interfaces, which are more oriented to free navigation than to strict processes adherence (e.g., users are enabled to jump back and forth on navigated pages). This means that users cannot be forced to perform any action or task, since Web architectures are meant to provide loosely coupled interactions between peers.

C. Dony et al. (Eds.):Exception Handling, LNCS 4119, pp. 101–120, 2006.
© Springer-Verlag Berlin Heidelberg 2006

In this chapter, we propose an approach to exception handling in this context. We identify the exceptions that may arise in Web applications, we classify them along various dimensions (e.g., type, target, detection time), and we provide a framework for exception handling based on the proposed classification. The methodology of our approach for traditional Web applications is described in [9] and has been extended in [6] for including business processes. It is basically an iterated process composed of (i) requirements analysis, (ii) process definition in terms of activities, actors and constraints, (iii) data design of the business objects, and (iv) hypertext modeling of the business activities in terms of Web interfaces. The steps of this methodology will be enriched to take into account the design of the identified exceptions and their integration into the final Web application modeling.

The implementation of our approach is based on a metadata model that describes the process enacted by the Web application and its status. A set of three models is built upon it: a capturing model (describing the mechanisms for capturing the exceptions), a notifying model (describing the options available for notifying the user about an exception occurrence), and a handling model (describing compensation actions that may be taken). Finally, we compare our framework with existing exception handling mechanisms with standards like BPMN[3], BPEL4WS[4], and XPDL[23].

Many works have addressed the problem of exception discovery and compensation. They mainly studied transactional properties for activities, which is not in our target. However, some works deal with weaker properties. For example, [13] is based on the concept of spheres, to make use of only those transactional properties that are actually needed; [16] is one of the first works that addresses the problem in the Web context, but it provides only a classification of exceptions. For the definition of the target and the expressive power of workflow primitives, our work is inspired by the pattern based workflow analysis by Van Der Aalst [18], and by industrial and academic standards like BPML /BPMN [3] and YAWL [19]. Other works on activity composition and coordination related to the Web have been considered; for example, [8] and others propose solutions on Web services interaction, for which we will propose some exception handling techniques.

Our previous work [6] studied the basic issues of the problem, with a specific focus on a Web application modeling language called WebML [20], while in [7] we considered a more general approach applicable to any underlying technology or design method. In this chapter we focus on the general mechanisms for managing exceptional behaviors on the Web and present some examples applied to WebML.

The chapter is structured as follows: in Section 2 we describe a model for Web applications implementing business processes; in Section 3 we introduce the main characteristics of the exceptions occurring in typical Web applications. Section 4 describes our approach for representing, capturing, notifying and handling the exceptions. Section 5 provides an overview of the implementation based on the Web Modeling Language; Section 6 compares our approach with existing standards, and, finally, in Section 7 we draw the conclusions.

2 Workflow-Driven Web Applications

In this section we describe a simplified model for Web applications implementing business processes, also called workflow-driven Web applications [6]. Typically, a workflow-driven Web application includes: (i) a business process model, and (ii) an hypertext model for specifying the composition of Web pages representing activities to be executed, and the user navigation path that determines the execution path.

2.1 The Case Study

We will exemplify our approach throughout the chapter by means of a case study describing a loan brokering Web application that provide users with the possibility to search for available loan options, fill loan applications, and be notified of their acceptance/rejection by the loan provider. The desired Web application should cover the whole process and allow the broker agent to evaluate the loan request, give a preliminary validation, check the details of loan applications (e.g. applicants' financial status, job history), and register his final decision for a given application. If the request is approved, the customer can accept it and proceed with the loan cashing and periodic installment payments. The scenario describes a simplified process executed on the Web by three actors: customers, brokering managers, and company employees. However, as we will see in the next sections, exceptional situations may occur during the execution of the process and lead the system to an uncertain state.

2.2 Business Process Modeling

For specifying business processes, we use the Workflow Management Coalition terminology [22] and the BPML/BPMN [3] notation. The workflow model is hence based on the concepts of Process (description of the business process), Case (process instance), Activity (elementary unit of work composing a process), Activity instance (instantiation of an activity within a case), Actor (user role intervening in the process), Event (punctual situation that happens in a case) and Constraint (logical precedence among activities and rules enabling activities execution). Processes can be internally structured using a variety of constructs: sequences of activities, gateways implementing AND, OR, XOR splits, respectively realizing splits into independent, alternative and exclusive threads; gateways implementing joins representing convergence points of more activities; activity iterations; and pre- and post-conditions of activities.

The workflow depicted in Fig. 1 describes the process model of the case study. Every Lane in the figure (horizontal containers) contains the Activities (rounded-corner rectangles) to be executed by a specific Actor. Events (small circles) may initiate (or terminate) the process execution, firing the activities execution ordered as indicated by the arrowhead lines and the gateways. The Actors in the process are the final users (customer, manager, employee) that will perform the described activities through a corresponding hypertext. Therefore, a mapping of the above process model to a hypertext model is needed.

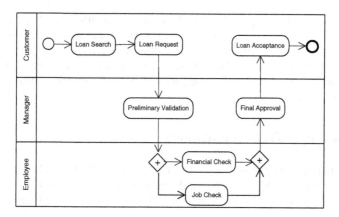

Fig. 1. Workflow modeling of the "Loan Request" process

2.3 Hypertext Modeling

Once the process model has been defined, each activity may be described through an hypertext model. The hypertext belonging to an activity for a user is broken down into pages. Pages are univocally identified within an activity and present the work to be executed. The links between subsequent pages indicate the permitted user navigation path that may be followed by server-side operations, and determine the activities execution order.

Fig. 2 depicts the first two activities of the customer modeled in Fig. 1. In particular, the Loan Search activity in the Loan Request process is composed of one hypertext page, identified as page 1. The Loan Request activity is composed of three pages: the Available Loans page is identified with 1, the Loan Details page with 2, and the Loan Ack page with 3. This hypertext allows the user to search for a loan with specific characteristics (Search Criteria page), to look at the results (Available Loans) and to see the details of a specific loan (Loan Details). Then, he may submit a request for that type of loan, and receive a confirmation (Loan Ack page). Between two subsequent pages, there can be a chain of operations executed at server-side (depicted as small circles in Fig. 2), which is not relevant for our purposes. Since we do not consider server-side failures, a chain of operations can be seen as an atomic element that never fails.

Another feature of workflow-based Web applications that we take into account is the invocation of Web Services within an activity, aiming at integrating remote

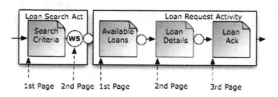

Fig. 2. Process hypertext modeling presenting pages numbering, navigation path, server side operations, and Web services interaction

services or data within the user hypertext. Between two subsequent pages, there can be a Web Service call whose unsuccessful execution can raise critical situations. As depicted in Fig. 2, the Web service interaction is considered as a numbered page within the activity. In the rest of the chapter, we assume that the Loan Search activity is actually implemented with a Web service call to a service which is outside of the bank offering the loans.

3 Exceptions in Web Applications

In order to handle exceptions, we try to clarify the conditions under which failures may occur. We present by example the different kinds of exceptions that may occur, and provide an exception classification that will be used later in our framework.

3.1 Examples of Events Generating Exceptions in Web Applications

Exceptions in process-centric Web applications may be caused by different types of events, like events generated from external sources (e.g., an incoming message of a Web service invocation), from data inconsistencies in shared data sources, or may be generated within the process execution from inconsistent user navigation, or from server/client infrastructure failures. For example, possible events that are not part of the normal flow in the Loan Request process Fig. 1 are presented in the following scenarios.

Within the Loan Request activity, the user presses the *back* button of the browser, thus reaching *another page within the same activity*, and tries to navigate a link repeating part of the Request or restarts its execution (see Fig. 3 (a)). This user navigation leads to a *Wrong Starting Page* exception. Once the Loan Request activity is completed, the user navigating some page *outside the process hypertext*, may press the *back* button of the browser, thus *reaching a page of the activity*, and may try to navigate a link repeating part of the Request or restart its execution (see Fig. 3 (b)). This navigation leads to an *Action By Completed Activity* exception.

Within the Loan Request activity, the user may press the *back* button of the browser, thus reaching the page of the Loan Search activity, and may try to navigate a link repeating part of the Search (see Fig. 4 (a)). This navigation occurs between two activities of the process and allows the user to quit an active activity and raises an *Activity Already Active* exception, since a running activity is abandoned. Within one of the activities, the user may stand on a page for a long time after which a timeout

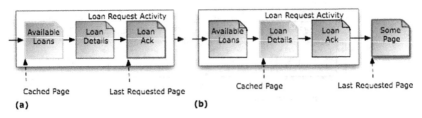

Fig. 3. Examples of (a) *Wrong Starting Page* and (b) *Action By Completed Activity* exceptions

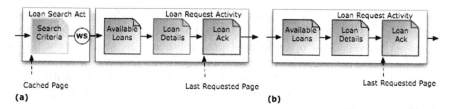

Fig. 4. Examples of (a) *Activity Already Active* exception and (b) *Session End* exception

may occur (see Fig. 4 (b)); thus, the user session ends generating a *Session End* exception. Within the Loan Request activity, the user may press the *back* button of the browser, thus reaching a page outside the process. Also, this case can be treated as a *Session end* exception. Within the Loan Request activity, the user may not be able to send his acknowledgement on the selected loan because of network unavailability. Therefore, a timeout occurs, generating a *Session End* exception.

A notification for the discount rate variation of a country may require changes in the loan conditions of requests fulfilled with the corresponding installment plans. In such a case, a *Discount Rate Variation* exception is raised. Anytime during the process execution, the user may ask the cancellation of the loan request. A *Cancel* exception is raised. In the Loan Search activity, when the Web Service is called to get the loans satisfying the criteria specified by the user, the loan amount may exceed the limits for which the loan can be approved. In such a case, a failure response is received from the Web service and an *Invalid Loan Amount* exception is raised. Anytime during the process execution, a modification of the expiration date of an installment plan may require that all the customers whose requested loans fulfilled the corresponding installment plan should revisit their loan options. In such a case, an *Expiration Date Modification* exception is raised.

3.2 Classification of the Exceptions

Exception handling may differ according to the characteristics of the exceptions introduced in the previous sections.

Exception Type. We distinguish three main categories of exceptions:

1. **Behavioral** (or user-generated) exceptions are driven by the improper execution order of process activities. The free user navigation through Web pages results in the client visiting older pages, trying to explore the hypertext of activities that have already been executed. The *Wrong Starting Page*, the *Action By Completed Activity* and the *Activity Already Active* exceptions belong to such category.
2. **Semantic** (or application) exceptions are driven by the unsuccessful logical outcome of activities execution. For example, the *Discount Rate Variation*, the *Cancel*, the *Invalid Loan Amount* and the *Expiration Date Modification* exceptions are semantic exceptions.
3. **System** exceptions are caused by the malfunctioning of the workflow-based Web application infrastructure both at server and at client side. Events that result in such exceptions are network failures and system breakdowns. In the current work, we do not consider server-side failures, since proposals for such an exception context

already exist for traditional data-storage and workflow technology. Client-side exceptions are caused either by data storage and client breakdowns, browser crashes, and network unavailability or by elapsed time between user interactions within a process (like in the last scenarios presented in the previous subsection). A client-side failure results either in the client not sending a request to the server, or in the server not responding to the client. Client-side failures are indistinguishable at application level and are recognized as *Session End* exceptions.

Exception Detection Time. Another important characterization of the exceptions in process-centric Web applications is related to the detection time: exception may occur while the users involved in the process are navigating through the activities of the workflow, or while they are visiting pages not belonging to the workflow, or, possibly, when they are disconnected. Exceptions can be therefore classified as synchronous or asynchronous:

1. **Synchronous** exceptions occur within an activity of the process, when a page representing the interface for that activity is requested to the server, or more in general, when the user clicks on a link within an activity. In this case, the user session is on, and therefore the exception can be immediately handled.
2. **Asynchronous** exceptions occur at any time during the process execution, independently of the state of activities in the case. In this case, the user session may be still on (and thus the user may be warned) or may be off (and the exception handling may be deferred).

According to these definitions, behavioral exceptions are always synchronous, because they occur during the navigation of an activity; semantic exceptions may be either synchronous or asynchronous; system exceptions may occur any time during the process execution (for example, when the user disconnects) and are therefore asynchronous.

Exception Target. The target identifies the part of the workflow that is affected by an exception occurrence. The ability to specify exceptional situations in individual or group of activities / cases within a process provides us with information about the exception context that will drive the exception handling. Upon a faulted condition, the recognized exception is caught at the following target levels:

1. **Activity Instance:** It refers to a specific activity instance. For example, the *Wrong starting Page, Action By Completed Activity* and *Session End* exceptions are raised for the appropriate instance of the Loan Request activity, and the *Invalid Loan Amount* exception occurs for the current instance of the Loan Search activity.
2. **Activities Instances:** It encloses a group of activities instances. For example, an *Expiration Date Modification* exception occurs for every instance of the Loan Acceptance activities of the cases in which the loan proposals have been fulfilled on the basis of the corresponding installment plan.
3. **Case:** It refers to a specific case. For example, the *Cancel* exception is raised for the case of the Loan Request process to be cancelled.
4. **Cases:** It encloses a group of cases. For example, a *Discount Rate Variation* exception occurs for every case of the Loan Request process in which the proposals have been fulfilled on the basis of the installment plans affected by such a variation.

Table 1 summarizes the characteristics of the exceptions of the Loan Request Process according to the three classifications.

Table 1. Classification of the Loan Request Process exceptions

Exception	Type	Detection Time	Target
Wrong Starting Page	Behavioral	Synchronous	Activity
Action By Completed Activity	Behavioral	Synchronous	Activity
Activity Already Active	Behavioral	Synchronous	Activities
Discount Rate Variation	Semantic	Asynchronous	Cases
Cancel	Semantic	Asynchronous	Case
Invalid Loan Amount	Semantic	Synchronous	Activity
Expiration Date Modification	Semantic	Asynchronous	Activities
Session End	System	Asynchronous	Activity

The different kinds of exceptions can be identified at design time. In particular, the behavioral and system exceptions can be examined during the process modeling where the affected activities and cases are identified. The semantic exceptions raised from data modifications can be recognized during the design of the application data, while those raised from the invocation of external services can be identified during the hypertext design.

4   A Framework for Exception Handling

In order to handle all the exceptions classified in the previous sections we propose a framework based on a *workflow meta-data model* and on three models for exception management. The workflow meta-data model is used to store and retrieve locally, at the application premises, state information about workflows. The three orthogonal models for exception handling builds upon it, as follws: (a) the *capturing model*, is used to capture the events generating the exceptions in the exceptions data model; such events may be triggered by remote services or by internal data (or metadata) values; (b) the *notifying model*, is in charge of notifying the occurred exceptions to the user inside the hypertext model; (c) the *handling model*, is used to resolve the exceptions, by applying a recovery policy, which typically impacts on the data model itself.

As we will see, the metadata and the mechanisms for capturing, notifying, and handling the exceptions depend on the different categories of exceptions.

4.1   Workflow Metadata Modeling

Managing exceptions in workflow-driven Web applications requires the storage and retrieval of state information about workflows and exceptions together with application data. The lower part in Fig. 5 represents the data model of the running example. Application data, following the Entity – Relationship model, is composed of entities describing domain objects and relationships among them imposing data connections. In our example, application data consists of *LoanProposals* whose conditions are imposed from a *Country*; each loan proposal can be fulfilled based on various *InstallmentPlans*; the customer may choose one of these plans and submit a

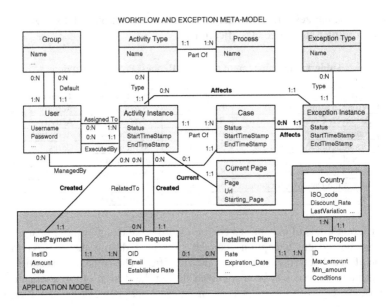

Fig. 5. Data model incorporating workflow and exception information

LoanRequest, and then, if the request is approved, he may proceed with the periodic payment of the instalment plans, which are recorded by the *InstPayment* entity.

In the E-R model of Fig. 5, the upper part contains the entities representing the basic concepts of a workflow, both at type level (Process, ActivityType, and Group) and at instance level (Case, ActivityInstance, and User). This metadata is inspired by the WFMC specification [22] and is described in detail in [6], [7]: entities describe the elements of a process and relationships represent the semantic connections between these elements. This model is sufficient to master the regular flow of processes, i.e., a flow without exceptions [9].

Exception execution context is captured in Fig. 5 by the exception metadata. Entity *Exception* denotes the classes of known exceptions that may occur during the process execution and are described by a name. The actual occurrence of an exception is presented in the entity *Exception Instance* and is described by its start time, end time and status which can be: active (the exception has occurred and has not been addressed yet), resolving (the exception is currently being solved by a predefined policy or a compensation chain) and resolved (the exception has been solved by some exception handling mechanism).

The above exception modeling is not enough to describe critical situations within a process execution. A mapping is also necessary in order to relate the generated exceptions to workflow concepts. For example, a variation in a country's discount rate is an exception that needs to be modeled for every process that has requested a loan whose conditions are imposed from the specific country. A behavioral exception within the Loan Request activity needs to be mapped to the corresponding activity instance. These mappings are modeled by the data connections *Affects* between the *Exception Instance* and *Activity Instance / Case* entities. In this way, it is always possible to retrieve the exceptions that are raised for an activity instance and (or) a case, and vice-versa.

Further objects in the exception metadata are introduced for exception handling. The executor of the appropriate exception handler is either the user who has actually performed the affected activity instance and is recognized by the "Executed By" connection, or the user denoted by the "Managed By" connection as the responsible to handle exceptions for the specific case. We define the *current page* of an active activity as the last page that the server has generated after a request by the client. This information is stored into the *CurrentPage* entity of the workflow metadata schema. For example, the identification of the current page for an activity in Fig. 2 occurs after a user request within the corresponding activity. Within a process case, it is always possible to retrieve the currently active activities, and, for each of them, the current page.

The current page has two important properties: (i) it is always uniquely defined for an active activity, and (ii) it gives us correct idea of the progress of the activity. Even if the client uses the back and forward buttons of the browser, the current page of the activity does not change: indeed, the client does not make any request to the server, it just reloads an old page.

Finally, the last object useful for applying recovery mechanisms is the *Created* relationship that connects the Activity Instance to the application data object that is managed within the workflow. It keeps track of the objects that have been created within the activity, at the purpose of allowing their possible removals when the activity is cancelled. Handling exceptions occurs at the price of managing such extra-information, which is a sort of process log.

4.2 Handling Approach

The workflow meta-data introduced in Section 4.1 can be used to manage exceptions. As already mentioned, our exception handling proposal is based on three models: (1) the *capturing model*, used to capture events and to store the exceptions data in the workflow meta-data model, (2) the *notifying model*, used to notify the occurred exceptions to the user inside the hypertext model, and (3) the *handling model*, used to apply a recovery policy and resolve the exceptions. In this scenario, the exception management remains apart from the normal workflow design.

The capturing model incorporates all the mechanisms used to capture events and generate exceptions in the workflow meta-model. We propose two different mechanisms for the exceptions classified in Section, namely, a) triggers, used for capturing exceptions caused by data modifications: b) Web services, used for capturing exceptions explicitly notified by external sources (or, possibly, by the application itself). Fig. 6 summarizes how these mechanisms can be used by the different kinds of exceptions.

Behavioral exceptions can be captured by the application by means of triggers defined on the workflow meta-data. For example, Fig. 6 shows the trigger for the generation of the behavioral exception "Wrong Starting Page", raised when the user reaches a page preceding the actual current page of the workflow, thus trying to repeat part of the same activity or an already completed activity. The *event* part of the trigger captures the exception event: the update of the current page for the current activity in

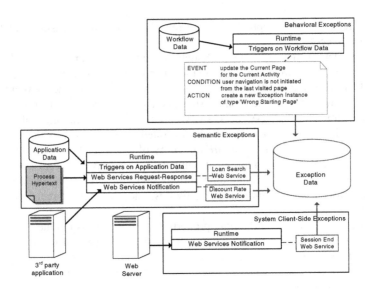

Fig. 6. Capture Model for Behavioral, Semantic and System client-side exceptions

the workflow meta-data. This update is performed every time a client request is made within an activity in order to identify the last page the server has generated for the activity. The *condition* part checks if the current client request does not come from the page identified as the actual current page in the database. If the condition holds, the *action* part of the trigger generates a new exception instance of type "Wrong Starting Page" and connects it to the current activity instance.

Semantic exceptions may instead be notified by external sources, and therefore be captured through Web services, as reported in Fig. 6[1]. Web services capture the two following kinds of exceptions: 1) an exceptional response received after calling a Web service (for example, if the loan search activity calls a Web Service to get the loans satisfying the criteria specified by the user, and the amount inserted by the user exceeds the limits for which the loan can be approved, a failure in the response may be raised); 2) an exception notified by an external application by means of a notification Web service (for example, the notification of the discount rate variation for a country). In both cases the Web services are responsible to generate the new exception instances and to connect them to the corresponding activity instances or cases. Semantic exceptions can also be captured by means of triggers defined on the application data. As an example, consider the modification of the expiration date of an installment plan. This event affects all the cases where the requested loan fulfilled such installment plan. In this case a trigger can be specified to generate a new exception instance of type "Expiration Date Modification" for every affected case and to connect it to the corresponding cases.

---

[1] Our choice of using Web services as opposed to other inter-process communication mechanisms is motivated by our focus on interoperability and portability. Web services are published by the Exception Manager and are invoked either by the workflow application itself or by external applications.

System (client-side) exceptions result in a communication failure between the client and the server. In such situations, the client unavailability is not immediately detected from the Web Server: such detection occurs after a timeout or after an unsuccessful communication from the server-side. Also the notification of such failures can be done by means of Web Services (see Fig. 6). When the Web Server detects the communication failure with the client, either because it cannot send the server's response or because the client does not make a request for a specific amount of time, it calls the Session Web Service published at server side, with the necessary parameters, like the identifiers of the activities that were in progress and have been interrupted. The Session End Web Service generates a new exception instance of type "Session End" and connects it to the corresponding activity instances.

The capturing model presented above can be designed separately from the process modeling. In the following, we will see how the generated exceptions are utilized and therefore integrated in the normal process flow in order to be handled.

The notifying model incorporates all the mechanisms used to present captured exceptions (stored into the database) to the user. Synchronous and asynchronous exceptions require different mechanisms. Indeed, if the exception occurs synchronously during the execution of the workflow activities, it can be notified immediately inside the affected activity; otherwise, the notification should take place outside the process flow. The process hypertext modeling introduced in Section 2.3 is extended with new primitives. In particular, for the detection of synchronous exceptions the concept of *exception-aware link* (graphically represented with the "E" label) is introduced: it is a navigational link extended with the ability to check the exceptions occurrence in the database and to redirect the process flow at execution time to the recovery mechanisms; in order to support asynchronous exceptions an *exception-control* mechanism is defined to be included in a generic page: it activates a hypertext link to the recovery mechanism in case of exception occurrence. These two mechanisms are illustrated in Fig. 7 (a) and (b).

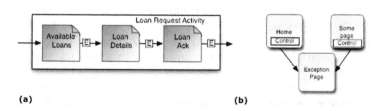

(a)   **(b)**

Fig. 7. Notification of the user in mode (a) synchronous, and (b) asynchronous

Fig. 7 (a) demonstrates the mechanism of notification for synchronous exceptions. The hypertext links outgoing from the pages within the Loan Request activity are marked as *exception-aware links*. The navigation of these links fires an automatic control to the database, checking the occurrence of behavioral exceptions for the current activity. If such an exception has occurred, the link leads the user to a recovery process, presented in the following subsection. Fig. 7 (b) shows an example of user notification in case of asynchronous exceptions; In the hypertext design an *exception-control primitive* can be inserted inside normal hypertext pages (e.g., in the

Home Page or in Some Page in the figure) to control exceptions occurrence before the page is loaded and to activate a hypertext link if such exceptions have been generated in the database. Navigating this link, the user is led to an Exception page where information about the above exceptions is retrieved.

The handling model represents the mechanisms used to recover the exceptions. It consists in recovery operations that take place on the affected activities or cases in order to bring the application to a consistent state, so that the process execution can proceed. The recovery policies can be either predefined or user-defined.

Predefined policies are server-side operations that receive initial input parameters about the exception to resolve. They are automated mechanisms that can be applied to different exception types. The process execution, after the exception is handled, is implicitly specified and routed from the predefined policy. We have identified five predefined policies:

(a) The *Accept* policy: it accepts all the operations done by the affected activity/case and concludes the activity/case execution by setting its status to Completed.

(b) The *Reject* policy: it deletes all the data created by the affected activity/case and enables its re-execution by setting its status to Inactive.

(c) The *Abort* policy: it accepts all the operations done by the affected activity/case and concludes the activity/case execution by setting its status to Aborted.

(d) The *Ignore* policy: it informs the user of the occurred exception with a message and resumes the flow execution.

(e) The *Resume* policy: it resumes the user navigation from the last visited page generated by the server for the affected activity; all the data created by the affected activity/case after the last visited page navigation are deleted.

User-defined policies are defined from the application designer to manage critical situations when automated mechanisms cannot restore the process state. For example, the exception caused by the discount rate modification may require the revision of the conditions of the loan proposals: such variations need to be explicitly modeled by the designer. User-defined policies specify: (i) the pages/operations to be executed to handle the exception and (ii) how to continue the process execution after the exception handling.

Fig. 8 (a) and (b) illustrate two examples of specification of the handling model to recover a synchronous and an asynchronous exception, respectively. Recovery policies are modeled as operations (graphically depicted as circles). Dotted curved lines represent the runtime calculation by the policy operation of the destination for returning to the normal workflow. Dotted lines are not part of the visual model.

The exception handling depicted in Fig. 8 (a) extends Fig. 7 (a) with the application of the Resume recovery policy. Suppose that the user visits page "Loan Ack", which is the last page of activity "Loan Request", and that he presses the *back* button of the browser twice, thus reloading the already visited page "Available Loans". If he navigates the outgoing link of that page, this link (marked as Exception-Aware) recognizes the "Wrong Starting Page" exception, and leads the user to the Resume policy, by means of an appropriate link. The resume policy leads the user to the last visited page, i.e., the "Loan Ack" page.

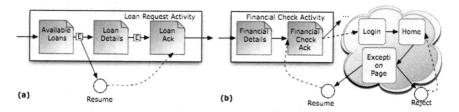

Fig. 8. (a) "Wrong Starting Page" handling for the "Loan Request" activity, and (b) "Session End" Handling for the "Financial Check" activity

Fig. 8 (b) extends Fig. 7 (b) with handling of the asynchronous exception "Session End", caused by the delayed user navigation within the "Financial Check" activity. Suppose that the employee remains inactive in the second page ("Financial Check Ack") of the activity Financial Check; after a timeout (e.g., 10 minutes of inactivity of the user), the Session End exception is generated into the database. When the user finally tries to navigate to the next page of the activity, he is redirected to the login page because his session has expired. After a successful login, the Home Page is loaded with the link to the "Exception" page activated by the Exception-control primitive. From the "Exception" page the user may choose: *(i)* to Resume the Financial check activity and be redirected to the last loaded page before the exception; (2) to Reject the "Session End" exception for the Financial Check activity and thus assign the Inactive status to the activity so that the activity may be re-executed.

5 Implementation in WebML

The approach for the exception handling illustrated in Section 4 has been specified using the WebML language [9], [20], a high-level notation for data- and process-centric Web applications, and has been implemented in a prototype that extends the CASE tool WebRatio [21], a development environment for the visual specification of applications in WebML and the automatic generation of code for the J2EE and Microsoft .NET platforms.

WebML is a conceptual language for specifying Web applications developed on top of database content described using the E-R model. A WebML schema consists of one or more hypertexts (site views), expressing the Web interface (pages) used to publish or manipulate the data specified in the underlying E-R schema. Pages enclose content units (either index units or data units), representing atomic pieces of information to be published from an underlying entity and filtered through complex logical conditions over the unit's entity. Pages and units can be connected with links to express a variety of navigation effects. Besides content publishing, WebML allows specifying predefined or customized operations represented by corner-rounded boxes: send an email, the creation and modification of instances for an entity (boxes with a roll in the center), the creation and deletion of instances for a relationship (boxes with an arc in the center), or the startup and termination of an activity (boxes with a circle in the center).

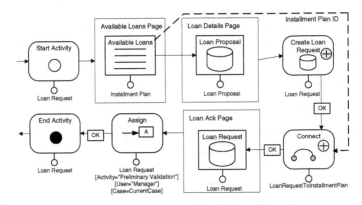

Fig. 9. WebML implementation of the "Loan Request" activity

In [6], [5] the language has been extended with operations supporting process specifications (but not exception handling), while in [15] also Web service calls and specifications have been included. Fig. 9 shows a fragment of hypertext specified in WebML. A *start activity operation* starts the Loan Request activity, setting its state to "active". Then, the user is allowed to see through an *index unit* all the available loans matching its search criteria from the previous activity in the Available Loans Page. Once a loan is selected, the Loan Details page shows the details of the selected loan to the user (Loan Proposal *Data unit*). If the user chooses to submit a request for the selected loan type, a *create operation* inserts a new instance in the Loan Request table and a *connect operations* creates the relationships between this new instance and the LoanRequestToInstallment relation. In the next Loan Ack page, the confirmation details of the newly created requested loan are shown to the user by the Loan Request *Data unit*. The activity ends with the assignment (*assign operation*) of the newly created instance to the manager and to the Preliminary Validation activity, which is therefore enabled for its execution, and with the *End activity operation*, which sets the status of the Loan Request activity to "completed".

The language is *extensible*, allowing for the definition of customized operations and units, implemented in the WebRatio CASE tool as plug-ins. In our prototype, the language has been therefore extended with new primitives to support exceptions. For a complete description of the language and of the architecture supporting WebML the reader may refer to [9], [20].

5.1   Extensions of WebML for Supporting Workflow Exception Handling

The specification of the exceptions in WebML and the implementation of all the policies require the following extensions.

Workflow metadata modelling. The data model of the Web application has been extended with the workflow and exception meta-models as described in Section 2.4.

Capturing model. Exceptions captured using the triggering mechanisms have been directly specified in the underlying database management system. Exceptions captured using the Web service mechanisms are instead specified using the WebML extensions for Web services, illustrated in [15]. Fig. 10 shows some examples of WebML specification for capturing exceptions.

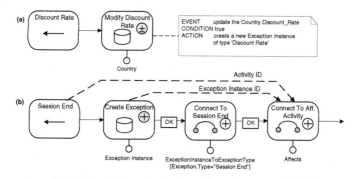

Fig. 10. Capturing an external exception with a Web service

The hypertext fragment (a) shows the capturing mechanism of a semantic asynchronous exception coming from an external application, representing the variation of the discount rate for a country. A notification service operation (Discount Rate) is published. When it is called, it modifies the Discount Rate attribute in the Country entity of the application data. Such an update fires an existing trigger, which generates a new exception instance of type "Discount Rate" and connects it to all the cases that have requested a loan with conditions imposed from the specific country. The hypertext fragment (b) shows the WebML implementation for capturing Session End exceptions. A notification service operation (Session End) is published. When it is called, a create operation inserts a new instance in the *Exception Instance* entity, connects the newly created instance with the exception type "Session End" (new instance of the relationship *Type*), and with the entity representing the affected activity (new instance of the *Affects* relationship).

Notifying and handling models. These two models have been implemented by adding new primitives to the WebML language, which will be introduced through examples. Further details about the implementation and our experience in WebML can be found in [7].

Fig. 11 presents the typical pattern for a synchronous exception: it implements the example of the behavioral exception "Wrong Starting Page" discussed in Section 2.3.1 and illustrated in Fig. 3. This exception is captured through a trigger (see Fig. 10 (a)). In the Available Loans Page, the customer receives a loans list (represented by an index unit) matching his search criteria. When the customer clicks on a link of the index the exception-aware link labeled with "E" is followed, which checks if the "Wrong Starting Page" exception has occurred. In such case, the Resume Policy, represented by the corresponding recovery unit, is applied; otherwise, the activity continues.

Fig. 12 depicts the typical pattern for an asynchronous exception: the "Session End" exception, discussed in Section 2.3.1 and illustrated in Fig. 4. This exception is captured by means of a Web service (see Fig. 10 (b)). The exception is not handled within an activity, but in the home page of the customer workflow. In this page an exception control unit checks if an asynchronous exception has occurred for activities assigned to the employee or for cases managed by the employee, and activates a link to the corresponding exception handler page. In the Exception Page an exception-aware index unit retrieves all the activities instances affected by a "Session End"

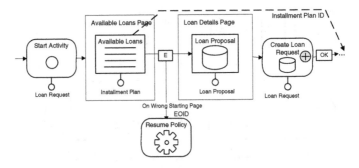

Fig. 11. Example of pattern for a synchronous exception

exception that can be recovered by the employee and shows also the recovery policies associated with it: in this example, the resume or the reject policies may be chosen by the employee. The selection of a particular policy for a particular activity instance yields to the execution of the corresponding recovery unit.

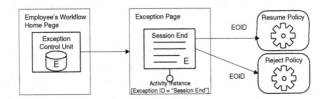

Fig. 12. Example of pattern for an asynchronous exception

6 Related Work

Our primary objective is the handling of exceptional situations that are not part of the normal flow of a Web-based process and may drive its execution to an uncertain state. The advantage of the present work is the ability to handle external and internal errors that may occur independently of the process state and therefore, their detection time and place cannot be expected. In the following paragraphs, we will present the process definition notation BPMN [3] and the process definition languages BPEL4WS [4] and XPDL [23], we will examine their behavior, and we will evaluate their ability to handle the exceptions of Section 2.

The Business Process Modeling Notation (BPMN) provides a business-oriented framework for describing both the internal implementation of a business process, and its interactions with other processes. The basic components are the atomic activities; they may be grouped to form a compound Activity, and exist only within a Process. Gateway elements control the sequence flow of the activities execution order. Every activity is associated with an event context that keeps track of specific events occurrence during its execution. While the activity is running, the event context captures events and redirects the user through the exception flow to the appropriate event handler. BPMN captures various types of exceptions either triggered from messages, timers, process data evaluations and application errors within the activity context, or thrown with the throw construct from any point of the process execution. Exceptions may be captured as message events attached to the boundary of the process; on exception occurrence, the user is directed to the appropriate message event handler; after exception handling, the process flow continues with the handler's exiting link. If the process is complete or inactive the message events will not be triggered and the exceptions will not be handled.

The Business Process Execution Language for Web Services (BPEL4WS) is an XML-based process definition language for Web services invocation. A process definition is composed of activities corresponding to WSDL operations for Web services calls. Basic control structures like those in BPMN control the execution order, and the state of activities/process is recorded at an enclosing scope level. Each scope has its own fault handlers that take control when exceptions occur. Situations that may raise exceptions in BPEL4WS are distinguished in application errors, in fault responses to invoke activities that correspond to WSDL operations, and in internal errors generated explicitly by the throw activity. Such faults are either captured and handled by the current scope or implicitly re-thrown to the scope of the upper level. Synchronous exceptions may be handled by means of fault handlers; although the exception is caught, the corresponding activity cannot repeat its execution and ends abnormally. Each scope may be also associated to event handlers. These are enabled when the associated scope starts, triggered when a message arrives and disabled when the associated scope ends. They may be used to capture asynchronous exceptions if the process is active at their occurrence time; in such a case the process execution may complete normally, otherwise the exception is not even captured.

The Xml-based Process Definition Language (XPDL) is the WfMC proposal for a process definition language. It is a graph-structured language in which nodes and edges represent the main work elements: activities, and transitions between activities respectively. The exceptions captured by an XPDL process are deadlines and other exception conditions controlled during the transition from one activity to the following. If an exceptional condition holds, the transition explicitly follows the appropriate exception flow. Exception activities are integrated into the workflow design in order to handle the undesired event.

The presented system exceptions cannot be captured by the above standards. Timer events in BPMN and event handlers of type alarm in BPEL4WS raise an exception upon the expiration of a fixed period of time for the associated activity and scope, respectively. Deadlines in XPDL are defined on a specific period of time that may be computed using workflow data for an associated activity. The mechanisms are enabled when the execution of the associated construct starts, and therefore, they cannot be used to check the expiration of a period of time that is being set dynamically, e.g., after user request. An extended version of these constructs could be used to capture a session end exception. Although the exception would be captured, it could not be handled immediately because of user's unavailability. BPMN, BPEL4WS and XPDL do not allow exception handling to be separated from the exception trigger and to take place asynchronous.

7 Conclusions

In this chapter we have presented the characteristics of the exceptions in a Web application driven by a workflow. We have seen that due to the nature of Web applications, new kinds of exceptions arise in such context, and that different ways for notifying and handling them should be available to the designer. We have provided some classifications of the exceptions and we have defined a framework for handling such exceptions based on workflow and exception meta-data, that comprises a capturing model, a notifying model, and a handling model.

We have also compared our framework with the primitives for exception handling provided by existing standards for business process modeling that can be applied in the Web context, such as BPMN, BPEL4WS and XPDL. Our analysis highlighted that only some kinds of Web exceptions can be handled by such process modeling languages. Our framework has been defined at an abstract level and therefore can be mapped either into more detailed design approaches based on Web modeling languages, or directly at the implementation level, leveraging the exception management features of programming languages. As an example, in [7] we have applied it to the WebML modeling language.

References

1. Atzeni, P., Mecca, G., Merialdo, P.: Design and Maintenance of Data-Intensive Web Sites. EDBT 1998, 436-450.
2. Baresi, L., Garzotto, F., Paolini, P.: From Web Sites to Web Applications: New Issues for Conceptual Modeling. ER Workshops 2000, 89-100.
3. BPML and BPMN site http://www.bpmi.org/
4. BPEL4WS site http://www-128.ibm.com/developerworks/library/specification/ws-bpel/
5. Brambilla, M.: Extending hypertext conceptual models with process-oriented primitives. In Proceedings of ER 2003, 22nd International Conference on Conceptual Modeling, Chicago, IL, USA, October 13-16, 2003. LNCS 2813, Springer, pp. 246-262.
6. Brambilla, M., Ceri, S., Comai, S., Fraternali, P., Manolescu, I.: Specification and Design of Workflow-Driven Hypertexts. Journal of Web Engineering (JWE), vol.1, number 2, 163-182, April 2003.
7. Brambilla, M., Ceri, S., Comai, S., Tziviskou, C.: Exception Handling in Workflow-Driven Web Applications. Int. Conf. WWW'05. Chiba, Japan, May 2005.
8. Bultan, T., Fu, X., Hull, R., Su, J. : Conversation specification: a new approach to design and analysis of e-service composition. WWW 2003, 403-410.
9. Ceri, S., Fraternali, P., Bongio, A., Brambilla, M., Comai, S., Matera, M.: Designing Data-Intensive Web Applications, Morgan-Kaufmann, 2002.
10. Conallen, J.: Building Web Applications with UML. Addison Wesley (OTS), 2000.
11. Fernandez, M. F., Florescu, D., Kang, J., Levy, A. Y., Suciu, D.: Catching the Boat with Strudel: Experiences with a Web-Site Management System. SIGMOD 1998, 414-425.
12. Gómez, J., Cachero, C., Pastor, O.: Conceptual Modeling of Device-Independent Web Applications. IEEE MultiMedia 8(2), 26-39, 2001.
13. Hagen, C., Alonso G.: Exception Handling in Workflow Management Systems. IEEE TSE 26(10), 943-958, 2000.

14. Hennicker, R., Koch, N.: A UML-based Methodology for Hypermedia Design. UML 2000, 410-424.
15. Manolescu, I., Brambilla, M., Ceri, S., Comai, S., Fraternali, P.: Model-Driven Design and Deployment of Service-Enabled Web Applications, ACM TOIT, Vol. 5(2), May 2005.
16. Miller, J. A., Sheth, A. P., Kochut, K. J., Luo Z. W.: Recovery Issues in Web-Based Workflow. CAINE-99, Atlanta, Georgia, 101-105, November 1999.
17. Schwabe, D., Rossi, G.: An Object Oriented Approach to Web Applications Design. TAPOS 4(4), 1998.
18. Van der Aalst, W. M. P., ter Hofstede, A. H. M., Weske: Business Process Management: A Survey. Business Process Management 2003.
19. Van der Aalst, W. M. P., Aldred, L., Dumas, M., ter Hofstede, A. H. M..: Design and Implementation of the YAWL system, CAiSE 04, Riga, Latvia, 2004. Springer Verlag.
20. WebML Web site http://www.webml.org
21. WebRatio site http://www.webratio.com
22. Workflow Management Coalition site http://www.wfmc.org
23. XPDL site http://www.wfmc.org/standards/XPDL.htm

Failure Handling in a Network-Transparent Distributed Programming Language

Raphaël Collet and Peter Van Roy

Université catholique de Louvain,
B-1348 Louvain-la-Neuve, Belgium
{raph, pvr}@info.ucl.ac.be

Abstract. This paper shows that asynchronous fault detection is a practical way to reflect partial failure in a network-transparent distributed programming language. In the network-transparency approach, a program can be distributed over many sites without changing its source code. The semantics of the program's execution does not depend on how the program is distributed. We have experimented with various mechanisms for detecting and handling faults from within the language Oz. We present a new programming model that is based on asynchronous fault detection, is more consistent with the network-transparent nature of Oz, and improves the modularity of failure handling at the same time.

1 Introduction

A network-transparent programming language tries as much as possible to make distributed execution look like centralized execution. This illusion cannot be complete, because distributed execution introduces new elements that do not exist in centralized execution, namely latency and limited bandwidth between sites, partial failure, resources localized on sites, and security issues due to multiple users and security domains. In our view, these new elements should not be considered as making network transparency an undesirable or unrealistic goal. On the contrary, we consider that network transparency can be a realistic approximation that greatly simplifies distributed programming, and that it should be part of the design of a distributed programming language. We find that a network-transparent implementation can be practical if it starts from an appropriate base language. The execution model of the base language is crucial, e.g., Oz is an appropriate choice [1] but Java is not [2].

This paper focuses on one part of network transparency, namely failure handling. We propose a solution to the issue of reflecting partial failures in the language that provides a way to build fault-tolerance abstractions in the language, while maintaining transparency and separation of concerns.

1.1 Context of the Paper

This work is done in the context of the Distributed Oz project, which is a long-term research project whose aim is to simplify distributed programming. This

C. Dony et al. (Eds.):Exception Handling, LNCS 4119, pp. 121–140, 2006.
© Springer-Verlag Berlin Heidelberg 2006

project started in 1995 with the goal of making a distributed implementation of the Oz language that is both network transparent and network aware [1,3]. That is, our main goal is to *separate* the distribution aspect from the functionality of the program. This was implemented in the Mozart Programming System, which was first released in 1999 [4].

In this system, an application is composed of several *sites* (i.e., system processes) that virtually share language entities. All language entities are implemented with distributed protocols that respect the language semantics in the case of no site failures. The difference between the protocols is in their network behavior. For example, objects were implemented with both a stationary protocol and a mobile (cached state) protocol. Single-assignment entities (dataflow variables) were implemented with a distributed binding protocol (that in its full generality is an implementation of distributed unification). These protocols were designed with a well-defined fault behavior, in the case of site failures, and the fault behavior was reflected in the language through a fault module.

The site and network faults are reflected as *data failures*, depending on how the faults affect the proper functioning of the data. For instance, a stationary object fails when the site holding its state crashes. The original fault module provided two ways to reflect failures in the language: a synchronous detection and an asynchronous detection. The present paper proposes a new model for reflecting partial failure based on our experience with this design.

1.2   Synchronous and Asynchronous Failure Handling

We make a clear distinction between two basic ways of handling entity failures, namely *synchronous* and *asynchronous* handlers. As we shall see, asynchronous failure handling is preferable to synchronous failure handling. A *synchronous* failure handler is executed in place of a statement that attempts to perform an operation on a failed entity. In other words, the failure handling of an entity is synchronized with the use of that entity in the program. Raising an exception is one possibility: the failure handler simply raises an exception. In contrast, an *asynchronous* failure handler is triggered by a change in the fault state of the entity. The handler is executed in its own thread. One could call it a "failure listener". It is up to the programmer to synchronize with the rest of the program, if that is required.

The following rules give small step semantics for both kinds of handlers. The symbol σ represents the store, i.e., the memory of the program. The system reflects the instantaneous fault state of an entity in the store through a system-defined function $\mathsf{fstate}(x)$, which gives the fault state of x. Each execution rule shows on its left side a statement and the store before execution, and on the right side the result of one execution step. Rule *(sync)* states that a statement S can be replaced by a handler H if the fault state of entity x is not ok, i.e., if x has failed. Rule *(async)* spawns a new thread running handler H whenever the fault state of x changes. Note that there may be more than one handler on x; we assume all handlers are run when the fault state changes.

$$\frac{S \| H}{\sigma \| \sigma} \quad \text{if} \quad \begin{array}{l} \text{statement } S \text{ uses entity } x \\ \text{and } \sigma \models \mathsf{fstate}(x) \neq ok \end{array} \qquad \text{(sync)}$$

$$\frac{H}{\sigma \wedge \mathsf{fstate}(x){=}fs \| \sigma \wedge \mathsf{fstate}(x){=}fs'} \quad \text{if} \quad fs \rightarrow fs' \text{ is valid} \qquad \text{(async)}$$

Synchronous failure handlers are natural in single-threaded programs because they follow the structure of the program. Exceptions are handy in this case because the failures can be handled at the right level of abstraction. But the failure modes can become very complex in a highly concurrent application. Such applications are common in Oz and they are becoming more common in other languages as well. Because of the various kinds of entities and distribution protocols, there are many more interaction schemes than the usual client-server scheme. Handlers for the same entity may exist in many threads at the same time, and those threads must be coordinated to recover from the failure.

All this conspires to make fault tolerance complicated to program if based on synchronous failure handling. This mechanism was in fact never used by Oz programmers developing robust distributed applications [5]. Instead, programmers relied on the asynchronous handler mechanism to implement fault-tolerant abstractions. One such abstraction is the "GlobalStore", a fault-tolerant transactional replicated object store designed and implemented by Iliès Alouini and Mostafa Al-Metwally [6].

1.3   Structure of the Paper

The present paper introduces a model based on asynchronous failure handling and shows how programming fault tolerance is simplified with this model. Section 2 explains the distributed programming model of Oz. Section 3 presents the design of a new fault module that takes our experience building fault-tolerance abstractions into account. Section 4 gives a detailed example of a group communication abstraction that shows minimal interaction between the failure handling and the abstraction's main functionality. Section 5 describes the implementation of the fault module. Finally, Sect. 6 explains the lessons we learned and Sect. 7 compares with related work.

2   The Programming Model of Oz

This section gives an overview of Oz as a programming language and its extension to distributed programming. We discuss an important property of the latter extension, namely the *network transparency*, which is convenient for separating distribution concerns from functional concerns of a program [3].

Oz is a high-level general-purpose programming language that supports declarative programming, object-oriented programming, and fine-grained concurrency as part of a coherent whole. It is dynamically typed and supports *multiparadigm* programming in a natural way. The Mozart Programming System implements the language and provides the support for its distributed implementation [4].

```
local X Y in
    thread X={Pow 2 100} end      % computes 2^100
    thread Y={Pow 5 10} end       % computes 5^10
    {Show X+Y}                    % blocks until X and Y are known
end
```

Fig. 1. An example of dataflow synchronization

To understand Oz and its distribution model, it is important to keep in mind that entities in Oz are classified into three kinds: stateless (including numbers, records, and procedures), stateful (cells and ports, see below), and single assignment (dataflow logic variables, see below).

2.1 Dataflow Concurrency

We briefly give the ideas underlying the Oz execution model. Oz can be defined by a process calculus based on concurrent constraints [7,8]. It provides lightweight threads and dataflow logic variables [9]. A logic variable is a placeholder for a value. Upon creation, the variable's value is unknown. The variable can be assigned at most once to a value, thanks to a unification mechanism. Note that unification is monotonic and there is no backtracking. A unification that fails simply raises an exception (see below).

A thread is created by an explicit statement **thread** S **end**, where S is the statement to be executed by the new thread. Threads communicate with each other by sharing logic variables, stateless entities (values), and stateful values (such as objects). A thread that attempts to use a variable's value automatically *blocks* if that variable is not bound yet. Once the variable is bound to a value, all threads blocking on that variable become runnable again. This synchronization mechanism is called *dataflow*. An example is shown in Fig. 1. We note that dataflow in Oz is monotonic (at most one token can appear on an input), whereas classic dataflow is nonmonotonic (new tokens can appear on an input).

2.2 Stateful Entities

Oz comes with a set of stateful entities that have a well-defined behavior in the presence of concurrency. The most primitive of them is the *cell*, which is a simple mutable pointer with an atomic value exchange operation. The first part of Fig. 2 shows the main operations on a cell. The exchange operation is provided as the multifix operator $x=y:=z$. In the example, the variable J is put in C, and the statement resumes by unifying I with the former contents of C. The new value of C is then determined. The last two lines of the example implement a thread-safe atomic increment of a counter.

Another important stateful entity is the *port*. The port defines a simple and efficient message-passing interface. The second part of Fig. 2 gives the typical use of a port. The *stream* S is a potentially infinite list that is built incrementally,

```
local C I J in
    C={NewCell 42}        % create a new cell C with contents 42
    {Show @C}             % print the contents of C (42)
    C:=7                  % assign 7 to C
    I=C:=J                % assign J to C, and unify I with 7
    J=I+1                 % bind J to I+1=8
end

local S P in
    P={NewPort S}         % create a port with stream S
    thread                % print every element appearing on S
        for X in S do {Show X} end
    end
    {Send P foo}          % send foo on P, S becomes foo|_
    {Send P bar}          % send bar on P, S becomes foo|bar|_
end
```

Fig. 2. Examples showing the cell and port entities

and whose elements are the messages sent to the port. In order to receive the messages, one simply has to read the list S. A list is either the empty list nil, or a pair $x \mid t$, where x is the head element, and the tail t is also a list. The dataflow synchronization automatically wakes up the threads reading the stream when new messages arrive.

2.3   Exceptions and Failed Values

The language provides a classical, thread-based exception mechanism. The block construct **try**...**catch**...**end** works as in most languages. When an exception is raised, all following statements are skipped until the closest **catch** delimiter. The exception is then handled by the code that follows the matching **catch**. Threads have no default handler, so uncaught exceptions are programming errors, which make the whole program fail.

An example is shown in Fig. 3. The keyword **fun** defines a new function. Notice that the exception value is the *record* divisionByZero(Y), and that the **catch** construct supports pattern matching.

Threads are independent of each other, and an exception can only be caught *within* the thread where it was raised. In order to propagate exceptions from thread to thread, we extend the basic model with *failed values*. A failed value is a special value that encapsulates an exception. A thread that attempts to use that value automatically raises the exception.

This model fits well with functional style programming. Suppose that a thread T computes some value, and binds a variable X to that result. That variable may be shared by other threads that are interested in the result. If the computation in T raises an exception E, the latter is caught, and X is bound to a failed value

```
fun {Divide X Y}
   if Y==0
   then raise divisionByZero(Y) end      % throw exception
   else X div Y                          % return result
   end
end

try
   {Show {Divide 42 0}}
catch divisionByZero(Y) then             % match exception
   {ShowError "error: division by zero"}
end
```

Fig. 3. An example of exception handling

```
fun {ConcurrentDivide X Y}
   thread  % return either the result, or a failed value
      try {Divide X Y} catch E then {FailedValue E} end
   end
end

try
   I={ConcurrentDivide 42 J}   % (1)
   J={ConcurrentDivide 7 13}   % (2)
in
   {Show I+1}       % blocks on I, which will raise an exception
catch E then
   {ShowError E}
end
```

Fig. 4. An example of exception passing between threads

containing E. Other threads trying to use X automatically raise the exception. An example is shown in Fig. 4. The statement (1) spawns a thread that blocks until J is known. Statement (2) spawns a thread that computes J, which is determined to be zero. Once this is known, I is bound to a failed value. The expression I+1 then raises the exception contained in I, which is caught in the main thread.

Failed values are strongly motivated by lazy computations in Oz. We model a lazy computation as a thread that waits until a result variable becomes *needed*. Another thread that blocks on the variable automatically makes it needed, which wakes up the lazy thread. A failed value allows to propagate the exception without forcing the user to add extra tests on the result.

2.4   Distribution Model

The distribution model of Oz allows several *sites* to share language entities. A site is simply a system process, and sites can be spread among a network of computers. The model gives all sites the illusion of a shared memory, with reference integrity. Well-chosen protocols implement the semantics of entity operations [10,11,1]. The power of the model is that it clearly distinguishes between the protocols for *stateless*, *stateful*, and *single-assignment* entities. The distribution strategies and implementation are chosen to be appropriate for each category.

Stateless entities, e.g., atomic values (numbers, literals), records, and procedures, are copied between sites that share them. Entities whose equality is referential (e.g., code) are given a globally unique identity, which ensures their referential integrity. Entities with structural equality (like integers and records) can be copied at will.

Stateful entities are given a global identity and use specific protocols to ensure the consistency of their state. For instance, ports use a stationary state. A stationary state requires each read/write operation to send a message to the state's home site. On the other hand, objects can use a mobile state [11]. The migratory protocol ensures that the state migrates where the operations are attempted. Once the state arrives on a site, a batch of operations can be performed locally without extra overhead. The state behaves like a cache. Protocols for a replicated state are also provided.

Single-assignment entities, i.e., logic variables, are implemented by a distributed unification algorithm [10]. Among the sites sharing a given variable, one of them is responsible for determining the final binding of the variable. Other sites that want to bind it send a message to that site, which propagates the binding to the other sites. The algorithm ensures the unicity of the binding, and the absence of cycles (when several variables are bound to each other).

In general, distributed entity references are acquired by transitivity. A bootstrapping mechanism allows a site to create a *ticket*, which is a public reference to an entity. The ticket is a character string that has the syntax of a URL, and can be transmitted by any other means (web page, email). The receiver program uses that ticket to retrieve the entity, and share it with its provider.

2.5   Network Transparency and Network Awareness

The distribution model has two important aspects: it is both *transparent* and *aware* with respect to the network. While these may look contradictory, they are in fact complementary. Let us give a definition for each one.

- *Network Transparency.* This property states that the semantics of a distributed entity is the same as if it were purely local. Primitive operations on that entity return the same results as if the whole computation was in the same address space. In other words, a programmer may reason about the functionality of a program without taking distribution into account.

– *Network Awareness.* This aspect gives the programmer some control over the non-functional behavior of the entity. For instance, different strategies for distributing a stateful entity will have different performances and robustness, depending on how they are used by the application.

A programmer cannot write a program without *ever* taking distribution into account. He or she should decide at some point where the various pieces of the code will be run, and which entities will be distributed among sites. But the network transparency will favor a separation of concerns, where the application's functionality is as independent as possible from its non-functional properties.

3   The Fault Model

This section proposes a language-level fault model that is compatible with network transparency. The model defines how site and network failures are reflected in the language. Because a failure may affect the proper functioning of a distributed entity, failures are reflected at the level of entities. Here are the principles defining our model, each being described in the corresponding subsection below.

1. Each site assigns a local *fault state* to each entity, which reflects the site's knowledge about the entity.
2. There is no synchronous failure handler. A thread attempting to use a failed entity blocks until the failure possibly goes away. In particular, no exception is raised because of the failure.
3. Each site provides a *fault stream* for each entity, which reifies the history of fault states of that entity. Asynchronous failure handlers are programmed with this stream.
4. Some fault states can be enforced by the user. In particular, a program may provoke a global failure for an entity.

This fault model is an evolution of the first fault model of Oz, and integrates parts of another proposal [5]. A comparison between the latter and this proposal is given in Sect. 6.

3.1   Fault States

First, each site defines a current *fault state* for each entity, which reflects the local knowledge of the system about the entity's global state. This implies that a given entity may have different fault states on different sites. We define four different fault states: ok, tempFail, localFail, and permFail. Their semantics are given below, and the arrows on the left show the valid state transitions.

ok	The entity behaves normally.
↓↑	
tempFail	The entity is currently unavailable locally. This is typically triggered by a communication timeout. It can be temporary (hence the name), or might hide a permanent failure. Basically the actual status of the entity is unknown.
↓	
localFail	The entity is permanently unavailable locally. This state reflects the fact that the site considers the entity to be failed, whatever its actual global status is. This state can always be enforced by the program.
↓	
permFail	The entity is permanently failed on a global scale. This final state comes with a strict guarantee: the entity will never recover. Usually this kind of diagnosis can only be performed on a LAN. We have extended the use of permFail by allowing an application to explicitly cause an entity to fail permanently. This allows an application to use permFail as a way to communicate between different parts of itself.

The absence of some state transitions is intensional. An entity going from ok to permFail will have to step through states tempFail and localFail before entering permFail. This simplifies the monitoring of the fault state of an entity, since observing the state localFail means that the state has reached localFail at least. This will become clear with the fault stream below.

Our experience shows that this simple model is in fact sufficient in practice. One can program abstractions in the language to improve the failure detectors by using local observations in a global consensus algorithm, for instance.

As the reader may guess, fault states are related to how the distribution of an entity is implemented. The more sophisticated the distribution's implementation, the more complicated the fault model. In this paper, we favor a simple fault model, therefore keeping the implementation simple. The programmer should be able to reason easily about the properties of the distribution. Complex fault-tolerant abstractions should be built at the higher user level, not at the low level.

The original fault model of Mozart was much more complex. It tried to extract the maximum information that could be deduced efficiently about failed entities [12]. Our experience with the original model showed that this extra information was in fact never used. We conclude that a simple model (such as defined by the present paper) is sufficient in practice.

3.2   No Synchronous Failure Handler

When the fault state of a given entity is not ok, operations on that entity have few chances to succeed. Raising an exception in that case might look reasonable, but our experience suggested that it is not. The main reason is that it breaks the transparency: such an exception would never occur if the application was not distributed. This is even worse for asynchronous operations, like sending a message on a port. Such operations should succeed immediately. With exceptions, the programmer cannot write a program without taking distribution into account from the start.

Another reason that exceptions are inadequate is because the exception mechanism assumes that you can *confine* the error. A partial failure in a distributed system can hardly be kept confined. Handling a distributed failure often requires some global action in the program. Moreover, because of the highly concurrent nature of Oz, the failure may affect many threads on a single site. Having many failure handlers for a single entity on a given site introduces too much complexity in the program.

In order to keep the network transparency, an operation on a failed entity simply blocks until the entity's fault state becomes ok again. The operation naturally resumes if the failure proves to be temporary. It will suspend forever if the failure is permanent (localFail or permFail).

3.3 Fault Stream

We propose a simple mechanism to monitor an entity's fault state and take action upon a state change. On each site, each entity is associated with a *fault stream*[1], which reflects the history of the fault states of the entity. The system maintains the *current* fault stream, which is a list $fs|s$, where fs is the current fault state, and s is an unbound variable. The semantic rule

$$\frac{}{\sigma \wedge \mathsf{fstream}(x){=}fs|s \, \Big\| \, \sigma \wedge s{=}fs'|s' \wedge \mathsf{fstream}(x){=}fs'|s'} \quad \text{if} \quad fs \rightarrow fs' \text{ is valid} \quad (1)$$

reflects how the system updates the fault state to fs'. The dataflow synchronization mechanism wakes up every thread blocked on s, which is bound to $fs'|s'$. An asynchronous handler can thus observe the new fault state.

The fault stream of an entity reifies the history of fault states of that entity. Moreover it transforms the nonmonotonic changes of a fault state into monotonic changes in a stream. It provides an almost declarative interface to the fault state maintained by the system.

To get access to the fault stream of an entity x, a thread simply calls the function GetFaultStream with x, which returns the current fault stream. A formal definition is given below. To read the current fault state, one simply takes the first element of the returned list.

$$\frac{y{=}\{\texttt{GetFaultStream } x\}}{\sigma} \, \Big\| \, \frac{y{=}fs|s}{\sigma} \quad \text{if} \quad \sigma \models \mathsf{fstream}(x){=}fs|s \quad (2)$$

Figure 5 shows an example of how an entity's fault stream may evolve over time. The stream is a partially known list, and the underscore "_" denotes an

---

[1] The fault stream is just like a port's stream.

```
     | FS={GetFaultStream E}
     | FS=ok|_
     | FS=ok|tempFail|_
     | FS=ok|tempFail|ok|_
time | FS=ok|tempFail|ok|tempFail|localFail|permFail|_
     ▼
```

Fig. 5. An example of a fault stream evolving over time

```
thread
   for S in {GetFaultStream E} do
      T = case S                              % pattern matching on S
            of ok        then "entity is fine"
            [] tempFail  then "some problem, don´t know"
            [] localFail then "no longer usable locally"
            [] permFail  then "no longer usable globally"
          end
   in
      {Show T}
   end
end
```

Fig. 6. A thread that prints messages when entity E's fault state changes

anonymous logic variable. Figure 6 shows a thread monitoring an entity E, and printing a message for each fault state appearing on the stream. The printed message is chosen by pattern matching. The thread is woken up each time the stream is extended with a new state.

3.4   Enforced Failure

Sometimes the system is unable to diagnose a distribution problem. And often, the actual impact of a distribution problem on a whole application is not reflected in the fault states. It is sometimes simpler to force a part of the application to fail, which causes it to launch a recovery mechanism.

We propose two operations to force an entity to fail, called KillLocal and Kill. The statement {KillLocal E} has a pure local effect. It forces the fault state of E to be at least localFail. The statement {Kill E} attempts to make the entity permanently failed. Execution of {Kill E} is asynchronous, i.e., it returns immediately. It initiates a protocol that attempts to make the entity globally failed. To succeed, this may require some of the other sites sharing the entity to be reachable at some point in the future. The local fault state of the entity becomes permFail upon confirmation of the failure. The next section gives an example that uses Kill.

4 An Example: A Robust Forwarder Tree

This section gives an example showing how to use the fault model defined in the preceding section. We present a simple and flexible group communication abstraction. The abstraction was tested on Mozart using the DSS implementation described in Sect. 5. The abstraction maintains a distributed tree whose nodes forward messages from the root to the leaves. Useful components are inserted as leaves in the tree. Depending on how the forwarding is defined at each internal node, one can broadcast messages or balance messages between components. In the latter case, each node forwards to one of its children only. With a small modification, one can also forward messages from the leaves to the root.

4.1 Architecture

Figure 7 depicts the architecture of the various components of the tree. The tree's nodes, shown as white circles in the figure, appear as Oz ports. They also use other entities (cells, and other ports) that are not visible outside the abstraction. The latter entities are not distributed, because they are never shared outside the site where they were created. This is implied by the fact that threads do not migrate by default.

We assume that the components are given as Oz ports, too. For each component, we create a leaf node, which is inserted in the tree by the root. For the sake of simplicity, the tree is built top-down. Every leaf first becomes a child of the root. When the root has six children, it groups them into two subtrees with three children each. The nodes of the tree can fail at any time, and the failure may be detected by the system or provoked by the program.

On the right of Fig. 7 we have illustrated some rules to follow when nodes fail. The main idea is that an internal node with less than two children makes itself fail. The failure will be propagated down the tree, and eventually forces new leaves to be created and inserted back in the tree. This avoids keeping "skinny" branches (linear chains) in the tree. The root of the tree is the only weak point in the architecture. Other algorithms could be used to make it robust.

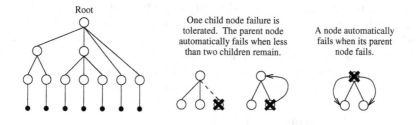

Fig. 7. Architecture of the forwarding tree

```
% create a leaf node
proc {MakeLeaf Root Component}
    Ms Leaf={NewNodeWithParent Ms}
in
    {Send Root insert(Leaf)}
    thread % forwarding messages to Component
        for M in Ms do {Send Component M} end
    end
    ┌─────────────────────────────────────────────────────────────────────┐
    │ thread % handling failures                                          │
    │     case {WaitTwo {WhenFailed Component} {WhenFailed Leaf}}          │
    │     of 1 then {Kill Leaf}                                            │
    │     [] 2 then {MakeLeaf Root Component}                              │
    │     end                                                             │
    │ end                                                                │
    └─────────────────────────────────────────────────────────────────────┘
end

% return a variable that is bound to true when E fails
fun {WhenFailed E}
    thread {Member permFail {GetFaultStream E}} end
end
```

Fig. 8. Creation of a leaf node in the tree

4.2   Leaf Nodes

Figure 8 shows a procedure that creates a leaf in the tree (identified with its root) for a given component. The code inside the box is the part that handles failures. It can be removed for a non-robust version.

As a first approximation, consider that NewNodeWithParent is equivalent to NewPort. The returned Leaf is effectively a port, and Ms is its stream of incoming messages. We will see more in detail how it works below. The code outside the box sends a message to the root node to insert the leaf in the tree, then a thread forwards all incoming messages to the component.

The boxed code handles failures from the leaf node and the component itself. If the component fails, the leaf is forced to fail, too. That leaf will be removed from the tree. If the leaf fails before the component, we simply recreate another leaf. The function WhenFailed returns a variable that is bound only when its argument has reached the fault state permFail. The function Member tests whether a value is an element of a list. The function WaitTwo is nondeterministic; it can return 1 if its first argument is bound and 2 if its second argument is bound.

4.3   Nodes Monitoring Their Parent

As we stated before, when a node's parent fails, the node itself must fail. The leaves should follow that rule, too. Figure 9 shows how to implement such a node, in a generic way. As the node must know its parent, we assume that every

```
% create a port node that kills itself when its parent fails
proc {NewNodeWithParent Ms Node}
    Strm
    DependOn = {MakeDependency Node}
    fun {CatchParent M|Ms}
        case M of parent(P) then {DependOn P} {CatchParent Ms}
        else M|{CatchParent Ms}
        end
    end
in
    Ms = thread {CatchParent Strm} end
    Node = {NewPort Strm}
end

% return a procedure that establishes a dependency for E
fun {MakeDependency E}
    CurrentD={NewCell none}
    proc {DependOn D}
        CurrentD := D
        thread
            {Wait {WhenFailed D}}
            if D==@CurrentD then {Kill E} end
        end
    end
in
    DependOn
end
```

Fig. 9. Creation of an Oz port that is the basis of a node in the tree

node in the tree receives a message of the form parent(P) with its parent P. That message is sent to the node when its parent changes, too. This is the case when a child of the root is put under a new node.

In NewNodeWithParent, a port is created for the node. Its stream Strm is filtered by the function CatchParent, which catches the parenthood message. Note that CatchParent is tail recursive, and its output is incremental. When a new parent is found on the stream, the loop calls the procedure DependOn, which establishes a link between the parent's failure, and the current node's failure. The procedure DependOn uses a hidden cell (CurrentD) to keep track of the current dependency. If a dependency D fails, and the dependency has not changed, the entity must fail. The procedure Wait blocks until its argument gets bound to a value.

4.4   Subtrees

The function MakeTree in Fig. 10 takes a list of nodes Cs in its argument, and returns a new node with Cs as children. That node must monitor its parent,

```
% create an internal node, initially with three children
fun {MakeTree Cs}
    Ms Node={NewNodeWithParent Ms}
    Children={NewCell Cs}
in
    thread % forwarding messages to children
        for M in Ms do {Forward Children M} end
    end
    for C in Cs do
        thread {Send C parent(Node)} end        % send parent message
        thread Cs Cs1 in       % handle child failures
            {Wait {WhenFailed C}}
            Cs = Children := Cs1
            Cs1 = {RemoveFromList C Cs}
            if {Length Cs1}<2 then {Kill Node} end
        end
    end
    Node
end

% forward message M to one or many of Children
proc {Forward Children M}
    for C in @Children do
        thread {Send C M} end
    end
end
```

Fig. 10. Creation of non-root internal nodes of the tree

so it is created by NewNodeWithParent. The cell Children contains the list of children of that node. The first thread created forwards messages to the children. The definition of Forward can be changed to forward to one child only, for instance. The procedure Forward is used by the root node as well.

For every child, a message parent is sent with the current node. The Send operation is performed in a separate thread, to make sure it does not block the main thread in case of a failure. The code that handles the failure is quite easy to read. It waits until the given child fails, then removes it from the children list. If the resulting list has less than two elements, the current node fails. This failure will be handled by Node's parent and remaining children.

4.5   The Root Node

Figure 11 shows the function that makes a root node. That node must be given to the components in order to create the leaves. The root node is similar to the subtree nodes. The first difference is that it has to insert leaves, which may

```
% make the root node of a tree
fun {MakeRoot}
   Ms Root={NewPort Ms}
   Children={NewCell nil}
   proc {Adopt C}
      thread {Send C parent(Node)} end      % send parent message
      thread Cs Cs1 in      % handle child failures
         {Wait {WhenFailed C}}
         Cs = Children := Cs1
         Cs1 = {RemoveFromList C Cs}
      end
   end
in
   thread % handle insertions, and forward messages
      for M in Ms do
         case M of insert(C) then Cs Cs1 in
            Cs = Children := Cs1
            case Cs of [C1 C2 C3 C4 C5] then
               % make two subtrees of the 6 children
               Cs1 = [{MakeTree [C1 C2 C3]}
                      {MakeTree [C4 C5 C]} ]
               for T in Cs1 do {Adopt T} end
            else % simply add another child
               Cs1 = C|Cs
               {Adopt C}
            end
         else {Forward Children M} end
      end
   end
   Root
end
```

Fig. 11. Creation of the root of the tree

force it to create subtrees. The second difference is that it does not fail when its children fail. Failed children are simply removed from its list.

4.6   Discussion of the Example

The first thing to notice is that the code that handles failures has been written so that it interacts as little as possible with the functional part of the abstraction. Keeping the failure handlers in separate threads improves their modularity, and they are quite easy to reason about. A consequence is that it is pretty easy to extend the functional part. If no extra entity is distributed, the failure handlers will not need to be modified.

Another interesting point is that the fault model encourages the programmer to think in terms of events and reactions. A failure is an event on its own, and

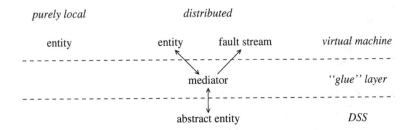

Fig. 12. The implementation's architecture

simple reactions are sometimes enough to make the program recover. The use of message passing also helps to simplify the reasoning.

One issue that has not been mentioned is *where the entities are*. Where should we place the nodes of the tree? The answer is: this is mostly an orthogonal issue. In other words, put them where you want. This works because of network transparency. Only the leaves of the tree should be placed on the site of their component. This is because the thread that monitors the leaf should preferably be on the same site as the component. The root node could keep track of a pool of machines that may host the intermediate leaves, and creates them there. We have not included this part in the code to keep it simple. The Mozart system provides a simple abstraction to create a remote process and execute code on it.

5   Implementation

The Mozart system contains a virtual machine that executes Oz programs and implements the distribution of Oz entities [4]. The distribution part of Mozart is currently being reimplemented with the Distribution SubSystem (DSS) library. The DSS is completely separate from the virtual machine emulator, with a well-defined interface between the two. The DSS provides generic distributed entities [13,14]. There are three types of abstract entities, namely *mutable, monotonic*, and *immutable*, and each type comes with a small set of abstract operations. The DSS makes a clear separation between communication protocols and the entity's semantics. The protocols are used internally by the DSS to implement generic operations, a distributed garbage collector, and failure detectors.

The way Mozart uses the DSS is sketched in Fig. 12. A purely local entity is managed exclusively by the virtual machine, while a distributed entity is mapped to an abstract entity in the DSS, which provides the basic support for its distribution. An intermediate object, called the *mediator*, defines the mapping between the virtual machine entity and the DSS entity. The mediator maps entity operations on abstract entity operations, and makes the virtual machine's garbage collector collaborate with the distributed garbage collector. It also reflects the abstract entity's failure state in the virtual machine, by building the fault stream of the entity and resuming threads that suspend because of a failure. The fault stream only has a small overhead in practice, because it is created on demand. Only monitored entities update their fault streams.

6   Lessons from the Past

Our argument against the use of exceptions to handle distribution failures comes from the original fault model used in Oz. The original model overlaps with the new model proposed in Sect. 3. The original model provided much more fault information (most of which was not used in practice) and provided both synchronous and asynchronous handlers. The major difference was the ability to define synchronous failure handlers, i.e., handlers that are called when attempting an operation on a failed entity. The programmer could either ask for an exception or provide a handler procedure that replaces the operation. The failure handler was defined for a given entity and with certain conditions of activation.

Instead of the synchronous handlers, programmers favored an asynchronous handler, called a *watcher*. A watcher is a user procedure that is called in a new thread when a failure condition is fulfilled. The fault stream we propose in this paper simply factors out how the system informs the user program. It also avoids race conditions related to the watcher registry system, which could make one miss a fault state transition. And finally, a watcher could not be triggered by a transition to state ok.

The original model had one further deficiency. There was no way to force an entity to be considered failed locally. As a result, there was a lack of control in case of erratic entity behavior (e.g., many transitions between ok and tempFail).

The original model is criticized in [5], which proposes an alternative model. That paper proposes something similar to our fault stream and an operation to make an entity fail locally. In order to handle faults, it proposes to explicitly break the transparent distribution of a failed entity. The local representative of the failed entity is disconnected from its peers and is put in a fault state equivalent to localFail. Another operation replaces that entity by a fresh new entity. This model has the advantage to avoid blocking threads on failed entities, because you can replace a failed entity by a healthy one. But this replacement introduces inconsistencies in the application's shared memory. We were not able to give a satisfactory semantics that takes into account these inconsistencies.

7   Related Work

Most mainstream programming languages use exceptions to reflect failures due to distribution faults. Those systems often propose less ambitious models for distributed programs. They usually do not favor concurrency, the distribution is often explicit, and failure handling is often mixed with the functionality of the program. A typical representative of those systems is Java's Remote Method Invocation (RMI) system. The exceptions thrown because of network failures are visible in the methods' signatures. Moving from a centralized to a distributed application requires to change API's explicitly. Making robust distributed abstractions is not impossible, but it comes at the price of a huge complexity increase in the program.

An interesting question is: how to implement the forwarder tree with the RMI approach? The problem is that no message is sent "upwards" the tree, hence a node never calls its parent. In order to detect the failure of its parent, a node would need to make regular dummy calls to it. Another possibility is to make the communication channel explicit, and catch problems at the receiving side. But this breaks the abstraction provided by RMI. Moreover, extra messages are required to simulate node failures, if those failures are not caused by site failures.

The Erlang programming language and system was designed at the Ericsson Computer Science Laboratory for building high availability telecommunication systems [15,16]. An Erlang program consists of a (possibly large) number of processes. An Erlang process is a lightweight thread with its own memory space. Processes are programmed with a strict functional language, and they communicate by asynchronous message passing.

Erlang provides asynchronous fault detection of permanent failures between processes. Two processes can be linked together. When one of them fails, the other one receives a message from the runtime system, provided it is declared as a supervisor. Erlang chooses to model all failures as permanent failures, in accordance with its philosophy of "Let it fail". That is, keeping the fault model simple allows the recovery algorithm to be simple as well. This simplicity is very important for correctness. We extend Erlang's model with temporary failures and with a fault stream. Furthermore, our model is designed for a richer language than Erlang, which only has stationary objects (in our terminology).

8   Conclusion

This paper proposes a simple fault model for the distributed execution of the Oz language. This distributed execution is network transparent, i.e., the semantics of a language entity does not depend on whether it is distributed or not. *Synchronous* failure handlers, like exceptions, break this transparency property. Moreover, they are no longer practical if the language is highly concurrent. We give evidence that *asynchronous* failure handlers are more adequate. They can be defined so that they do not break the network transparency of the language. In our design, each language entity produces a stream giving its fault state transitions. Monitoring an entity is done by reading the stream. One can also force a failure either locally or globally, which allows to implement simple abstractions for handling partial failure.

Acknowledgments

We thank our colleagues Kevin Glynn and Boris Mejías for fruitful discussions about the model and careful proofreading of the paper. This work is supported by the CoreGRID Network of Excellence (contract number 004265) and the EVERGROW Integrated Project (contract number 001935), both funded by the European Commission in the 6th Framework program.

References

1. Haridi, S., Van Roy, P., Brand, P., Schulte, C.: Programming languages for distributed applications. New Generation Computing **16**(3) (1998) 223–261
2. Waldo, J., Wyant, G., Wollrath, A., Kendall, S.: A note on distributed computing. Technical Report SMLI TR-94-29, Sun Microsystems Laboratories, Mountain View, CA (1994)
3. Van Roy, P.: On the separation of concerns in distributed programming: Application to distribution structure and fault tolerance in Mozart. In: International Workshop on Parallel and Distributed Computing for Symbolic and Irregular Applications (PDSIA 99), Sendai, Japan (1999) 149–166
4. Mozart Consortium (DFKI, SICS, UCL, UdS): The Mozart programming system (Oz 3) (1999) http://www.mozart-oz.org.
5. Grolaux, D., Glynn, K., Van Roy, P.: A fault tolerant abstraction for transparent distributed programming. In: Second International Mozart/Oz Conference (MOZ 2004), Charleroi, Belgium (2004) Springer-Verlag LNCS volume 3389.
6. Al-Metwally, M.: Design and Implementation of a Fault-Tolerant Transactional Object Store. PhD thesis, Al-Azhar University, Cairo, Egypt (2003)
7. Saraswat, V.A.: Concurrent Constraint Programming. MIT Press (1993)
8. Van Roy, P., Haridi, S.: Concepts, Techniques, and Models of Computer Programming. MIT Press, Cambridge, MA (2004)
9. Smolka, G.: The Oz programming model. In: Computer Science Today. Lecture Notes in Computer Science, vol. 1000. Springer-Verlag, Berlin (1995) 324–343
10. Haridi, S., Van Roy, P., Brand, P., Mehl, M., Scheidhauer, R., Smolka, G.: Efficient logic variables for distributed computing. ACM Transactions on Programming Languages and Systems **21**(3) (1999) 569–626
11. Van Roy, P., Haridi, S., Brand, P., Smolka, G., Mehl, M., Scheidhauer, R.: Mobile objects in Distributed Oz. ACM Transactions on Programming Languages and Systems **19**(5) (1997) 804–851
12. Van Roy, P., Haridi, S., Brand, P.: Distributed programming in Mozart – A tutorial introduction. Technical report (1999) In Mozart documentation, available at http://www.mozart-oz.org.
13. Klintskog, E., El Banna, Z., Brand, P.: A generic middleware for intra-language transparent distribution. Technical Report T2003:01, Swedish Institute of Computer Science (2003)
14. Klintskog, E., El Banna, Z., Brand, P., Haridi, S.: The DSS, a middleware library for efficient and transparent distribution of language entities. In: Proceedings of HICSS'37. (2004)
15. Armstrong, J., Williams, M., Wikström, C., Virding, R.: Concurrent Programming in Erlang. Prentice-Hall, Englewood Cliffs, N.J. (1996)
16. Armstrong, J.: Making Reliable Distributed Systems in the Presence of Software Errors. PhD thesis, Royal Institute of Technology (KTH), Kista, Sweden (2003)

Ambient-Oriented Exception Handling

Stijn Mostinckx*, Jessie Dedecker**, Elisa Gonzalez Boix,
Tom Van Cutsem**, and Wolfgang De Meuter

Programming Technology Laboratory
Vrije Universiteit Brussel, Belgium
{smostinc, jededeck, egonzale, tvcutsem, wdmeuter}@vub.ac.be

Abstract. Writing ambient-oriented software for mobile devices connected through wireless network connections provides new challenges in the field of exception handling. It involves dealing with issues such as asynchronous communication, moving hardware and software, only to name a few. Building on an analysis of the fundamental differences between mobile networks and their stationary counterparts, this paper establishes a set of criteria for an ambient-oriented exception handling mechanism. We subsequently present ambient conversations, a novel distributed exception handling mechanism that adheres to the prescribed criteria, and describe its realisation in the experimental ambient-oriented programming language AmbientTalk.

1   Introduction

Recently, mobile hardware has evolved to become ever cheaper, smaller and yet more powerful. The current crop of mobile devices have wireless network provisions (such as Bluetooth and WiFi) that allow them to collaborate with one another in open, mobile and highly dynamic networks. Such networks of mobile devices are crucial to achieve Weiser's vision of ubiquitous computing [24], where computers are seamlessly integrated in the fabric of everyday life. Similarly, the spontaneous interaction between both mobile and embedded devices plays an important role in the various Ambient Intelligence (AmI) scenarios proposed by the IST Advisory Group of the European Union [7].

At present, little experience exists in developing applications that fully exploit the potential of mobile networks of wirelessly connected devices. A significant obstacle impeding the construction of such applications is the fact that contemporary programming languages lack proper support to deal with the specific properties that distinguish mobile networks from their stationary counterparts. The most important ones are that disconnection is the rule rather than the exception (because the communication range of wireless technology is limited) and that the network is open (because devices can appear and disappear unheraldedly).

The goal of our work is to uncover the necessary language abstractions and implementation techniques that ease the development of applications which are

---

* Funded by a doctoral scholarship of the Institute for the Promotion of Innovation through Science and Technology in Flanders (IWT-Vlaanderen), Belgium.
** Research Assistant of the Fund for Scientific Research Flanders, Belgium (F.W.O.).

C. Dony et al. (Eds.):Exception Handling, LNCS 4119, pp. 141–160, 2006.

based on spontaneous interaction between different mobile devices. Since little software engineering experience exists in developing such systems, our research is based on a conceptual analysis of the hardware phenomena that fundamentally distinguish mobile from stationary networks. In previous work, this analysis led us to propose a number of fundamental programming language characteristics that define a novel ambient-oriented programming (AmOP) paradigm [5]. This paradigm – based on asynchronously communicating actors provided with innate mechanisms for discovering services in the ambient (*i.e.* its immediate environment) as well as reversible computing – was embodied in the AmbientTalk language [4].

This paper focusses on the handling of exceptions which may occur during such spontaneous interactions of mobile devices. The next section establishes the essential differences between mobile and stationary networks and illustrates how they affect an exemplar collaborative editing application deployed on mobile hardware. Subsequently, we derive a set of criteria for future ambient-oriented exception handling mechanisms and relate them to the example application (section 3). Section 4 provides an overview of existing distributed exception handling techniques and evaluates them with respect to the proposed criteria. Based on this analysis of the (shortcomings of) existing approaches, section 5 proposes ambient conversations as a first tentative ambient-oriented exception handling mechanism.

2   Motivation

As mentioned in the introduction, our goal is to cater for spontaneous interaction between different mobile devices. The hardware properties of such mobile devices engender a number of phenomena that need to be dealt with when writing ambient-oriented software. These phenomena have led us to propose a novel ambient-oriented programming paradigm tailored toward prescribing such spontaneous interactions of mobile devices [5]. This section recapitulates the hardware phenomena that lie at the basis of the ambient-oriented programming paradigm and illustrates the repercussions of the various hardware phenomena on an exemplar collaborative editing application.

2.1   Hardware Phenomena

With the current state of commercial technology, mobile devices are often characterised as having scarcer resources (such as lower CPU speed, less memory and limited battery life) than traditional hardware. However, in the last couple of years, mobile devices and full-fledged computers like laptops are blending more and more. That is why we do not consider such restrictions as fundamental as the following phenomena which are inherent to networks of mobile devices:

Connection Volatility. Collaborating devices cannot assume a stable connection due to the limited communication range of the wireless technology combined with the fact that users can move out of range. Therefore, disconnection of a device should not necessarily be interpreted as a failure.

Often, the task is expected to resume when the disconnected party returns within a reasonable amount of time. An alternative might be to continue the interaction with a replacement service. These examples merely serve to illustrate that ambient-oriented software is typically expected to perform its task in the presence of volatile connections.

Ambient Resources. When developing software for mobile devices, it is important to realise that, as the device roams, new resources will become dynamically (un)available in its ambient. It is therefore unrealistic to encode knowledge about the availability of a service explicitly (*e.g.* storing a server address). Instead a mechanism is needed to dynamically manage the set of ambient resources.

Autonomy. Mobile devices should be able to act as autonomous computing devices. First of all, this implies that it should be possible for a device to collaborate with other devices, without requiring to be connected to infrastructure (*e.g.* a server) to either discover other participants or to coordinate the interaction. Similarly, the device must be able to recover when one of its communication partners disconnects, such that the device does not remain blocked until that communication partner returns.

Natural Concurrency. The autonomy phenomenon clearly stimulates different devices to collaborate in an entirely concurrent fashion. Typically these concurrent devices communicate using asynchronous communication since waiting for the result of synchronous invocations undermines the autonomy of the waiting device. When specifying collaborations between different mobile devices, it is necessary to orchestrate the naturally concurrent devices.

In previous work, the implications of these hardware phenomena on the design of distributed programming languages have been thoroughly analysed [5]. To enhance the construction of applications for networks of mobile devices, the *Ambient-Oriented Programming* paradigm was established. Languages adhering to this paradigm have distribution characteristics which are designed with respect to the hardware phenomena summarised above. First of all, ambient-oriented programming languages break with the tradition of structuring programs using classes which are instantiated at run-time into objects. Rather, these languages employ a *classless object model*: code and data are packed together directly in an object, rather than storing the code separately in a class. When distributing objects across a network, this has proven to be a more flexible approach and forgoes much of the problems related to class versioning [23]. Secondly, ambient-oriented programming languages must safeguard the autonomy of all concurrent processes. That is to say that no process should be blocked when one of its communication partners goes out of earshot. This property can be achieved when the language's concurrency model relies solely on *non-blocking communication primitives*. Concretely, this implies that message sending is asynchronous and that the language explicitly prohibits blocking until a result becomes available. Thirdly, ambient-oriented programming languages facilitate collaborating processes to continue working to preserve their autonomy. This may yield inconsistencies between the different processes. To resolve these inconsistencies, processes store an explicit representation (i.e. a reification) of their communication details. Such *reified communication state* allows a process to properly recover from an inconsistency by reversing (part of) its computation. Finally, ambient-oriented programming languages need to provide support for distributed naming [6] to dynamically discover ambient resources without knowing their address beforehand. Complemented with a mechanism to keep track of the communication partners that become unavailable, this yields an *ambient acquaintance management* system.

This paper provides a similar analysis of the implications of the hardware phenomena on the design of an exception handling mechanism. Whereas an ambient-oriented programming language will provide some rudimentary exception handling support by means of its *reified communication traces*, an additional mechanism is clearly needed to be able to handle both functional exceptions (which are raised explicitly) as well as non-functional ones (*e.g.* long-lasting disconnections). To ground the discussion, the remainder of this section describes an illustrative example application which highlights the effects of the hardware phenomena on both the application logic and on how one expects exceptions to be raised, propagated and handled in the system.

2.2   A Sample Application: Collaborative Editing

When developing ambient-oriented applications, the effect of the hardware phenomena described above permeates the entire application. This is illustrated using a classic distributed application, namely a collaborative text editor. The application consists of participant editors which are distributed over various mobile devices. Each participant has its own copy of a document which is synchronised regularly with the versions of the other editors. To create a collaborative editing session, a single editor may publish a document, and specify which users may join to edit the document. These users will receive an invitation containing a copy of the document. The way the hardware phenomena influence the construction of such an editor is discussed next.

Connection Volatility. Editors should not be excluded from the collaboration when they go out of communication range. Despite being disconnected, the editor may continue making local changes. When reconnecting within a reasonable amount of time, the changes made locally are synchronised and the editor is once again working on the same document as the other participants.

Ambient Resources. In networks of mobile and frequently disconnecting devices, invitations are preferably issued based on high-level information such as the user's name rather than low-level network addresses. This makes it possible to invite users whose devices are currently not reachable or whose device's address is not known (the address of a mobile device may change frequently). The ambient resource management is responsible for spontaneously discovering devices based on such high-level information. Once such a device is found, it can be provided with an initial version of the document.

Autonomy. The autonomy of the device implies that it can function, even when it is no longer connected with any other participant. Concretely, this implies that the collaboration is not aborted when the device is temporarily disconnected. Instead it can continue making local changes and rest assured that these changes will percolate to the other participants upon reconnecting.

Natural Concurrency. Since participants concurrently edit the joint document without necessarily being able to synchronise, different versions of the document may be in circulation. When the different versions are to be merged during synchronisation, editing conflicts may arise. For instance, if the collaborative editor is line-based, conflicts arise when one participant edits a line which the other participant had either edited or deleted. These application-specific conflicts will be signalled using the exception handling mechanism.

We consider the collaborative editor presented in this section to be an epitome of a class of ambient-oriented applications where state is replicated across different collaborating devices which are entitled to make independent updates. When these independent updates prove to be incompatible, an exception is raised. The next section outlines a set of criteria for an exception handling mechanism which can be applied in an ambient-oriented setting.

3   Ambient-Oriented Exception Handling

This section presents a collection of criteria that need to be exhibited by an ambient-oriented exception handling mechanism. Whereas some of the criteria described below can be observed in various distributed exception handling mechanisms, no single exception handling mechanism exhibits all of them.

Asynchronous Exception propagation. Exception handling mechanisms define a *context* in which dynamically raised exceptions are to be handled. For instance, when an editor detects merge conflicts while it was asked to synchronise, the editor that requested the synchronisation needs to be brought back into the correct context for handling these conflicts. In an ambient-oriented setting, such contexts cannot be described using classic **try-catch** blocks since the processes making up an ambient-oriented application communicate using *non-blocking communication primitives*. This implies that the calling process may have left the context of its **try** block before the exception was propagated by the invoked process. The most basic criterion for an ambient-oriented exception handling mechanism is therefore that it provides an adequate mechanism for ensuring that exceptions raised by a concurrent process are caught in the correct context.

Concerted Exceptions. Exception handling mechanisms typically allow specifying a single context for exception handling for an entire block of code consisting of several instructions. The combination of *non-blocking communication primitives* with block-level handling implies that all processes invoked by expressions listed in the block may concurrently raise exceptions. In the

collaborative editor example, this situation may occur during the synchronisation which basically consists of broadcasting local changes to the other
editors. Each editor may independently raise exceptions, which might have
to be handled jointly. An ambient-oriented exception handling mechanism
should therefore allow the programmer to examine all concurrently raised
exceptions (*e.g.* to evaluate whether they are symptoms of a common problem) and to subsequently propagate a *concerted* exception [11] which best
captures the particular combination of raised exceptions.

Collaborative Exception Handling. Ambient-oriented programs are devised as a collaboration of processes which should be able to continue working in the face of volatile connections. Therefore, the individual processes
typically make optimistic assumptions while performing their tasks. As a
consequence, an exception raised by one process may violate these assumptions and therefore should be handled by all participating processes. The
synchronisation in the collaborative editor application is an excellent example of this optimism. When synchronising, each editor will merge in all
changes that do not produce local conflicts. The design choice not to wait for
confirmation from all participants, improves the resilience of the application
to disconnection. However, it also implies that conflict handling is a collaborative activity, not only involving the editors which signalled a conflict, but
also those who already performed the merge.

Loosely-coupled Exception Handling. An ambient-oriented exception handling mechanism should be able to guarantee the autonomy of the processes
for which it handles exceptions. This implies that it may not rely on a centralised node to coordinate the exception handling. Furthermore, it needs to
provide a mechanism to discover long-lasting disconnection, in order to prevent processes from waiting indefinitely for an unreachable communication
partner. Long-lasting disconnection is signalled using an exception, albeit
one raised by the environment rather than by the program.

4   Related Work

A diverse spectrum of approaches exists to handle exceptions in a distributed or
concurrent setting. This section groups these existing approaches according to
the level of granularity at which they operate and evaluates them with respect
to the criteria for ambient-oriented exception handling mechanisms outlined in
the previous section.

4.1   Message-Level Handling

A single asynchronous message send is the finest level of granularity at which
a distributed exception handling mechanism can operate. The flavour of an exception handling mechanism at this level depends largely on the underlying
mechanism for communication. The non-blocking communication prescribed by
the ambient-oriented programming paradigm can be achieved using two different
communication mechanisms. Processes may communicate in a non-blocking way

with one another directly using asynchronous messages or indirectly by reading and writing tuples in a shared distributed tuple space [18].

Asynchronous Messages. Exception handling can be aligned with asynchronous message sending by passing a complaint address along with every message [9]. When an exception occurs, a predefined message (*e.g.* **handle**) is sent to the object denoted by that address, passing the exception object as a parameter. When futures are used to represent the results of asynchronous invocations, these futures need to be integrated into the exception handling mechanism. An example of such an integration is witnessed in the E language which provides a **when-catch** construct to specify how to handle results as well as exceptions raised from a particular asynchronous invocation [15].

Tuple Spaces. Serugendo and Romanovsky [20] argue that exception propagation for distributed systems communication using tuple spaces is best handled using an external mechanism to ensure that each exception is correctly handled, rather than depending on the fact that the appropriate process will read the exception tuple and handle it. The CAMA system [10] therefore requires every tuple to be equipped with a reference to a *tuple space trap* to which exceptions are signalled. Such tuple space traps can transform the received exception and choose to propagate it to the "caller", a dedicated handler agent or an ensemble of (affected) agents.

Whereas these exception handling mechanisms may provide a fertile basis to develop an ambient-oriented exception handling mechanism, they lack support for funnelling concurrently raised exceptions to a single *concerted exception*, since they consider only one message send and thus one exception at a time.

4.2   Block-Level Handling

Various distributed exception handling mechanisms offer a variation of the well-known **try-catch** construct, to bind a single exception handler to a sequence of asynchronous message sends. As we have indicated in section 3, the fact that the messages are sent asynchronously implies that different exceptions may be raised concurrently. Different mechanisms exist to reduce these concurrent exceptions to a single *concerted exception* :

ProActive aims to hide the induced concurrency and therefore only handles the first exception to be raised inside the **try** block [3]. The underlying assumption is that all asynchronous invocations are closely related (*e.g.* they depend on one another's results) such that the first exception to be reported is a good representative of the underlying error.

SaGE deals with exceptions raised from asynchronous invocations in a multi-agent system [21]. It requires handlers to provide a **concert** method that is invoked for every exception raised. Based on the current exception and the log of previous exceptions it can choose to either log the exception for future reference or to immediately propagate a concerted exception.

Arche aggregates *all* concurrently raised exceptions and feeds them to a *resolution function* that in its turn raises the concerted exception [11,12]. The main difference with SaGE is that, in Arche the decision which concerted exception is thrown is based on complete information, which greatly simplifies the decision process. However, the use of an Arche-like construct quite naturally incurs a performance penalty.

DOOCE [22] varies on the semantics of the **try-catch-finally** construct by allowing all exceptions raised by asynchronous invocations in a particular **try** block to be handled by the associated **catch** blocks. Exceptions that cannot be handled by these most closely nested **catch** blocks are aggregated and passed to the **finally** block after all asynchronous calls have returned.

Despite their provisions for producing *concerted exceptions*, these mechanisms do not qualify as an ambient-oriented exception handling mechanism, since they require the concerted exception to be handled solely by the sender of the messages. In other words, the mechanisms discussed above offer no provisions for *collaborative exception handling*, as prescribed in section 3. This implies that the techniques described above are only applicable when the different processes make no optimistic assumptions. In an ambient-oriented setting however, optimistic assumptions are often required to cope with the effects of volatile connections.

4.3   Collaboration-Level Handling

Finally, some exception handling mechanisms allow structuring an application in a complex interplay of different processes. In addition to the mechanisms they provide for structuring such interactions, they also provide mechanisms for handling exceptions that may be raised concurrently by those processes.

Open Multi-threaded Transactions (OMT transactions) structure a group of collaborating threads within the boundaries of a transaction [13]. The threads communicate using shared objects which maintain their own consistency to ensure that exceptions caused by one thread cannot influence any other thread. This form of communication is opted for to allow each thread to handle exceptions locally. This design decision implies that OMT transactions provide no support for *collaborative exception handling*.

Coordinated Atomic Actions (CA actions) are a well-established technique for describing a collaboration between different processes. The exception handling mechanism produces *concerted exceptions* using an exception graph [25] and raises this concerted exception in all participating processes. Whereas a lot of experience exists on how to distribute CA actions [19,26], the model proves to be too rigid for our purposes since it requires every participant to exit the CA action with the same result. This implies that once a participant disconnects, the entire collaboration must be aborted.

The Guardian Model shuns the use of transaction-like mechanisms to structure applications for exception handling. Instead a process can explicitly manipulate its own context by pushing symbolic names on the context stack. Similarly, when raising an exception, the exception needs to be tagged with a handling context. All processes which are currently in this context will collaborate to handle this exception. However, since each process may change its context independently, the model needs to contact all processes whenever exceptions are raised. In order to ensure a timely response to exceptions, the guardian model relies on being able to contact all processes in a bounded time [16]. This requirement implies that the exception handling mechanism depends on the presence of *all* processes, which clearly conflicts with the *loosely-coupled exception handling* characteristic.

This section has provided a general overview of the different approaches to handle exceptions that were raised within the context of a collaboration of various processes : OMT transactions opt for a particular communication scheme that minimises the effect of a single exception, so that it may always be handled locally. CA actions on the other hand implement transaction-like guarantees to ensure that the effect of errors can be adequately handled collaboratively by its participants. Unfortunately this semantics is hard to reconcile with the characteristics of an ambient-oriented setting. Finally, the guardian model offers collaborative handling without imposing the use of a transaction-like structure, yet it proves to be impracticable precisely because of this lack of imposed structure.

4.4   Conclusion

Our overview of the existing distributed exception handling mechanisms has failed to identify a single exception handling approach that adheres to all of the criteria for an ambient-oriented exception handling mechanism. This shortcoming forms the main motivation for our work. On the other hand, the approaches discussed in this section provide a solid basis on which to base our own approach. For example, we have opted to employ an E-like mechanism [15] to allow exceptions to be propagated from one actor to another one. This model was then extended with a language construct to protect a block of asynchronous invocations, whose exceptions are fed to an Arche-like resolution function. Finally, we have constructed a distributed mechanism for structuring collaborating actors, in a manner that is reminiscent of CA actions.

5   Ambient Conversations

This section describes ambient conversations, a first exception handling mechanism for ambient-oriented software. The ambient conversation model consists of an ensemble of four language constructs which directly correspond to the four criteria described in section 3. First of all, the **when-catch** construct allows *asynchronous exception propagation* at the granularity of a single asynchronous invocation. Secondly, exceptions raised in a sequence of several asynchronous invocations may be dealt with using a single exception handler by wrapping this sequence in a **group-resolve** construct. This construct allows treating such a sequence as a single asynchronous invocation, funnelling all concurrently raised exceptions into a single *concerted exception*. Thirdly, *collaborative exception handling* is achieved using the **conversation** language construct. This construct specifies a set of participants and will ensure that exceptions raised by a single participant will be handled by all available participants. Finally, the ambient conversation model provides for *loosely-coupled exception handling* through the introduction of the **when-catch-due** construct.

5.1   Ambient-Oriented Programming in AmbientTalk

The ambient conversation model was realised as a reflective extension of the AmbientTalk language kernel, which was designed as a language laboratory to uncover new features for ambient-oriented programming languages. An in-depth description of the language is outside the scope of this paper, and can be found elsewhere [4]. For the sake of comprehending the exception handling mechanism explained below it suffices to know that AmbientTalk's concurrency model is based on actors [1] which communicate with one another using asynchronous message passing. Asynchronous messages are processed one by one by an actor's thread. This serial treatment of messages precludes actors from suffering from race conditions on their internal state. AmbientTalk's actors are also the unit for distribution. Hence, an ambient-oriented application in AmbientTalk consists of a suite of actors that are possibly located on different devices and that transparently send asynchronous messages to one another over a volatile connection. When these connections are temporarily broken, messages sent are accumulated with the sender and are automatically flushed upon re-establishing that connection. AmbientTalk's asynchronous messages are denoted with the # operator. In what follows, we use a pseudo-syntax in order to avoid having to explain AmbientTalk's technical details. The low-level technical details of the reflective implementation of the constructs described in this paper can be found in a companion technical report [17].

Since AmbientTalk's concurrency model stems from the actor model, asynchronous messages do not have a return value. This necessitates the use of callback methods to return results or exceptions. To allow for a more direct style of programming, AmbientTalk has been extended with the notion of futures (or promises) [8,14,2] – placeholder objects which are immediately returned upon sending an asynchronous message. When the actual result has been computed the future is said to be *resolved* and its value can be used freely. Using a future prior to its resolution will typically yield *wait-by-necessity* semantics [2], leaving the caller *blocked* until the future it attempted to use gets resolved. As explained in section 2.1, the ambient-oriented programming paradigm dictates both non-blocking send *and* receive operations, prohibiting such a wait-by-necessity strategy. Instead, AmbientTalk adopts the non-blocking futures as proposed in the language E [15]. Messages sent to such futures are buffered and automatically forwarded to the actual result once the future gets resolved. A key ingredient in this scenario is that messages sent to a future need to be asynchronous and thus are equipped with a future of their own. Since the resolution of the latter future depends on the resolution of the former, they are said to be pipelined. Future pipelining allows one to "chain" asynchronous message sends, even though the intermediate results are not yet computed.

Whereas it is crucial to uphold the non-blocking characteristic of the ambient-oriented paradigm, the future pipelining technique alone is no panacea. Often the application logic dictates that certain actions should only be taken when a reply to an asynchronous message has been received (*i.e.* when its future is resolved). Surely, this action can be implemented as a method of the expected return value, yet this would inevitably lead to cluttered code. Therefore AmbientTalk, like E, features a **when** language construct that takes two parameters: a future and a **becomes** clause consisting of a formal parameter name for the resolved value and a code block. The **becomes** clause denotes a closure (*i.e.* a function with the specified formal parameter and full access to local variables) which is *registered* with the future. The **when** language construct immediately returns a future itself which acts as a placeholder for the result of executing the **becomes** clause. This closure will be invoked after the future it was registered with has been resolved. As such, **when** allows one to send an asychronous message resulting in a future (i.e. the first argument) and to specify what should be done upon getting a result (i.e. the **becomes** clause), without resorting to blocking and without having to manually establish a connection between the time of sending the message and the time of receiving a result.

The following code excerpt exemplifies how a **when** construct can be registered on a future resulting from an asynchronous message send. Executing this code excerpt will immediately display "first" on the screen. When the future itself is eventually resolved by the actor, "second" will be displayed along with the computed result.

```
{ f = actor # compute();
  when(f) becomes(result) {
    display("second", result)};
  display("first")
}
```

5.2 Supporting Asynchronous Exception Propagation

Exceptions in AmbientTalk are represented as objects[1] which understand the **match** message. This message takes one argument which is expected to be another exception object. The **match** message is invoked by the exception handling mechanism to determine whether a raised exception matches the exception object specified by a particular handler. The introduction of this reflective hook allows programmers to make their own variants of exceptions as long as these implement a **match** method.

AmbientTalk's basic exception handling mechanism consists of a **raise** primitive and a **try-catch** construct. The former allows exceptions to be raised,

---

[1] Apart from actors, AmbientTalk also features 'normal' objects that do not have any concurrency provisions. For the details we refer to [4].

whereas the latter can be used to handle exceptions within the scope of a single actor method invocation [17]. When a raised exception is not handled by the actor that raised it, the invoked method is said to *propagate an exception* instead of returning a value. The propagated exception then *ruins* the future corresponding to that method invocation. The fact that futures can be ruined by exceptions changes the future pipeling semantics described above. As explained, when a message **m** is sent to a future f_1, a new future f_2 is returned that will be resolved by the result of sending **m** to the resolution of f_1. However, when f_1 is eventually ruined, f_2 will be ruined by the same exception. A similar phenomenon exists in the E language where it is called broken promise contagion [15].

The transitive ruining of pipelined futures enables the propagation of exceptions along a chain of subsequent asynchronous message sends. Defining handlers for such asynchronously propagated exceptions can be achieved using AmbientTalk's **when-catch** construct. This extension of the **when** construct described above allows attaching **catch** blocks to handle the exceptions propagated by the associated future. The **when-catch** construct thus requires three constituents: a future, a closure to handle the value the future will eventually resolve to and a list of **catch** blocks to handle possible exceptions. The construct looks as follows.

```
when(f) becomes(result) {
    when-block
} catch(Exception1) {
    catch-block1
} catch(Exception2) {
    catch-block2
    ...
}
```

The idea is that a **when-catch** construct can be registered with a future **f** and in its turn denotes a future **f'**. If **f** gets resolved with a value, the becomes clause of the **when-catch** will be executed and its result will be used to resolve **f'**. If **f** is ruined by an exception, the **when-catch** construct is notified of this exception and will identify the first catch clause capable of handling the raised exception (using the **match** message described above). If such a catch clause exists, the value of **f'** depends on whether the catch clause returns a value or raises an exception in its turn. If no matching catch clause is found, **f'** is ruined by the same exception that ruined **f**.

5.3   Supporting Concerted Exceptions

By default, the result of a method is aligned with the value of the last expression in its body. As a consequence, exceptions raised from asynchronous message sends will only be taken into account if they transitively ruin the future of the last expression (using the propagation rules explained above). This default semantics may lead to exceptions being overlooked if they are resulting from independent (*i.e.* not pipelined) message sends, which is clearly not a desirable outcome. In the collaborative editor example, such independent messages are sent when local editors broadcast their local changes to synchronise with the other participants of the editing session. This synchronisation consists of sending independent **merge** messages to all editors participating in the writing session. In this case, the synchronisation is only to be considered successful if *none* of the participants has propagated an exception. It is precisely in such cases that a mechanism is required to funnel all possible concurrent exceptions and produce a single *concerted exception*.

AmbientTalk's exception handling mechanism provides the **group-resolve** construct as an alternative mechanism to group the exception handling of multiple asynchronous invocationswithin a block. Unlike an "ordinary code block", the **group** clause does not immediately return the value of its last expression. Instead a future is returned, the value of which will be determined only after *all* futures created within the **group** clause either have been resolved with a return value or ruined by an exception. When none of the futures was ruined, the result of the **group-resolve** construct is equivalent to that of an ordinary code block, namely the value of the last expression. However, if exceptions were propagated, the **resolve** clause will be triggered with an array of concurrently raised exceptions. The **resolve** clause may either return a value (if the reported exceptions can be tolerated) or raise a *concerted exception*. Using the **group-resolve** construct, the synchronisation between different editors can be written as follows:

```
method synchroniseDocument(document) {
  group {
    for editorActor in editorActors {
      editorActor#merge(document);
    }
  } resolve( concurrentExceptions ) {
    // compute and raise a concerted exception based on concurrentExceptions
}}
```

Needless to say, when using a **when-catch** construct inside a **group** clause, exceptions that have ruined a future but were subsequently handled by that nested **when-catch** will not be considered any more by the **group-resolve** construct.

5.4   Supporting Collaborative Exception Handling

The criteria for an ambient-oriented exception handling mechanism defined in section 3 stipulate that a mechanism is needed to inform a set of collaborating actors when one of them has propagated an exception. Such an exception might invalidate the optimistic assumptions the actors have to make to achieve a *loosely-coupled exception handling* mechanism. The **synchroniseDocument** method described in the previous section, contains an example of such an optimistic operation in the collaborative editor example. The **merge** method which is invoked on all collaborating editors, allows each editor to merge the changes under the assumption that none of the other participants will have encountered conflicts. This assumption allows editors to autonomously merge changes without communicating with the other participants, thereby tolerating the temporary disconnection of some of the collaborating editors. However, when one of the editors *does* propagate an exception back, all editors need to be notified of this event, and be able to collaboratively handle the exception.

Our ambient conversation model achieves *collaborative exception handling* through the introduction of a **conversation** abstraction. The conversation's task is to provide a mechanism to propagate exceptions to all participants of the collaboration it embodies. Conversations are represented as actors and are automatically created by the **conversation** construct shown below.

```
conversation( participants ) {
  // Additional behaviour for the conversation
}
```

When creating a **conversation** the actors that are to participate in the conversation are passed along in an array. The conversation actor itself offers a **propagate** method which, when passed an exception object, broadcasts this exception to all participants such that it can be handled collaboratively. The participants are notified of such broadcasted exceptions by installing **when-catch** observers on the conversation actor. A **conversation** can thus be thought of as a special kind of future which can be 'ruined multiple times'. In addition to providing the **propagate** method, the conversation also has access to the participants, and it can be provided with additional behaviour that is to be specified in the body of the **conversation** construct.

Although a conversation is conceptually thought of as a single actor, the *loosely-coupled exception handling* criterion clearly prohibits an ambient-oriented exception handling mechanism to introduce dependencies on a single "leader" device (*i.e.* the device hosting the conversation). Such dependencies are avoided by providing each participant of the conversation with its own local replica of that conversation actor. Each participant is given a reference to its local replica using the **startConversation** method. A participant can broadcast an exception to all other participants in the conversation by invoking the **propagate** method on its local replica. Section 6 illustrates how conversations are used in the editor case in order to broadcast a merge exception to all participating editors.

5.5   Supporting Loosely-Coupled Exception Handling

An ambient-oriented exception handling model must provide for exceptions to be handled in a loosely-coupled fashion. This implies that tight coupling between devices (which harm that device's autonomy) should be avoided whenever possible. It is for this reason that we have introduced replication in the design of the **conversation** language construct, to minimize the dependencies between the participants other than those inherent to the task at hand.

Dependencies between devices are also created when the actors they host send messages to one another. Although such dependencies cannot leave a device blocked and therefore unable to respond to requests, the inability to communicate with its communication partner may prohibit the application from making any progress. An extreme example hereof is the **group-resolve** construct which observes a collection of futures and will only end when *all* futures have been either resolved or ruined. In order to make this construct more suitable for an ambient-oriented setting, support is needed to differentiate between temporary (tolerable) and long-lasting (presumably permanent) disconnections. This technique allows loosening the coupling between collaborating actors and *e.g.* allows actors to find replacement services for unavailable collaborators.

In previous work, we have already proposed the **due** language construct [4] which addresses the problem described above by putting an expiration deadline (in milliseconds) on the transmission of outgoing messages. In this context, we are not interested in the ability to send messages to a particular actor, but rather in the resolution (or ruining) of the future corresponding to that message. Therefore, we present a variant of the **due** language construct, which annotates **when-catch** blocks, rather than messages, with deadlines. When the future is neither resolved nor ruined within the expiration period, the **due** clause will be executed. The resulting construct, called **when-catch-due** can be used in the editor example to exclude editors from the collaborative editing session when they have been disconnected for too long a period.

```
when(editorActor#merge(document)) becomes(result) {
   // merge performed successfully
} catch ( MergeException ) {
   // handle merge conflicts
} due ( MAX_TIMEOUT ) {
   // remove editor from the collaborative editing session
}
```

6   Implementation of the Collaborative Editor

This section illustrates how the ambient conversation model presented in the previous section can be used to realise the collaborative editor described in section 2.2. Such a collaborative editor can be embodied in the ambient-oriented programming paradigm as a suite of collaborating editor actors. Each editor is provided with its own copy of the document which it may edit locally. For simplicity we assume the collaborative editor to be line-based with a public interface consisting of an **insert**, a **delete** and a **replace** method. These methods allow the editor to make local changes on its copy of the document. At regular intervals the editor will synchronise its local document with the version of its collaborators.

The synchronisation of one editor with its collaborators is achieved by sending each editor a **merge** message with one's own document. The merge operation can encounter two kinds of conflicts while combining the changes in two documents:

either one editor has replaced a line that was deleted by another participant or both of them have replaced the same line. These conflicts are reported by raising the **DeleteException** and **EditException** exceptions respectively.

In order for editors to collaborate, they need to establish a conversation listing all participants invited to join the editing process. This is performed by the **publish** method listed below, who receives an array of the editor participants and creates a conversation grouping them.

```
method publish(editorActors) {
  conversation(editorActors) {
    method synchroniseDocument(document){
      group{
        for editorActor in editorActors {
          editorActor#merge(document)
        }
      } resolve( concurrentExceptions ) {
        //manage conflicts received from all the participants
        thisActor#propagate(aMergeException);
      }}
  }
}
```

As explained in section 5.4, the conversation actor sends a **startConversation** message to each participant passing along a replica of itself. The body of the conversation defines the protocol for broadcasting their changes to the different participant editor actors. Since the merge phase may report overlapping conflicts, the **group-resolve** construct is used here to handle and resolve them in a single concerted conflict. Note that while the **synchroniseDocument** method is clearly application-dependent, the propagation of exceptions to the participants will be triggered by the default **propagate** method implicitly defined by the conversation actor.

Each editor must also implement the **startConversation** method with the code that follows. As mentioned, upon reception of a **startConversation** message, all the participants will receive a replicated actor representing the collaborative editing session. Editors can then register a **when-catch** block on their local conversation replica to handle the exceptions raised during the synchronisation phase. If the synchronisation succeeds, the editor checkpoints its document.

```
method startConversation(conversationActor) {
  when(conversationActor) becomes(val) {
    //code to update the checkpoint
  } catch( DeleteConflict ){ // application-dependent handler code
  } catch( EditConflict ){ // application-dependent handler code
}}
```

The **when-catch-due** construct can be used in the context of the collaborative editor example to detect the inability to synchronize with some participants. This is interpreted as a long-lasting disconnection and the participant is subsequently forced to leave the conversation. The code below introduces a **when-catch-due** construct guarding every **merge** message sent in the **publish** method explained above. This technique allows detecting that a particular future may be neither resolved nor ruined after a timeout period of **maxTimeOut** milliseconds. In this case, the **due** clause is used to remove the participant to which the timed out message was sent from the conversation. Note that exceptions which are reported within the specified timeout period will still be handled by the **resolve** block since in this particular example the **when-catch-due** construct does not specify any exception handlers.

```
method publish(editorActors) {
  conversation(editorActors) {
    method synchroniseDocument(document){
      group{
        for editorActor in editorActors {
          when( editorActor#merge(document) ) becomes (val) { ...
          } due( maxTimeOut ){
            // the participant is removed from the conversation
          }
        }
      }
    } resolve( concurrentExceptions ) {
      //manage conflicts received from all the participants
      thisActor#propagate(aMergeException);
  }}
  }
}
```

The implementation of the collaborative editor application validates the language constructs designed for the ambient-oriented exception handling mechanism. Furthermore, the implementation also illustrates that it is relatively straightforward to combine the different constructs to build an ambient-oriented application which is resilient to both deliberately raised exceptions as well as exceptions raised due to lost participants.

7   Future Work

The ambient conversation exception handling mechanism does not deal adequately with all aspects of exception handling for ambient-oriented software. Further research to improve the model is currently focussing on the following tracks:

Augmenting the Expressiveness. The ambient conversation model consists of a set of primitives which need to be combined in order to effectively deal with exceptions in ambient-oriented software. In order to yield a set of more expressive language constructs for exception handling, one track of future research focuses on finding abstractions for recurring exception handling strategies. Additionally, this track investigates the porting of existing distributed exception handling techniques (as described in section 4) to an ambient-oriented context.

Handler Communication. A problem that is currently not addressed by the ambient conversation model is the regulation of how handlers that are invoked concurrently using the **conversation** construct may communicate with one another. Currently, we are investigating a mechanism that allows handlers to reuse the communication infrastructure of the actors in which they reside. Since AmbientTalk is an actor-based programming language, our early experiments use the **become** primitive to install "handler behaviours" in all actors that host one of the collaborating handlers. However, further research is necessary to explore the practicability of this approach in realistic applications.

8   Conclusion

This paper has focussed on the integration of exception handling into an ambient-oriented language called AmbientTalk. Having unravelled the hardware characteristics that fundamentally discriminate mobile networks from their stationary counterparts, we have identified four criteria for novel ambient-oriented exception handling mechanisms. We have then proposed the ambient conversation exception handling model as a suite of exception handling language features in which each language feature addresses one of the criteria. The essence of the ambient conversations exception handling model consists of the **when-catch** language construct which correctly propagates and handles exceptions resulting from an asynchronous message send between several actors that are possibly located on different devices linked by a volatile connection. Based on this language construct, the **group-resolve** mechanism was proposed to group several such asynchronous message sends when these occur in a block of code. Their concurrently raised exceptions can then be funneled into a single concerted exception. Third, the **conversation** exception broadcasting construct was described that allows one to specify that different actors are collaborating and to ensure that all available participants are involved in the exception handling process. Finally, the distribution properties of the proposed constructs were evaluated in the face of long-lasting disconnections. The introduction of **due** clauses as part of the **when-catch-due** construct provides an adequate mechanism to detect and deal with such long-lasting disconnections. The four constructs were validated by using them in the design of an ambient-oriented collaborative editor that allows several editors deployed on autonomous hardware to participate in a shared writing session. The exception handling constructs have been used to make this editor resilient to distributed merge conflicts without relying on a shared infrastructure.

References

1. G. Agha. *Actors: a Model of Concurrent Computation in Distributed Systems.* MIT Press, 1986.
2. D. Caromel and M. Rebuffel. Object based concurrency: Ten language features to achieve reuse. In R. Ege, M. Singh, and B. Meyer, editors, *Proceedings of TOOLS-USA'93, Santa Barbara, (CA), USA*, pages 205–214. Prentice-Hall, Englewood Cliffs (NJ), USA, 1993.

3. D. Caromel and G. Chazarain. Robust exception handling in an asynchronous environment. In *Exception Handling in Object-Oriented Systems: Developing Systems that Handle Exceptions*, Technical Reports 05-050 - Laboratoire d'Informatique, de Robotique et Micro-Electronique de Montpellier, 2005.

4. J. Dedecker, T. Van Cutsem, S. Mostinckx, W. De Meuter, and T. D'Hondt. Ambient-oriented programming in AmbientTalk. In *Proceeding of the 20th European Conference on Object-Oriented Programming (ECOOP)*, Dave Thomas (Ed.), Lecture Notes in Computer Science Vol. 4067, pp. 230–254, Springer-Verlag, 2006.

5. J. Dedecker, T. Van Cutsem, S. Mostinckx, T. D'Hondt, and W. De Meuter. Ambient-Oriented Programming. In *OOPSLA '05: Companion of the 20th annual ACM SIGPLAN conference on Object-oriented programming, systems, languages, and applications*. ACM Press, 2005.

6. D. Gelernter. Generative communication in Linda. *ACM Transactions on Programming Languages and Systems*, 7(1):80–112, Jan 1985.

7. IST Advisory Group. Ambient intelligence: from vision to reality, September 2003.

8. R. Halstead, Jr. Multilisp: a language for concurrent symbolic computation. *ACM Trans. Program. Lang. Syst.*, 7(4):501–538, 1985.

9. Y. Ichisugi and A. Yonezawa. Exception handling and real time features in an object-oriented concurrent language. In *Proceedings of the UK/Japan workshop on Concurrency : theory, language, and architecture*, pages 92–109, New York, NY, USA, 1991. Springer-Verlag New York, Inc.

10. A. Iliasov and A. Romanovsky. Exception handling in coordination-based mobile environments. In *Proceedings of the 29th Annual International Computer Software and Applications Conference (COMPSAC 2005)*, pages 341–350. IEEE Computer Society Press, 2005.

11. V. Issarny. An exception handling mechanism for parallel object-oriented programming: toward reusable, robust distributed software. *Journal of Object-Oriented Programming*, 6(6):29–40, 1993.

12. V. Issarny. Concurrent exception handling. In *Advances in Exception Handling Techniques (Lecture Notes in Computer Science)*, volume 2022, pages 111–127. Springer-Verlag, 2000.

13. J. Kienzle, A. Ströhmeier, and A. Romanovsky. Open multithreaded transactions: Keeping threads and exceptions under control. In *Workshop on Object-Oriented Real-Time Dependable Systems (WORDS'01)*, page pp. 197, 2001.

14. B. Liskov and L. Shrira. Promises: linguistic support for efficient asynchronous procedure calls in distributed systems. In *Proceedings of Conference on Programming Language Design and Implementation*, pages 260–267. ACM Press, 1988.

15. M. Miller, E. D. Tribble, and J. Shapiro. Concurrency among strangers: Programming in E as plan coordination. In R. De Nicola and D. Sangiorgi, editors, *Symposium on Trustworthy Global Computing*, volume 3705 of *LNCS*, pages 195–229. Springer, April 2005.

16. R. Miller and A. Tripathi. The guardian model and primitives for exception handling in distributed systems. *IEEE Trans. Software Eng.*, 30(12):1008–1022, 2004.

17. S. Mostinckx, J. Dedecker, E. Gonzalez Boix, T. Van Cutsem, and W. De Meuter. Ambient-oriented exception handling in AmbientTalk. Technical report, Vrije Universiteit Brussel, 2006.

18. A. Murphy, G. Picco, and G.-C. Roman. Lime: A middleware for physical and logical mobility. In *Proceedings of the The 21st International Conference on Distributed Computing Systems*, pages 524–536. IEEE Computer Society, 2001.

19. A. Romanovsky and A. F. Zorzo. On distribution of coordinated atomic actions. *SIGOPS Oper. Syst. Rev.*, 31(4):63–71, 1997.

20. G. Di Marzo Serugendo and A. Romanovsky. Using exception handling for fault-tolerance in mobile coordination-based environments. In *ECOOP Workshop on Exception Handling in Object Oriented Systems: towards Emerging Application Areas and New Programming Paradigms*, 2003.

21. F. Souchon, C. Dony, C. Urtado, and S. Vauttier. Improving exception handling in multi-agent systems. In *Advances in Software Engineering for Multi-Agent Systems*. Springer-Verlag, 2003.

22. S. Tazuneki and T. Yoshida. Concurrent exception handling in a distributed object-oriented computing environment. In *Seventh International Conference on Parallel and Distributed Systems Workshops (ICPADS'00 Workshops)*, 2000.

23. R. Tolksdorf and K. Knubben. Programming Distributed Systems with the Delegation-based Object-oriented Language dSelf. In *Proceedings of the 2002 ACM Symposium on Applied Computing*, pages 927–931. ACM Press, 2002.

24. M. Weiser. The computer for the twenty-first century. *Scientific American*, pages 94–100, september 1991.

25. J. Xu, A. Romanovsky, and B. Randell. Coordinated exception handling in distributed object systems: From model to system implementation. In *International Conference on Distributed Computing Systems*, pages 12–21, 1998.

26. A. F. Zorzo and R. J. Stroud. A distributed object-oriented framework for dependable multiparty interactions. In *OOPSLA '99: Proceedings of the 14th ACM SIGPLAN conference on Object-oriented programming, systems, languages, and applications*, pages 435–446, New York, NY, USA, 1999. ACM Press.

Exception Handling in CSCW Applications in Pervasive Computing Environments

Anand R. Tripathi*, Devdatta Kulkarni, and Tanvir Ahmed

Department of Computer Science,
University of Minnesota, Minneapolis, MN 55455 U.S.A.
{tripathi, dkulk, tahmed}@cs.umn.edu

Abstract. In this paper we present conceptual foundations of an exception handling model for context-aware CSCW applications. Human participation in the recovery actions is an integral part of this model. Role abstraction is provided with an exception interface through which the role members can perform exception handling actions. Exception handling involving multiple role members is also supported through inter-role exception propagation mechanisms provided in the model.

1 Introduction

There is a growing interest in building context-aware applications and pervasive computing environments that allow mobile users to seamlessly access computing resources to perform their activities while moving across different computing domains and physical spaces [1,2,3]. A typical user is generally involved in many activities such as office workflow tasks, distributed meetings, collaborative tasks, personal activities such as shopping or entertainment. Many of these activities may involve multiple users collaborating on some shared tasks. Applications built for such environments are characterized by dynamic integration of large number of components based on the user context and ambient conditions. These characteristics impart a malleable nature to these applications giving rise to different kinds of error conditions and abnormal situations which are caused by following kinds of failures:

- Context-based dynamic resource discovery and binding may fail because of unavailability of required type of resources in the environment.
- Failures could arise while accessing the resources/services because of incompatible resource access protocols or insufficient security privileges. Also a resource may encounter internal failures.
- Some users working towards a common goal in a collaborative application may fail to perform certain obligated tasks. This may affect other users in the collaboration.
- Events occurring in the physical world may affect the application. These events may violate the application's assumptions about the state of the external world.

---

* This work was supported by NSF grant 0411961.

In such applications context can be classified into two categories: *internal* and *external*. The internal context of a CSCW (computer supported collaborative work) application is related to the execution state of its various tasks. The external context represents the attributes that are related to the physical environment. A user's external context may be defined in terms of a number of different kinds of attributes, such as the user's current physical location (GPS, presence in a building or room, proximity to certain devices or users), the Internet domain in which the user is currently present, or devices through which the user is interacting with the environment.

We have developed a programming framework for building context-aware CSCW applications in pervasive computing environments [4,5]. In this framework, such applications are built from their high level specifications expressed in XML and realized through a distributed middleware [6]. The specification model provides the abstraction of *roles* for users to participate in an *activity*. This specification model is essentially a composition framework for integrating users, application-defined components, and infrastructure services/resources to build the runtime environment of a context-aware CSCW application.

In this paper we present a methodology for handling error conditions and abnormal situations arising in context-aware CSCW applications. The methodology is based on programmed error handling wherein exceptions are used for representing different types of failures encountered by an application and exception handlers are built into the application to perform recovery actions. We present different failure categories to motivate the exception handling requirements in context-aware CSCW applications. Human participation in exception handling is an integral part of error recovery in such applications. Towards that end, the exception handling model provides mechanisms for involving role members in handling exceptions and for propagating exceptions from one role to another.

Section 2 describes our specification model for building context-aware CSCW applications in pervasive computing environments. In Section 3 we present a categorization of the error conditions arising in these applications. We also present the exception handling requirements for context-aware CSCW applications in this section. In Section 4 we present a model for exception handling in our role-based programming framework and we demonstrate its capabilities through two examples in Section 5. In Section 6 we discuss related work and conclude in Section 7.

2   Specification Model for Context-Aware CSCW Systems

We present here an overview of the collaboration specification model which we have developed [5,4]. A CSCW application is modeled as an activity. Activity defines three things: a set of objects representing shared resources and infrastructure services, a set of roles through which a group of users cooperate towards some common objectives by performing tasks involving shared resources and infrastructure services, and a set of actions (called reactions) that are triggered by events occurring within an activity or events occurring in the external physical environment.

The shared resources/services required by an activity may be created by the activity or discovered in the environment. Resources are described using RDD, which is an XML schema based on RDF [7] and WSDL [8]. An RDD for a resource includes the attribute-value pairs describing the resource, the interfaces, and the events that are exported by the resource.

A user joins one or more roles in the activity, and a role represents authorization of its members to invoke a set of operations on shared objects to perform tasks in the collaboration space. A precondition associated with a role operation must be satisfied to execute the operation. These preconditions are based on both internal and external events.

Both internal and external context can affect various aspects of the activity. The binding of the shared resources/services may need to be changed based on the context, and the role operation precondition may also depend on the context.

Activity activityName
    {**Parameter** objName}
    {**Object** [**Collection**] *objName* **RDD** *rddSpec* }
    {**Bind** *Binding-Definition*}
    {**Reaction** *Reaction-Definition*}
    {**Role** *Role-Definition*}

Fig. 1. Activity Syntax

We represent activity specifications through an XML schema. Here, rather than using XML, we use a notation that is conceptually easy to follow. In Figure 1, the syntax for the XML schema for *activity* definition is shown, where [ ] represents optional terms, { } represents zero or more terms, | represents choice, and boldface **terms** represent tags for elements and attributes in XML schema. In this paper we do not address exception handling with nested activities.

Specification of a sample CSCW application, an exam session activity, is shown in Figure 2. Two roles are defined in the exam session activity, *Student* and *Examiner*. Multiple users can be present in both the roles. The *Student* role is provided with operations for taking the exam such as: *StartExam*, *WriteExam*, and *SubmitExam*. The *Examiner* role is provided with the operation *GradeExam* for grading the exam. We use the exam session activity to demonstrate the specification model in this section and extend it to incorporate the exception handling model in Section 4.

2.1   Event Based Coordination Model

Events are used for task coordination within an activity. Three types of events are defined in the model: system defined events, application defined events, and

```
1.  Activity ExamSession
2.     Object examPaper
3      Object Collection StudentAnswers
4.     Bind examPaper With direct (//ExamPaperURL)
5.     Role Student
6.        Object answerBook
7.        Bind answerBook With new (//AnswerBookCodeBase)
8.        Operation StartExam
9.           Precondition true
10.          Action answerBook.startExam()
11.       Operation WriteExam
12.          Precondition #StartExam.start(invoker=thisUser) > 0
13.          Action answerBook.writeExam()
14.       Operation SubmitExam
15.          Precondition #StartExam.start(invoker=thisUser) > 0
16.          Action Bind answerBook With StudentAnswers
17.    Role Examiner
18.       Operation GradeExam
19.          Precondition #Student.SubmitExam.finish > 0
20.          Action StudentAnswers.gradeExam()
```

Fig. 2. Exam Session Activity Specification

external world events. System defined events are *start* and *finish* events associated with each role operation, and they are generated by the middleware implicitly. Application defined events are signaled explicitly using the *NotifyEvent* construct defined in the specification model. The role name, role member name, and the event to be notified are given as parameters to this construct. The external world events are notified to the activity through the shared resources and services bound in the activity scope.

Operation *start* and *finish* events have two predefined attributes: *invoker* and *time*. The history of occurrences of an event type is represented by an event list. The specification model supports various functions on event lists. The count-operator # returns the number of events of a given type that have occurred so far, and a sublist of these events can be obtained by applying a selector predicate.

2.2   Role, Operation, and Reaction

A *role* in an activity defines two things: an object space for the role members and a set *operations* that are executed by the role members on objects defined within the activity scope or the role scope. The objects declared within a role represent a separate namespace created for each member in the role, and binding of these names is performed independently for each member.

A role operation can only be invoked by a member in the role. A role operation can have precondition that must be satisfied before the operation is executed.

These preconditions are expressed in terms of predicates based on events occurring within the activity, role memberships of participants, and query methods of the environmental resources representing external context information. In contrast to an operation, a reaction is not invoked by a user but is automatically executed when certain events occur. Reactions are specified in the activity scope. Similar to an operation, a reaction is executed only when its precondition is true. Figure 3 presents the syntax of a role definition.

The variable `thisUser` is used in our specification framework for identifying the role member who is invoking a particular role operation. A boolean function `member(thisUser, roleId)` is defined for checking the role membership of the user invoking the role operation. The function `members(roleId)` returns the role member list. Set operations can be performed on role member lists. A *count* operator, `#`, can be applied on a member list. The count of the members in a role is `#(members(roleId))`.

In the exam session activity, the operations *WriteExam* and *SubmitExam* can only be performed by a *Student* role member if that role member has previously performed *StartExam* role operation. This is specified as the preconditions for *WriteExam* (line 12) and *SubmitExam* operations (line 15). The *Examiner* can perform *GradeExam* operation only after *Student* role members have *finished* executing the *SubmitExam* role operation. This is specified as precondition to the *GradeExam* role operation (line 19).

A role also has *admission constraints* and *activation constraints* associated with it. We do not discuss them here as they are not related to the exception handling model presented here.

Role roleName
    {**Object** [**Collection**] *objName* **RDD** *rddSpec* }
    {**Bind** *Binding-Definition*}
    {**Operation** *Operation-Name*}
      [**Precondition** *Condition*]
        [**Action** {objId methodSignature methodParameter}]

Fig. 3. Syntax for role definition

2.3   Binding Specification

Resources and services required as part of the activity or a role can be specified using the *Bind* primitive in four different ways as shown below.

1. Binding to a new object: The binding primitive with **new** specifies that a new resource of the specified codebase type should be created. For example, in the exam session activity, an *AnswerBook* object is created and bound to the name *answerBook* as shown in line 7 of Figure 2. This binding is specified inside the *Student* role scope since a separate *answerBook* object needs to be created for each *Student* role member.

2. Binding to an existing resource through URL: This form of binding primitive with `direct` specifies that the resource identified by the given URL should be used in binding. For example, in the exam session activity, the URL of the *ExamPaper* might be well-known. Such a direct binding is shown in line 4 of Figure 2.

3. Binding to another object: This type of binding is used to export a resource, created as part of a role, to the activity scope. For example, in the exam session activity the *answerBook* object for every *Student* role member is exported to the *StudentAnswers* collection (defined in line 3) as part of the *SubmitExam* role operation (line 16).

4. Binding through discovery: This form of the binding primitive is useful when a resource with a particular set of attributes is needed to be discovered in the environment. In the example below, we present specification of a museum information desk activity. A separate activity is instantiated for each museum visitor. In this activity, the audio channel of user's device needs to be bound with the audio player based on the user's location and also taking into consideration the user's choice of the language. In this example, the *audioChannel* object is re-binded when there is a change in the user's location, indicated by the *LocationChangeEvent* generated by the *locationService* when the visitor's location changes. Discover primitive used in binding the *audioChannel* object specifies the location attribute and the preferred language in the *Audio-Channel-Description* to be used during resource discovery.

Activity Museum Infodesk
  Object locationService **RDD** Location-Service-Description
  Parameter userPreference
  Bind locationService **With direct** *(//LocationServiceURL)*
    Role Visitor
        Object audioChannel **RDD** Audio-Channel-Description
        Bind audioChannel **When** LocationChangeEvent(thisUser)
          With discover *(<location=locationService.getLocation(thisUser),*
                  language=userPreference.preferredLanguage>)
      Operation ListenAudio
        Precondition true
                Action audioChannel.listenAudio()

3   Failures in Context-Aware CSCW Applications

An activity encounters *error conditions* as a result of various failures occurring in resources/infrastructure services being used by the activity [9]. *Exceptions* are *raised* in the activity by the middleware to indicate these failures. Exception handling actions are programmed in the activity to recover from the error conditions. The exception based approach for handling failures decouples the activity from the failure monitoring tasks corresponding to various resources/services being used by the activity.

In this section we identify various failure categories for context-aware CSCW applications. We use several examples to demonstrate the nature of failures. We identify requirements that need to be supported by an exception handling model for handling these failures.

3.1   Resource Discovery and Binding Failure

Dynamic discovery and binding of resources based on the user context or application context is one of the important aspects of context-aware applications. An activity encounters an error when the discovery of the required type of resource in the environment fails. Such errors are to be anticipated for applications in the pervasive computing environments because of their highly dynamic nature. Alternate resources may need to be discovered and bound to handle these errors. In the worst case, if no appropriate resources are found, then users must be involved in handling these errors.

Consider a museum infodesk activity in which users can bind to the audio commentary of an artifact when they move close to the artifact. This discovery and binding may fail if the audio commentary resource is not available in user's preferred language or if the audio commentary resource is not available at all. The exception handling mechanism should allow the application to transparently handle this exception by discovering and binding with audio commentary in another language or may provide alternative operations to the user by binding to the textual commentary for the artifact. The exception handling mechanism thus needs to have the ability to perform *automatic rebinding actions* and should also support *alternate interfaces* that are enabled depending on the objects that are bound.

3.2   Resource Interaction Failure

Resource interactions may fail because of insufficient security privileges, incompatible interaction protocols, resources being busy, or internal resource failures. For example, consider the exam session activity involving different students. Multiple students may encounter errors while performing one of the operations provided for the *Student* role because of operation failures. Each corresponding exception should be handled separately for each student in its appropriate context. There can be multiple ways to handle this exception. One way would be to allow the student to re-execute the failed operation. Another way would be to require the examiner to grant appropriate permission to the student to allow retake of the exam. If there are multiple examiners, then any examiner may approve retaking of the exam. Still another way would be to require the particular examiner who gave out the exam to approve a retake.

The exception handling mechanism needs to support exception propagation across different roles as the recovery actions may require participation of members in different roles. Furthermore, there should be a provision to specify whether the exception should be handled by any of the role members or a specific role member. This further requires that each role supports a special interface, i.e. a set of operations, for handling exceptions. This interface would be enabled only for those role members that have to be involved in exception handling.

3.3   Obligation Failure

Obligation failures occur when the participants in a particular task fail to perform the required actions causing the progress of the task to stall. Consider the exam session activity. There might be an obligation that once the exam is started it must be submitted by the student before the alloted time is over. An obligation failure occurs when a student taking the exam does not submit it within the specified time. The handling of such an exception may consist of performing a default action for the obligated role operation, without requiring any user participation. Alternatively, it may also be communicated to some role members for some human assisted recovery.

3.4   Environmental Failure

A task may depend upon external events for its progress. For example, consider a workflow task for car reservation application involving two roles, *Agent* and *Renter*. A task is started when a renter requests a car to be booked. The agent reserves a car for the renter which the renter can pickup at the reservation time. At the reservation time it may happen that the particular rented car is not available because it may not be returned yet by the prior renter or because an accident might have occurred to the car.

Such external events represent error conditions regarding an activity's assumptions about the state of its environment. These errors may be handled in multiple ways. The workflow task can be structured so that it handles such errors by providing an alternate car to the customer without involving the agent or the renter. On the other hand, the customer might want to negotiate the type of the alternate car with the rental facility. This requires restructuring the workflow such that one of the *Agent* role members is involved in assigning an alternate car to the renter.

Appropriate mechanisms are required for translating the external world events to exceptions that represent failure of activity's assumptions about the external physical environment. Mechanisms are required for handling these exceptions without any human intervention. Mechanisms are also required for propagating these exceptions to different roles defined within an activity when human intervention is needed in performing any restructuring of the workflow for recovery.

3.5   Summary of Error Handling Requirements in Context-Aware CSCW Applications

Exceptions occur in three scopes corresponding to: *role operation*, *role*, and *activity*. There is an hierarchical relationship between the three scopes. Activity is the outermost scope. It encapsulates the role scope which encapsulates the role operation scope.

Exceptions occurring in the role operation scope pertain to resource interaction failures and obligation failures. Exceptions pertaining to resource discovery and binding failures occur in the role scope. Exceptions occurring in the activity scope pertain to resource discovery and binding failures and environmental failures.

For developing an exception handling model for performing programmed error recovery in context-aware CSCW applications we need to answer the following questions:

- What mechanisms should be provided for handling exceptions in different scopes?
- What mechanisms should be provided to support exception handling involving role members? Furthermore, how to restrict the exception handler invocation by a specific role member, any role member, or all role members?
- What mechanisms should be provided for propagating exceptions from one role to another role?
- What mechanisms should be provided for restructuring an activity in response to exceptions and external world events?

4   Model for Exception Handling in Context-Aware CSCW Applications

We present the exception model that addresses the requirements identified in Section 3. We extend the programming framework presented in Section 2 with the exception handling model.

- There are three types of exception handlers: (1) those that are attached with role operations and object binding constructs; (2) those that are attached to the role abstraction; (3) those that are provided at the activity-level. Exception handlers attached to the role abstraction require participation from role members for exception handling.
- Exceptions may need to be propagated from the role operation scope to the role scope or may need to be signaled from the activity scope to the role scope. Exceptions may also be propagated from one role to another role.
- An exception encapsulates relevant information about the error occurrence that is essential for exception handling. For example, an exception occurring in the role operation scope, encapsulates the following information tuple: <role name, role member name, role operation name>.

4.1   Exception Handling in the Role Operation Scope

Exceptions in the role operation scope arise due to the failures in executing the associated action or failures corresponding to the non-execution of an obligated operation. An exception handler is statically associated with each role operation, following the *termination model*. The control-flow of the thread executing the operation is automatically transfered from the operation's action to the exception handler associated with the operation.

Exceptions are propagated from the role operation scope to the role scope if there is no exception handler attached with the operation or if the handler encounters an exception or if the handler explicitly signals the exception. A handler may explicitly signal an exception if handling the exception requires some role member to perform certain actions. The inability to handle the exception completely in the scope of the role operation indicates that it cannot be handled automatically and an external human intervention is required to handle it. Hence the exception is propagated to the role scope and the operation execution context, corresponding to the failed operation, is terminated. Figure 4 shows the exception handling in the role operation scope and role scope.

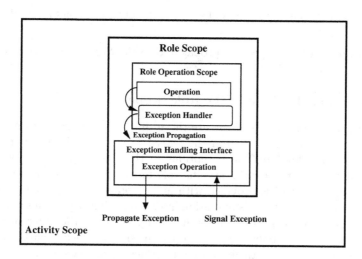

Fig. 4. Exception Handling in the scope of Role

The role operation specification is extended to include the specification of an *exception handler* as shown in Figure 5. The exception handler is specified using the *OnException* clause. The exception handler may perform a sequence of actions specified through the *Action* clause, such as resource interaction, or binding action, or it may signal the exception to the role scope using the *Signal* clause. The signaling target is specified through the *Target* clause. The role that encapsulates the role operation is used as the default target if no *Target* clause is specified.

The role operation specification is extended to incorporate the specification of an *obligation* as shown in Figure 5. The obligation specification consists of the specification of an event whose occurrence after the occurrence of *Event-of-Interest* causes the obligation to fail.

Figure 6 shows the exam session activity in which role operations are provided with exception handlers. The *SubmitExam* role operation is specified to be an *obligation* operation. The obligation exception is handled separately for each role member. The exception handling action consist of automatically performing the action specified as part of the operation (lines 9-12). It may also be propagated to the role scope by re-signaling it. On the other hand, the *WriteExam* operation failure is handled by allowing the student to retake the exam. Correspondingly

---

Operation *opName*
    [**Obligation** {**Before** *Event* **After** *Event-of-Interest*}]
    [{**OnException** *exceptionObject* **Type** *ExceptionType*
      (**Action** *sequence of actions* |
      Signal (*exceptionObject*) **Target** *TargetName*) }]

Fig. 5. Operation Syntax: Modified to incorporate Exception Specification

the *WriteExamFailedException* is propagated to the *Student* role scope through the *Signal* clause (line 16-17).

4.2   Exception Handling in the Role Scope

Exceptions raised in the role scope are those that are propagated from the role operation's scope or signaled from the activity's scope. Role member participation is required for handling exceptions in the role scope. Exceptions may be required to be handled by a specific role member, any role member, or all role members. Each role is provided with an *exception interface*. The exception interface is similar to the role's operation interface in that it provides a set of operations to be performed for exception handling. However, the difference is that the exception interface operation can be executed only when a particular type of exception is delivered to the exception interface. Every exception operation is preceded by a *When* clause that specifies the exception which will enable that operation. The exception interface supports a *queuing model* for exception delivery and handling. Every exception delivered to the exception interface queue is handled separately. In conjunction with enabling the exception interface operation, the delivered exception may also be further propagated to the activity scope if exception handling needs to involve some other role's members.

Consider again the exam session activity specification in Figure 6. An exception, *WriteExamFailedException*, is raised to indicate the failure of *WriteExam* operation. *Student* role is provided with *RetakeExam* operation as part of its exception interface. This operation is enabled when an *WriteExamFailedException* object is delivered to the exception interface of the *Student* role (line 19).

There are two requirements for handling this exception. First, we require that students must receive an approval from the *Examiner* before they can invoke the *RetakeExam* operation. Hence the *WriteExamFailedException* is propagated to the activity scope (line 20) through which it is further propagated to the exception interface of the *Examiner* role. Second, we require that the *Retake-Exam* operation be enabled for only those role members who have encountered the failure. Such an access restriction on the invocation of exception interface operations is achieved through the specification of a special qualifier *Invoker* in the *Enable-For* clause (line 21). In our specification model three qualifiers are defined to be used in the *Enable-For* clause. These correspond to *Invoker*, *ANY*, and *ALL*. The qualifier *Invoker* restricts the accessibility of the exception operation to only that role member whose invocation of an operation resulted in

---

1. **Activity** ExamSession
2.   **Object** examPaper
     Object Collection StudentAnswers
     Bind examPaper **With direct** (//ExamPaperURL)
3.   **Role** Student
4.   **Object** answerBook
       Bind answerBook **With new** (//AnswerBookCodeBase)
5.   **Operation** StartExam
       ...
6.   **Operation** SubmitExam
7.   **Precondition** #StartExam.start(invoker=thisUser) > 0
8.   **Action Bind** answerBook **With** StudentAnswers
9.   **Obligation**
10.   **Before** TimerEvent(3:00:00 hours)
           After StartExam.start(invoker=thisUser)
11.   **OnException** ExceptionObject **Type** ObligationFailedException
12.   **Action Bind** answerBook **With** StudentAnswers
13.   **Operation** WriteExam
14.   **Precondition** #StartExam.start(invoker=thisUser) > 0
15.   **Action** answerBook.writeExam()
16.   **OnException** ExceptionObject **Type** OperationFailedException
17.   **Signal** (**new** WriteExamFailedException)
18.   **Exception Interface**
19.   **When** ExceptionObject **Type** WriteExamFailedException
20.   **Signal** (ExceptionObject)
21.   **Enable-For** Invoker
22.   **Operation** RetakeExam
23.   **Precondition**
             #Examiner.RetakeApprovedEvent(user=Invoker) > 0
24.   **Action**
25.   **Bind** answerBook **With new** (//AnswerBookCodeBase)
26.   answerBook.writeExam()

27. **Role** Examiner
28.   **Exception Interface**
29.   **When** ExceptionObject **Type** ExamInterruptedException
30.   **Enable-For** ANY
31.   **Operation** ApproveRetakeExam
32.   **Precondition** true
33.   **Action NotifyEvent**
34.   (Student, ExceptionObject.getRoleMemberName(),
               RetakeApprovedEvent)

35. **Reaction** HandleOperationFailedException
36.   **When** ExceptionObject **Type** WriteExamFailedException
37.   **Precondition** member(ExceptionObject.getRoleName(), Student)
38.   **Signal** (**new** ExamInterruptedException) **Target** Examiner

---

Fig. 6. Exam Session Activity Specification

raising the exception which is being handled. The qualifier *ANY* allows any role member to perform the exception operation, and the qualifier *ALL* requires all the role members to perform the exception operation.

Thus a *Student* role member can invoke *RetakeExam* operation only when the following two conditions are satisfied. First, the particular student role member must have encountered *OperationFailedException* while performing the *WriteExam* operation. Second, the *Examiner* role member must have explicitly approved retaking the exam for that particular *Student* role member. The second condition is specified as a precondition for the *RetakeExam* operation (lines 22-23). This precondition gets satisfied when the *Examiner* role member notifies the *RetakeApprovedEvent* as part of the exception handling action corresponding to the *ExamInterruptedException* delivered to it by the activity (lines 31-34).

4.3   Exception Handling in the Activity Scope

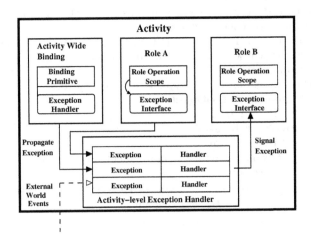

Fig. 7. Activity-level Exception Handling Model

Figure 7 shows the activity-level exception handling model. An activity-level exception handler is modeled as a reaction. There are three kinds of exceptions that occur in the activity scope: (1) the exceptions corresponding to the abnormal events occurring external to the activity; (2) exceptions occurring due to binding failures corresponding to the activity-level resource binding requirements; (3) exceptions that are propagated from the role scope.

In Figure 6, the activity-level exception handler for the *ExamSession* activity is shown in lines 35-38. This activity-level exception handler signals *ExamInterruptedException* to the *Examiner* role if the *WriteExamFailedException* occurred as part of some *Student* role member executing the *WriteExam* operation. The exception interface specification for the *Examiner* role is shown in lines 27-34 in Figure 6. The *ApproveRetakeExam* operation can be performed by any member of the *Examiner* role. This is specified through the qualifier *ANY* meaning that any member of the *Examiner* role can perform this operation. The *Examiner* role member uses the *ApproveRetakeExam* operation for approving retaking of the examination.

There can be multiple *Student* role members who may have encountered failures while executing the *WriteExam* operation and may require appropriate approval. A *RetakeApprovedEvent* is generated corresponding to each such failure and is notified to the appropriate *Student* role member. This event causes the precondition of the *RetakeExam* operation in the exception interface of the *Student* role to become true (lines 23 of Figure 6) for that role member.

An activity-level exception handler may seem similar to the Guardian like exception handler [10] for concurrent object-oriented systems. However there is a crucial difference between the two. The guardian model of exception handling is suited for timed asynchronous systems. The guardian handles an exception by suspending all the participant processes and signaling appropriate exceptions to the processes. Each process handles the exception according to its execution context. CSCW applications are loosely coupled and asynchronous in nature. Exception handling in such applications may require participation from human users. Also, the generated exceptions may not be relevant immediately. Their effect may be felt by the application at some later stage. This is unlike synchronous systems where exceptions affect the immediate execution of the application and hence the exceptions need to be dealt with immediately.

The exception propagation model presented here loosely resembles the one developed for mobile agent systems [11,12]. A scope defines a logical space of roles through which agents coordinate with one another in [11]. Exceptions arising in inter-agent coordination are propagated to all the agents present in the scope. In [12] a specific agent is designated as the exception handling agent to which, all the exceptions arising in an agent's context, are propagated.

4.4   Discussion

Our exception propagation model does not propagate exceptions along the dynamic call chain. Instead, exceptions are propagated along the handlers that are statically associated [13] with different scopes. We use this approach for the following reasons:

- Exception propagation along the handlers that are statically associated with different scopes allows determination of the complete exception handling path for an exception at the activity design time.
- Restructuring of an activity, as part of the exception handling actions, is specified at the activity design time. Such restructuring actions are relevant only in the scope where an exception occurs and hence such actions should be performed in the exception handlers associated with that scope.
- Propagating exceptions arising in the role operation scope along dynamic call chain would mean propagating them directly to the role member who invoked the operation. This is not appropriate in our role-based framework

where users hold only as much privileges as are provided to them by the role abstraction. Users may not have sufficient privileges or mechanisms for handling exceptions that are directly propagated to them.

Concurrent exceptions may occur in an activity. We use a simple queuing model which ensures that all the concurrent exceptions are handled in some serial order. For example, multiple students may encounter failures while executing the *WriteExam* operation. All the corresponding *WriteExamFailedExceptions* are delivered to the exception interface queue of the *Student* role where they are handled separately for each *Student* role member. Our current exception handling model does not support exception resolution.

All the exceptions requiring participation of members from multiple roles are propagated through the activity scope. This is a conscious design decision. The set of roles that can participate in handling a particular exception can be changed easily in a design by altering the activity-level exception handler for that exception type.

5   Examples of Exception Handling in CSCW Applications

In this section we present modeling examples of two context-aware CSCW applications. For each of these, we identify different error conditions and show how these errors are programmatically addressed through the exception handling model presented in Section 4.

5.1   Case Study 1: Car Rental Activity

The purpose of this example is to demonstrate handling of exceptions arising due to external world events. Consider the car rental activity consisting of an *Agent* role and a *Renter* role. A renter can reserve a car to be picked up at some time. One of the error conditions in this workflow corresponds to the case where the car is involved in an accident or has encountered a mechanical failure. Such an error condition is handled as follows. An alternate car is searched and given to the renter, if available. This action may fail if no alternate car is available. In that case, the agent needs to be involved for providing alternate car by discussing with the renter.

The specification of this activity is shown in Figure 8. The renter can book a car through the *BookCar* operation (line 6). The *carBooking* object is used to describe the requirements of the car. It is declared to be of type *carRDD* which is a *RDD* of the car. A car satisfying the requirements specified in the RDD is discovered from the car database and assigned id of the renter (lines 4-8).

The activity-level exception handler is defined as a reaction *CarFailureReaction* (line 16). This reaction gets triggered when it receives *CarFailedEvent* which is an external event. The *carRDD* (not shown) specifies that this event is imported from a *car* resource. This event is generated when there is any failure associated with a car such as an accident.

```
1.  Activity CarRental
2.      Object carBooking RDD carRDD
3.      Object carDatabase
4.      Role Renter
5.          Bind carBooking With discover (category=<car-category>)
6.          Operation BookCar
7.              Precondition true
8.              Action carDatabase.reserveCar(carBooking, bookingId=thisUser)
9.      Role Agent
10.         Exception Interface
11.             When ExceptionObject Type BookedCarFailureException
12.                 Enable-For ANY
13.                 Operation HandleCarRelatedFailure
14.                     Precondition true
15.                         Action // discuss with the renter
16.     Reaction CarFailureReaction
17.         When ExceptionObject Type CarFailedEvent
18.         Precondition true
19.         Action
20.             carDatabase.provideAlternateCar(CarFailedEvent.getBookingId())
21.             OnException ExceptionObject Type
                AlternateCarNotAvailableException
22.                 Signal (new BookedCarFailureException) Target Agent
```

Fig. 8. Car Booking Activity Specification

The exception handling action consists of providing an alternate car to the renter (lines 17-20). This action may also encounter failure. In that case, *Booked-CarFailureException* is signaled to the *Agent* role (lines 21-22). This exception enables the *HandleCarRelatedFailure* operation provided as part of the exception interface of the *Agent* role. Any member of the *Agent* role can handle this event. This is specified through the qualifier *ANY* for the *Enable-For* clause (line 12).

5.2   Case Study 2: Museum Infodesk Activity

The purpose of this example is to demonstrate handling of exceptions related to resource discovery/binding and resource interaction.

Consider the museum infodesk activity where a *Visitor* role member discovers and binds to the audio commentary object of an artifact based on the user's location. We consider two representative error conditions that can arise in such context-based discovery and binding. First type of errors correspond to the case where audio commentary is not available in the user's desired language. This failure occurs because there is a mismatch between the resource specification and available resources. It can be handled by changing some aspects of resource requirements and retrying resource discovery. Alternate resource specifications may be specified at the activity design time. The museum infodesk activity can bind with an audio commentary resource in another language.

```
1.  Activity Museum Infodesk
2.     Object locService RDD Location-Service-Description
3.     Bind locService With direct(//LocationServiceURL)
4.     Object audioChannel RDD Audio-Channel-Description
5.     Object textInterface RDD Text-Interface-Description
6.       Role Visitor
7.          Bind audioChannel When LocationChangeEvent(thisUser)
8.          With discover(<location=locService.getLocation(thisUser),
9.          language="ENGLISH">)
10.         OnException ExceptionObject Type ResourceDiscoveryException
11.                 Action Bind audioChannel
12.                 With discover
13.                 (<location=locService.getLocation(thisUser),
14.                 language="SPANISH">)
15.         Operation ListenAudio
16.                 Precondition true
17.                 Action audioChannel.listenAudio()
18.       Exception Interface
19.          When ExceptionObject Type AudioServiceFailedException
20.          Enable-For Invoker
21.          Operation ReadText
22.                 Precondition true
23.                 Action Bind textInterface With Direct
24.                 (//textInterfaceURL)
25.                 textInterface.readText()
```

Fig. 9. Museum Infodesk Activity Specification

Second type of errors correspond to the case where audio commentary object encounters a failure while the user is listening to the commentary. As part of exception handling, the museum infodesk activity may bind to the textual commentary resource and present the appropriate interfaces to the role member.

The specification of this activity is shown in Figure 9. The activity consists of a *Visitor* role. The objects corresponding to audio interface (*audioChannel*) and text interface (*textInterface*) are declared in the activity scope. Binding of the *audioChannel* object is performed whenever an event indicating a change in the *Visitor* role member location is delivered (lines 7-9). A resource that matches *Audio-Channel-Description* for the new location and which provides commentary in English language is searched. This discovery and binding action fails if the audio commentary is not available in English. An exception, *ResourceDiscoveryException*, is raised to denote this failure. The recovery action consists of automatically retrying the discovery process by changing the requirement from English language to Spanish language (lines 10-14).

The *Visitor* role member is provided *ListenAudio* operation (line 15) through which the role member can listen the audio commentary. This operation encounters a *AudioServiceFailedException* if the audio object fails for some reason. No exception handler is attached to this operation. Hence this exception is propagated to the *Visitor* role's exception interface (line 18-25). An operation *ReadText* is defined (line 21) in the exception interface which gets enabled on the receipt of *AudioServiceFailedException*. This operation allows the role member to bind and use the textual interface of the artifact.

6   Related Work

Our work is related to research concerning exception handling in workflow systems [14,15,16,17,18]. In [14] a model for workflow failure handling that includes both forward error recovery based on exception handling and backward error recovery based on the notion of atomic workflow tasks is presented. Exceptions generated in a subtask are propagated to its encapsulating task and are handled there. Our exception handling model differs from this model along two aspects. First, exception handlers are directly associated with role operations, roles, and activities. Second, the model in [14] propagates exceptions along the task invocation hierarchy. Our exception propagation model allows exception propagation across roles. Such inter-role exception propagation is required because of the asynchronous and multi-user nature of CSCW applications.

A language for exception modeling based on event-condition-action (ECA) paradigm, independent of any particular workflow system, is presented in [15]. Exception rules are compiled from this language and integrated with the underlying workflow system. In contrast to this, exceptions and exception handlers are directly integrated with the activity specification in our approach.

A uniform framework for addressing data and process irregularities in workflow systems based on context-sensitive exception handling is presented in [16]. In their model, *unanticipated* exceptions are handled by human agents. Thus human assistance is enlisted as a last failure handling option. Human involvement in exception handling is an intrinsic part of our model. Exception interfaces are associated with roles and these interfaces are enabled only for those role members that need to participate in exception handling.

Failures arising in pervasive computing environments are considered in [19]. The failure categories presented in [19] correspond to *device failures, application failures, network failures,* and *service failures*. The resource interaction failure defined in this paper can effectively model application, network and service failures. We also consider errors arising due to failures in context-aware resource discovery and binding, obligation failures, and errors corresponding to the external world events that represent violations of application's assumptions about the external world. They propose failure handling through heart-beat based status monitoring, redundant provisioning of alternate services/applications, and restarting failed applications. In contrast to this, we present application level exception handling mechanisms for programmed error recovery in such applications.

The interference issues arising in software services deployed in home environments are considered in [20]. Interference can be considered as a form of failure occurring in concurrent resource access in home environments. A resource access model based on locking primitives for preventing such interferences is presented in [20]. Such concurrent resource access can be modeled as error conditions corresponding to the external world events that represent resource interference.

7 Conclusions

In this paper we have presented an exception handling model for programmed error recovery in context-aware CSCW applications. The salient feature of this model is the exception interface abstraction through which role members can participate in exception handling. The exception propagation model consists of propagating exceptions along the handlers that are statically determined based on the exception occurrence scope. Our earlier specification model [5] is extended to incorporate the exception handling model. Capabilities of the exception handling model are demonstrated through three different context-aware CSCW applications.

References

1. MIT: (Project Oxygen) Available at url http://oxygen.lcs.mit.edu/.
2. Satyanarayanan, M.: Pervasive Computing: Vision and Challenges. IEEE Personal Communications **8** (2001) 10–17
3. Schilit, B., Adams, N., Want, R.: Context-Aware Computing Applications. In: IEEE Workshop on Mobile Computing Systems and Applications, Santa Cruz, CA, US (1994) 85–90
4. Tripathi, A., Kulkarni, D., Ahmed, T.: A Specification Model for Context-Based Collaborative Applications. Elsevier Journal on Pervasive and Mobile Computing **1** (2005) 21 – 42
5. Tripathi, A., Ahmed, T., Kumar, R.: Specification of Secure Distributed Collaboration Systems. In: IEEE International Symposium on Autonomous Distributed Systems (ISADS). (2003) 149–156
6. Tripathi, A., Ahmed, T., Kumar, R., Jaman, S.: Design of a Policy-Driven Middleware for Secure Distributed Collaboration. In: Proceedings of the 22nd International Conference on Distributed Computing Systems (ICDCS). (2002) 393 – 400
7. RDF: Resource Description Framework (RDF) (1999) Available at url http://www.w3.org/RDF/.
8. WSDL: Web Services Description Language (WSDL) 1.1 (2001) Available at url http://www.w3.org/TR/wsdl.
9. Randell, B., Lee, P., Treleaven, P.C.: Reliability Issues in Computing System Design. ACM Comput. Surv. **10** (1978) 123–165
10. Miller, R., Tripathi, A.: The Guardian Model and Primitives for Exception Handling in Distributed Systems. IEEE Transactions on Software Engineering **30** (2004) 1008 – 1022
11. Iliasov, A., Romanovsky, A.: CAMA: Structured Coordination Space and Exception Propagation Mechanism for Mobile Agents. In: ECOOP Workshop on Exception Handling. (2005)

12. Tripathi, A., Miller, R.: Exception Handling in Agent-Oriented Systems. In: Advances in Exception Handling Techniques, LNCS 2022, Berlin Heidelberg, Springer-Verlag (January 2001) 128–146
13. Knudsen, J.L.: Better Exception-Handling in Block-Structured Systems. IEEE Software **4** (1987) 40 – 49
14. Hagen, C., Alonso, G.: Exception Handling in Workflow Management Systems. IEEE Transactions on Software Engineering **26** (2000) 943–958
15. Casati, F., Ceri, S., Paraboschi, S., Pozzi, G.: Specification and Implementation of Exceptions in Workflow Management Systems. ACM Trans. Database Syst. **24** (1999) 405–451
16. Murata, T., Borgida, A.: Handling of Irregularities in Human Centered Systems: A Unified Framework for Data and Processes. IEEE Transactions on Software Engineering **26** (2000) 959–977
17. Li, J., Mai, Y., Butler, G.: Implementing Exception Handling Policies for Workflow Management System. In: Software Engineering Conference, 2003. Tenth Asia-Pacific. (2003) 564 – 573
18. Chiu, D.K.W., Li, Q., Karlapalem, K.: Exception Handling with Workflow Evolution in ADOME-WFMS: a Taxonomy and Resolution techniques. SIGGROUP Bull. **20** (1999) 8–8
19. Chetan, S., Ranganathan, A., Campbell, R.: Towards Fault Tolerant Pervasive Computing. IEEE Technology and Society **24** (2005) 38 – 44
20. Kolberg, M., Magill, E., Wilson, M.: Compatibility Issues Between Services Supporting Networked Appliances. IEEE Communications Magazine **41** (2003) 136 – 147

Structured Coordination Spaces for Fault Tolerant Mobile Agents

Alexei Iliasov and Alexander Romanovsky

School of Computing Science, University of Newcastle
Newcastle upon Tyne, NE1 7RU, United Kingdom
alexei.iliasov@ncl.ac.uk, alexander.romanovsky@ncl.ac.uk

Abstract. Exception handling has proved to be the most general fault tolerance technique as it allows effective application-specific recovery. If exception handling is to make the programmer's work more productive and less error-prone, however, it requires adequate support from programming and execution environments. Scoping is a dynamic structuring technique which makes it easier for developers to deal with the complexity of system execution by narrowing down the context visible to individual system components.This study is specifically concerned with scoping that supports error confinement and allows system error recovery to be limited to the area confining the error. The approach we propose is designed to assist in rigorous development of structured multi-level fault tolerant agent systems.

Keywords: exception handling, scopes, exception propagation, middleware.

1 Introduction

Such intrinsic virtues of mobile agents as mobility, loose coupling and ability to deal with disconnections make them useful for structuring large-scale distributed systems. Yet agents have to face all kinds of communication media failures as well as those of software in their fellow agents and, of course, internal ones. System openness raises even more concerns, such as interoperability, security and trustworthiness. Mobile agent system failures can be grouped into the following categories:

1. *the hosting environment failing to deliver service*
2. *failures in one of the collaborating agents*
3. *internal agent failures*
4. *environment failures.*

Having discussed a similar classification in [1], in this paper we are introducing different categories of faults in order to focus on interoperability issues and to capture in a more practical and detailed way all possible kinds of environment failures.

Failures of the first category include all types of transient failures, such as disconnection, migration, spawning, inability to deliver messages, etc. Such failures may be caused by changes in the environment, e.g. because of component migration, and are better handled by application logic. It has often been said that recovery actions for such

C. Dony et al. (Eds.):Exception Handling, LNCS 4119, pp. 181–199, 2006.

situations must be developed at the initial stages of agent design. And, unlike traditional software, mobile agents have, thanks to mobility and code migration, a broad range of recovery possibilities.

The second category consists of very interesting failures. One of the appealing features of mobile agents is dynamic composition. Agents do not have to know what other agents they will cooperate with, and this allows extreme flexibility in agent system design. In open systems, where agents discover their partners dynamically and where each agent has its own interest in cooperation, there must be some mechanism to encourage communication among matching agents and prevent it among incompatible ones. In addition to the means of communication among agents, we also need those for inter-agent exception propagation and cooperative exception handling. We believe that this is essential to disciplined and fault-tolerant composition of mobile agent systems.

The abnormal situations of the third category are detected inside an agent. Most traditional recovery techniques developed for sequential programming are applicable in this case. If an agent fails to recover from a failure individually, then there is a need for cooperative exception handling by all the involved agents.

The last category of failures corresponds to exceptional situations in the environment that are beyond the control of a mobile agent. Examples of these are failures of hardware components, administrative restrictions, software bugs in the underlying middleware and in the core components of the environment.

All these are typical of the mobile agent software domain as mobile agents cannot anticipate or avoid all of them. In this paper we focus on the second category of failures to propose two fault tolerance solutions. The first one is an exception handling technique for coordination space-based mobile agents. The second solution is a scoping mechanism for mobile coordination spaces. In our approach we combine these two solutions in one fault tolerance development method.

Exception handling has proved [2] to be the most general fault tolerance technique as it allows effective application-specific recovery. If exception handling is to make the programmer's work more productive and less error-prone, however, it requires adequate support from the programming and execution environments. Scoping is a dynamic structuring technique which makes it easier for developers to deal with the complexity of system execution by narrowing down the context visible for individual system components. In this work we are specifically concerned with scoping that supports error confinement and allows error recovery to be limited to the area surrounding the error.

2   Related Work

MobileSpaces [3] is a middleware with a hierarchical organisation of agents. The notion of agent nesting and the approach proposed to migration is similar to those used in the Ambient Calculus [4] algebra. An agent in MobileSpaces communicates only with its parents or descendants (nested agents). Whole branches of the agent tree migrate, changing their parent nodes. This approach presents quite a flexible form of isolation.

Agent communication in Mole [5] is based on the event model ensuring agent anonymity. Using the event service synchronised objects are introduced as the main means for propagating events among agents and for agent synchronisation. Synchronisation objects are active components that provide synchronisation of the entire application or its part. Typed and untyped event channels are implemented in Mole by using synchronisation objects. These channels are be created at run-time and the creating agent decides whom pass the channel reference. Although these features encourage closer cooperation among several agents they are not designed as an isolation mechanism supporting nested system structuring.

Paper [6] discusses an extension of the publish/subscribe scheme with the scope concept. Scopes are nested and they regulate event propagation and publishing. Agents create, join and leave scopes dynamically. The purpose of scopes in this model is to limit visibility of published events to a subset of agents from the same tree of scopes (all scopes in the system form a forest). Another important implication of the scope notion is the introduction of the administrator role. Administrator is a utility agent that controls event flow inside a scope and across its boundaries according to the rules statically defined for the scope.

A different approach is taken in the ActorSpace system [7,8], where the communication space is structured using an abstract agent container called ActorSpace. Special entities called managers may control visibility of agents and ActorSpaces with respect to some other ActorSpaces. Each agent has a set of patterns describing its interests. There are three basic ways of sending a message: using a pattern which non-deterministically describes a destination agent, using a unique agent name and using a pattern-based broadcast which delivers messages to all the agents satisfying the specified pattern. In addition it possible to create very complex visibility structures by placing a reference to an ActorSpace in another ActorSpace.

Coordination with Scopes [9] discusses a scoping mechanism developed for coordination-based systems built in the way similar to ActorSpace. However the scope here is not a container but a viewpoint of an agent on otherwise flat tuple space. The most interesting aspect is possibility of dynamically create new scopes by using several predefined operations on already known scopes forming a kind of scope algebra. In addition to the obvious joining and nesting operations, new scopes can calculated through intersection and subtraction. This gives extreme flexibility in structuring tuple space and adapting it to an agent needs. A dedicated scope initially known to all agent is used to exchange scope names.

3   CAMA Scoping Mechanism

In this work we deal with distributed applications consisting of the mobile software components called agents. These components are developed independently and pursue their own goals during execution. To achieve these goals they typically need to move, which can be done either by logical migration of the component or by physical movement of the device on which the component is located, and to cooperate with other agents, for example, to use their services or resources provided by them.

We are specifically focusing on the coordination mobile environments, which have become very popular in developing mobile agent applications. All these environments rely on the Linda approach to coordination of distributed processes [10]. Linda provides a set of language-independent coordination primitives that can be used for communication between and coordination of several independent pieces of software. Thanks to its language neutrality, Linda is quite popular, and its coordination primitives have been implemented in many programming languages. First used for parallel programming, Linda later became the core component of many mobile software systems because it fits in nicely with the main characteristics of mobile systems: openness, dynamicity and loose coordination. Linda coordination primitives allow processes to put *tuples* in a tuple space shared by these processes, get them out and test for them. A tuple is a vector of typed data values, some of which can be empty, in which case they match any value of a given type. Certain operations, like *get* (or in) and *test* (or inp), can be blocking. This provides effective inter-process coordination and allows other kinds of coordination primitives, like semaphores or mutexes, to be simulated in a straightforward way.

3.1 The CAMA Model

The CAMA (context-aware mobile agents) is a middleware for supporting rapid development of agent systems. It uses the Linda paradigm for agent coordination. A CAMA system consists of a set of *locations*. A location can be associated with a particular physical location (such as lecture theatre, warehouse or meeting room). Location is the core part of the system as it provides means of agent communication and coordination. *Agents* are the active entities of the system.

Agents communicate through a special construct of coordination space called *scope*, which we discuss in details in the next section. Two agents can cooperate only if they are participating in the same scope. A location can have certain restrictions on the types of the scopes it supports.

Each agent is executed on its own *platform*. Platform provides an execution environment and an interface to the location middleware. Examples of platforms are smartphones, PDAs and laptops.

Agents represent the basic structuring unit of a CAMA application. To deal with various functionalities provided by the individual agent, CAMA introduces agent role as a finer unit of code structuring. A role is a structuring unit of an agent, and being an important part of the scoping mechanism, it allows dynamic composition of multi-agent applications and ensures agent interoperability and isolation.

A set of agents playing different roles can dynamically instantiate a multi-agent application. A simple example is a client-server model where a distributed application is constructed when agents playing two roles meet and collaborate. An agent can have several roles and use them in different scopes. A server agent can provide the same service in many similar scopes. In addition it can also implement a client role and act as a client in some other scopes. For example in a flea market application there can be roles of seller and buyer. It is possible for a single agent to combine both roles. When a predefined number of sellers and uyer meet in a location they can instantiate a flea market scope and thus start cooperation within this multi-agent application.

CAMA agents can logically and physically migrate from a location to a location. Migration from a platform to a platform is also possible using logical mobility.

Figure 1 demonstrates the relationship among the introduced abstractions.

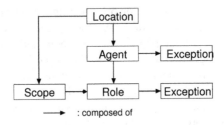

Fig. 1. CAMA abstractions relationship

In the rest of the paper we use term *scope* to refer to a run-time scope in the coordination space. More details on building formal specification of roles using the B Method and general description of the CAMA system can be found in [11].

3.2 Scoping Mechanism

The ultimate aim of our work is to support behaviour and information hiding in the ways that ensure fault tolerance during rigorous development of complex agent systems. After analysing a number of existing approaches to introducing structuring of mobile agents (see Section 2) we have came to the conclusion that the best way to do it to meet our aim is by *structuring agent activity* (dynamic behaviour). This should allow us to introduce communication structuring with a clean semantics and a number of other benefits discussed below.

By structuring activity we mean arranging agents in groups according to agent intentions and *afterwards* configuring their communication to meet to the requirements of these groups. Reconfigurations happen automatically thus allowing agents (and developers) to solely focus on collaboration with other agents participating in the group. The distinctive features of this approach are outlined below:

– *high-level abstraction of communication structuring;*
– *impossibility to create incorrect, malfunctioning or cyclic structures;*
– *strong relationship with interoperability and exception handling;*
– *simple semantics facilitating formal development.*

In a very basic view scope is a dynamic data container. It provides an *isolated* coordination space for *compatible* agents by restricting visibility of tuples contained in a scope to the participants of the scope. The concept of agent compatibility is based on the concepts of role and scope. A set of agents is compatible if there is a composition of their roles that forms an instance of an abstract scope model.

Agents may issue a request for a scope creation and, at some point, when all the precondition are satisfied, the scope is atomically instantiated by the hosting location. A scope has a number of attributes divided into categories of scope *requirements* and scope *states*. Scope requirements essentially define type of a scope, or, in other words, the kind of activity supported by the scope (see Figure 2). Scope requirements are derived from a formal model of a scope activity and together with the agent roles form an instance of the abstract scope model. State attributes characterise a unique scope instance.

Requirements	State
- *list of roles*	- *currently enrolled roles*
- *restriction on roles*	- *owner*
	- *name*

Fig. 2. Scope attributes

In addition to these attributes, the scope contains *data* (*tuples*), as well as *subscopes* defining the *nested activities* that may happen inside it.

Restrictions on roles dictate how many agents can play any given role of a scope. Requirements are defined by the two numbers - the minimum required number of agents for a given role and the maximum allowed number of agents for a given role. A scope state tracks the number of currently taken roles and determines whether the scope can be used for agent collaboration or not.

R_1	R_1^{min}	R_1^{max}
R_2	R_2^{min}	R_2^{max}
...		
R_k	R_k^{min}	R_k^{max}

$R_i^{min} \leq N_{R_i} \leq R_i^{max}$	(taken roles)
n	(scope name)
A	(owner)

Fig. 3. Scope requirements (left). Scope state (right)

In addition to obvious $R_i^{min} \leq R_i^{max}$ we also require that $R_i^{max} > 0$.

There are three important states of a scope. Their summary is given on Table 4. A scope in the *pending* state does not allow agents to communicate because there are some essential roles missing. When all the required roles are taken the scope becomes *expanding* or *closed*. In the expanding state a scope supports communication among agents while still allowing other agents to join the scope. In the closed state there are no free roles and no additional agent may join the scope.

Some scope configurations present interesting cases. A scope with zero required number of agents for all the roles is called *blackboard*. It exists even without any participating agents and all the contained data are persistent. With this scope the agents do not have to wait for any other agents to communicate, they may put some information into

State name	Definition
pending	$\exists r \cdot (r \in R \wedge N_r < r^{min})$
expanding	$\forall r \cdot (r \in R \Rightarrow N_r \geq r^{min}) \wedge \exists r \cdot (r \in R \wedge N_r < r^{max})$
closed	$\forall r \cdot (r \in R \Rightarrow N_r = r^{max})$

Fig. 4. Three important states of a scope

Scope class	Definition
blackboard	$\forall r \cdot (r \in R \wedge r^{min} = 0)$
container	$card(R) = 1 \wedge (r \in R \wedge r^{min} = r^{max} = 1)$
bag	$card(R) = 1 \wedge (r \in R \wedge r^{min} = 0 \wedge r^{max} = 1)$
unrestricted	$\exists r \cdot (r \in R \Rightarrow r^{max} = \infty)$

Fig. 5. Some interesting classes of scopes

the blackboard scope and leave. Note, that there is an important difference between a blackboard scope and a generic tuple space. For a blackboard scope only agents implementing the roles specified by the blackboard requirements may enter and put or read any data whilst in a tuple space anyone may always put and read any tuples. *Container* is a scope with a single role for which only single agent is allowed and required. This is an important case since such kind of a scope acts as a private and protected data container of an agent. A variant of container scope that survives change of owners without losing all the contents is called *bag*. Bags are used to privately pass some bulk data between two agents.

An *unrestricted* scope permits an unlimited number of agents for one or more of its roles. It is used, for example, for the a client-server communication when there are no restrictions on number of clients.

All system scopes form a tree. Due to the specifics of our approach the tree is mostly shallow and wide since the depth is determined by the nesting level of actions that is usually not large. All the high-level scopes are united by the dedicated scope λ. Any scopes other than λ are subscopes of λ. Scope λ has two predefined roles: role λ_A of agent requesting services from location and and role λ_L of location. Functionality of role λ_A is arbitrary and defined by agent developers. However there is a fixed set of operations called λ_L^0 that must be included into implementation of each λ_L. λ_L^0 operations are described below.

Since the CAMA system allows an agent to communicate in several locations at the same time we use a location name when referring to a scope. Moreover the scope names have to be unique only inside the containing scope. Thus the full name of a scope includes the names of all the containing scopes. We are omitting name of λ scope for convenience of notation. Sometimes we have to explicitly state in what location a scope is contained and what are its parents (containing scopes). A unique scope name starts with the name of a location, followed by the outer-most parent scope then the next parent and so on, ending with the name of the scope in question.

λ_L^0 operations:

- engage(id) - issue a new location-wide unique and unforgeable name for agent id. This name as agent identifier in all other role operations.
- disengage(a) - issued name a becomes invalid.
- create(a, n, R)@s (n $\not\subseteq$ 1.s) - creates a new sub-scope of scope s with the name n and given scope requirements R. The created scope becomes a private scope of agent n.

- destroy(a, n)@l.s (n ∈ l.s ∧ a *is owner of* l.s.n) - destroys sub-scope with the name n contained in the scope s. This operation always succeeds if the requesting agent is the owner of the scope. If the scope is not in the pending state then all the scope participants receive EDestroy exception as the notification of the scope closure. This procedure is executed recursively for all the subscopes contained in the scope.

- join(a, n, r)@s (n ∈ l.s ∧ r ∈ n ∧ n *is pending or expanding*) - adds agent a into scope n contained in l.s with roles r. Succeeds if scope l.s.n exists and it is possible to take the specified roles in the scope. This operation may cause state change of the scope.

- leave(a, n, r)@s (a *is in* l.s.n *with role(s)* r) - removes agent roles r from scope l.s.n. The calling agent must be already participating in the scope. This operation may also change the state of the scope.

- put(a, n)@s: advertises scope n contained in scope s thus making it a public scope. A public scope is visible and accessible by other agents. contained in scope l.s and supporting role(s) r.

- get(a, r)@s: enquires names of the scopes contained in scope l.s and supporting role(s) r.

- handshake(a, t)@s: allows agents to safely exchange their names.

3.3 Naming

This section clarifies how names of various resources are used and passed between agents. One essential requirement our approach meets is that a scope name is known to an agent only if the agent has joined the parent scope. Passing the scope name in a message may violate this rule so we have to take special care of the names used by agents. However, we still allow agents to learn names of other agents, scopes, locations and traps (discussed further below) through communication with other agents. To make it impossible for an agent to use incorrect names and pass names to third parties without permission we do not use any absolute names or references. Instead the naming mechanism is based on *tickets* issued by locations. Whenever an agent needs to have a name for some resource (e.g. a new scope created by its request) a location generates a new structure consisting of the agent name and the resource reference. This structure is associated with a random ticket number which is passed to the agent. The location issuing a ticket is the only entity that is able to translate ticket numbers into resource references. Location has the full control over name passing and prevents issuing and usage of incorrect names. Note that a legitimately owned name may become invalid if a resource is destroyed or the agent no longer has rights to access it. Assuming that agent names are unforgeable (we need some additional scheme to ensure agent names validity) tickets numbers may be exposed without any risk for the owner. When an agent wants to share or pass a resource to another agent it requests the location to issue additional ticket for another agent. The major advantage of this scheme is that the agent requesting a new ticket still has, being the owner of the ticket, the full control over the resource access through this new ticket. At any moment it can request the location to invalidate the ticket and it has the immediate effect on the ticket user. In addition an owner of a resource may add other agents to the list of owners and remove itself from the list. When an agent becomes a resource owner it controls resource usage and may issue new tickets.

This procedure cannot be used to exchange agent names since to do that agents would have to already know names of each other. This is why we introduce the handshake operation implementing secure and atomic exchange of names within a group of agents. Each agent receives names of all its peers made specifically for the agent. Each name is a ticket number usable only by the agent and referring to a name of another agent. The second argument of the handshake operation is the list of tuples received from the fellow agents within one scope. The location support knows how to identify agents from tuples they produce (see [12]). The handshake operation must be symmetrically executed by all the agents with the same list of agents as an argument (although tuples in the list may be different for each agent). The operation fails for *all* agents if there is at least one agent not executing the handshake or executing it with a different set of agents. Unsuccessful handshakes are unblocked after a timeout defined by the location.

4 Exception Propagation Via Coordination Space

Previously we have developed a mechanism for propagating exceptions among independent, anonymous and asynchronously-communicating agents [12]. In this section we give only a brief overview of the work to allow us to discuss the problems of exception propagation between scopes. The detailed discussion of the mechanism and its experimental implementation for the Lime mobile agents system [13] can be found in [12].

4.1 Motivation

Exception handling in CAMA introduces fast and effective application recovery by supporting a flexible choice of the handling scope and of the exception propagation directions. The mechanism of the exception propagation is complementary to the application-level exception handling. All the recovery actions are implemented by application-specific handlers attached to the agents involved in handling. The ultimate task of the propagation mechanism is to transfer exceptions between agents in a reliable and secure way. However the enormous freedom of agent behaviour in agent-based systems does not allow any guarantees of reliable exception propagation to be given in a general case. To this end we attempt to identify all the situations when exceptions may be lost or not delivered within a predictable time period. This is why if an application requires cooperative exception handling at certain moments then for that time, agents behaviour must be constrained in some way at the application level to prevent any unexpected migrations or disconnections.

The following example illustrates how the CAMA exception propagation can be used for handling exceptions in multi-agent applications.

Two agents, Agent 1 and Agent 2, communicate through a tuple space. Agent 1 issues two requests and then waits for a result. The second agent reads requests one by one and does some calculations on each. In case an exception happens in the second agent (e.g. because of wrong request data) the first agent must be notified of the situation so it does not continue with useless calculations or even get stuck on the in() operation. One may think of an Agent 2 programmed so that it puts a special tuple whenever an

```
out(req₁);                      t₁ = in(req₁*);
e₁ = inp(err₁*);                if (t₁ is invalid) { out(err₁); stop; }
if (e₁ not null) { recover }    ...
out(req2);                      t₂ = in(req₂*);
e₂ = inp(err₂*);                if (t₂ is invalid) { out(err₂); stop; }
if (e₂ not null) { recover }    ...
r = in(res*);                   out(res);
```

Fig. 6. Coordination without a support for an exception propagation mechanism

```
try {                           try {
  out(req₁);                      t = in(req₁*);
  ...                             ...
  out(req₂);                      t = in(req₂*)
  r = in(res*);                   out(res);
} catch(E1 e) { recover }       } catch(E2 e) { raise(t, E1); }
```

Fig. 7. Coordination supported by the exception propagation mechanism

it detects a problem (see Figure 6, where $tuple*$ stands for a template matching a tuple $tuple$). Then the first agent at some moment should test for such tuple and do appropriate recovery. This solution is not only inelegant but also wrong. With asynchronous communication it turns out that there is no single proper place for checking for an exception presence. Agent 2 is slow with processing the first request and when it writes an exception tuple for it the first agent might has already produced the second request and expects a different type of exception. Or it might be it has already started executing operation in() and gets deadlocked since a result tuple from the second agent never arrives. Testing for abnormal situations, already being a poor technique for sequential programs, is inapplicable in asynchronous systems. The exception propagation mechanism gracefully solves the problem of exception discovery and also separates recovery code from normal behaviour. The main idea follows the general principle of exception handling - providing recursively nested recovery blocks.

Figure 7 shows how agents from the example above are represented using the CAMA exception propagation. The source code is more readable and now it really does what it is supposed to do.

4.2   Mechanism

There are three basic operations that agents can use to receive and send inter-agent exceptions. This functionality is complementary the functionality of the application-level exception handling mechanism.

raise	wait	check

The first operation, raise, propagates an exception to an agent or a scope. The important requirement is that the sending agent prior to raising an exception must receive a message from the destination agent and they both must be in the same scope. There are two variants of the operation:

- `raise(m, e)` - throws exception e as a reaction to message m. The message is used to trace the producer and to deliver it the exception. The operation fails if the destination agent has already left the scope in which the message was produced.
- `raise(s, e)` - throws exception e to all the participants of the scope s.

The crucial requirement to the propagation mechanism is to preserve all the essential properties of agent systems such as agents anonymity, dynamicity and openness. The exception propagation mechanism does not violate the agent anonymity since we prevent disclosure of agent names at any stage of the propagation process. Note that the `raise` operation does not deal with agent names. Moreover we guarantee that our propagation method cannot be used to learn names of other agents.

Also the mechanism itself does not introduce any limitations on agent activities. Though agents dynamicity and reliability of exception propagation are conflicting we believe that it is the developers who must take the final decision to favour either of them. Notion of openness is the key for building large-scale agent systems. Proper exception handling has proved to be crucial for proper component composition. It is even more so for mobile agent systems where composition is dynamic and parts of the system are developed independently. We are working now on introducing a formal step-wise development procedure which supports composition of large scale agents handling exceptions, but this work is outside of the scope of this paper.

Two other operations, `check` and `wait` are used to explicitly poll and wait for inter-agent exceptions:

- `check` - checks for pending exceptions and throws the oldest. Does not do anything if there are no exceptions for the agent.
- `wait` - waits until any inter-agent exception appears for the agent and raises it in the same way as the previous operation.

The exception handling mechanism alters semantics of blocking Linda operations so that they unblock whenever an exception appears for a n agent. They return with the exception instead of a result and the exception is thrown at the point of the operation call using a native exceptions mechanism.

4.3 Traps

The propagation procedure expressed only with the primitives above would be too restrictive and inflexible for the mobile agent systems. To control the propagation process in a way that accounts for various agent behaviour scenarios we introduce a notion of *trap*. A trap is a set of rules created by agents to control exception propagation. Traps exist independently of the creating agent as they are stored and manipulated by a location that provides the coordination space. A trap is essentially a list of rules that choose a reaction for a coordination space exception. It is represented as a CASE construct where rules are associated with exceptions (see Figure 8). Exception matching and comparison are non-trivial issues which are typically dictated by the language of choice.

A trap is enabled when there is an incoming message for the agent created the trap. Agent may have several traps and traps are automatically organised into an hierarchical structure. When an exception appears, the most recently added trap is activated. If the

```
case e is
    when E₁ => op₁
    when E₂ => op₂
    ...
    when Eₙ => opₙ
    when others => abort
endcase
```

Fig. 8. Trap is a CASE-style construct

trap fails to find a matching rule for the exception, the exception is propagated to the second most-recent trap and so on. Agents may dynamically create, add and remove traps. The following operations are used to express trap structure:

- deliver - delivers the exception to the destination agent. The exception is stored until the destination agent is ready to react to it or the containing scope is destroyed;
- relay(t) - propagates the exception to a trap t which may be a trap of another agent. Name of a trap is learnt only through negotiations with the trap owner. Owner of the trap becomes the destination the propagated exception;
- abort - leaves the current trap and transfers control to the next trap in the hierarchy.
- if *(condition)* then *ac* - action *ac* is applied conditionally;
- . *(concatenation)* - forms a new action by concatenation of two other actions.

The deliver operation is introduced to deal with agent migration and connectivity fluctuations. It introduces some level of asynchrony and makes the whole exception propagation scheme more suitable to the asynchronous communication style of coordination space. The relay operation is a tool for building linked trap structures supporting a disciplined cooperative exception handling. Discussions and examples related to this approach can be found in [12]. Preconditions for the if operation are formed from the following primitives:

- local - holds if the owner of the trap is joined to the current scope
- local(a) - holds if agent a is joined to the current scope
- tuple(t) - holds if there is a tuple matching template t
- ¬, ∨, ∧ - logical operations that are used on the predicates above

Rule preconditions and concatenation provide an expressive mechanism that may create traps for many interesting and useful scenarios. For example, a rule in a trap could make multiple deliveries to involve several agents, or, depending on the locality of the trap owner, another agent or even a trap in a different location.

5   Exception Propagation Through Scope Boundaries

The exception propagation mechanism described above works well within the boundaries of a scope. However in many cases a scope corresponds not to a completely isolated activity but rather forms a part of a more general activity of the containing scope.

In such a case a failure of a scope may disrupt activity of the containing scope and require agents of the containing scope to execute some recovery actions. Our intention is to introduce exception propagation outside of scope boundaries in such a way that it smoothly integrates with the concepts of the scoping and exception propagation mechanisms discussed above.

It is very natural to try to take the advantage of the scope nesting mechanism and build a scope-based exception recovery. However the specifics of the mobile agents and the scoping mechanism introduce a number of challenges and make the design of such mechanism far from trivial. We start by discussing problems that we have identified and briefly present several possible solutions, after that we discuss the one we have found to be the most applicable for our system.

5.1 Background

Exception propagation in agent systems is very much different from propagation in sequential, parallel or conventional distributed systems.

In the agent systems there is no centralised control. Though we introduce cooperative recovery, agents are still *autonomous*. They cannot be orchestrated in cooperative recovery by a single manager. Instead they must exclusively rely on communication to coordinate their recovery.

In the general case, agents are *multi-threaded*. One consequence of this is that they can participate in several scopes at the same time, possibly with different roles and in different locations. Recovery in one of the scopes might lead to recovery in other scopes.

An agent may work at the same time in a containing and a *nested* scope. This has an impact on recovery of the scopes and the agent. Unrecoverable failure of a contained scope must abort all the nested scopes.

A number of unrelated scopes, may be from different locations, can be *linked by a state* of an agent which works in these scopes. An error in one of them might affect the execution of the agent in another scope. Thus failure in one of the scopes may require recovery in some other scopes.

In the general case, an activity of a subscope in CAMA is not linked by any construct to the activity of the containing scope. Subscope is an isolated tuplespace visible to the participants of the containing scope. A scope and a subscope activities are concurrent and there is no simple way to initiate a recovery should a contained scope fail.

Scopes and agents can be related to each other in different ways. In addition to the hierarchy of scopes, introduced by the scoping mechanism, there is a relationship introduced by agents participating in several scopes. An agent communicating with other agents in a scope can also indirectly communicate with agents in other scopes.

One simple solution is to propagate an exception through an hierarchy of scopes. That is, whenever a nested scope fails its container automatically gets involved into recovery. Which can be achieved by placing an exception in the container. Agents working in the containing scope must interrupt their current activity and switch to recovery. The major problem of this approach is absence of the context associated with an exception at the moment of recovery. Hence agents must be ready to recovery from a subscope exception at any moment which typically means that the recovery needs to be very general.

We can attempt to solve the problem of context with the traps structure. Instead of placing an exception in a containing scope agents can use a tree of traps which propagates an exception through scopes in a disciplined manner. Through a negotiation, agents exchange trap names and link them in a common trap tree structure. The root of the tree is initially created by one of the agents and then the tree is configured by all the scope participants. An exception indicating a scope failure is propagated through a chain of traps and, if it is an unrecoverable one, it reaches the root of the tree. This leads to the termination of the scope. To delegate recovery to the containing scope the trap tree is linked to a branch of a similar tree of the containing scope. This gives more control over propagation of exceptions in the contained scope. For instance, a trap tree can configured to involve only some of the agents or it can be mapped into a different exception.

5.2 Internal Propagation

The solution we propose is based on propagation of exceptions through a state of an agent. This approach is both simple and general. It does not require any centralised control or a global agreement (which is needed for the common trap tree), is neutral to multi-threading and covers all the propagation scenarios. One of its most attractive features is that in spite of being expressive it is simple and does no require any support from the middleware.

Taking into account the fact that each agent participating in a nested scope is also present (though does not necessarily active) in the containing scope it is always possible to propagate exceptions through an agent internal state. When an agent fails in a nested scope the participants attempt a cooperative recovery. If it is unsuccessful the scope is closed and each scope participant attempts to recovery individually from this failure. Some agents might succeed and others not. Those who failed to recover involve their other roles in the recovery. Consequently this leads to a new exception thrown in some other scope. In case when agent works only in one location and in a single scope and its subscopes this recovery process is similar to the solutions discussed above. However there are important differences. Agent may map an exception in a different one during its internal recovery. The roles involved into recovery are selected arbitrary by an agent. Thus an agent may choose to not involve a containing scope into recovery, though a failed scope was a subscope. Another interesting problem is that exception from the same failure (failure of a subscope) may appear at different moments, in true asynchronous fashion of the agent systems. We are going to address this problem with the exception resolution technique where several concurrent exceptions are mapped into a single one which is used for the recovery process.

One of the motivation for using this style of recovery is its ability to involve a number of otherwise independent scopes into a recovery process. By independent we mean scopes that are not nested into each other and may be even hosted on different locations. The idea of recovery involving independent scopes might seem counterintuitive at first since the role of scopes is to isolate different activities of agents. However a general case of a multi-agent application is a number of scopes linked by agents working in these scopes. Such scopes does not have to be nested thus there is a new kind of relation between scopes, which is purely dynamic. An example of such application is an agent selling in scope sell on location l_1 and buying in scope buy on location l_2. Failure of sell may force the agent to initiate recovery at scope buy. The logic controlling propagation is contained in agents. Each agent has its own rules for exception propagation according to its activities in different scopes. The mechanism of the propagation is quite simple. When a role fails to recover in a scope it informs some other roles of the agent about a failure. Since roles are developed independently (they are parts of different multi-agent applications) an exception must be mapped into one of the predefined common exceptions. In the shared state of the agent there is a function which for any given failed role returns a set of roles which must be involved into a recovery. Combined with the exception mapping these process can be expressed as follows. A role r throwing exception e forces roles r_m to recover from exception e_m where

$$map : E \times R \rightarrow E_s \quad route : R \rightarrow \mathcal{P}(R)$$

$$e_m := map(r, e) \quad r_m := route(r)$$

To implementation the discussed propagation mechanism it is enough to define two exception mapping functions map and $route$. Functions map must be defined for all the roles and all the exceptions which can be thrown by each agent role. It can be interpreted as a number of functions each attached to its corresponding role. Function $route$ expresses relationship between roles of an agent. In case when agent roles are truly independent and failure of any role can be ignored by the rest, $route$ maps each role into an empty set.

6 Implementation

The CAMA middleware has asymmetric design. Its functionality is distributed over two unequal parts - server and client. The server part provides coordination, the scoping mechanism, exception handling and a number of other features. The client part offers an adaptation layer for an access to the server part of the middleware. A client is designed specifically for a given combination of a platform and programming language.

Agent connects to a location by initiating a a TCP connection on a fixed port to the host running the location middleware. If the client platform supports multi-threaded agents the second connection is initiated on the same port (Figure 9). The role of the second channel is to support several concurrent activities of an agent in the location. It allows an agent issuing a potentially blocking request, like in to use communication primitives in other threads. The design is also dictated by the lack of robust support for asynchronous input-output in many programming languages [1].

The second channel is not needed if the agent does not uses concurrent requests to a location. This simplifies the client part for environments which does not support multi-threading.

There are two modes of connection to a location - normal connection and reconnection. Agent uses normal connection mode when it first arrives to a location. Reconnection allows an agent to recover from the connectivity failures or to suspend an activity and return to it later. One notable use of this feature is using a location as a permanent storage service.

---

[1] Java asynchronous input-output package (java.nio) is not supported by the major JVM implementations for mobile platforms.

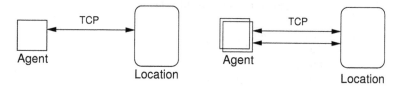

Fig. 9. Single and double channel configurations

6.1 CAMA Protocol

The client and server parts of the CAMA middleware talk to each other using a well-defined protocol. Being an abstract model of the client-server, this protocol is the core of CAMA. This facilitates development of the server and client parts for different platforms. It is also possible to combine roles of the server and the client in a single implementation. This would result in a symmetric middleware suitable for peer-to-peer or MANET networks.

The protocol has three layers.

The First Layer. This layer implements locations discovery mechanism, basic handshaking, reconnection and heartbeating. The discovery mechanism is used by agents to get names of locations to which they are able to connect. An agent sends a broadcast packet announcing its name. A location replies with its name.

Before a client and a location start communication they check each other versions in order to determine if they are compatible. We plan to investigate possibility of automated update of the client middleware. There are a number of security and compatibility issues to be researched.

Heartbeating is supported on the double-channel configuration only. Implementation of heartbeating in non-multitasking environments is rather difficult and requires elaborate asynchronous input-output, that, as mentioned above, is often missing. Before the heartbeating protocol is initiated, a client and server declare their requirements to the hearbeating. A client sends value t_c (see Figure 10) which is the maximum interval permitted for location heartbeats. Symmetrically, a location sends t_s which the maximum interval between the client heartbeats.

Reconnection allows an agent to reuse its old name and restore the contents of the scopes that it previously created on the location. Location identifies an agent using a 128-bit value issued during a previous connection. The agent must keep this value while disconnected.

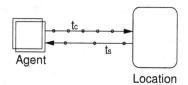

Fig. 10. Heartbeating protocol

Table 1. CAMA second-level protocol

operation code	format	blocking
IN	**f p**	+
INN	**f p**	+
INA	**f p**	+
OUT	**t**	-
OUTA	**l**	-
CREATE	**S d**	-
DESTROY		-
JOIN	**n S**	+
LEAVE		-
GET	**S t**	-
PUT	**s**	-
SWITCH	**s**	-
DISENG		-
COMMAND	**S**	-
TYPE	**S**	-
CMD	**?**	-
server reply operations		
OUT	**a t**	
OUTA	**a l**	
DONE		
ERROR	**I**	
JOIN	**I**	
CREATE	**n**	
COMMAND	**I**	
TYPE	**I**	

notation	description	size, bytes
B	signed integer	1
W	signed integer	2
I	signed integer	4
F	float	4
S	string	variable
B	binary	variable
C	custom	variable
f	flags, {remove, wait}	1
p	template	variable
a	public agent id	4
t	tuple	variable
l	tuple list	variable
s	scope handler	4
n	scope name	variable

CAMA *command format*			
opcode(5)	fmod(1)	fbor(1)	unused(1)

The Second Layer. The second level of the protocol provides a set of operations implementing coordination between agents and the scoping mechanism. Many operations of this layer directly correspond to the methods in the API of the client part of the middleware. An operation is made of an operation code and a number of arguments. The set of arguments is fixed for each operation. The summary of the operations along with the argument types is given in Table 1. All the input operations are potentially blocking. The JOIN operation blocks if scope liveness requirements are not satisfied at the moment.

Server replies by passing an operation result to a client in a form of another operation. Any flavour of IN results in OUT operation from a server, scope creation is answered with the CREATE and so on. If operation has a delayed result, such as **in** not matching any tuple, it is considered to be a blocking one. In the single channel configuration the client must be suspended until result is available. In the double channel mode the delayed result is sent over the second channel.

Operations COMMAND, TYPE and CMD are a gateway to the custom extension of the middleware. Such extensions form the third level of the CAMA protocol.

The Third Layer. The middleware functionality is extended through *plugins*. A plugin is a dynamically loadable code which exports some functionality. For the CAMA middleware they are written in C or Java languages. Extensibility of CAMA is based on *hooks*. A hook is a special mechanism which invokes a routine before or after execution of a certain operation. Plugins can dynamically configure hooks to define new operations or change behaviour of the existing ones. A routine associated with a hook receives all the arguments of the invoked operation and the context associated with the operation invocation. It analyses the arguments and either takes the responsibility for the command execution or passes control to the next hook or to a built-in operation implementation.

Plugins define new operations to be used by agents. They do this by setting a hook for the COMMAND and CMD operations. Operation COMMAND allows an agent to get a code for a particular operation which is used later with CMD. This has two purposes. The first is to save on network traffic by using efficient representation of a command name. The second is to add flexibility to this binding procedure. It could happen that an agent can get a similar service with another operation. If a particular COMMAND call fails, an agent can retry with another name.

One of the important CAMA plugins provides a support for the exception handling mechanism described in this paper. The plugin provides three new operations: **raise**, **wait** and **check**. It also configures hooks to alter behaviour of many other operations. An agent willing to use the exception handling mechanism requests operation codes. For the **raise** operation the request is:

COMMAND uk.ac.ncl.csr.exceptions.raise

Use of the authority domains in operation names is optional but highly recommended. As described above, the exception handling mechanism changes behaviour of many operations to allow them to be interrupted by an exception. This is implemented by setting hooks on these operations and aborting an operation whenever there is a pending exception. The mechanism semantics also requires interruption of the blocking input operations. This is implemented by sending an exception instead of a result with the ERROR command while intercepting using the hook mechanism the result from the original operation and cancelling its effect (i.e. by putting a tuple back into the tuplespace).

7   Conclusion

The paper introduces a novel exception handling mechanism which suits the main characteristics of agent systems, including openness, multifunctionality of the agent behaviour, communication asynchrony and anonymity. In particular, the paper makes the following contributions. It proposes a scoping mechanism for structuring complex coordination-based agent applications. This mechanism is in the core of an advanced exception handling mechanism in which the nested scopes represent the exception contexts containing the errors and localising recovery. Another part of the proposed exception mechanism is a support for flexible exception propagation between agents participating in the same scope. The third part of the mechanism is a flexible schema allowing agents to dynamically choose the direction of exception propagation when recovery inside the current scope is not possible. The exception handling mechanism proposed is provided to the application programmers as a set of easy-to-use abstractions and a specialised supporting coordination-based middleware.

Acknowledgements

This research has been supported by the EC IST project on Rigorous Open Development Environment for Complex Systems (RODIN - rodin.cs.ncl.ac.uk) and by the School of Computing Science at the University of Newcastle upon Tyne (UK). A. Iliasov is partially supported by the ORS award (UK).

References

1. Di Marzo, G. and Romanovsky, A. *Designing Fault-Tolerant Mobile Systems*. In Proceedings of the International Workshop on Scientific Engineering for Distributed Java Applications (FIDJI 2002), Luxembourg-Kirchberg, Luxembourg, 28-29 November 2002 Guelfi, N., Astesiano, E. and Reggio, G. (eds.). LNCS 2604 pp.185-201. Springer-Verlag 2003.
2. F. Cristian. *Exception Handling and Fault Tolerance of Software Faults*. Software Fault Tolerance. Wiley, NY, pp.81-107, 1995.
3. I. Satoh. *Mobile agent-based compound documents*. Proc. of the ACM Symposium on Document Engineering 2001, pp.76-84. 2001.
4. L. Cardelli, A. Gordon. *Mobile Ambients*. Foundations of Software Science and Computational Structures, volume 1378 of Lecture Notes in Computer Science. Springer-Verlag, pp.140-155, 1998.
5. J. Baumann, F. Hohl, K. Rothermel, M. Straßer. *Mole - Concepts of a Mobile Agent System*. World Wide Web Journal. 1(3), pp.123-137. 1998.
6. L. Fiege, M. Mezini, G. Muhl, A. P. Buchmann. *Engineering Event-Based Systems with Scopes*. Proceedings of European Conference on Object-Oriented Programming (ECOOP'2000), pp.309-333. 2002.
7. G. Agha and C. J. Callsen. *ActorSpace: An Open Distributed Programming Paradigm*. Proceedings 4th ACM Conference on Principles and Practice of Parallel Programming, ACM SIGPLAN Notices, pp.23-323, 1993.
8. C. J. Callsen and G. Agha. *Open Heterogeneous Computing in ActorSpace*. Journal of Parallel and Distributed Computing, vol. 21,3, pp.289-300, 1994.
9. I. Merrick, A. Wood. *Coordination with Scopes*. Proceedings of the 2000 ACM symposium on Applied Computing,Como, Italy, pp.210-217, 2000.
10. D. Gelernter. *Generative Communication in Linda*. ACM Transactions on Programming Languages and Systems, volume 7, pp.80-112, 1985.
11. A. Iliasov, L. Laibinis, A. Romanovsky, E. Troubitsyna. *Towards Formal Development of Mobile Location-based Systems*. Proceedings of the International Workshop on Rigorous Engineering of Fault Tolerant Systems. Newcastle upon Tyne, UK. School of Computing Science, Technical Report Series, CS-TR-915, 2005. ISSN 1368-1060
12. A. Iliasov, A. Romanovsky. *Exception Handling in Coordination-based Mobile Environments*. Proceedings of the 29th Annual International Computer Software and Applications Conference Edinburgh, Scotland, July 26-28, 2005. IEEE CS Press. 2005.
13. G. P. Picco, A. L. Murphy, G.-C. Roman. *Lime: Linda Meets Mobility*. Proceedings of the 21st International Conference on Software Engineering (ICSE'99), Los Angeles (USA), May 1999.

Practical Exception Specifications

Donna Malayeri and Jonathan Aldrich

Carnegie Mellon University, Pittsburgh, PA 15213, USA
{donna+, aldrich+}@cs.cmu.edu

Abstract. Exception specifications can aid in the tasks of writing correct exception handlers and understanding exceptional control flow, but current exception specification systems are impractical in a number of ways. In particular, they are too low-level, too heavyweight, and do not provide adequate support for describing exception policies.

We have identified the essential properties of a practical exception specification system and we present a methodology and tool that provides integrated support for specifying, understanding, and evolving exception policies. The annotations required of the programmer are lightweight and easier to maintain than those of current systems; in our studies we observed a 50% to 93% reduction in annotations. By leveraging these annotations, our system provides scalable support for understanding exception flow and for modifying exception annotations.

1 Introduction

Exceptions can be very useful for separating normal code from error handling code, but they introduce implicit control flow, complicating the task of understanding, maintaining, and debugging programs. Additionally, testing is not always effective for finding bugs in exception handing code, and these bugs can be particularly problematic (for example, a program that crashes without saving the user's data).

For programmers to write correct exception handlers, they need precise information about all exceptions that may be raised at a particular program location. Documentation is inadequate—it is error prone and difficult to maintain. On the other hand, precise information can be obtained through a whole-program analysis of exception flow (including analysis of all libraries used), but this is not a scalable solution, nor is it even applicable in situations where the whole program is not available. Moreover, relying on whole program exception analysis would complicate team development; if one programmer changes exception-related code, the control flow in apparently unrelated parts of the program may change in surprising ways.

1.1 A Motivating Example

We now present an example to motivate the need for practical exception specifications, and to illustrate the way a programmer would use our tool, ExnJava. Consider a module whose intended abstraction is that it present to its clients a high-level view for managing user preferences. The module is to hide implementation details of how the preferences are actually stored; clients should not depend on such details.

C. Dony et al. (Eds.):Exception Handling, LNCS 4119, pp. 200–220, 2006.

```
1    public class UserPrefs {
2      public Object getValue (String key) {
3        ...
4        return PrefKeys.getValue(this.userID, key);
5      }
6      public void setValue (String key, Object value) {
7        ...
8        PrefKeys.setValue(this.userID, key, value);
9      }
10   }

11   class PrefKeys {
12     // class' methods are package-private
13     void Object getValue (String userID, String key) {
14       ...
15       return Serializer.readValue(userID, key);
16     }
17     static void setValue (String userID, String key, Object value) {
18       ...
19       Serializer.writeValue(userID, key, value);
20     }
21   }

22   class Serializer {
23     // class' methods are package-private
24     static Object readValue (String id, String key) {
25       ...
26       // old code: return registry.getValue(key);
27       return theDB.get(id, key);
28     }
29     static void writeValue (String id, String key, Object value) {
30       ...
31       // old code: registry.save(id);
32       theDB.set(id, key, value);
33     }
34   }
```

Fig. 1. Excerpts of Java code for managing user preferences. The classes are part of the package `util.userPrefs`.

See Figure 1 for the corresponding code, written in Java. The classes UserPrefs, PrefKeys and Serializer reside in the util.userPrefs package, for which the programmer supplies the following package exception specification:

`package util.userPrefs may only throw util.PrefException`

This specifies the policy that PrefException is the only checked exception that can be thrown from the public methods of util.userPrefs. This is to prevent an interface method from throwing a low-level exception, in which case clients would not be able to write a meaningful exception handler without knowing the module's implementation details.

The class `UserPrefs` is the interface to the package; `PrefKeys` and `Serializer` are package-private. `PrefKeys` just passes through to `Serializer`, which previously stored preferences in the registry (lines 26 and 31), but now uses a database (lines 27 and 32). Note that preferences values are stored in the database as soon as `UserPrefs.setValue` is called.

Suppose that in the old version of the code, the calls to `registry`'s methods in lines 26 and 31 did not throw an exception. If the registry did not contain a value for a particular key, the `registry` object simply returned an appropriate default. Similarly, a failed save to the registry was simply logged by the `registry` class.

Now, however, `theDB.get` (line 27) and `theDB.set` (line 32) *can* throw an exception—a `SQLException` in this case. Since in Java, uncaught exceptions are automatically propagated up to the caller, all 6 methods now also throw this exception: `UserPrefs.getValue`, `UserPrefs.setValue`, `PrefKeys.getValue`, `PrefKeys.setValue`, `Serializer.readValue` and `Serializer.writeValue`.

Accordingly, the Java typechecker would require that all of these methods update their exception declarations. Though only 2 lines of code have been changed, programmers must now manually update the exception declarations of 6 methods—a threefold increase even in this simple example. This factor only increases in larger programs with more complex control flow. In Section 3, we will explore this problem in more detail, as well as look at the problems of other exception specification systems.

In contrast, in ExnJava, programmers need not add all of these `throws` declarations; `throws` annotations are only required on the public interface of a package. Since only the methods of `PrefKeys` are visible outside the package, these are the only methods that need to have a `throws` declaration; the `throws` declarations are automatically inferred for the other 4 methods. However, ExnJava will not accept the definition of `UserPrefs` as is—its package exception specification does not allow `SQLException` to be thrown from public methods. This error prompts the programmer to make a decision regarding how `SQLException` should be handled. The programmer realizes that line 27 in `Serializer.readValue` should be wrapped in a `try-catch` block:

```
catch (SQLException e) {
    return DefaultsManager.getDefault(key); }
```

For the exception originating from `Serializer.writeValue`, the correct behavior is that the exception be caught in `UserPrefs.getValue` and rethrown, so a handler is added around line 8:

```
catch (SQLException e) { throw new PrefException(e); }
```

1.2 Exception Specifications

As shown in the example, exception specifications can be a useful tool for reasoning about exceptions (see, for example, [18, 15, 2, 7]). They serve to document and enforce a contract between abstraction boundaries, which facilitates modular software development, and can also provide information about exception flow in a scalable manner. In Section 2 we describe the essential properties that we believe a practical exception specification system must have: it should be lightweight while sufficiently expressive, and should facilitate creating, understanding, and evolving specifications.

We have provided an integrated methodology for practical use of exception specifications and have designed a tool, described in Section 4 that leverages this. The tool combines user annotations, program analysis, refactorings, and GUI views that display analysis results. Our methodology and tool raise the level of abstraction of exception specifications, making them more expressive, more lightweight, and easier to modify. As we saw in the example above, this can aid programmers in writing better exception handlers.

Note that we focus on the problem of *specifying* various properties of exception behavior, rather than a proposal for a new exception handling mechanism. Additionally, though our work is performed in the context of Java, much of our basic design would be applicable to languages with similar exception handling mechanisms. There are two key properties of Java's exception handling mechanism: handlers are bound dynamically (the call stack is searched to find the handler, and cannot in general be statically determined), and exception propagation is performed automatically (if a method does not handle an exception, it is automatically propagated to its caller). The exception handling mechanisms of many popular languages have these properties, such as Ada, Eiffel, C++, C#, and ML.

The contributions of system are as follows:

- It performs a modular exception analysis and allows developers to easily browse the exception control flow within an application. This allows developers to easily answer questions about non-local exception behavior, and shows information about exceptions that are not provided by the host language.
- It allows developers to express and check exception specifications at the level of program modules. This raises the level of abstraction of exception specifications, helping developers to use exceptions consistently across many functions or methods in a module.
- It makes exceptions more lightweight by allowing developers to omit exception specifications from methods internal to a module, and providing refactoring tools that support transitive changes to the remaining specifications. These tools reduce the overhead of exception specification in general, and make evolving exception specifications as lightweight as the corresponding edits to throw and catch clauses in the code.

Additionally, in Section 5 we report both quantitative and qualitative data on the use of exception specifications in open source Java applications. These data motivate and validate the design of our tool.

2   Practical Exception Specifications

If an exception specification system is to be practical, we believe that it must posses several essential properties; we enumerate these here. We use the general term "exception policy" to refer to programmers' design intent regarding how exceptions should be used and handled. An exception policy specifies the types of exceptions that may be thrown from a particular scope and the properties that exception handlers must satisfy. We use the general term "module" to refer to a set of logically related compilation units to which access control can be applied (i.e., the module can have a public interface, and private implementation details).

In our view, a good exception specification system, which may include both language features and tools, should be lightweight while sufficiently expressive, and should facilitate creating, understanding, and evolving specifications.

2.1 Specification Overhead

The specification system must be lightweight. Programmers are not fond of writing specifications, so the benefits must clearly outweigh the costs. Additionally, incremental effort should, in general, yield incremental results. If a specification system requires that an entire program be annotated before producing any benefit, it is unlikely to be adopted.

2.2 Expressiveness

The system should allow specifying exception policies at an appropriate level of abstraction. It should support the common policy of limiting the exception types that may be thrown from some scope. Such scopes need not be limited to a method or a class. Rather, they could consist of a set of methods, a set of classes, or a module. In our example in Section 1.1, we illustrated how a programmer might use such a policy.

Additionally, there should be a way to specify a policy independently of its implementation, though an implementation may perhaps be generated from a policy (e.g., code to log exceptions, or wrap some exception and rethrow). Solutions that make it easy to implement a policy are useful, but they do not obviate the need for one. Until it is possible to generate all desired implementations automatically—which may not ever be fully achievable—we believe that the distinction between specification and implementation is an important one.

2.3 Ease of Creating and Understanding Policies

The solution should provide tools that aid programmers in creating new exception policies and understanding existing policies. Without the aid of such tools, reasoning about exceptions is difficult due to their non-local nature. Such tools may, for example, include information on exception control flow.

2.4 Maintainability

The specification scheme should support evolving specifications as the code evolves, possibly through tool support. This differs from the property of being lightweight; a system may be lightweight but inflexible. The cost involved in changing specifications should generally be proportional to the magnitude of the code change.

In Java and in other commonly-used languages, exceptions automatically propagate up the call chain if there is no explicit handler. A specification system for these languages should take these semantics into account, so that small code changes do not require widespread specification changes.

3   Related Work

Previous solutions have failed to meet one or more of the criteria described above; we describe each of these here.

3.1   Java

One well-known exception specification scheme is that of Java, which requires that all methods declare the checked exceptions that they directly or indirectly throw.[1]

Though we believe it is useful to separate exceptions into the categories of checked and unchecked (see, for example, [14, 2]), the Java design has a number of problems that make it impractical. Java `throws` declarations are too low-level; they allow specifying only limited exception policies at the method level. This leads, in part, to high specification overhead. It is notoriously bothersome to write and maintain `throws` declarations. Simple code modifications—a method throwing a new exception type; moving a handler from one method to another—can result in programmers having to update the declarations of an entire call chain.

There is anecdotal evidence that this overhead leads to bad programming behaviors [4, 26, 10]. Programmers may avoid annotations by using the declaration `throws Exception` or by using unchecked exceptions inappropriately. Worse, programmers may write code to "swallow" exceptions (i.e., catch and do nothing) to be spared the nuisance of the declarations [19, 13].

Eclipse[2] provides a "Quick Fix" for updating a method's `throws` declaration if it throws an exception that is not in its declaration, but this can only be applied to a single method at a time. Consequently, programmers would have to iteratively update declarations until a fixpoint was reached. Eclipse also includes an optional warning that will list methods whose `throws` declarations are imprecise, but this too applies to a single method at a time.

Empirical results. Based on our experience with Java programs, we hypothesized that even if programmers use checked exceptions as the language designers intended, exception declarations can easily become imprecise. To verify this, we analyzed several open-source Java programs. Descriptions of the programs analyzed, along with their code size, are displayed in Table 1.

In this discussion, we use the following definitions: a *throws conjunct* is an individual exception type listed in a `throws` declaration. For example, in the declaration "`throws` E_1, E_2", E_1 and E_2 are throws conjuncts. A throws conjunct E of a method m is *imprecise* if the analysis determines that m throws a proper subtype of E, but not E itself; E is *superfluous* if m does not throw E nor any of its subtypes. An *imprecise*

---

[1] In Java, the class `Exception` is the supertype of all exception types. One of its subtypes is `RuntimeException`, which represents *unchecked* exceptions. Exceptions that are a subtype of `Exception` but not a subtype of `RuntimeException` are *checked* exceptions; subtypes of `RuntimeException` are *unchecked exceptions*. A method must declare all checked exceptions that it throws (directly or transitively) in its `throws` declaration; unchecked exceptions may be omitted.

[2] Available at www.eclipse.org.

Table 1. Description of programs analyzed, along with lines of code (LOC denotes the non-comment, non-blank lines of code) and number of classes and methods. The program *Tapestry* refers to the Apache Jakarta Tapestry project.

Program	LOC	Classes	Methods	Description
LimeWire	61k	1291	8346	p2p filesharing client
Columba	40k	1054	5654	e-mail client
Tapestry	20k	515	3186	framework for developing web applications
JFtp	13k	104	1005	graphical network browser
Lucene	10k	178	1335	text search engine library
Metrics	7k	203	1378	Eclipse plugin, computes program metrics

Table 2. The number of throws conjuncts that were imprecise (proper subtype thrown), and superfluous (not thrown at all), the total number of throws conjuncts, and the percentage of throws conjuncts that were imprecise or superfluous. Within the *imprecise* and *superfluous conjuncts* columns, the total is displayed, as well as the number of instances where the imprecise or superfluous throws conjunct was the exception supertype `Exception`. The *subsume* sub-column within the *imprecise conjuncts* column indicates the number of exception types that were subsumed by the `Exception` declaration.

Program	Imprecise conjuncts			Superfluous conjuncts		Total throws	Percent
	Total	e = Exception		Total	e = Exception	conjuncts	of Total
		occurrences	subsume				
LimeWire	26	2	4	120	0	917	16%
Columba	275	274	1130	301	272	826	70%
Tapestry	16	10	30	93	20	231	47%
JFtp	5	5	9	17	1	27	81%
Lucene	7	2	5	209	0	598	37%
Metrics	1	0	0	17	0	78	23%

throws declaration contains one or more imprecise or superfluous throws conjuncts; a *superfluous throws declaration* is comprised entirely of superfluous throws conjuncts.

Table 2 summarizes the number of imprecise and superfluous throws conjuncts, the total number of throws conjuncts, and the percentage of throws conjuncts that were either imprecise or superfluous. The table also lists the number of cases where the imprecise or superfluous conjunct was `Exception`. The declaration `throws Exception` is particularly problematic: aside from providing no information about exception flow, it precludes the method's client from writing anything other than a general exception handler.

In our subject programs, there were numerous imprecise and superfluous throws conjuncts; their totals range from 19% to 85% of the total throws conjuncts. Averaged over all the programs, one out of every 2 throws conjuncts is imprecise or superfluous. The number of occurrences of `throws Exception` was also quite high in Columba and Tapestry, relative to the exception declarations.

In the cases where the declaration `throws Exception` was imprecise, we computed the number of exception types that it subsumed, which is a measure of *how* imprecise the declaration is. For example, if method m declares that it throws `Exception`, but can actually throw `SMTPException`, `WrongPassphraseException`, and `ParserException` (all exception types defined by Columba), then in a sense, m's declaration is more imprecise than if it only threw `SMTPException`. The three exception types represent three opportunities for writing a handler that is specific to the error condition that was raised, but this is obscured by m's throws declaration.

Table 2 includes the total number of throws conjuncts that were subsumed by a more general type (e.g., for m, 3 conjuncts were subsumed). In Columba, the 274 instances of the imprecise declaration throws Exception subsumed 1130 exception types; an average of 4.1 per occurrence. We also observed several cases where 7 or 8 exception types, each of which appeared to represent semantically distinct error conditions, were subsumed by the type Exception. Thus, the imprecise throws declarations were large in both number and magnitude.

Aside from illustrating the difficulty of maintaining throws declarations, these results cast doubt on whether they are even a good tool for understanding exception flow and exception policies—though advocates often claim that this is one of their very benefits [8, 25, 2, 24]. Imprecise and superfluous throws declarations can obscure exception flow, leading to violations of intended exception behavior or catch blocks that are dead code.

3.2   Other Work

There are several proposals for specifying method post-conditions on exceptional exit [5, 15, 1], but these are even more heavyweight than Java throws declarations. These solutions do provide powerful verification capabilities, but it is unclear whether these benefits will outweigh the significant cost of annotating an entire program.

Some researchers have proposed languages and language extensions to facilitate the implementation of a policy, but these solutions provide no way to *specify* the policy. These include languages with first-class exception handlers [3] and languages that allow applying handlers to some set of methods or classes [12, 16]. However, unless new tools are created, these features will further complicate the task of reasoning about exceptions. It is also unclear how these schemes would work with programmer-supplied specifications; as far as we are aware, this problem has not been addressed.

Robillard and Murphy [21] provide a good methodology (though not a tool) for specifying exceptions at module boundaries; our tool builds on this work. A number of researchers have developed exception analysis tools [22, 23, 11, 6], and while most of these analyses are more sophisticated in terms of either precision or efficiency, they all perform a whole-program analysis which has inherent scalability problems [20]. Most of these analyses are superior to the one that we have implemented in our prototype tool, as the goal of our work is not to perform exception inference but rather to provide tools and a methodology for lightweight exception specifications.

For the task of understanding exception flow, Sinha et al. [23] propose a set of views that display the results of their exception analysis, but for these they provide only a high-level design.

4   Features of ExnJava

We have designed and implemented an exception specification system for Java 1.4 that satisfies the initial criteria outlined in Section 2. Our design raises the level of abstraction of exception specifications, while remaining lightweight.

Our current simplifying assumption is to take a Java package as a unit of modularity. Thus, methods with public or protected visibility are the package's interface methods; private and package-private[3] methods are internal methods.

Our system, ExnJava, is implemented as an Eclipse plugin. It contains one language change: the Java rules for method `throws` declarations are relaxed such that only package *interface methods* require a `throws` declaration. ExnJava also includes package-level exception specifications, checked on every compilation. This is implemented as an extra-linguistic feature. Additionally, there is a Thrown Exceptions view to facilitate creating and understanding exception policies. Three refactorings help programmers evolve specifications: Propagate Throws Declarations, Convert to Checked Exception, and Fix Imprecise Declarations. In the subsections below, we describe each of these features.

4.1 Exception Inference

The main goal of ExnJava's exception inference is to determine the checked exceptions that each method throws, and use these to ensure that methods adhere to package exception specfications and to infer the `throws` declarations for private and package-private methods. Our analysis does compute the unchecked (i.e. "runtime") exceptions that are explicitly thrown by the program, but this analysis is unsound and intended merely to provide additional information. The reason for this design choice is that the goal of our work is to allow programmers to specify and check exception *policies*, and unchecked exceptions are not suitable for this task.

Analysis Modes. ExnJava can be run in two modes: *per-package mode* or *whole-program mode*. Programmers can choose the former for a more scalable analysis, or the latter for more detailed information. Both analyses provide complete information about the checked exceptions that each method throws, but the whole-program analysis provides information about exception control flow between packages. The same views and refactorings are available in either mode (with the exception of the Convert to Checked Exception refactoring).

Per-package analysis. This is the main mode of operation for ExnJava. This analysis is quadratic in the size of the largest package and scales well to large programs.

Whole-program analysis. This analysis is useful in cases where a programmer requires a detailed understanding of exception flow, and for the Convert to Checked Exception refactoring. However, its worst-case complexity is quadratic in the size of the program and therefore may not be efficient enough for frequent interactive use.

Analysis Algorithm. Since ExnJava does not require throws declarations on all methods, there is an inference algorithm to determine the checked exceptions thrown by internal methods. ExnJava analyzes each package as a whole and performs a conservative intra-procedural dataflow analysis, similar to that of previous systems [22]. The analysis determines the checked exceptions thrown by each internal method (through

---

[3] Also known as "default" or "friendly" access.

either a `throws` statement or a call to an interface method or a library method) and iterates until a fixpoint is reached. For calls to non-final (i.e., virtual) methods, the union of the exceptions thrown by all known overriding methods are considered.

4.2   Specifying Exception Policies

In ExnJava, programmers specify exception policy at the package level. We believe this is a more appropriate level of abstraction than the low-level declarations of previous solutions, such as method-level declarations in Java. A package has two kinds of exception policy: one applies to each individual interface method, the other to the package as a whole.

Interface Method Policies. The exception policy of interface methods is specified using Java `throws` declarations. In contrast to Java however, the declarations for internal methods need not be specified—they are inferred by ExnJava.[4] Consequently, this design raises the level of abstraction of `throws` declarations.

To determine the checked exceptions thrown by internal methods, ExnJava performs an intra-package dataflow analysis. Within a package, the implementation of our analysis is similar to the whole-program analyses of previous systems [22, 23]. However, our analysis is scalable, as it depends on the size of each package rather than the size of the entire program. The results of this analysis, as well as additional information about exception control flow, are displayed in the Thrown Exceptions view, described below in Section 4.3.

There are several advantages to this scheme. First, annotations are more lightweight. As we describe in Section 5.1, in our subject programs we found that inference reduces the number of required declarations by a range of 50% to 93%. Also, inference gives programmers more precise information. Rather than examine Java `throws` declarations, programmers use the Thrown Exceptions view to determine the checked exceptions thrown by internal methods. And, in contrast to a pure exception inference tool, programmers can enforce exception policies by specifying `throws` declarations on interface methods.

Package Exception Policies. Our design of package exception policies extends the work of Robillard and Murphy [21]. Their work, in turn, builds on work by Litke [17], who provides recommendations for designing systems with good exception structure (in the context of Ada). Litke's recommended software engineering practice is that exceptions that can occur at module boundaries to be precisely and completely specified.[5] Litke argues that using modules reduces complexity, making it easier for programmers to reason about program behavior and to write and modify error handlers. He also recommends the use of automated methods for checking conformance of the program against the module specifications.[6]

---

[4] It may sometimes be useful to include `throws` declarations on internal methods; this is supported.

[5] Litke uses the term "compartment", but this is equivalent to our definition of "module."

[6] As far as we are aware, Litke did not publish any work regarding such a tool, though one paper [17] mentioned that an implementation was in progress.

org.columba.mail.pop3	IOException, CommandCancelledException, ParserException, POP3Exception
org.columba.mail.smtp	IOException, CommandCancelledException, SMTPException
org.columba.mail.pgp	IOException, WrongPassphraseException, JSCFException
org.columba.mail.plugin	java.lang.ClassNotFoundException, java.lang.IllegalAccessException, java.lang.InstantiationException, java.lang.NoSuchMethodException, java.lang.reflect.InvocationTargetException, java.net.MalformedURLException, PluginHandlerNotFoundException

Fig. 2. Excerpt of our package exception specification for the Columba application. IOException refers to java.io.IOException. The other unqualified exception names refer to application-defined checked exceptions.

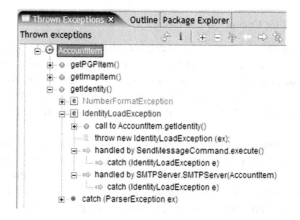

Fig. 3. The Thrown Exceptions view in method level mode

For simplicity, our approach considers each Java package as a module; the package's public and protected methods are the module boundaries.[7] For each package, its exception specification (which corresponds to Litke's module specification) consists of a list of entries that are either exception class names or regular expressions (e.g., java.lang.*). An exception type E can be thrown from a package interface method if either E or a supertype of E is listed in the specification, or if E's fully-qualified name matches a regular expression in the specification.

Unchecked exceptions can be included in the specification; however, to ensure conformance, the entire program, including any libraries that are used, would have to be analyzed. Therefore, the analysis can find some violations of such specifications, but cannot assure complete conformance with the specified policy.

---

[7] It would also be possible to devise a module specification language, where a module could consist of a set of packages or classes; we will consider this in future work.

Package exception specifications thus ensure that the exception policy of each interface method (the types of exceptions that they throw) also conforms to the general exception policy of the package. Recall the example of Section 2.2 where the storage details of the user preferences package were to be hidden from clients. This package's specification would include perhaps `PreferenceStoreException` but would *not* include `FileNotFoundException`. If such an exception were thrown within the package, the exception could be wrapped as a higher-level exception type (such as `PreferenceStoreException`). This idiom, called exception translation, is recommended by Bloch [2] (among others) and is common in Java programs.

Figure 2 is a representative excerpt of our package exception specification of the Columba program; we defined this specification while performing the case study described below (Section 5.2). The entry for the `org.columba.mail.plugin` package is particularly interesting, as it suggests that some low-level exceptions are inappropriately thrown, while they should probably be wrapped by a more abstract exception type. We will revisit this issue in Section 5.2.

4.3   Understanding Exception Policies

The Thrown Exceptions view (Figure 3) displays the details of exception control flow, to help programmers understand the implemented exception policies. Without the information provided by this view, we believe that it would be difficult to correctly create and modify exception policies. We believe that the general difficulty of programming with exceptions is partly due to lack of information on a program's exceptional control flow.

The Thrown Exceptions view displays information computed by either a whole-project analysis or a per-package exception analysis (as described above); the former will provide more information, but the latter is more scalable. The view has two modes: method level and package level. The method level view, inspired by the work of Sinha et al [23], displays a tree view of the project's methods, grouped by package and class. For each method, the checked and unchecked exceptions[8] thrown by the method are listed, as well as the lines of code that cause the exception to be thrown. Using this view, the programmer can jump to method definitions that throw exceptions, and can also quickly jump to the ultimate sources of a particular exception (i.e., the original throw statements or library method calls that caused an exception to flow up to this part of the code.) Additionally, for each exception that a method throws, the view displays all catch blocks that may handle that exception. (This is limited, of course, to catch blocks in code available to the analysis.)

The package level view displays, for each package, the checked exceptions that are thrown by its interface methods. For each exception type, the methods that throw the exception are listed, as well as the detailed exception information described above. The package view can be useful for creating a package's exception policy. (In fact, we used it to define Columba's exception policy in Figure 2.) The view can also help identify possible errors in the exception policy. For example, if a particular exception type is

---

[8] Information on unchecked exceptions will not be complete, due to the fact that a whole-program analysis (including all libraries used) would be required. However, even partial information on unchecked exceptions can be useful.

only thrown by one or two methods, it is possible that the exception should have been handled internally or wrapped as a different exception type.

4.4 Evolving Exception Policies

Our system raises the unit of abstraction to which an exception specification applies; this alone makes it easier to evolve specifications. If the set of exceptions thrown by an internal method changes, no `throws` declarations need to be updated, unless one or more interface methods throw new exceptions. This often occurs when an exception handler is moved from one method to another in the same package. Though this is a conceptually simple modification, a number of internal methods may now throw a different set of exceptions. In standard Java, the `throws` declaration of each of these methods would have to be manually updated.

Propagating Declarations. Still, if a code change causes an *interface* method to throw new exceptions, the same "ripple effect" of Java `throws` declarations may result—requiring changes to the declarations of the transitive closure of method callers. To avoid this problem, ExnJava provides a Propagate Throws Declarations refactoring (accessible as an Eclipse "Quick Fix") that will propagate declarations up the call graph (see Figure 4). The goal of this refactoring is to help programmers find the correct location for new exception handlers, rather than tempting them to carelessly propagate declarations to every method that requires them. To this end, the refactoring displays a checkbox tree view of the call graph (which includes only methods whose declarations need to be changed), which is initially collapsed to show only the original method whose declaration needs to be updated. The programmer then expands this one level to display the method's immediate callers (and callers of the methods that it overrides), and so on for each level in the tree. Checking a particular method in the tree will add the declaration to both that method and all the overridden superclass methods (so as not to violate substitutability).

The refactoring also incorporates the package exception specification; if updating the `throws` declaration of a particular method would violate the package specification, the method is displayed in a different color, with a tooltip describing the reason for the inconsistency. The declaration for the method can still be changed, but ExnJava will display an error until the package specification is modified.

Unchecked Exceptions. Sometimes, unchecked exceptions are used where checked exceptions are more appropriate. In fact, some programmers prefer to use unchecked exceptions during the prototyping phase, and then switch to checked exceptions later. ExnJava includes a Convert to Checked Exception refactoring which changes an exception's supertype to `Exception` and updates all `throws` declarations in the program accordingly.

Imprecise Exceptions. As previously noted, `throws` declarations can become unintentionally imprecise as code evolves: they may include exception types that are never thrown or types that are too general. (Of course, sometimes imprecise declarations are

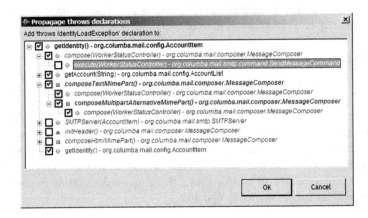

Fig. 4. The dialog for propagating throws declarations. Methods that are typeset in italics are those for which the package specification does not allow throwing this particular exception type.

an intentional design choice, to provide for future code changes. Our tool allows programmers to retain such declarations.)

When a `catch` block is moved from one package to another, for example, a number of interface methods may include an exception type that they will consequently never throw. New callers of these methods will then have to include handlers for these exceptions—which would be dead code—or must themselves add superfluous exceptions to their `throws` declarations. Such problems do occur in actual code; for example, Robillard and Murphy found a number of unreachable catch blocks in their analysis of several Java programs [22].

To solve this problem, ExnJava includes an Fix Imprecise Declarations refactoring, which can be run on a package or set of packages. The refactoring first lists the exception types which appear in imprecise declarations; the programmer chooses an exception type from this list. The exception type is chosen first so that the view can show the propagation of this exception declaration. For this exception, the view displays all methods where that type appears in an imprecise declaration. The view displays a call graph tree (similar to that of the Propagate Throws Declarations refactoring) showing the propagation of imprecise declarations. This allows the programmer to determine the effect of fixing (or not fixing) a particular imprecise declaration. Initially all methods are checked, indicating that their declarations will be updated; the programmer can choose to not change the declarations for particular methods by unchecking them. (We chose this design as we hypothesize that most imprecise declarations are out-of-date rather than intentional design choices.) The view ensures that a consistent set of methods is chosen; if a method is unchecked, all of its transitive callers will also be unchecked.

Our tool could be extended to include a "Fix Imprecise" refactoring at the package specification level, to inform the programmer of specifications that may no longer be valid. Such a tool would display each package whose specification lists one or more exceptions that are not actually thrown in the implementation.

5   Evaluation

We evaluated ExnJava with quantitative analyses and with case studies. Exception inference was evaluated for 1) its potential annotation savings and 2) its impact on reducing
the incidence of imprecise and superfluous `throws` declarations. We also analyzed the
annotation overhead of package exception specifications. Finally, we conducted case
studies to determine how ExnJava could be used to improve a program's exception
structure and ease program understanding and maintenance.

5.1   Quantitative Results

Package-Private Inference. ExnJava's checked exception inference is most useful for
programs with well-encapsulated packages with as few public members as possible. We
hypothesized that the visibility of classes and methods are often not restrictive enough;
that is, many classes and methods are public when in fact they should be package-
private or private. To this end, we have developed an Eclipse plugin that changes the
visibility modifiers on classes and methods to *package-private* wherever possible (i.e.,
when they are not accessed outside of their defining package).

Table 3. Percentage of methods that were private or package-private before and after visibility modifier refactoring. The results show that a significant percentage of methods have weaker
visibility modifiers than are necessary.

Program	Methods	Package-private and Private Methods	
		before refactoring	after refactoring
LimeWire	8346	38%	67%
Columba	5654	10%	57%
Tapestry	3186	14%	75%
JFtp	1005	14%	58%
Lucene	1335	46%	73%
Metrics	1378	27%	72%

We found that the percentage of package-private methods increases dramatically
when this refactoring is applied; results are displayed in Table 3. Grothoff et al. found
similar results in their work on confined types [9]. Note that in computing this data, we
considered the *actual* visibility of methods, not merely the method's access modifier
(e.g., a method with `public` visibility in a `private` class was counted as a private
method). Before refactoring, an average of 25% of methods were private or package-
private, as compared to an average of 67% after refactoring. However, for some of
these programs (for example, Tapestry and Lucene), the refactoring may have been
too aggressive: it is likely that some of the classes and methods that were changed
to package-private were intended to be used by library clients. On the other hand,
classes in the programs LimeWire, Columba, JFtp, and Metrics were not intended to
be used directly by clients (aside from some plugin capabilities in Columba and Metrics that were excluded from the refactoring), so the refactoring for these was likely
accurate.

Effectiveness of Inference. In the discussion that follows, *inferable checked exceptions* denote checked exceptions that could be inferred by our analysis, and therefore omitted by the programmer (that is, exceptions thrown by private and package-private methods). Table 4 compares the number of inferable checked exceptions before and after the package-private refactoring was performed, as computed by a whole-program analysis. As expected, the percentage of inferable exceptions was closely related to the percentage of private and package-private methods in the program. In these programs, 50% to 93% of thrown checked exceptions could be omitted with ExnJava.[9]

Table 4. Total number of exceptions thrown, and percentage of inferable checked exceptions before and after package-private refactoring. Each exception type thrown by a method was counted separately. Exceptions thrown were computed using the whole-program exception analysis.

Program	Checked Exns Thrown	Percent Inferable Exceptions	
		before refactoring	after refactoring
LimeWire	966	45%	**72%**
Columba	1510	44%	**50%**
Tapestry	146	12%	**75%**
JFtp	14	44%	**93%**
Lucene	492	56%	**81%**
Metrics	54	23%	**72%**

We also found that many occurrences of imprecise and superfluous throws conjuncts are on private and package-private methods; see Table 5. The data suggests that 53% to 78% of these could be eliminated without any additional tool support. That is, by simply removing all `throws` declarations from private and package-private declarations, ExnJava will eliminate more than half of the imprecise declarations through its exception inference. Of course, there are still a number of public and protected methods with imprecise or superfluous declarations, for which ExnJava does not perform inference. As it would be very error-prone and tedious to correct these by hand, we believe that tool support such as our Fix Imprecise Declarations refactoring would be beneficial.

We computed the average number of exceptions thrown by packages in our subject programs, and our results indicate that package exceptions specifications have a very low annotation overhead: in most applications, packages generally throw a small number of exception types—fewer than 2 exceptions per package, on average.

5.2   Case Studies

We used the programs Columba and LimeWire as subjects of our case studies, as they are the largest two programs and contain the most uses of exceptions. The two programs were quite different in their exception structure: Columba had very poor exception structure and exception handling. Though it had no application-defined unchecked exceptions, the declaration `throws Exception` was ubiquitous. In contrast, LimeWire had a well-designed exception structure. Despite the fact that it was the largest program we analyzed and contained the most uses of exceptions, it had the fewest percentage of imprecise and superfluous exceptions (see Table 2).

---

[9] This data essentially assumes that all `throws` declarations are precise. However, we derived very similar results when considering the actual, imprecise `throws` declarations.

Table 5. The number of imprecise or superfluous throws conjuncts and the number of superfluous `throws` declarations; the percentage of each these that are on private or package-private methods (and that could therefore be inferred). Data was gathered after package-private refactoring was performed.

Program	Imprecise/ superfluous conjuncts	Private or pkg-private	Superfluous "throws" decl	Private or pkg-private
LimeWire	146	53%	108	42%
Columba	576	42%	291	40%
Tapestry	109	68%	72	69%
JFtp	22	59%	16	44%
Lucene	216	75%	209	75%
Metrics	18	78%	13	69%

Columba. As described in Section 3.1, Columba had many imprecise `throws` declarations, and these subsumed an average of 4.1 exception types that were actually thrown. Thus, in this program, `throws` declarations are useless for inferring a package exception policy; considering `throws` alone, of the 61 packages that threw exceptions, 38 of them contained `Exception`, or 62%.

We therefore examined the package exception specification for Columba as inferred by the whole-program analysis. We found that two packages, `org.columba.mail.plugin` and `org.columba.core.plugin`, appeared to be throwing exceptions that were inappropriate to the abstraction (see Figure 2). These packages were involved with loading user-defined plugins and were each throwing 5 low-level exceptions related to class loading. Inspecting the `throw` point for each of these exception revealed that they all originated from the `org.columba.core.loader` package, which actually performed the class loading operation. Further, there were no specific handlers for the 5 low-level exceptions in clients of the plugin packages, while there were handlers for an existing exception `PluginLoadingFailedException`. In the plugin packages, we found a few cases where the low-level exceptions were translated to this type. This all suggests that the intended policy was that the class loading-related exceptions be wrapped as the more meaningful `PluginLoadingFailedException`, but this policy was inconsistently applied.

Adding just two handlers to perform this exception translation had the effect that only the `core.loader` package threw the low-level exceptions and the `plugin` packages threw only plugin-related exceptions. The total number of exceptions thrown by each package was reduced from 201 to 193 (at the very start of our refactoring, this total was 229); the resulting exception structure is simpler and better modularized. This could probably be improved further, but would require an understanding the design intent of the various packages.

We were also surprised to discover that our inference determined that the supertype `Exception` was thrown by 7 different packages. Similar to a throws declaration of `throws Exception`, a package specification that includes `Exception` provides no information and essentially circumvents the package specification checking. The source of the problem was two abstract methods relating to the operation of encoding a MIME attachment in an e-mail message. We will discuss one of these methods, renderMimePart, though the discussion applies to the other method as well (in fact, the same catch block handled exceptions from both methods).

The abstract method renderMimePart was presumably given the declaration throws Exception to provide implementers with maximum flexibility. However, this flexibility comes at a high cost: none of its clients would be able to write specific exception handlers, unless they knew that some particular mime encoder object was used. Most of the implementations of this method did not throw any exceptions, but the implementation in MultipartEncryptedRenderer could throw a checked exception, EncryptionException. This exception was a direct subtype of Exception.

Using our exception view (Figure 3) which shows the handlers that may handle a particular exception, we determined that there was only one catch block c that could catch exceptions from this source, and that it did not catch any instances of EncryptionException originating from other throw points. The handler c was contained within code that was responsible for sending an e-mail message. If an EncryptionException was thrown, the message composer window would be displayed along with an error message. Note that the action that was taken was related to the fact that an exception occurred during MIME rendering, not that there was a problem during encryption. We therefore created a new exception type MimePartRenderException and wrapped the instance of EncryptionException.

Note that it would not be easy for a developer to produce a correct implementation for the original handler c. He could not simply look at throws declarations to determine that EncryptionException could be thrown from the operation of MIME rendering. There were many methods (including several that were called indirectly) between the catch and the corresponding throw points, and all were annotated with throws Exception. We speculate that this exception handler was added after testing uncovered this execution path.

We updated the throws declarations in the methods that we changed and after full exception inference the imprecision of throws declarations were even more pronounced. There were an additional 81 imprecise or superfluous throws conjuncts—now 80% of all throws conjuncts were imprecise or superfluous (up from 70%). Somewhat unsurprisingly, there were 168 catch handlers that caught the type Exception, comprising 31% of all catch handlers. Manual inspection of a subset of these handlers revealed that most did little more than log a message to the console. We suspect that more specific error handlers would make the program more robust, but it is obviously difficult to write such handlers if 80% of throws conjuncts do not provide accurate information.

LimeWire. As mentioned previously, LimeWire had a very good exception design and contained much fewer imprecise exceptions declarations than Columba. There were only two application-defined unchecked exceptions, one of which represented an assertion failure. We converted the other one to a checked exception using our refactoring, though this required few new annotations (the exception was always being caught by the immediate callers).

There were no obvious cases where a package in LimeWire was throwing inappropriate exception types. Many packages threw IOException, which made this task more difficult. LimeWire had 12 application-defined subtypes of IOException, so it is likely that some packages should have been throwing one of these subtypes. It is also unclear whether it was appropriate for all of these exceptions to be subtypes of IOException, since some of them were generated by actual I/O operations, while others were generated in response to a higher-level network event. However, as in Columba, considering actual throws declarations made it difficult to understand the exception behavior of each package; according to the declarations, packages threw a total of 50 exceptions, as compared to 80 as computed by inference. The discrepancy was caused by imprecise exception declarations.

5.3 Performance

Analysis times for our prototype whole-program and per-package analysis are displayed in Table 6, as measured on a 3.2 GHz Pentium 4. We measured only the time for the exception analysis itself, after the AST was loaded and dependencies were computed. The average time to analyze each package in the per-package analysis is reasonable, and optimizations would likely improve this quite a bit.

We were limited by the high memory consumption of the program analysis infrastructure that we used, and were unable to analyze programs that were much larger than LimeWire, though this is not a problem inherent in our analysis. We are currently working to address this issue.

Table 6. Analysis times for whole-program analysis, total per-package analysis (entire program), and average time to analyze one package in the per-package analysis

Program	LOC	Whole program	Total per-package	Average per-package
LimeWire	61k	180 s	126 s	2210 ms
Columba	40k	68 s	51 s	411 ms
Tapestry	20k	29 s	17 s	304 ms
JFtp	13k	10.4 s	10 s	1250 ms
Lucene	10k	9.6 s	9.5 s	950 ms
Metrics	7k	10 s	9 s	563 ms

6   Summary and Future Work

We have described a novel exception specification methodology which combines inferred and programmer-specified annotations and illustrated how this scheme can be used to display a variety of analysis results to the user. The basic design of this scheme is applicable to any language with dynamically bound exception handlers, and where exception propagation is performed automatically. We have also provided quantitative evidence that our design addresses many of the problems of a commonly used exception specification system—that of Java.

Future work includes support for Java 1.5 generics, which will require changes to both our underlying algorithm and the implementation. We would also like to support richer exception specifications. The expressiveness of exception specifications would be greatly increased if they would be applicable to *modules* rather than Java packages. A module would consist of a set of Java classes, and there would be support for hierarchical modules with support for controlling visibility. We are currently designing such a module system, and our initial experiments indicate that performing exception inference over a module rather than a package can reduce the number of programmer-supplied annotations by up to an order of magnitude.

We are also considering support for a lightweight notation for specifying the high-level properties of handlers in the module exception specification (such properties need not be exposed to clients, as they may express implementation details). Some examples of policies we would like to support include: "handlers for exceptions of type E should be non-empty"; "thrown exceptions of type E should be logged"; "exceptions of type E should always be wrapped as type F before they escape the interface of this scope."

Acknowledgments

We would like to thank David Garlan and George Fairbanks for their comments on an earlier version of this paper, and Bill Scherlis for his suggestions and discussions.

This work was supported in part by NASA cooperative agreements NCC-2-1298 and NNA05CS30A, NSF grant CCR-0204047, and the Army Research Office grant number DAAD19-02-1-0389 entitled "Perpetually Available and Secure Information Systems."

References

[1] Mike Barnett, K. Rustan M. Leino, and Wolfram Schulte. The Spec# programming system. In *Cassis International Workshop, Ed. Marieke Huisman*, 2004.

[2] Joshua Bloch. *Effective Java*. Addison-Wesley Professional, 2001.

[3] Christophe Dony. A fully object-oriented exception handling system: rationale and Smalltalk implementation. In *Advances in exception handling techniques*, pages 18–38, New York, NY, USA, 2001. Springer-Verlag New York, Inc.

[4] Bruce Eckel. *Thinking in Java, 3rd edition*. Prentice-Hall PTR, December 2002.

[5] C. Flanagan, K. Leino, M. Lillibridge, C. Nelson, J. Saxe, and R. Stata. Extended static checking for Java. In *Proceedings of PLDI 2002*, 2002.

[6] Chen Fu, Ana Milanova, Barbara Ryder, and David Wonnacott. Robustness testing of Java server applications. In *IEEE Transactions on Software Engineering*, pages 292–312, April 2005.

[7] Alessandro F. Garcia, Cecília M. F. Rubira, Alexander B. Romanovsky, and Jie Xu. A comparative study of exception handling mechanisms for building dependable object-oriented software. *Journal of Systems and Software*, 59(2):197–222, 2001.

[8] James Gosling, Bill Joy, Guy Steele, and Gilad Bracha. *Java(TM) Language Specification, The (3rd Edition) (Java Series)*. Addison-Wesley Professional, July 2005.

[9] Christian Grothoff, Jens Palsberg, and Jan Vitek. Encapsulating objects with confined types. In *Proceedings of the 16th ACM SIGPLAN Conference on Object-Oriented Programming, Systems, Languages, and Applications (OOPSLA '01)*, pages 241–255. ACM Press, 2001.

[10] Anson Horton. Why doesn't C# have exception specifications? Available at http://msdn.microsoft.com/vcsharp/ team/language/ask/exceptionspecs.

[11] Jangwoo Jo, Byeong-Mo Chang, Kwangkeun Yi, and Kwang-Moo Choe. An uncaught exception analysis for Java. *Journal of Systems and Software*, 2004.

[12] Gregor Kiczales, Erik Hilsdale, Jim Hugunin, Mik Kersten, Jeffrey Palm, and William G. Griswold. An overview of AspectJ. In *ECOOP '01: Proceedings of the 15th European Conference on Object-Oriented Programming*, pages 327–353, London, UK, 2001. Springer-Verlag.

[13] Joseph R. Kiniry. Exceptions in Java and Eiffel: Two extremes in exception design and application. In *Proceedings of the ECOOP 2003 Workshop on Exception Handling in Object-Oriented Systems*, 2003.

[14] Jorgen Lindskov Knudsen. Fault tolerance and exception handling in BETA. In *Advances in exception handling techniques*, pages 1–17, New York, NY, USA, 2001. Springer-Verlag New York, Inc.

[15] K. Rustan M. Leino and Wolfram Schulte. Exception safety for C#. In *SEFM*, pages 218–227. IEEE Computer Society, 2004.

[16] Martin Lippert and Cristina Videira Lopes. A study on exception detecton and handling using aspect-oriented programming. In *Proceedings of the 22nd International Conference on Software Engineering (ICSE '00)*, pages 418–427. ACM Press, 2000.

[17] John D. Litke. A systematic approach for implementing fault tolerant software designs in Ada. In *Proceedings of the conference on TRI-ADA '90*, pages 403–408. ACM Press, 1990.

[18] Robert Miller and Anand Tripathi. Issues with exception handling in object-oriented systems. In *ECOOP*, pages 85–103, 1997.

[19] Darell Reimer and Harini Srinivasan. Analyzing exception usage in large Java applications. In *Proceedings of the ECOOP 2003 Workshop on Exception Handling in Object-Oriented Systems*, 2003.

[20] Martin P. Robillard, May 2005. Personal communication.

[21] Martin P. Robillard and Gail C. Murphy. Designing robust Java programs with exceptions. In *Proceedings of the 8th ACM SIGSOFT International Symposium on Foundations of Software Engineering (FSE '00)*, pages 2–10. ACM Press, 2000.

[22] Martin P. Robillard and Gail C. Murphy. Static analysis to support the evolution of exception structure in object-oriented systems. *ACM Trans. Softw. Eng. Methodol.*, 12(2): 191–221, 2003.

[23] Saurabh Sinha, Alessandro Orso, and Mary Jean Harrold. Automated support for development, maintenance, and testing in the presence of implicit control flow. In *Proceedings of the 26th International Conference on Software Engineering (ICSE '04)*, pages 336–345. IEEE Computer Society, 2004.

[24] Bill Venners. *Interface Design: Best Practices in Object-Oriented API Design in Java*. Available at http://www.artima.com/interfacedesign, 2001.

[25] Bill Venners. Failure and exceptions: a conversation with James Gosling, Part II. Available at http://www.artima.com/intv/solid.html, September 2003.

[26] Bill Venners and Bruce Eckel. The trouble with checked exceptions: A conversation with Anders Hejlsberg, Part II.
Available at http://www.artima.com/intv/handcuffs.html, August 2003.

Exception-Aware Requirements Elicitation
with Use Cases

Aaron Shui, Sadaf Mustafiz, and Jörg Kienzle

School of Computer Science, McGill University,
Montreal, Quebec, Canada
aaron@rome.com, sadaf@cs.mcgill.ca, Joerg.Kienzle@mcgill.ca

Abstract. During the execution of an application many exceptional situations arise that interrupt the normal interaction of the system with its environment. When developing dependable software, the first step is to foresee these exceptional situations and document how the system should deal with them. Any such exception that is not identified during requirements elicitation might potentially lead to an incomplete system specification during analysis, and ultimately to an implementation that lacks certain functionality, or even behaves in an unreliable way, or in a way that is not expected by the users of the system. This paper outlines an approach that extends use case based requirements elicitation with ideas from the exception handling world. After defining the actors and the goals they pursue when interacting with the system, our approach leads a developer to systematically investigate possible exceptional situations that the system may be exposed to: exceptional situations arising in the environment that change user goals and system-related exceptional situations that threaten to fail user goals. The process requires the developer to specify means that detect such situations, and define the recovery measures, i.e. the exceptional interaction between the actors and the system, necessary to recover from such situations in handler use cases. To conclude the requirements phase, an extended UML use case diagram summarizes the standard use cases, exceptions, handlers and their relationships. In addition, all exceptional situations are carefully documented in an exception table.

1   Introduction

Most main stream software development methods define a series of development phases – requirements elicitation, analysis, architecture and design, and finally implementation – that lead the development team to discover, specify, design and finally implement the main functionality of a system. This main functionality dictates the system's behavior most of the time. However, there are also many exceptional situations that may arise during the execution of an application. When using a standard software development process there is no guarantee that such situations are considered during the development. Whether the system can handle these situations or not depends highly on the imagination and experience of the developers. In addition, even if the application can actually deal with these

C. Dony et al. (Eds.):Exception Handling, LNCS 4119, pp. 221–242, 2006.

special situations, the particular way that the developer chose to address that situation might not be the one that a typical user of the system would expect. As a result, the final application might not function correctly in all possible situations or react in unexpected ways. This can at best annoy or confuse the user, but can also have more severe repercussions.

When developing dependable systems, i.e. mission- or safety-critical systems where a malfunction can cause significant damage, nothing should be left to chance. Following the idea of integrating exception handling into the software life cycle [1,2], this paper describes an extension to standard *use case*-based requirements elicitation that leads the developers to consider all possible exceptional situations that the system under development might be exposed to. We believe that thinking about exceptional behavior has to start at the requirements phase, because it is up to the users of the system to decide how they expect the system to react to exceptional situations. Only with exhaustive and detailed user feedback is it possible to discover and then specify the complete system behavior in a subsequent analysis phase, and decide on the need for employing fault masking and fault tolerance techniques for achieving run-time reliability during design.

This paper is an extended version of the work presented in [3]. Section 2 provides background information on exceptions and exception handling as found in modern programming languages. Section 3 describes our proposed process, and illustrates the ideas by means of an elevator control case study. Section 4 shows how we integrated our ideas with UML. Section 5 presents related work in this area, and the last section draws some conclusions.

2   Exceptions

2.1   Background on Exceptions

An exceptional situation, or short *exception*, describes a situation that, if encountered, requires something exceptional to be done in order to resolve it. Hence, an *exception occurrence* during a program execution is a situation in which the standard computation cannot pursue. For the program execution to continue, an extraordinary computation is necessary [4].

A programming language or system with support for exception handling, subsequently called an *exception handling system* (EHS) [5], provides features and protocols that allow programmers to establish a communication between a piece of code which detects an exceptional situation while performing an operation (a *signaler*) and the entity or context that asked for this operation. An EHS allows users to signal *exceptions* and to define *handlers*. To *signal* an exception amounts to:

1. identify the exceptional situation,
2. to interrupt the usual processing sequence,
3. to look for a relevant handler and
4. to invoke it while passing it relevant information about the exception.

Handlers are defined on (or attached to, or associated with) entities, such as data structures, or *contexts* for one or several exceptions. According to the language, a context may be a program, a process, a procedure, a statement, an expression, etc. Handlers are invoked when an exception is signaled during the execution or the use of the associated context or nested context. To *handle* means to set the system back to a coherent state, and then:

- to transfer control to the statement following the signaling one (*resumption model* [1]), or
- to discard the context between the signaling statement and the one to which the handler is attached (*termination model* [1]), or
- to signal a new exception to the enclosing context.

2.2   Exceptions and Requirements

The previous section described exceptions and exception handling mechanisms as defined at the programming language level. During requirements elicitation, an activity that is carried out very early during the software development cycle, the focus of the developer is on discovering and documenting essential functionality and behavior of a (software) system that does not yet exist.

Since their introduction in the late 80's [6], use cases are a widely used formalism for discovering and recording behavioral requirements of software systems [7]. A use case describes, without revealing the details of the system's internal workings, the system's responsibilities and its interactions with its environment as it performs work in serving one or more requests that, if successfully completed, satisfy a goal of a particular stake-holder. The external entities in the environment that interact with the system are called *actors*. The actor that initiates a use case in order to pursue a goal is called the *primary actor*, actors that the system interacts with in order to provide a service are called *secondary actors*.

In short, use cases are stories of actors using a system to *meet goals*. Typical goals are, for instance, withdrawing money from a bank account, placing an order for a book on an online store, or using an elevator to go to a destination floor (see Fig. 1). The standard way of achieving a goal is described in the *main success scenario*. Alternatives or situations in which the goal is not achieved are usually described in *extensions*. Use cases are in general text-based, but their strength is that they both scale up or scale down in terms of sophistication and formality, depending on the need and context. They can be effectively used as a communication means between technical as well as non-technical stake-holders of the software under development.

Use cases can be described at different levels of granularity [8]. *User-goal* level use cases describe how individual user goals are achieved. Optional *summary* level use cases provide a general overview of how the system is used. Finally, *subfunction* level use cases can be written that encapsulate subgoals of higher level use cases.

As explained above, an individual use case describes the sequence of interaction between the system and the environment that leads to the fulfillment of the primary actor's goal. Sometimes, however, a system is exposed to exceptional situations or conditions that *interrupt* the flow of interaction leading to the fulfillment of the actor's goal. From now on, we'll use the word *exception* to refer to such exceptional situations. It is important to point out that the meaning of exception at the requirements level is *not* directly related to exceptions as defined by modern programming languages. The term exception is used at a higher level of abstraction here. An exception occurrence endangers the completion of the actor's goal, suspending the normal interaction temporarily or for good.

2.3 Fault Assumptions

During requirements elicitation, the developer can assume that the system itself, once it has been built, will always behave according to specification – in other words, it will not contain any faults, and will therefore never fail. As the development continues into design and implementation phases, this assumption is most certainly not realistic. Dependability assessment and fault forecasting techniques have to be used to estimate the reliability of the implemented system. If needed, fault tolerance mechanisms have to be built into the system in order to increase system dependability.

Although the system is assumed to function perfectly, a reliable system can not assume that it will operate in a fault free environment. Actors can fail to provide essential input to the system: for instance, a floor sensor in an elevator system might not tell the system when the cabin has reached the destination floor. Actors can also fail to provide services that the system under development requests from them. If this service is essential, then the system under development must be able to compensate for such an actor failure, and the need for this compensation must be documented in the system requirements.

Even if the actors are reliable, the communication between the system under development and the actors might fail due to physical damage, electromagnetic perturbations, faults in the network protocol, etc.

Finally, in certain situations it might be impossible for the system to provide a requested functionality due to environmental constraints or business rules. For example, it might be impossible to withdraw money from an empty bank account. Such a situation can also be looked at as an interaction protocol violation: the user should not have requested to withdraw money from the empty bank account in the first place.

Our exception-aware requirements elicitation process considers environmental faults, communication problems and protocol violations in detail (see sections 3.3 and 3.3), since they affect the interaction of the system with the environment significantly.

2.4 Importance of Exception-Awareness

Discovering and documenting all possible exceptions that can interrupt normal system interaction is of tremendous importance in the context of dependable system development. Any exception that is not identified during requirements elicitation might potentially lead to an incomplete system specification during analysis, and ultimately in an implementation that lacks certain functionality, or even behaves in an unreliable way, or in a way that is not expected by the users of the system.

This is why our exception-aware process extends traditional use case-driven requirements elicitation with additional steps to make sure that all exceptional interactions that the system must support are discovered and documented. The process is described in section 3. The description is split into 4 tasks. We suggest to begin with standard use case-driven requirements elicitation (described in task 1 of section 3.2), followed by the elicitation of exceptions arising in the environment (described in task 2 of section 3.3), followed by the elicitation of exceptions internal to the system which prevent the system from providing the requested service (described in task 3 of section 3.4).

3   Exception-Aware Process

3.1   Elevator System Description

For illustration purpose, our exception-aware process is applied to a simple case study, a reliable and safe elevator system. For the sake of simplicity, there is only one elevator cabin that travels between the floors. The job of the development team is to decide on the required hardware, and to implement the elevator control software that processes the user requests and coordinates the different hardware devices. So far, only "mandatory" elevator hardware has been added to the system:

- a motor that the elevator control software can use to make the elevator cabin go up, go down or stop
- a cabin door that the elevator control software may ask to open and close
- floor sensors that detect when the cabin is approaching a floor
- two buttons on each floor (except for the top and ground floors) to call the lift, one for going up, one for going down
- a series of buttons, one for each floor, inside the cabin

Fault Assumptions in the Elevator System All elevator hardware components might fail:

- The motor might not react when asked to move the cabin.
- The cabin door might not react when asked to open or close.
- Sensors might fail to detect the approaching cabin.
- Buttons might be out of order and not send floor requests to the system.
- All communication channels might fail.

3.2   Standard Use Case Driven Requirements Elicitation

Task 1: Describing Normal Interaction

The first task of our exception-aware process consists in performing standard use case driven requirements elicitation for the system under development in order to discover the requirements that the system has to meet under normal conditions.

We define a textual use case template that the analyst has to fill out when elaborating a use case. It is based on the template used by the object-oriented, UML-based development method Fondue [9]. Using a predefined template forces the developer to document all important features of a use case, e.g. the *primary actor* (the one that wants to achieve the goal), the *level* of the use case, the potential concurrent execution of the use case (*Frequency & Multiplicity* section) [10], the *main success scenario* (a numbered step of interactions between the system and external actors) and the *extensions*.

The extension section of standard use cases may contain alternative ways that achieve the primary actor's goal, but often also describe situations in which the primary actor's goal is not achieved. Since we want to make a clear distinction between normal interaction and exceptional interaction, the extensions of the standard use cases should *only* describe alternative ways to achieve the goal, or interactions in which the primary actor *voluntarily abandons* his goal with the system. This voluntary abortion is documented by stating "Use case abandoned" at the end of the extension section.

Just like the steps in the main success scenario, extension steps are numbered. The number is the same as the interaction step number of the main success scenario to which the extension defines an alternative, followed by the letters 'a', 'b', 'c', etc.

Normal **Interactions with the Elevator System.** In the elevator system there is initially only one primary actor, the *User*. A user has only one goal with the system, namely to take the elevator to go to a destination floor, described in the user-goal level use case *TakeElevator* shown in Fig. 1.

As we can see from the main success scenario, the *User* first calls the elevator (step 1), and then rides it to the destination floor (step 2). The potential concurrent use of the elevator is documented in the *Frequency & Multiplicity* section.

The *CallElevator* use case is shown in Fig. 2. To call the elevator, the *User* pushes the up or down button and waits for the elevator cabin to arrive.

The *RideElevator* use case is shown in Fig. 3. To ride the elevator the *User* enters the cabin, selects a destination floor, waits until the cabin arrives at the destination floor and finally exits the elevator.

The extensions of the standard use cases of the elevator system only describe alternative ways to achieve the goal (as shown in step 2a of Fig. 2), or interactions in which the primary actor voluntarily abandons the interaction (as shown in steps 1a and 2a of Fig. 3).

Use Case: TakeElevator
Scope: Elevator Control System
Primary Actor: User
Intention: The intention of the *User* is to take the elevator to go to a destination floor.
Level: User Goal
Frequency & Multiplicity: A *User* can only take one elevator at a time. However, several *Users* may take the elevator simultaneously.
Main Success Scenario:
    1. User **CallsElevator**.
    2. User **RidesElevator**.
Extensions:
    1a. The cabin is already at the floor of the *User* and the door is open. *User* enters elevator; use case continues at step 2.
    1b. The user is already inside the elevator. Use case continues at step 2.

Fig. 1. *TakeElevator* Use Case

Use Case: CallElevator
Primary Actor: User
Intention: *User* wants to call the elevator to the floor that he / she is currently on.
Level: Subfunction
Main Success Scenario:
    1. *User* pushes button, indicating in which direction he / she wants to go.
    2. System acknowledges request.
    3. System schedules **ElevatorArrival** for the floor the *User* is currently on.
Extensions:
    2a. The same request already exists. System ignores the request. Use case ends in success.

Fig. 2. *CallElevator* Use Case

CallElevator and *RideElevator* both include the *Elevator Arrival* use case shown in Fig. 4. It is a subfunction level use case that describes how the system directs the elevator to a specific floor: once the system detects that the elevator is approaching the destination floor, it requests the motor to stop and opens the door.

The use cases that describe the normal interaction between the user and the elevator control system can be summarized in a standard UML use case diagram as shown in Fig. 5. The primary actor *(User)* is the one that initiates the *TakeElevator* use case. All secondary actors (the *Door*, the *Motor*, the *Exterior* and *Interior Floor Buttons*, as well as the *Floor Sensors*) that collaborate to provide the user goal are also depicted together with their multiplicities.

3.3   Actor-Signaled Exceptions

Each user-level use case describes a unit of useful functionality that the system under development provides to a particular actor. It details all interaction steps that an actor has to perform in order to achieve his / her goal. Sometimes, however, *exceptional situations arising in the environment*, i.e., situations that

Use Case: Ride Elevator
Primary Actor: User
Intention: The *User* wants to ride the elevator to a destination floor.
Level: Subfunction
Main Success Scenario:
1. *User* enters elevator.
2. User selects a destination floor.
3. System acknowledges request.
4. System requests door to close.
5. System receives confirmation that door is closed.
6. System schedules **ElevatorArrival** for the destination floor.
7. *User* exits the elevator at destination floor.

Extensions:
1a. *User* does not enter elevator. System times out and closes door. Use case abandoned.
2a. *User* does not select a destination floor. System times out and closes door. System continues processing pending requests or awaits new request. Use case abandoned.
7a. *User* selects another destination floor. System acknowledges new request and schedules **ElevatorArrival** for the new floor. Use case continues at step 5.

Fig. 3. *RideElevator* Use Case

Use Case: ElevatorArrival
Primary Actor: N/A
Intention: System wants to move the elevator to the *User*'s destination floor.
Level: Subfunction
Main Success Scenario:
1. System asks motor to start moving the cabin in the direction of the destination floor.
2. System detects elevator is approaching destination floor.
3. System requests motor to stop.
4. System opens door.

Fig. 4. *ElevatorArrival* Use Case

cannot be detected by the system itself, might cause actors to interact with a system in an exceptional way. The situations are exceptional in the sense that they occur only rarely, and they change the goals that actors have with the system, either temporarily or permanently. We call these exceptions *actor-signaled exceptions*. Sometimes even new actors – *exceptional actors* – start interacting with the system in order to signal the exception, or to help during handling of the situation.

Very often, such situations are related to safety issues. In an elevator system, for example, a fire outbreak in the building causes the elevator operator, an exceptional actor, to activate the fire emergency mode (see Fig. 6), in which all elevator cabins go down to the lowest floor to prevent casualties or physical damage in case the ropes break. Activating the emergency behavior is an *exceptional goal* for the elevator operator, since this happens only in very rare occasions.

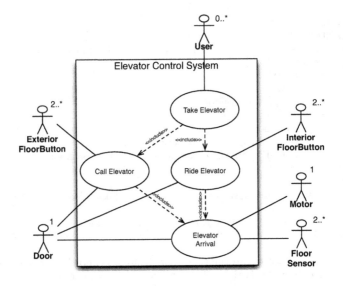

Fig. 5. Standard Elevator Use Case Diagram

Actor-signaled exceptions are communicated to the system by special actions of actors – hence their name. A dependable system must react to actor-signaled exceptions in a well-specified way. If the handling requires exceptional interaction steps with the primary actor or other secondary actors, then a handler use case (see below) must be defined. The handler is then linked to the context, i.e. the use case in which the exception can occur. Upon reception of the exception, the normal interaction is interrupted and the exceptional interaction begins.

Handler Use Cases. Just like it is possible to encapsulate several steps of normal interaction in a separate subfunction-level use case, an exceptional interaction that requires several steps of handling can be described separately from the normal system behavior in a *handler use case*. The major advantage of doing this is that from the very beginning, exceptional interaction and behavior is clearly identified and separated from the normal behavior of the system. This distinction is even more interesting if it can be extracted at a glance from the use case diagram (see section 4).

Separation of handlers also enables subsequent reuse of handlers. Just like a subfunction-level use case can encapsulate a subgoal that is part of several user goals, a handler use case can encapsulate a common way of handling exceptions that might occur while processing different user goals. Sometimes even, different exceptions can be handled in the same way.

Handler use cases for actor-signaled exceptions, i.e. handlers that describe exceptional goals, are self-contained, just like standard use cases. But of course, handlers can include sub-level handler use cases.

Just like in standard exception handling, where exception handlers are associated with exception handling contexts, handler use cases apply to a base use case, in this case any standard use case or other handler use case. When an exception occurs in a context, the associated handler can temporarily take over the system interaction, for instance to perform some compensation activity, and then switch back to the normal interaction scenario, similar to the resumption model described in section 2. Some exceptional situations, however, cannot be handled smoothly, and cause the current goal to fail. This is similar to the classic termination model.

Task 2: Actor-Signaled Exception Discovery

After having completed the standard use cases, the analyst should think of any exceptional situations or conditions in the environment that could make actors deviate from their initial goal, or change their goals completely. Actor-signaled exception discovery is done in a top-down manner, starting at the system-level.

System Level. At the system level, the analyst should focus on what could prevent the system as a whole from being operational. Interesting things to consider include: the operational needs of the system, e.g. power source, accessibility, connectivity; and anything that will draw away the attention of an actor, e.g. emergencies, safety concerns, malicious behavior. For example, in the elevator system, a fire outbreak should cause the elevator system to stop processing requests and come to a safe halt.

Use Case Level. At the use case level, the analyst should consider situations that could (temporarily) change the goal of the primary actor (without considering the failure of individual interactions contained within). Sometimes it even makes sense to consider sub-function level use cases and how their interaction could be interrupted due to external conditions. For example, in the elevator system, the user might feel unsafe while riding the elevator and wants to perform an emergency stop.

Interaction Step Level. There are rarely actor-signalled exceptions that are discovered at the interaction step level. This is due to the fact that these exceptional situations occur in the environment, and therefore can happen anytime. It only makes sense relate them to a single interaction step if all other interaction steps of the use case are not affected by the exception.

Actor-signaled Exceptions in the Elevator System. In the elevator case study we identified two actor-signaled exceptions. *EmergencyStop* is signaled by the *User* actor pushing the emergency button in the elevator in case he wants to interrupt the movement of the cabin. *EmergencyOverride* is signaled by an exceptional actor, the elevator operator, using the emergency override key on the ground floor in case of an emergency, for example a fire outbreak in the building. In our case, both exceptions can interrupt the normal system operation at any time, so their context is *TakeElevator*.

Handler Use Case: UserEmergency
Contexts & Exceptions: TakeElevator{EmergencyStop}
Primary Actor: User
Intention: *User* wants to stop the movement of the cabin.
Level: User Goal
Frequency & Multiplicity: Since there is only one elevator cabin, only one *User* can activate the emergency at a given time.
Main Success Scenario:
1. System initiates **EmergencyBrake**.
2. System clears all pending requests.
3. *User* toggles off emergency stop button.
4. System deactivates brakes and awaits the next request.

Handler Use Case: ReturnToGroundFloor
Contexts & Exceptions: TakeElevator{EmergencyOverride}
Primary Actor: Elevator Operator
Intention: *Elevator Operator* wants to call the elevator to the ground floor because the elevator operation is too dangerous.
Level: User Goal
Frequency & Multiplicity: Only one *ReturnToGroundFloor* use case can be active at a given time.
Main Success Scenario:
1. System clears all requests and requests motor to go down.
2. System detects that elevator is approaching the ground floor.
3. System requests motor to stop.
3. System opens elevator door.

Fig. 6. *UserEmergency* and *ReturnToGroundFloor* Handler Use Case

Fig. 6 shows the handler *UserEmergency* that handles the exception *EmergencyStop*. Handler use cases have an additional field in the use case template named *Contexts & Exceptions* that is used to document by which exception occurring in what context the handler is triggered. In our case, an emergency stop occurring in take elevator interrupts and fails the goal of the use case. As a first handling step, the emergency brakes are activated. Then the pending requests are cleared. Subsequently, the *User* can toggle off the emergency button to reactivate the elevator.

The *EmergencyOverride* exception is handled by the *ReturnToGroundFloor* handler use case, also shown in Fig. 6. *ReturnToGroundFloor* interrupts and fails the *TakeElevator* use case.

3.4 System-Detected Exceptions

Even if all actors interact with the system in a normal way, *system-related exceptional situations* might prevent the system from providing the desired functionality to the actor. For example, insufficient funds can prevent a successful withdrawal, an order might not be fulfillable because the book is currently out of stock, or a motor failure might prevent a user from taking the elevator. In such cases, the goal of the actor cannot be fulfilled.

Handler Use Case: RedirectElevator
Context & Exception: ElevatorArrival{MissedFloor}
Primary Actor: N/A
Intention: System redirects the elevator to a different floor because the destination floor is unreachable.
Level: Subfunction
Main Success Scenario:
   1. System cancels request to stop at destination floor.
   2. System schedules a new request to stop at next floor.

Handler Use Case: EmergencyBrake
Context & Exception: TakeElevator{MotorFailure}
Primary Actor: N/A
Intention: System wants to stop operation of elevator and secure the cabin.
Level: Subfunction
Main Success Scenario:
   1. System stops motor.
   2. System activates the emergency brakes.
   2. System turns on the emergency display.

Fig. 7. *RedirectElevator* and *EmergencyBrake* Handler Use Case

In general, this sort of exceptional situation also triggers some exceptional interaction steps with the environment. One of the steps is (or should be!) to inform the actor of the impossibility to achieve the goal. Once informed, the actor can decide how to react to the situation. The system itself might also be capable of handling the problem, for instance by suggesting to withdraw a smaller amount of money, or by suggesting to buy some other book, or by activating the emergency brakes and calling the elevator operator (see Fig. 7).

Task 3: System-Detected Exception Discovery

After having discovered the actor-signaled exceptions, each use case must now be examined to see if there are any system-related exceptional situations that can make the use case goal fail. Up to now we have assumed that actors are reliable, that hardware never fails, and that communication with hardware / actors is reliable as well. However, this is an unrealistic assumption that a safety-critical application such as the elevator control software cannot make.

Inputs and outputs may fail (see fault assumptions in section 2.3), and the consequences and ways of dealing with such a failure must be identified. If the consequences endanger the accomplishment of the user goal, then the system must detect the failure – hence the name *system-detected exception* – and address the situation. Detection might require the use of additional hardware or timeouts.

Once the exception is detected, ways of addressing the exception have to be investigated. Some situations require actions to be taken that ensure system safety. Sometimes, actions can be taken in order to allow the system to continue to provide service, and hence ensure system reliability.

In both cases, however, actors – especially humans – are "surprised" when they encounter an exceptional situation, and are subsequently more likely to make mistakes when interacting with the system. Exceptional interactions during exception handling must therefore be as intuitive as possible, and respect the actor's needs. Again, all interaction steps addressing an exception have to be recorded in handler use cases. In contrast to actor-signaled handlers, handlers that address system-detected exceptions may not necessarily be meaningful by themselves, but only within the context of another use case.

System-detected exceptions are usually found at the interaction step level. Our process therefore suggests to perform system-detected exception discovery in a bottom-up manner.

Interaction Step Level. Each sub-level use case must be looked at step by step, and every interaction classified into either an *input* or an *output* interaction. Then, depending on the kind of interaction, the following issues have to be considered:

Input Problems. If omission of input from an actor can cause the goal to fail, then, once the omission has been detected, different options of handling the situation have to be considered. For instance, prompting the actor for the input again after a given time has elapsed, or using default input are possible options. Safety considerations might make it even necessary to temporarily shutdown the system in case of missing input. Invalid input data is another example of input problem that might cause the goal to fail. Since most of the time the actors are aware of the importance of their input, a reliable system should also acknowledge input from an actor, so that the actor realizes that she is making progress in achieving her goal.

Output Problems. Whenever an output triggers a critical action of an actor, then the system must make sure that it can detect eventual communication problems or failure of an actor to execute the requested action. For example, the elevator control software might tell the motor to stop, but a communication failure or a motor misbehavior might keep the motor going. Again, additional hardware, for instance, a sensor that detects when the cabin stopped at a floor, or timeouts might be necessary to ensure reliability.

Use Case Level. Once every step has been inspected, the analyst should concentrate on system-detected exceptions that prevent the execution of sub-function level goals. It might help to ask the opposite question: what preconditions must be fulfilled in order to achieve the sub goal?

System Level. There are rarely system-detected exceptions that prevent the *entire* system from providing its services, unless the entire system functionality depends on, for instance, a single secondary actor.

System-Detected Exceptions in the Elevator Case Study. To illustrate the process of discovering system-detected exceptions, let us go step by step through the use case *ElevatorArrival* (see Fig. 4). The first step involves the floor sensor informing the system that the elevator is approaching a floor. This is an input interaction, and its omission leads to an exceptional situation. A floor

Use Case: ElevatorArrival
Primary Actor: N/A
Intention: System wants to move the elevator to the *User*'s destination floor.
Level: Subfunction
Main Success Scenario:
1. System asks motor to start moving in the direction of the destination floor.
2. System receives confirmation that cabin is moving.
3. System detects elevator is approaching destination floor.
4. System requests motor to stop.
5. System receives confirmation that cabin is stopped at destination floor.
6. System requests door to open.
7. System receives confirmation that door is open.
Extensions:
2a. Exception{MotorFailure}
3a. Exception{MissedFloor}
5a. Exception{MotorFailure}
7a. Exception{DoorStuckClosed}
System displays message to *User* (it is up to the user to select a new destination floor or press the emergency button). Use case ends in failure.

Fig. 8. Updated *ElevatorArrival* Use Case

sensor defect might cause the elevator to miss a destination floor. In this case, the corresponding handler *RedirectElevator*, shown in Fig. 7, stops the cabin at the next floor.

In Step 2 of *ElevatorArrival* the system requests the motor to stop. This is an output interaction that requests a service from a secondary actor, in this case the motor. In case the motor malfunctions and does not stop, the emergency brakes have to be activated immediately. This is done by the *EmergencyBrake* handler, also shown in Fig. 7.

Finally, in step 3 of *ElevatorArrival*, the system requests the door to open. This output can only be sent *after* a successful stop of the motor. For reliability reasons, a "stop detection" mechanism, such as an additional sensor that monitors the cabin speed, must be added to the system. Additionally the door might fail to open in step 3. We have to add an additional sensor to detect this failure. If the door does not open, the elevator could move to a different floor and try to open the door there. Without threatening reliability, we can also choose to ignore the failure and continue processing the next request, and hence leave it up to the user in the elevator to decide to either retry the floor, go to a different floor or push the emergency button. Fig. 8 shows the updated, reliable version of the *ElevatorArrival* use case.

Looking at the *CallElevator* and *RideElevator* use case, we can detect a common problem that might prevent the goals from succeeding: the elevator door might be stuck open, for instance because an obstacle prevents it from closing. This case is handled by the *DoorAlert* handler use case. Another exceptional situation occurs when there are too many passengers in the elevator. The *OverweightAlert* handler addresses this exception. The *DoorAlert* and *OverweightAlert* handlers are shown in Fig. 9.

Handler Use Case: DoorAlert
Primary Actor: N/A
Context & Exception: TakeElevator{DoorStuckOpen}
Intention: System wants to alert the passengers that there is an obstacle preventing the door from closing.
Level: Subfunction
Main Success Scenario:
1. System displays "door open".
2. System turns on the buzzer.
3. System requests the door to close.
Step 3 is repeated until the door closes.
4. System detects that the door is now closed.
5. System turns off the buzzer.
6. System clears the display.

Handler Use Case: OverweightAlert
Primary Actor: N/A
Context & Exception: RideElevator{Overweight}
Intention: System wants to alert the passengers that there is too much weight in the elevator.
Level: Subfunction
Main Success Scenario:
1. System displays "overweight".
2. System turns on the buzzer.
3. System detects that the weight is back to normal.
4. System turns off buzzer.
5. System clears display.

Fig. 9. *DoorAlert* and *OverweightAlert* Handler Use Case

Task 4: Recursion

The step-by-step analysis of the use cases must then be recursively applied to all the handlers, because handlers may themselves be interrupted by exceptions. In our system, the *EmergencyBrake*, *OverweightAlert* and *DoorAlert* handler use cases all wait until the situation is resolved. In case the problem persists for a certain amount of time, the elevator control system should notify an elevator operator. The elevator operator can then evaluate the situation and, if necessary, call a service person. Similarly, if there are problems such as a door that does not open that prevents the *RedirectElevator* handler use case from completion, a service person can be notified. This functionality is described in the handler use case *CallElevatorOperator* shown in Fig. 10.

Similar to *ElevatorArrival*, the *ReturnToGroundFloor* handler use case has to be refined with acknowledgment steps to detect a possible motor failure as shown in Fig. 11.

3.5   Completing the Exception Table

For traceability and documentation reasons, all discovered actor-signaled and system-detected exceptions should be recorded in a table. For each exception

Handler Use Case: CallElevatorOperator
Context & Exception: EmergencyBrake{ElevatorStoppedTooLong],
  OverweightAlert{OverweightTooLong}, DoorAlert{DoorStuckOpenTooLong}
  RedirectElevator{DoorStuckClosed}
Intention: The system wants to alert the elevator operator, so that the elevator operator can come and assess the damage.
Level: Subfunction
Main Success Scenario:
  1. System cancels all pending requests.
  2. System displays "calling operator ".
  3. System calls operator.

Fig. 10. *CallElevatorOperator* Handler Use Case

Handler Use Case: ReturnToGroundFloor
Contexts & Exceptions: TakeElevator{EmergencyOverride}
Primary Actor: Elevator Operator
Intention: *Elevator Operator* wants to call the elevator to the ground floor because the elevator operation is too dangerous.
Level: User Goal
Frequency & Multiplicity: Only one *ReturnToGroundFloor* use case can be active at a given time.
Main Success Scenario:
  1. System clears all requests and requests motor to go down.
  2. System receives confirmation that cabin is moving.
  3. System detects that elevator is approaching the ground floor.
  4. System requests motor to stop.
  5. System receives confirmation that cabin is stopped at destination floor.
  6. System opens elevator door.
  7. System receives confirmation that door is now open.
Extensions:
  2a. Exception{MotorFailure}
  3a. Exception{MissedFloor}
  5a. Exception{MotorFailure}
  7a. Exception{DoorStuckClosed}

Fig. 11. Refined *ReturnToGroundFloor* Handler Use Case

this table should contain a small textual description of the exceptional situation, the exception contexts in which it can occur, the associated handler(s), and the mechanism of detecting the situation.

The exception table for the elevator system with the detailed descriptions of each exception is shown in Tab 1.

4   Integration with UML

The Unified Modeling Language (UML) [11] defines a *notation* for specifying, constructing, visualizing, and documenting the artifacts of a software-intensive system. UML is intentionally process-independent. However, it offers a variety

Table 1. Exceptions of the Elevator Control System

Exception	Description	Context	Handler	Detection
Emergency Stop	An emergency situation in the elevator cabin makes the User want to stop the elevator	Take Elevator	User Emergency	Triggered by User actor pressing the emergency button
Emergency Override	An external emergency situation, for example a fire outbreak, makes the operation of the elevator too dangerous.	Take Elevator	ReturnTo GroundFloor	Triggered by ElevatorOperator actor using the emergency override key.
Missed Floor	Due to a floor sensor or communication failure, the elevator control does not get notified when the cabin approaches or stops at a floor	Elevator Arrival	Redirect Elevator	Sensor detects elevator is approaching a floor beyond destination floor - OR - timeout expires after a stop request has been sent to motor
Motor Failure	Due to a motor or communication failure, the motor does not react to requests	Take Elevator - OR - ReturnTo Ground Floor	Emergency Brake	Sensor detects elevator is approaching a floor beyond destination floor after a stop request has been sent to motor - OR - timeout expires and no sensor input has been received after a up/down request has been sent to motor
Door Stuck Open	The door does not respond to a close request because of a door failure, a communication failure or an obstacle blocking the door	Take Elevator	DoorAlert	Timeout expires after a close request has been sent to the door
Overweight	There is too much weight in the elevator for safe operation	Ride Elevator	Overweight Alert	Overweight sensor in the elevator cabin
DoorStuck Closed	The door does not respond to a close request because of a door failure, a communication failure or an obstacle blocking the door	Elevator Arrival - OR - Redirect Elevator	none - OR - Call Elevator Operator	Timeout expires after an open request has been sent to the door
Elevator Stopped TooLong	The emergency brakes have been active for too long	Emergency Brake	Call Elevator Operator	Timeout
Door Stuck Open TooLong	The door has been open for too long	Door Alert	Call Elevator Operator	Timeout
Overweight TooLong	The elevator has been overloaded for too long	Overweight Alert	Call Elevator Operator	Timeout

of diagrams that unify the scores of graphical modeling notations that existed in the software development industry in the 80's and 90's. The diagram we are focussing on in this work is the *use case diagram*.

Whereas individual use cases are text-based, the UML use case diagram provides a concise high level view of all (or a set of) use cases of a system. It allows the developer to graphically depict the use cases, the actors that interact with the system, and the relationships between actors and use cases.

In parallel to the elaboration of the individual use cases and handlers, we propose to build an extended exception-aware use case diagram providing a detailed and precise summary of the partitioning of the system into normal and exceptional interactions.

In a use case diagram, standard use cases appear as ellipses (see Fig. 13), associated with the actors whose goals they describe. We propose to identify handler use cases with a `<<handler>>` stereotype, which differentiates them from the standard use cases. To allow developers to identify exceptional behavior at a glance, handler use cases can be represented in the use case diagram with a special symbol or using a different color.

A handler that is attached to a context use case is shown by a directed relationship (dotted arrow) in the diagram. This relationship is very similar to the standard UML `<<extends>>` relationship. It specifies that the behavior of the context use case may be affected by the behavior of the handler use case in case an exception is encountered. Similar to the explicit extension points introduced in UML 2.0, the context use case can specify the specific steps in which the exception might occur (see Fig. 8 step 7a), but does not need to. In the latter case, the exceptional situation can affect the base processing at any time.

In case of an occurrence of an exceptional situation, the base behavior is put on hold or abandoned, and the interaction specified in the handler is started. A handler can temporarily take over the system interaction, for instance to perform some compensation activity, and then switch back to the normal interaction scenario. In this case, the relationship is tagged with a `<<interrupt & continue>>` stereotype. Some exceptional situations, however, cannot be handled smoothly, and cause the current goal to fail. Such dependencies are tagged with `<<interrupt & fail>>`. This is similar to the resumption and termination models reviewed in section 2.

The `<<interrupt & continue>>` and `<<interrupt & fail>>` relationships also differ from the `<<extends>>` relationship in the sense that they apply also to all sub use cases of a base use case. In the elevator example presented in the next section, for instance, an *Emergency Override* can interrupt *Take Elevator*, and therefore also any of the included use cases of *Take Elevator*, namely *Call Elevator*, *Ride Elevator* and *Elevator Arrival*.

Finally, the exceptions that activate the handler use case are added to the interrupt relationship in a UML comment. The notation follows the same notation that was introduced in UML 2.0 to specify extension points for use cases.

Fig. 12 shows how all the aforementioned extensions are integrated with the UML 2.0 metamodel.

HandlerUseCase is defined as a stereotyped extension of *UseCase*, and therefore inherits all properties and associations of standard use cases. An *Interrupt* relationship is modeled in a similar way as *Extend* and *Include* relationships.

An *Interrupt* relationship, however, must be associated with exactly one *HandlerUseCase* (*triggeredHandler*), and interrupts exactly one standard or handler use case (*interruptedCase*). The two different interrupt relationships, i.e. *interrupt and continue* and *interrupt and fail*, are modeled as subclasses of *Interrupt*. Finally, *Exception* inherits from *RedefinableElement*, just as *ExtensionPoint* does. An *Interrupt* relationship can be triggered by one or multiple exceptions (*triggeredException*).

4.1   Extended Use Case Diagram of the Elevator System

Fig. 13 illustrates the integration with UML by showing the extended use case diagram of the Elevator System. All exceptional interactions are tagged with the <<handler>> stereotype, and all exceptional situations that trigger these interactions are documented using notes attached to the <<interrupt>> relationships. For space reasons, the secondary actors have been omitted from the diagram.

A UML CASE tool supporting our process and the extended use case diagrams should allow the developer to selectively display the normal interactions, the handlers attached to actor-signaled exceptions, or the handlers that address system-detected exception. This makes it possible for developers to focus on the main functionality, on exceptional functionality, or on recovery of system-related exceptions.

5   Related Work

Main stream software development methods currently deal with exceptions only at late design and implementation phases. However, several approaches have

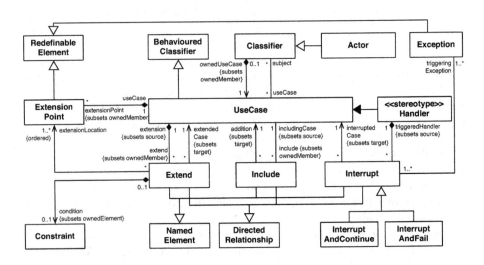

Fig. 12. Extended Use Case UML 2.0 Metamodel

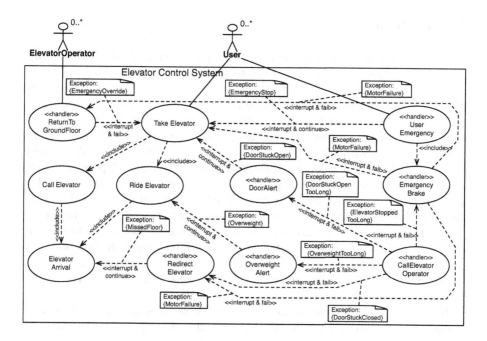

Fig. 13. Reliable Elevator Use Case Diagram

been proposed that extend exception handling ideas to other parts of the software development cycle.

De Lemos et al. [2] emphasize the separation of the treatment of requirements-related, design-related, and implementation-related exceptions during the software life-cycle by specifying the exceptions and their handlers in the context where faults are identified. The description of exceptional behavior is supported by a cooperative object-oriented approach that allows the representation of collaborative behavior between objects at different phases of the software development.

Rubira et al. [12] present an approach that incorporates exceptional behavior in the development of component-based software by extending the Catalysis software development method. The requirements phase of Catalysis is also based on use cases, and the extension augments them with exception handling ideas.

Our approach is different from the above for several reasons. Firstly, we help the requirements engineers to discover exceptions and handlers by providing a detailed *process* that they can follow. Without a process, the only way a developer can discover exceptions is based on her imagination and experience. Secondly, our process increases reliability even more by helping the developers detect the need for adding "feedback" and "acknowledgment" interaction steps with actors to make sure that there were no communication problems. Additionally, the process recommends adding of hardware to monitor request execution of secondary actors when necessary. Finally, our handler use cases are stand-alone, and can therefore be associated with multiple exceptions and multiple contexts.

6   Conclusion

We believe that when developing reliable systems, exceptional situations that the system might be exposed to have to be discovered and addressed at the requirements elicitation phase. Exceptional situations are less common and hence the behavior of the system in such situations is less obvious. Also, users are more likely to make mistakes when exposed to exceptional situations.

In this paper we propose an approach that extends use case based requirements elicitation with ideas from the exception handling world. We define a process that leads a developer to systematically investigate all possible exceptional situations that a system may be exposed to. First the use cases are looked at in a top-down manner, focussing on external exceptional situations that could change or interrupt user goals. During this step, additional exceptional actors can be discovered. In a second step, the use cases are looked at in a bottom-up manner, focussing on system-related exceptions that prevent the individual interactions and sub-goals from completing successfully. The process ensures that the system is capable of detecting such situations, for instance by using time-outs, or by adding additional hardware. Finally, the process leads the developer to discover and then document how the users of the system expect the system to react in such situations. The discovery of all exceptional situations and detailed user feedback at an early stage is essential, saves development cost, and ultimately results in a more dependable system.

We also show how to extend UML use case diagrams to separate normal and exceptional behavior. This allows developers to graphically show the dependencies among standard and handler use cases.

Based on our exception-aware use cases, a specification that considers all exceptional situations and user expectations can be elaborated during a subsequent analysis phase. This specification can then be used to decide on the need for employing fault masking and fault tolerance techniques when designing the software architecture and during detailed design. For more detailed information on our exception-aware process, the interested reader is referred to [13], where we discuss advanced issues, such as handler priorities.

References

1. Goodenough, J.B.: Exception handling: Issues and a proposed notation. Communications of the ACM **18** (1975) 683 – 696
2. de Lemos, R., Romanovsky, A.: Exception handling in the software lifecycle. International Journal of Computer Systems Science and Engineering **16** (2001) 167 – 181
3. Shui, A., Mustafiz, S., Kienzle, J.: Exceptional use cases. In: 8th International Conference on Model Driven Engineering Languages and Systems – MoDELS 2005, Montego Bay, Jamaica, Oct. 2-7, 2005. Number 3713 in Lecture Notes in Computer Science, Montego Bay, Jamaica, Springer Verlag (2005) 568 – 583
4. Knudsen, J.L.: Better exception-handling in block-structured systems. IEEE Software **4** (1987) 40 – 49

5. Dony, C.: Exception handling and object-oriented programming: Towards a synthesis. In Meyrowitz, N., ed.: 4th European Conference on Object–Oriented Programming (ECOOP '90). ACM SIGPLAN Notices, (ACM Press)
6. Jacobson, I.: Object-oriented development in an industrial environment. In: Conference proceedings on Object-oriented programming systems, languages and applications, ACM Press (1987) 183 – 191
7. Larman, C.: Applying UML and Patterns: An Introduction to Object-Oriented Analysis and Design and the Unified Process. 2nd edn. Prentice Hall (2002)
8. Cockburn, A.: Writing Effective Use Cases. Addison–Wesley (2000)
9. Sendall, S., Strohmeier, A.: Uml-based fusion analysis. In: UML'99, Fort Collins, CO, USA, October 28-30, 1999. Number 1723 in Lecture Notes in Computer Science, Springer Verlag (1999) 278–291
10. Kienzle, J., Sendall, S.: Addressing concurrency in object-oriented software development. Technical Report SOCS-TR-2004.8, McGill University, Montreal, Canada (2004)
11. Object Management Group: Unified Modeling Language: Superstructure. (2004)
12. Rubira, C.M.F., de Lemos, R., Ferreira, G.R.M., Fliho, F.C.: Exception handling in the development of dependable component-based systems. Software — Practice & Experience **35** (2004) 195 – 236
13. Shui, A.: Exceptional use cases - Master Thesis, School of Computer Science, McGill' University (2005)

An Approach to Defining Requirements for Exceptions

William Bail

Software Engineering Center
The MITRE Corporation
7515 Colshire Drive
McLean, VA 22102, USA
wbail@mitre.org

Abstract. When exception handling is required for a software system, the defining the requirements of the desired behavior in the presence of exceptional conditions is generally defined as an add-on to the core requirements. This is necessary because by definition, requirements define desired behavior, and exceptions are undesired, abnormal situations. Consequently, by using separate mechanisms to define :normal" processing and "exceptional" processing, the requirements statements do not provide a unified way of analyzing behavior, potentially allowing undesired effects during execution. This paper proposes a new approach, based on usage modeling, to unifying the specification of normal behavior and exceptional behavior into one model.

Keywords: exception handling, usage models, state machines, requirements specification.

1 Introduction

Exception handling has become a standard feature in modern programming languages. Using such features facilitates being able to provide continuous operation by allowing the programmer to predict and handle conditions of execution that are anomalous. Rather than allowing the system to crash or otherwise fail to provide service, programmers can detect anomalous conditions and provide logic to mitigate any undesired effects, including correction of the problem as well as graceful degradation.

Generally, the desired responses of systems to exceptional situations are defined separately from the definition of the desired responses to normal situations. Clearly, exceptions are not normal processing. They are usually defined in terms of the exceptional conditions and a prescription of how the system needs to behave when encountering such conditions. While there are various ways of describing the desired exception handling behavior, these are usually expressed in English or some other natural language. Several researchers have devised approaches to defining the exceptional conditions using a formal approach. Such formalism facilitates generation of exception handling code. But to date, there have been no unified mechanisms to define both requirements and exception handling behaviors in a single model [1]. [2]

C. Dony et al. (Eds.):Exception Handling, LNCS 4119, pp. 243–254, 2006.
© Springer-Verlag Berlin Heidelberg 2006

recognized the value of having all requirements information in a single model. The advantages to unifying these aspects of a system's behavior include the ability to verify the consistency of the defined behaviors as well as to exploit a model driven development approach and automatically generate code.

When we require that a system use exception handling as a mechanism to achieve reliable behavior, we are imposing a specific design approach. When we specify the desired behavior of a system, including its behavior in erroneous conditions, and omit constraining the design approach to a specific design pattern, we allow the developers more flexibility in implementation, generally a preferred approach.

2 Requirements and Exception Handling

The requirements for a system describe what is expected of a system. Strictly speaking, requirements express the desired externally-visible behaviors of a system, as observable by users and other systems [3]. We generally refer to the description of the requirements of a system as the system's specification.

However, in common use, requirements specifications often include other attributes of a system, such as design patterns, expectations for quality, and other aspects that may be thought to be of importance. For example, an organization may contract for the development of a system that implements a customer-supplied algorithm, or may require that a system be developed using fault-tolerant design features.

It is important, when we discuss a system's requirements, to be clear about those that refer simply to its externally visible behavior, and those that refer to other aspects such as design. Such an external view treats the system as a black box, which can be verified by observing its responses to stimuli without having to look at the internal processing of the system, potentially simplifying how the system can be tested.

Requirements can be created at multiple levels within a system. We can define the requirements for the system as a whole. We can also define the requirements for individual components within the system, as a part of defining the system's architecture. The overall behavior of the system is then a composition of the behaviors of its constituent components, as illustrated in figure 1.

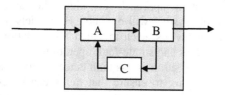

Fig. 1. System Composed of Components

When developing complex systems, precisely defining requirements for each layer of subcomponents is an important activity and is inherent to the design process. It is important to facilitate design and integration of the system across multiple development teams, to promote the reusability of these components to other systems, or to reuse components that were developed previously. Knowing the behavior of components is essential to being able to interact with those components.

Exceptions are a feature of a programming language that provide the ability to detect anomalous conditions in the execution state, and to recover from such states under control, potentially without failure, but at least under a controlled degradation. We use the term *exception handling* to refer to a class of mechanisms and design approaches that have the purpose of dealing with and mitigating the effects of embedded and latent defects in software.

When we require that a system make use of exception handling in order to ensure reliable behavior, we are imposing a design constraint on the developers, potentially reducing their design flexibility. However, it is not necessary to explicitly require that exception handling be used. Rather, the requirements can describe conditions that are abnormal, and define appropriate reactions to these conditions, letting the developers devise design approaches to handle these conditions.

3 Previous Work

There has been a significant amount of work analyzing the relationships between requirements and exception handling. In much of this work however, the focus was on applying requirements definition to the identification of where exception handling was required. In some cases, the models created assisted in automatically generating code to identify the exceptional conditions and in handling them. Refer to [4] for one such approach.

[5] Identifies two aspects of requirements, goals and the requirements that are derived from the goals. He notes that goals and requirements tend to be too ideal and do not recognize the reality that during operation many unexpected conditions may occur. He recommends identifying *obstacles* to the goals, where an obstacle is an undesirable condition. By integrating these at an earlier stage, developers are better able to design exception handling mechanisms into the overall design rather than retrofitting them after the design has been completed.

[6] proposes what he refers to as a "history-based specification" where each requirement is defined based on the input histories of the input parameters. He advocates a closed system approach in which he describes the operational environment in which the system will operate. He models the system's operational state as a sequence of behaviors, each modeled by a relation, and he differentiates between fault-free operations and single-fault operations.

[7] [8] also describe the need to assess fault detectability characteristics of systems. Reasoning that it is necessary to ensure that faults can be effectively detected, he analyses ways of characterizing the criteria needed to determine the feasibility of detection. Regardless of the quality of a system's fault tolerance design, if the anomalous states cannot be reliably identified during operation, the system will fail.

[9] describes a concept that he calls "misuse" cases. He observes that Use Cases have become popular as a way of eliciting requirements, but may have limitations. Some practitioners, for example, employ them informally, minimizing their effectiveness. He observes however that use cases and scenarios can help to elicit more detailed requirements. He then suggests that the idea of a *misuse* case could also

be useful. In a misuse case, a non-desirable situation is described. By explicitly describing such situations, additional requirements can be identified to avoid negative outcomes.

[10] [11] describes an approach to specification-based software verification based on temporal logic. In his approach, formal statements define the constraints under which a system is to operate. These are automatically converted into code and used to detect at run-time the violation of any of the constraints, thereby providing a mechanism to support error-handling processes.

4 Proposed Approach

This paper proposes to integrate the specifications of exception handling into the same model as being used to define normal (non-erroneous) operations. In this approach for any potential input or sequence of inputs, both normal responses and erroneous responses will be defined. To avoid what may appear to be ambiguous specifications of requirements, each of the multiple responses will be associated with probabilities of occurrence, the total adding to 100% (certainty). This approach fits in with the intuitive concept that exceptions should occur rarely. Being able to specify how rarely provides a level of control to the owners of the requirements, and allows a natural mechanism for the defining of the desired reliability of the system. The technique to be used is based on using an extension of state machines to define operational behavior. This technique is called *usage modeling* [12,13]. [14] describes a similar approach using a different technique.

Usage modeling is used to assist in the verification that a system meets it reliability requirements. It is also valuable to assist developers in performing trade-offs during the design process. Basically, usage models allow defining of the relative likelihoods of various input patterns in a system's operational environment. As such they facilitate defining the system's operational scenarios, a necessary step when testing for reliability. With a usage model, test cases can be defined in a proportion that approximates the expected usage of the system. When exception handling requirements are integrated into such models, testing for normal behavior and for exceptional behavior can be combined, reducing time and increasing fidelity.

This approach borrows from the previous work both in the areas of exception handling but also in statistical testing.

5 Usage Models

A usage model is a derivation of a state transition model used to describe the behavior of a software component or system. [2] recommends the state machines as a way of unambiguously defining the requirements of a system and handling them as black boxes without involving design features. To support this approach, she used a state-based language called RSML (Requirements State Machine Language).

Using state machines to define requirements has become popular, especially with the increasing use of model driven development techniques [2] [10] [15]. To illustrate how usage models are related to state machines, consider the following example.

We need to develop a software component (to be named *abc*) to be built with the following behavior:

The component shall examine the input stream as each symbol appears. After each symbol, the component shall return a value of 0 if the most recent three symbols do not form the pattern "abc", and a value of 1 if the most recent three symbols form this pattern. The input symbols consist solely of the letters a through z.

We can define a state machine that more formally expresses these requirements, as shown in table 1.

Table 1. State Machine Specfication of Component abc

State	Input	Next State	Output
unseen	a	a_seen	0
	¬ a	unseen	0
a_seen	a	a_seen	0
	b	ab_seen	0
	¬ a ∧ ¬ b	unseen	0
ab_seen	a	a_seen	0
	c	abc_seen	1
	¬ a ∧ ¬ c	unseen	0
abc_seen	a	a_seen	0
	¬ a	unseen	0

or, as shown pictorially in figure 2:

In this diagram, each state transition arc is labeled with the stimulus provided to the system (in this case, the next letter in the input stream), and the response (or output) of the system in response to the stimulus. This state machine provides a concise mechanism for defining the required behavior, and can be used as a template for the creation of test cases, simply by traversing the state transitions, selecting the inputs as appropriate, and, verifying that the correct responses are returned.

With a simple extension, this state model can be used to estimate the expected reliability of the system once developed. Estimating the reliability requires creating an expected operational scenario against which the component can be tested. This is the case because the reliability of a system depends on the distribution of inputs to that system. The probability of a failure equals the probability that an input sequence occurs that encounters an embedded defect, causing a failure. Usage models provide a mechanism for expressing such operational profiles.

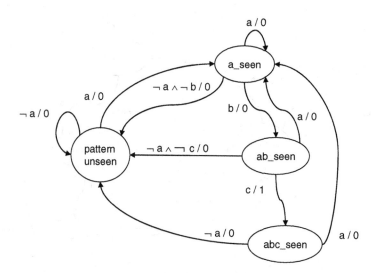

Fig. 2. State machine model of component *abc*

Specifically, we can convert this state machine into a usage model by defining the likelihood of each input as a part of the definition, as shown in table 2.

Table 2. Usage model for pattern recognizer

State	Input	Prob	Next State	Output
unseen	a	**0.10**	a_seen	0
	¬ a	**0.90**	unseen	0
a_seen	a	**0.10**	a_seen	0
	b	**0.05**	ab_seen	0
	¬ a ¬ b	**0.85**	unseen	0
ab_seen	a	**0.40**	a_seen	0
	c	**0.05**	abc_seen	1
	¬ a ∧ ¬ c	**0.55**	unseen	0
abc_seen	a	**0.10**	a_seen	0
	¬ a	**0.90**	unseen	0

This table is the same as the previous one, but with an additional column that defines the likelihood that any specific input symbol will be encountered. According to the table, at any random point in the input stream, the likelihood of seeing an "a" is 0.10. Once an "a" is encountered, the likelihood of seeing a "b" is 0.05, and of then seeing a "c" is 0.05. That is, the likelihood of seeing the pattern "abc" is 0.00025. Note that in this case, the likelihood is much larger than one would expect by random chance where there is a uniform probability of each letter's appearing.

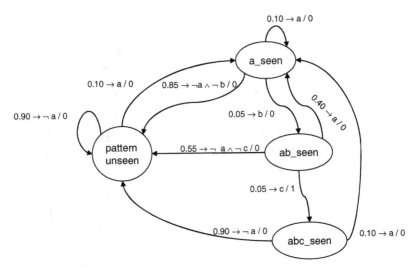

Fig. 3. Usage model diagram

Usage models can also be drawn as an extended state machine (figure 3).

In this figure, each state transition is labeled with the likelihood of the input, the input itself, and the resulting output.

The likelihoods can be determined in many ways, including historical observations of the input stream as seen by previous software components. Once such a usage model is defined, the process of defining test cases that conform to the operational profile can be done mechanically and automatically. Note that these usage models form finite-state discrete parameter Markov chains [16, 17, 18].

6   Applying Usage Models to Specifying Exceptions

The state machine shown above concisely and unambiguously defines the expected behavior for the component - but it is not complete. Refer back to figure 1 which illustrates components within a system. If we have defined the behavior of each of the constituent components using state machines (see figure 4), we can accurately characterize how they behave and interoperate under normal circumstances. But the state machines do not define what the responses should be if an exceptional condition is encountered in one of the components. If, for example, component A encounters a storage error (*e.g.*, running out of memory), the output is not defined in this model. We might want the output to be a 0 under normal circumstances, but in the presence of an exception, the output is likely to be something other than what the state machine defines. This may result in the other components failing as well.

If the component is written in Ada (for example), such an exception would cause normal execution to halt, control to be passed to an exception handling portion of the component's code, and possibly propagated to calling component. In this situation,

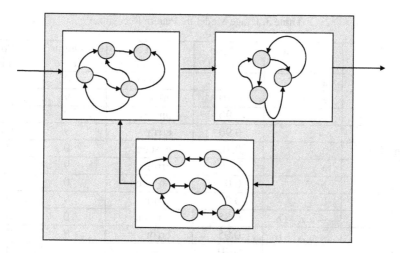

Fig. 4. Components with State Machines

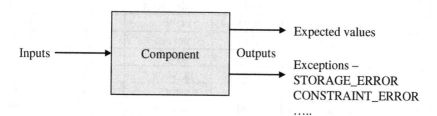

Fig. 5. Stimuli and Responses for a Sample Component

the external component needs to know that such a propagation is possible – it should be naturally part of the components requirements specification. Refer to figure 5.

We might use English as the way of defining this behavior, something like:

> If the component should experience an exception, a value of 9 shall be returned.

or

> If the component should experience a STORAGE_ERROR, processing will cease and the exception shall be propagated to the calling procedure.

Clearly, incorporating these requirements into a single form, such as a state machine, encounters the same challenge that other techniques encounter when trying to define exceptional behavior – defining exceptional conditions is performed as an add-on, not as an integral part of defining behavior in a single model.

If we wish to enforce certain design features, such as fault tolerance, we can define design constraints on the component, guiding the developers in a specific direction. We might for example, require that the developers make use of exception handling techniques to detect and mitigate any erroneous states in which the component finds

Table 3. Usage Model for Pattern Recognizer

State	Input	Prob Input	Next State	Output	Prob Output
unseen	a	0.10	a_seen	0	0.99
	a	0.10	error	9	0.01
	¬ a	0.90	unseen	0	0.99
	¬ a	0.90	error	9	0.01
a_seen	a	0.10	a_seen	0	0.99
	a	0.10	error	9	0.01
	b	0.05	ab_seen	0	0.99
	b	0.05	error	9	0.01
	¬ a ∧ ¬ b	0.85	unseen	0	0.99
	¬ a ∧ ¬ b	0.05	error	9	0.01
ab_seen	a	0.40	a_seen	0	0.99
	a	0.05	error	9	0.01
	c	0.05	abc_seen	1	0.99
	c	0.05	error	9	0.01
	¬ a ∧ ¬ c	0.55	unseen	0	0.99
	¬ a ∧ ¬ c	0.55	error	9	0.01
abc_seen	a	0.10	a_seen	0	0.99
	a	0.10	error	9	0.01
	¬ a	0.90	unseen	0	0.99
	¬ a	0.90	error	9	0.01
error	#	0.90	unseen	0	0.99
	#	0.10	error	9	0.01

itself. If handling the exception can be performed internally to the component, there might be no visible effects. But invisibility cannot be guaranteed, and might not be desired. We may want the appearance of exceptional conditions to be visible externally. This requires incorporating the desired results on the exception handling into the behavioral requirements.

Our proposed approach for this situation is based on an augmented usage model. We wish to incorporate not only the probability of occurrence of the inputs, but also the likelihood of the responses. As such this model takes on the form of a nondeterministic finite state machine, but instead of random state transitions (with a uniform distribution) in the case of duplicates, we assign a probability to each alternative.

Consider the usage model defined above for the "abc" system. We add a column to this model titled "probability of output" (refer to table 3). This column represents the likelihood that the input will produce the specified output. While this feature could be used for any distribution of outputs, we will use it specifically for anomalous conditions. As such, it describes the desired action of the system should an exceptional condition occur. It augments the normal processing requirement by providing for exceptional conditions, and for constraining the frequency when such conditions actually occur. In this way, the expected reliability of the system can be specified in conjunction with its desired behavior under error conditions.

In this table, for each input we have two potential outcomes (responses) – one for normal processing, the other for exception processing. We define our expectations (i.e., *requirements*) for how the system should behave when exceptions occur. As a part of this specification, we are also defining what we expect in terms of the reliability of the component. Specifically, for each input, we require that the likelihood of an exception's being raised is 0.01. With this approach, we are need to add a new state (*error*) that captures the notion of an exceptional condition's having occurred. Once entering this state, we can then require that to exit the error state and return to normal processing, any character input can be provided (indicated by the # symbol in the table).

7 Advantages and Disadvantages of this Approach

There are several distinct advantages to integrating the definition of normal processing requirements together with those of exceptional processing. Primarily, an integrated model provides a definition of behavior that can be analyzed and modeled as a unit. The interaction of normal and exceptional processing can be more clearly observed, as opposed to providing separate definitions. In addition, being in the form of a state machine, the behavior can be simulated using any one of many commercially available tools.

A second advantage is that the requirements development process is forced to directly examine both normal and abnormal behaviors up front, as a part of the requirements elicitation and analysis phase, rather than deferring the analysis of abnormal behaviors until later in the development cycle. Considering abnormal behaviors later in the development cycle raises the risk of inefficient and inappropriate error processing.

A third advantage to this approach is the mechanism by which expectations of reliability can be defined. The form of the enhanced state machine supports the explicit assignment of exception handling rates as a part of the requirements process. This allows the developers and the future users to perform trade-off analyses and make such decisions based on an objective consideration of the alternatives.

A fourth advantage is the support that such models give to the verification and test process. Once a model for a specific system or component is completed, it provides a way of selecting test cases to apply to the product such that the test cases conform to the expected operational profile of how the product will be used. The test cases would be selected by traversing the state machine, with the selection of inputs based on the likelihoods defined for each of the state transitions. While this approach is already used for normal usage models, by incorporating the exception handling features, the test process will challenge to software product in a much more realistic manner.

As currently defined, there are also some shortcomings to this technique. First, the way that the appropriate exception rates are to be determined is not clearly defined. Associated with this shortcoming is the challenge of correlating overall failure rates to the individual likelihoods assigned to each of the exception occurrences.

A second shortcoming is due to the lack of familiarity that most users have in applying this technique. When developing requirements, most users think about what they want the system to do. Trying to also consider what might go wrong is not a common practice. By introducing this thought process into the requirements elicitation activity, users might get confused and fail to adequately capture their true needs. It is expected however that once users become familiar with this approach they will easily learn how to use it effectively.

8 Conclusions

The inclusion of error handling behaviors in specifying requirements is not a straightforward process. A tight integration of the error handling actions with the normal processing actions is not generally possible with current specification models and techniques. While there is ample support for defining what the exceptional conditions are, not only by using natural language but also by employing formal notations, this process still remains as a disjoint part of the total requirements analysis activity. It appears however that with a slight enhancement of the usage modeling technique, the behavior of a system can be defined for not only normal processing but also abnormal and exceptional processing. By integrating these two aspects of a systems behavior, the ability to verify adherence of a system to its desired behavior is facilitated. In addition, this approach provides a natural mechanism for defining the desired error rate for the system, and also supports automatic generation of test cases to verify attainment of this error rate. More research however needs to be performed to characterize the most effective ways that this approach can be applied.

References

1. Fernandez, E. B., and R. B. France. "Formal Specification of real-time dependable systems". *Proceedings of the First IEEE International Conference on the Engineering of Complex Computer Systems*, 1995. Held jointly with 5th CSESAW, 3rd IEEE RTAW and 20th IFAC/IFIP WRTP. pp. 342 - 348
2. Levenson, Nancy G., Mats Per Erik Heimdahl, Holly Hildreth, and Jon Damon Reese. "Requirements Specification for Process-Control Systems". *IEEE Transactions on Software Engineering*, vol 20, No. 9, September 1994.
3. Bail, William G. "Requirements Management for Dependable Software Systems". In: Zelkowitz, Marvin (ed): *Advances In Computers*, 66. Academic Press: (2006).
4. Feather, M.S.; S. Fickas, A. van Lamsweerde, C. Ponsard. "Reconciling system requirements and runtime behavior." *Proceedings of the Ninth International Workshop on Software Specification and Design, 1998*. pp. 50 - 59
5. van Lamsweerde, Axel.; Darimont, R.; Letier, E. "Managing conflicts in goal-driven requirements engineering". *IEEE Transactions on Software Engineering*. vol 24, issue 11, Nov. 1998. pp. 908 - 926
6. Del Gobbo, Diego, and Ali Mali. "Re-engineering Fault Tolerance requirements: A Case Study in Specifying Fault Tolerant Flight Control Systems". *Proceedings of the Fifth IEEE International Symposium on Requirements Engineering, 2001*. pp. 236 - 245

7. Del Gobbo, Diego, Bojan Cukic, Marcello R. Napolitano, and S. Easterbrook. "Fault Detectability Analysis for Requirements Validation of Fault Tolerant Systems". *Proceedings of the 4th IEEE International Symposium on High-Assurance Systems Engineering, (1999)*. pp. 231 – 238.

8. Del Gobbo, Diego, and M. R. Napolitano. "Issues in Fault Detectability for Dynamic Systems".*Proc of the 2000 American Control Conference, Jun2000*. Vol 5, pp.3203 - 3207

9. Alexander, Ian. "Misuse Cases Help To Elicit Non-Functional Requirements". *Computing and Control Engineering*. (Feb 2005).

10. Drusinsky, Doron and Klaus Havelund "Execution-Based Model Checking of Interrupt-Based Systems". In *Workshop on Model Checking for Dependable Software Intensive Systems*. pp. 22--25, (2003)

11. Drusinsky, Doron. "Formal Specs Can Handle Exceptions". *Embedded Developers Journal*. Nov 2001.

12. Trammell, Carmen. "Quantifying the reliability of software: statistical testing based on a usage model". Proceedings., *Second IEEE International Software Engineering Standards Symposium, 1995*. (ISESS'95) 'Experience and Practice'. pp. 208 – 218

13. Simmons, Erik. "The usage model: a structure for richly describing product usage during design and development". *Proceedings of the 13th IEEE International Conference on Requirements Engineering, 2005*. pp. 403 – 407

14. Regnell, Björn.; Kristofer Kimbler, and Anders Wesslen. "Improving the use case driven approach to requirements engineering". *Proceedings of the Second IEEE International Symposium on Requirements Engineering, 1995*. pp.40 - 47

15. Börger, Egon, Elvinia Riccobene, and Joachim Schmid. "Capturing Requirements by Abstract State Machines: The Light Control Case Study". *Journal of Universal Computer Science*, vol 6, issue 7, (2000).

16. Prowell, S.J. "Using Markov Chain Usage Models to Test Complex Systems". *Proceedings of the 38th Annual Hawaii Int'l Conf on System Sciences, 2005*. HICSS '05. pp. 318c - 318c

17. Whittaker, James. A.,and Jesse. H. Poore. "Markov Analysis of Software Specifications" *ACM transactions on Software Engineering and Methodology*. Jan 1993.

18. Jiong Yan; Ji Wang; Huo-wang Chen. "Automatic generation of Markov chain usage models from real-time software UML models". *Proceedings of the Fourth International Conference on Quality Software, 2004*. pp. 22 – 31

Aspectizing Exception Handling: A Quantitative Study

Fernando Castor Filho[1], Cecília Mary F. Rubira[1],
Raquel de A. Maranhão Ferreira[1], and Alessandro Garcia[2]

[1] Institute of Computing - State University of Campinas
P.O. Box 6176. CEP 13083-970, Campinas, SP, Brazil
{fernando, cmrubira}@ic.unicamp.br,
raquel.maranhao@convergys.com
[2] Computing Department - Lancaster University
South Drive, InfoLab 21, LA1 4WA, Lancaster, UK
garciaa@comp.lancs.ac.uk

Abstract. It is usually assumed that the implementation of exception handling
can be better modularized by the use of aspect-oriented programming (AOP).
However, the trade-offs involved in using AOP with this goal are not yet well-
understood. To the best of our knowledge, no work in the literature has attempted
to assess whether AOP really promotes an enhancement in well-understood quality attributes other than separation of concerns, when used for modularizing
non-trivial exception handling code. This paper presents a quantitative study of
the adequacy of aspects for modularizing exception handling code. The study
consisted in refactoring part of a real object-oriented system so that the code responsible for handling exceptions was moved to aspects. We employed a suite
of metrics to measure quality attributes of the original and refactored systems,
including coupling, cohesion, and conciseness. We found that AOP improved
separation of concerns between exception handling code and normal application
code. However, contradicting the general intuition, the aspect-oriented version of
the system did not present significant gains for any of the four size metrics we
employed.

1 Introduction

Aspect-oriented programming (AOP) [15] has been proposed recently as a means for
improving the modularization of systems that include crosscutting concerns. A crosscutting concern can affect several units of a software system and usually cannot be
isolated by traditional object-oriented programming techniques. A typical example of
crosscutting concern is logging. The implementation of this concern is usually scattered across the modules in a system, and tangled with code related to other concerns,
because some contextual information must be gathered in order for the recorded information to be useful. Other common examples of crosscutting concerns include profiling
and authentication [18].

It is usually assumed that the exceptional behavior of a system is a crosscutting
concern that can be better modularized by the use of AOP [15,18,19]. The first study
on the subject, performed by Lippert and Lopes [19], had the goal of evaluating if
AOP could be used to separate the code responsible for detecting and handling exceptions from the normal application code in a large object-oriented (OO) framework. The

C. Dony et al. (Eds.):Exception Handling, LNCS 4119, pp. 255–274, 2006.

authors found out that the use of AOP brought several benefits, such as tangling in the program texts and a drastic reduction in the number of lines of code (LOC). However, this first study did not investigate the "aspectization" of application-specific error handling, which is often the case in large-scale software systems. Moreover, in spite of the assumption made by many authors that using AOP for separating exception handling code from the normal application code is beneficial, the trade-offs involved in using AOP with this goal are not yet well-understood. To the best of our knowledge, no work in the literature has attempted to assess whether AOP really promotes an enhancement in well-understood quality attributes such as separation of concerns, coupling, cohesion, and conciseness, when used for modularizing non-trivial exception handling code.

This paper presents a study performed to assess the adequacy of AspectJ [18], a general purpose aspect-oriented extension to Java, for modularizing exception handling code. The study consisted of refactoring part of a real OO system so that the code responsible for handling exceptions was moved to aspects. This study differed from the Lippert and Lopes study in the following points:

- The target of the study is part of a complete, deployable system, not a reusable infrastructure, like a framework. Hence, the exception handling code implements non-uniform, complex strategies, making it harder to move handlers to aspects.
- We employ the metrics suite proposed by Sant'Anna and his colleagues [23] to assess attributes such as coupling, conciseness, cohesion, and separation of concerns in both the original and the refactored system.
- We assess the overall quality of both the error handling aspects and the application classes affected by them.
- We do not attempt to move error detection code to aspects.

We have found that, in general, AOP improved separation of concerns between exception handling code and normal application code. Moreover, we noticed that aspects promote handler reuse, but reusing handlers requires careful design planning. Otherwise, the behavior of the system may be unintentionally altered when the handlers are extracted to aspects. Furthermore, contradicting the general intuition, we observed that, for systems with application-specific exception handling strategies, an aspect-oriented (AO) solution does not result in a reduced number of LOC. For the system we have refactored, the AO version had almost the same number of LOC as the OO version. Another consequence of using aspects was that, in many cases, it was necessary to refactor the application code to expose join points that AspectJ can capture. This produced code that did not appropriately express the intent of the programmer and had a negative impact in the overall cohesion of the system.

This paper is organized as follows. The next section 2 describes the setting of our study. The results of the study are presented in Section 3. Section 4 analyzes the obtained results and points some constraints on the validity of our study. Section 5 discusses related work. The last section rounds the paper and points directions for future work.

2   Study Setting

This section describes the configuration of our study. Section 2.1 briefly describes the AO programming language we have used, AspectJ. Section 2.2 briefly explains how we moved exception handling code to aspects. Section 2.3 describes the Telestrada system, the target of our study. Section 2.4 presents the metrics we have used to evaluate the OO and AO versions of Telestrada.

2.1 AspectJ Overview

AspectJ [18] is a general purpose aspect-oriented extension to Java. It extends Java with constructs for picking specific points in the program flow, called join points, and executing pieces of code, called advice, when these points are reached. Join points are points of interest in the program execution through which crosscutting concerns are composed with other application concerns.

AspectJ adds new constructs to Java, in order to support the selection of join points and the execution of advice in these points. A *pointcut* picks out certain join points and contextual information at those join points. Join points selectable by pointcuts vary in nature and granularity. Examples include method call and class instantiation. Advice may be executed *before*, *after*, or *around* the selected join points. In the latter case, execution of the advice may potentially alter the flow of control of the application, and replace the code that would be otherwise executed in the selected join point. AspectJ also allows programmers to modify the static structure of a program by means of static crosscutting. With static crosscutting, one can introduce new members in a class or interface, or make a checked exception unchecked.

Aspects are units of modularity for crosscutting concerns. They are similar to classes, but may also include pointcuts, advice, and static crosscutting. The code of an aspect-oriented application written in AspectJ consists of two parts: (i) base code that is written in written in Java and implements the non-crosscutting concerns of the system; and (ii) aspect code that implements the crosscutting concerns of the system and comprises a set of aspects and auxiliary classes. Aspect code is combined with base code by means of a process called weaving. Therefore, the tool responsible for performing weaving is called *weaver*.

Figure 1 presents a trivial aspect named `ConnectionPoolHandler`. Lines 2 and 3 declare a pointcut named `setManualCommitHandler` that captures calls to the method `setAutoCommit()` of class `Connection`, independently of return type ("*") or list of parameters (".."). Line 4 *softens* `SQLException` for the join points selected by `setManualCommitHandler`. This means that `SQLException` is not statically checked by the Java compiler. At run time, if `SQLException` is raised in a call to `setAutoCommit()`, it is wrapped with an unchecked exception named `SoftException`, defined by AspectJ. Lines 5-8 declare an advice that is executed after the join points selected by `setManualCommitHandler` if their execution ends by throwing `SQLException` (Line 5). This advice captures contextual information on the selected join points by specifying that the target of the calls to `setAutoCommit()` can be referred to through variable `con`.

2.2 Aspectizing Exception Handling

Our study focuses specifically on the handling of exceptions. We moved all the `try-catch`, `try-catch-finally`, and `try-finally` blocks in the selected portions of Telestrada to aspects. Method signatures (`throws` clauses) and the raising

```
1  public aspect ConnectionPoolHandler {
2    pointcut setManualCommitHandler() :
3      call(* Connection.setAutoCommit(..));
4    declare soft : SQLException : setManualCommitHandler();
5    after(Connection con) throwing (SQLException e) :
6        setManualCommitHandler() && target(con) {
7      con.close();
8    }
9  }
```

Fig. 1. A very simple aspect

of exceptions (throw statements) were not affected because these elements are more related to exception detection than to exception handling.

Handlers moved to aspects were implemented by means of after and around advice, depending on whether or not the handler ended its execution by raising an exception, respectively. Whenever possible, we used after advice, since they are simpler. After advice are not appropriate, though, for implementing handlers that do not raise (or re-raise) an exception because these advice cannot alter the flow of control of a program. In cases where this was necessary, we employed around advice. New advice were created on a per-try-block basis, excluding cases where handlers could be reused. Depending on the number and complexity of the handlers in the classes of a package and the amount of reuse that could be achieved, we created an aspect implementing handlers for a single class or for a whole package.

We used the Extract Fragment to Advice [20] refactoring to move handlers to aspects. On several occasions, it was necessary to modify the implementation of a method in order to expose join points that aspects could select. Usually, this amounted to extracting new methods whose body is entirely contained within a try block. After extracting all the handlers to advice, we looked for reuse opportunities and eliminated identical handlers. Figure 2 shows a trivial example of aspectization of handlers using an around advice.

After refactoring, method closeResultSet() consists of the body of the original try block, plus a return statement. In the GOHandler aspect, we define a pointcut named crsHandler to select the execution of closeResultSet(). The around advice implementing the handler is executed at this join point. This advice invokes closeResultSet() by means of the proceed() statement of AspectJ and, if no exceptions are raised, returns the result of the method execution. If an SQLException is raised, the exception handler is executed. In this example, SQLException is softened at crsHandler. This is required because the body of closeResultSet() can still raise SQLException but, from the viewpoint of the Java compiler, the exception is not handled and does not appear in the signature of closeResultSet().

In several occasions, it was necessary to modify the implementation of a method in order to expose join points that AspectJ can select. For example, in the snippet in Figure 2, we had to remove references to the local variable r from the try-catch block before moving the latter to an advice.

```
1  // OBJECT-ORIENTED VERSION - ORIGINAL
2  public class GenericOperations {
3    public static boolean closeResultSet(ResultSet aResultSet) {
4      boolean r = true;
5      try { ...  // body of the "try" block.
6      } catch (SQLException e) { System.out.println(e.toString());
7      r = false;
8      }
9      return r;
10   }  ... // implementation of the class
11 }
12
13 // ASPECT-ORIENTED VERSION - AFTER REFACTORING
14 public class GenericOperations {
15   public static boolean closeResultSet(ResultSet aResultSet) {
16       ... // body of the original "try" block.
17       return true;
18   } ... // implementation of the class
19 }
20 public aspect GOHandler { // another source file
21   pointcut crsHandler() :
22       execution(public static boolean closeResultSet(..));
23   boolean around(ResultSet rs) : crsHandler() && args(rs){ //
           advice
24     try { return proceed(rs);
25     } catch (SQLException e) { System.out.println(e.toString());
26     return false;
27     }
28   }
29   declare soft : SQLException : crsHandler();
30 }
```

Fig. 2. An example of aspectization of exception handlers

In our study, we have tried to simulate the oblivious approach [9] to AO software development. The latter dictates that one can build a system without ever thinking about aspects and later in the development process add the aspects as required. This approach represents the current state of the practice in AO software development [26]. It had to be simulated because, in Telestrada, the concern to be aspectized was already implemented using OO constructs. Since we measured the system before and after refactoring, however, we believe that the results presented in Section 3 are realistic. Furthermore, it is important to stress that throughout the study, we always attempted to produce high quality code when moving exception handlers to aspects. In many cases, different strategies for refactoring were attempted and their pros and cons were taken into account in order to chose which one to adopt. This gives us confidence that the obtained results were as close to what would happen in practice as possible.

2.3 Telestrada: Our Case Study

Telestrada [4] is a large traveler information system being developed for a Brazilian national highway administrator. It comprises five subsystems: Central Database Subsystem, GIS (Geographic Information System) Subsystem, Call-Center Operations Subsystem, Roadside Operations Subsystem, and Complaint Management Subsystem.

For our study, we have selected some self-contained packages of the Complaint Management Subsystem (CMS). The implementation of the CMS comprises more than 12000 LOC and more than 300 classes. The packages we selected for the study comprise approximately 3350 LOC (excluding comments and blank lines) and more than 200 classes and interfaces. It is important to note that, due to implementation conventions, the system has a large number of very simple interfaces. This explains the small LOC/number of classes and interfaces ratio.

The classes and interfaces of the selected portion of the CMS include more than 45 `try-catch` blocks of varied complexity. They implement diverse exception handling strategies that range from trivial to sophisticated, for example: (i) do nothing (empty catch block); (ii) log and close database connection; (iii) log the exception, perform a rollback, close the database connection, and raise a different exception; (iv) use Java's reflection API to create a new `Method` object and use it for logging.

2.4 Metrics Suite

We have employed a suite of metrics for separation of concerns, coupling, cohesion, and size [23] to evaluate both OO and AO implementations. These metrics have already been used in various different experimental studies [2,13,12,14,17,24] and have been effective in assessing several internal quality attributes of Java and AspectJ programs. Some of them have been automated in the context of a measurement tool [27]. This metrics suite was defined based on the reuse and refinement of some classical OO metrics [7,8]. The original definitions of the OO metrics [7] were extended to be applied in a paradigm-independent way, supporting the generation of comparable results.

The employed metrics suite includes metrics related to four quality attributes: separation of concerns, coupling, cohesion, and size. The separation of concerns metrics were used in our study to measure the degree to which the exception handling concern in Telestrada maps to the design components (classes, interfaces, and aspects), operations (methods and advice), and lines of code.

Separation of concerns refers to the ability to identify, encapsulate, and manipulate those parts of software that are relevant to a particular concern. Coupling provides an indication of the strength of interconnections between the components in a system. Highly coupled systems have strong interconnections, with program units dependent on each other. The cohesion of a component is a measure of the closeness of the relationship between its internal components. The size metrics measure the length of the design and code of software systems.

Table 1 presents a brief definition of each metric, and associates them with the attributes measured by each one. In general, the higher the value of a measure, the worse the performance of the assessed system with respect to that metric. Detailed descriptions of the metrics appear elsewhere [23].

Table 1. The Metrics Suite

Attributes	Metrics	Definitions
Separation of Concerns	Concern Diffusion over Components	Counts the number of classes and aspects whose main purpose is to contribute to the implementation of a concern plus the number of other classes and aspects that access them.
	Concern Diffusion over Operations	Counts the number of methods and advice whose main purpose is to contribute to the implementation of a concern plus the number of other methods and advice that access them.
	Concern Diffusion over LOC	Counts the number of transition points for each concern through the lines of code. Transition points are points in the code where there is a "concern switch".
Coupling	Coupling Between Components	Counts the number of components declaring methods or fields that may be called or accessed by other components.
	Depth Inheritance Tree	Counts how far down in the inheritance hierarchy a class or aspect is declared.
Cohesion	Lack of Cohesion in Operations	Measures the lack of cohesion of a class or an aspect in terms of the amount of method and advice pairs that do not access the same field.
Size	Lines of Code (LOC)	Counts the lines of code.
	Number of Attributes	Counts the number of fields of each class or aspect.
	Number of Operations	Counts the number of methods and advice of each class or aspect.
	Vocabulary Size	Counts the number of components (classes, interfaces, and aspects) of the system.

3 Study Results

This section presents the results of the measurement process. The data have been collected based on the set of defined metrics (Section 2.4). The presentation is broken in three parts. Section 3.1 presents the results for the separation of concerns metrics. Section 3.2 presents the results for the coupling and cohesion metrics. Section 3.3 presents the results for the size metrics.

We present the results by means of tables that put side-by-side the values of the metrics for the OO and AO version of Telestrada. Results are broken in two parts, in order to make it clear the contribution of classes and aspects to the value of each metric. Hereafter, we use the term "class" to refer to both classes and interfaces.

3.1 Separation of Concerns Measures

Table 2 shows the obtained results for the three separation of concerns metrics. The AO version of Telestrada performed better for two of the three metrics, Concern Diffusion over Components and Concern Diffusion over LOC. The OO version had a slightly better result for Concern Diffusion over Operations. In the AO version of Telestrada, all

Table 2. Separation of Concerns Metrics

Metrics	# components	OO version	AO version
Concern Diffusion over Components	classes	22	0
	aspects	-	18
	total	22	18
Concern Diffusion over Operations	classes	42	0
	aspects	-	44
	total	42	44
Concern Diffusion over LOC	classes	208	0
	aspects	-	0
	total	208	0

the code related to exception handling concern was moved to aspects. Therefore, for all the metrics, the number of classes implementing exception handling was zero.

The measure of Concern Diffusion over Components in the AO version of Telestrada was approximately 18% lower than in the OO version. This result is a direct consequence of our strategy for creating new handler aspects. Various different approaches are possible. For example, we could adopt extreme alternatives, such as putting all the exception handling code in a single aspect or creating several simple aspects that encapsulate the possible handling strategies for each type of exception. More moderate approaches include creating a handler aspect per class that has exception handling code in the OO version, or one aspect for each package whose classes implement exception handling. All of these approaches have pros and cons that revolve around the code size vs. modularity trade-off. This trade-off is also faced by developers applying design patterns [11] to unstructured OO systems. Our design choice was a middle-ground. For complex classes with 7 or more `catch` blocks, we created a new aspect whose sole responsibility is to implement the handlers for that class. Furthermore, each package includes an aspect that modularizes exception handling code for simpler classes.

In Concern Diffusion over Operations, surprisingly, the AO version of Telestrada exhibited worse results. The value of this metric in the AO version was almost 5% higher than in the OO version. For various components, the AO solution was either equivalent or superior to the OO one. For example, even though class `GenericOperations` had some methods with more than one `try-catch` block, the handler aspect associated to this class in the AO version exhibited a lower value in Concern Diffusion over Operations, since some of the handler advice could be reused. However, in some packages, reuse of handler code was virtually inexistent and some classes had operations with more than one `try-catch` block. Hence, when exception handling code in these classes was moved to aspects, each handler had to be put in a separate advice, contributing to the increase in the value of the metric.

Concern Diffusion over LOC was the metric where aspects performed best. The AO version of Telestrada did not have any concern switches and therefore had value 0 for this metric. This result was expected and confirms the findings of the study conducted by Lippert and Lopes [19]. The authors claim that the use of aspects decreases interference between concerns in the program texts.

3.2   Coupling and Cohesion Measures

Table 3 shows the obtained results for the two coupling metrics, Coupling between Components and Depth of Inheritance Tree, and the cohesion metric, Lack of Cohesion in Operations. The OO and AO versions of Telestrada exhibited very similar measures for the coupling metrics. The Depth of the Inheritance Tree increased by less than 1% in the AO version. This was expected, since the use of aspects alone does not interfere with this metric. The increase of 2 in the value of the metric was due to the creation of a new aspect from which two handler aspects inherit. The super-aspect was created in order to avoid duplicated code.

Table 3. Coupling and Cohesion Metrics

Metrics	# components	OO version	AO version
Coupling between Components	classes	179	142
	aspects	-	39
	total	**179**	**181**
Depth of Inheritance Tree	classes	186	186
	aspects	-	2
	total	**186**	**188**
Lack of Cohesion in Operations	classes	408	524
	aspects	-	0
	total	**408**	**524**

Coupling between Components in the two versions was almost identical (the result in the AO version was only 1.1% higher). New couplings were introduced only when aspects had to capture contextual information from classes. In these cases, at most one new coupling is created per aspect, due to a reference from the aspect to its corresponding class. Furthermore, in the AO version of Telestrada, the aspects contributed with approximately 22% of the value of the metric. This means that coupling between classes was 21.3% lower in the AO version.

Among all the metrics, Lack of Cohesion in Operations was the one for which the AO version of Telestrada presented the worst results. Lack of cohesion in the operations of the AO version was approximately 28% higher than in the OO version. This is due to the large number of operations that were created to expose join points that AspectJ can capture. These new operations are not part of the implementation of the exception handling concern (and therefore do not affect Concern Diffusion over Operations), but are a direct consequence of using aspects to modularize this concern. Refactoring to expose join points is a common activity in aspect-oriented software development [21], since current aspect languages do not provide means to precisely capture every join point of interest.

It is interesting to note that the goal of the Lack of Cohesion in Operations metric is to capture a partial view of cohesion: it considers only the explicit relationships between the attributes and operations. It does not consider direct inter-operation relationships and the semantic closeness between elements of a component. Moreover, even though cohesion was worse in the AO version, this was caused solely by the classes.

The value of Lack of Cohesion in Operations for the aspects in the AO version was 0. This happened because none of the handler advice accesses fields of the classes they refer to and the aspects do not define new fields.

3.3 Size Measures

Contradicting the general intuition that aspects make programs smaller [18,19], the OO and AO versions of Telestrada had very similar results in three of the four size metrics: LOC, Number of Attributes, and Vocabulary Size. Moreover, the Number of Operations of the AO version was 13.7% higher than the OO version. Table 4 summarizes the results for the size metrics.

Table 4. Coupling and Cohesion Metrics

Metrics	# components	OO version	AO version
Lines of Code (LOC)	classes	3352	2885
	aspects	-	459
	total	3352	3334
Number of Attributes	classes	127	127
	aspects	-	0
	total	127	127
Number of Operations	classes	423	437
	aspects	-	44
	total	423	481
Vocabulary Size	classes	224	224
	aspects	-	18
	total	224	242

The similar values for LOC were expected. As mentioned in Section 3.1, reusing handler aspects in Telestrada was much harder then we had originally predicted. Hence, although some reuse could be achieved, this was not anywhere near the results obtained by Lippert and Lopes in their study. Moreover, most handlers comprise just a few LOC and the use of AspectJ incurred in a slight implementation overhead because it was necessary to specify join points of interest and soften exceptions in order to associate handlers to pieces of code. In the end, the economy in LOC achieved due to handler reuse was compensated by the overhead of using AspectJ.

The 8% increase in the vocabulary size of the AO version was entirely due to the aspects. No new classes were introduced or removed. Similarly to Concern Diffusion over Components (Section 3.1), Vocabulary Size depends heavily on how the implementation of the exception handling concern is partitioned among the aspects.

The number of operations in the AO version of Telestrada was 13.7% bigger than in the OO version. The main reason for this result was the creation of advice implementing handlers. Since there is a one-to-one correspondence between `try` blocks and advice (except for cases where handlers are reused) and handlers do not count as methods in the OO version, this increase was expected. Another reason for the increase in the Number of Operations was the refactoring of methods to expose join points that AspectJ can capture.

4 Discussion

This section provides a qualitative analysis of the results presented in Section 3, some examples of scenarios we encountered during the study, and discussions about the constraints on the validity of our empirical evaluation.

4.1 General Analysis

In general, we found out that reusing handlers is much more difficult than is usually advertised [19]. Handler reuse depends directly on: (i) the type of exception being handled; (ii) what the handler does and whether it ends its execution by returning or raising an exception; (iii) the type of contextual information required, if any; and (iv) what the method that raises the exception returns and what exceptions appear in its throws clause.

The difficulty of reusing handler code is illustrated by Figure 3. The figure shows three advice that look similar, but cannot be merged into a single one because of small differences. Advice #1 and #2 cannot be combined because they log different error messages and handle different exceptions. A possible solution to the second problem is to implement a single advice that catches a supertype of both CVSException and IOException. Since the nearest common supertype is Exception, it would also be necessary to modify the catch clause in order for it to reraise unchecked exceptions. Although this solution works, it does not solve the problem of logging different error messages and is far from ideal. For the same reasons, advice #2 and #3 cannot be combined. It is also not possible to combine advice #1 and #3. The former returns a value that depends on the call to proceed() (Line 3) while the latter always returns false (Lines 17 and 19).

When exception handlers are non-trivial, it may be difficult to fully understand the implications of moving a handler to an aspect. Hence, reusing handlers requires careful design, in order to avoid changing the exceptional behavior semantics of the system. The same issue applies for exception softening. Softening an exception that is a supertype of another exception raised within the same context causes the subtype to be softened as well, possibly with unexpected effects. We believe that developers should never soften exceptions that are supertypes of many other exceptions, such as Exception and Throwable in Java.

Although the Coupling between Components in both versions of Telestrada was almost identical, this does not mean that components are as coupled to each other in the AO version as in the OO version. The measures of Coupling between Components for the classes in the AO version were lower than in the OO version. Moreover, the sums of the measures of Coupling between Components for the classes and their corresponding aspects in the AO version were similar to the measures for the respective classes in the OO version. Therefore, we can say that the AO version has more components but they are, in general, less strongly coupled to one another.

As seen in Section 3.3, handler advice accounted for a 10.4% increase in the number of operations. As with all size metrics, this value cannot be evaluated in isolation. Although a developer getting acquainted to the AO version will have to understand more operations, these operations are smaller, have less dependencies, and do not mix the

```
1  // ADVICE #1
2  boolean around() : ...  {
3    try { return proceed();
4    } catch (CVSException e) { CVSProviderPlugin.log(e); }
5    return false;
6  }
7  // ADVICE #2
8  boolean around() : ...  {
9    try { return proceed();
10   } catch (IOException e) {
11     CVSProviderPlugin.log(IStatus.ERROR, e.getMessage(), e);
12   }
13   return false;
14 }
15 // ADVICE #3
16 boolean around() : ...  {
17   try { proceed();
18   } catch (CVSException ce) { CVSProviderPlugin.log(ce); }
19   return false;
20 }
```

Fig. 3. Three similar advice that cannot be merged into a single one

system's normal activity with the code that handles exceptions. Therefore, the increase in the Number of Operations caused by the handler advice should not be seen as a negative factor.

The number of operations extracted in order to expose join points that AspectJ could capture corresponded to 3.3% of the total Number of Operations. Unlike the increase caused by handler advice, the increase caused by refactored operations, albeit small, is definitely negative. These new operations are not part of the original design of the system and possibly do not clearly state the intent of the developer. In some cases, the refactored operations comprised just a couple of lines that did not make much sense when separated from their original contexts. This problem may suggest that there is still room for improving AspectJ so that more join points of interest can be captured.

4.2 Representative Scenarios

In this section, we present some examples of scenarios that were identified during the process of refactoring Telestrada. These scenarios represent recurring situations with which a developer would have to deal if faced with the task of modularizing exception handling code using aspects. Each scenario consists of two parts: (1) a code snippet including some exception handling code from the OO version of Telestrada; and (ii) a code snippet from the AO version showing the result of moving exception handling to an aspect. We identified 14 different scenarios in Telestrada and classified each one of them as beneficial or harmful, according to the quality of the AO implementation, when compared to the OO one.

A Beneficial Scenario. Figure 4 shows a scenario where the use of aspects is advantageous. In this scenario, the `try-catch` block in the OO version (Lines 4-8) wraps the whole implementation of method `log()` and the handler does not do anything. Therefore, it is straightforward to implement this block as an around advice in the AO version. The only factor that complicates refactoring in this case is the need to soften `Exception`, as `log()` does not have a `throws` clause. As pointed out in Section 4.1, softening `Exception` can alter the behavior of the system in unforeseen ways. To avoid this problem, we discovered and softened the checked exceptions that method `log()` actually throws (Lines 19-20). We used the Java compiler to discover these exceptions. The Java compiler points out when a checked exception is not caught or declared in the throws clause of a method that signals it. In cases where the `throws` clause of a method included only the generic exception `Exception`, we removed the `throws` clause and, based on the error messages provided by the Java compiler, discovered what were the specific checked exceptions thrown by the method.

It is easy to see that the effect of the scenario presented in Figure 4 on the values of some of the metrics is either neutral or positive. The separation of concerns metrics, except for Concern Diffusion over LOC which is affected positively, are not affected by this refactoring. Also, the value of the cohesion metric does not change, as the advice does not access any attributes. The same applies to Depth of Inheritance Tree,

```
1  // OBJECT-ORIENTED VERSION - ORIGINAL
2  public class ConnectionPool extends GenericPool {
3    public void log(String aMsg) {
4      try {
5        Object[] params = new Object[1];
6        params[0] = aMsg;
7        logMethod.invoke(logObject, params);
8      } catch (Exception e) {} // ignore exceptions when logging
9    } ...
10 }
11 // ASPECT-ORIENTED VERSION - AFTER REFACTORING
12 public class ConnectionPool extends GenericPool {
13   public void log(String aMsg) {
14     ... // contents of the try block from the original version.
15   } ...
16 }
17 privileged public aspect ConnectionPoolHandlers {
18   pointcut logHandler() : execution(public void log(..));
19   declare soft : InvocationTargetException : logHandler();
20   declare soft : IllegalAccessException : logHandler();
21   void around() : logHandler() {
22     try { proceed();
23     } catch (Exception e) {} // ignore exceptions when logging
24   } ...
25 }
```

Fig. 4. A scenario where aspectization is beneficial

since `ConnectionPoolHandlers` extends `Object`. Furthermore, in the AO version, method `log()` has fewer couplings than in the OO version, because it does not refer to `Exception`. Finally, the measures for the size metrics are worse in the AO version. This is expected, though, since the refactoring requires the creation of a new operation (the handler advice) and, since no reuse is possible when only one operation is taken into account, the number of LOC also grows.

A Harmful Scenario. Figure 4 shows a scenario where aspectization brings more harm than good. Due to space constraints, the resulting handler aspect is not included in the code of the AO version. In this scenario, method `init()` in the OO version has four `try-catch` blocks, three of them nested within an outermost one. Modularizing exception handling with aspects is harmful in this scenario because it is necessary to create two new methods (`setProperties()` and `obtainAndSetLogMethod()`) and three different handler advice (`try-catch` blocks #2 and #3 can be implemented by a single advice).

As in the previous scenario, aspectization has a negative influence on Number of Operations and Number of LOC. In this case, the increase in the Number of Operations is substantial - 1 in the OO solution against 6 in the AO solution. Furthermore, the use of aspects also affects the separation of concerns metric Concern Diffusion over Operations, as the OO version has only one operation implementing exception handling, whereas the AO version has three. Finally, the extraction of the try-catch blocks from method `init()` promoted an increase in the Lack of Cohesion in Operations, though it is not possible to infer this just by looking at Figure 5. This was caused by the creation of methods `setProperties()` and `obtainAndSetLogMethod()`.

4.3 Limitations of this Study

Arguably, the employed metrics suite is a limitation of this work. There are a number of other existing metrics and other modularity dimensions that we could be exploited in our study. We have to decided to focus on the metrics described in Section 2.4 because they have already been proved to be effective quality indicators in several case studies [2,13,14]. In fact, despite the limitations of these metrics, they complement each other and are very useful when analyzed together. In addition, there is no way in a single study to explore all the possible measures. For every possible metrics suite there will be some dimensions that will remain uncovered. In addition, future case studies can use additional metrics and assess the aspectization of exception handling using different modularity dimensions.

Our study focuses on a single aspect-oriented language, namely, AspectJ. Although many ideas presented here also apply to other AO languages, some surely do not. For example, it is not necessary (or possible) to soften exceptions in Eos [22], an aspect-oriented extension to C#, because C# does not have checked exceptions.

Not all possible strategies for implementing exceptional behavior of systems are covered. In Telestrada, handlers are implemented exclusively by means of `catch` blocks. However, more complex applications may include methods and fields which are specific to the implementation of the exceptional behavior. Moving these additional elements to aspects would probably affect the quality attributes of the refactored system.

```
1  // OBJECT-ORIENTED VERSION - ORIGINAL
2  public class ConnectionPool extends GenericPool {
3    public void init() throws PoolException {
4      try {        // try-catch block #1
5        ... // 5 LOC
6        try { setPoolSize(...);      // try-catch block #2
7        } catch (NumberFormatException e) {}
8          catch (MissingResourceException e) {}
9        ... // try-catch block #3, similar to the one above.
10       setLogMethod(null, null);
11       try {      // try-catch block #4
12         ... // 17 LOC
13       } catch (Exception e) { ... // 7 LOC handler }
14       Class.forName(getDbClass());
15     } catch (Exception e) { throw new PoolException(...);}
16   }
17   ... // rest of the code.
18 }
19 // ASPECT-ORIENTED VERSION - AFTER REFACTORING
20 public class ConnectionPool extends GenericPool {
21   public void init() throws PoolException {
22     ... // Invokes obtainAndSetLogMethod() and setProperties().
23   }
24   void obtainAndSetLogMethod(...) throws NoSuchMethodException {
25     ... // Extracted from try-catch block #4 of the OO version
26   }
27   void setProperties(ResourceBundle dbBundle) {
28     ... // Extracted from try-catch block #1 of the OO version
29         // Includes try-catch blocks #2 and #3 of the OO version
30   }
31   ... // rest of the code.
32 }
```

Fig. 5. A scenario where aspectization is harmful

We do not attempt to evaluate the scalability of aspects for modularizing exception handling. Although the target of our study implements non-trivial exception handling policies, it is still just part of a system and comprises less than 3500 LOC. Moreover, we only modularize exception handling using aspects. We do not evaluate interactions between exception handling aspects and aspects implementing other concerns.

5   Related Work

Related work can be categorized into two groups: those that assess the use of aspect-oriented techniques to modularize exception handling code and those that evaluate aspect-oriented techniques to structure other fault tolerance mechanisms, most notably transactional execution.

5.1 Aspect-Oriented Programming and Exception Handling

Even though introductory texts [15,18,28] usually cite exception handling as an example of the (potential) usefulness of AOP, only a few works attempt to evaluate the suitability of this new paradigm to modularize exception handling code. The study of Lipert and Lopes [19] employed an old version of AspectJ to refactor exception handling code in a large OO framework, called JWAM, to aspects. The goal of this study was to assess the usefulness of aspects for separating exception handling code from the normal application code. The authors presented their findings in terms of a qualitative evaluation. Quantitative evaluation consisted solely of counting LOC. They found that the use of aspects for modularizing exception detection and handling in the aforementioned framework brought several benefits, for example, better reuse, less tangling in the program texts, and a decrease in the number of lines of code.

The Lippert and Lopes study was a important initial evaluation of the applicability of AspectJ in particular and aspects in general for solving a real software development problem. However, it has some shortcomings that hinder its results to be extrapolated to the development of real-life software systems. First, the target of the study was a system where exception handling is generic (not application-specific). However, exception handling is an inherently application-specific error recovery technique [1]. In other words, the real exception handling would be implemented by systems built using JWAM as an infrastructure and not by the framework itself. The authors report that most of the handlers in JWAM implemented policies such as "log and ignore the exception". This helps explaining the vast economy in LOC the authors achieved by using AOP.

Second, the qualitative assessment was performed in terms of quality attributes that are not well-understood, such as (un)pluggability and support for incremental development. The authors did not evaluate some attributes that are more fundamental and well-understood in the Software Engineering literature, such as coupling and cohesion.

Third, quantitative evaluation was performed only in terms of number of LOC. Although the number of LOC may be relevant if analyzed together with other metrics, its use in isolation is usually the target of severe criticisms [29]. In the context of the Lippert and Lopes study, the use of LOC as the sole metric provided a narrow view of the effects of the aspectization of exception handling on the program quality. It portrayed the AO solution as very superior to the OO solution even though, as described previously, this owed more to the nature of the target of the study than to the quality of the AO solution.

In a previous work [6], we described our experience implementing an aspect-based framework that complements the exception handling mechanism of Java with coordinated exception handling [3]. The goal of the study was to analyze the benefits and disadvantages of using aspects to build a framework for coordinated error recovery, instead of relying on an exclusively object-oriented implementation. This previous work does not measure the impact of using aspect-oriented techniques to modularize exception handling code.

The book on AspectJ by Laddad [18] presents a design pattern for organizing exception handling code using AspectJ. The author only presents trivial examples of the application of the pattern and does not attempt to analyze the benefits and problems involved in applying it to more complex cases.

5.2   Aspect-Oriented Programming and Fault Tolerance

One of the first studies of the applicability of AOP for developing dependable systems was conducted by Kienzle and Guerraoui [16]. The study used AOP techniques to separate concurrency control and failure management concerns from other parts of a distributed application. It employed AspectJ and transactions as a representative of AOP languages and a fundamental paradigm to handle concurrency and failures, respectively. The authors attempted to achieve three goals, from the most to the least ambitious: (i) to completely hide transactional semantics from programmers, so that these semantics can be associated to the program a posteriori and automatically; (ii) to completely separate transactional interfaces (being, commit, abort, etc.) from the main (functional) objects methods and have these interfaces invoked through specific aspects; and (iii) to aspectize transaction mechanisms, that is, to separate the mechanisms responsible for ensuring the ACID properties of transactions from the main (functional) program and encapsulate these mechanisms within code invoked through aspects. The authors state that the first goal is impossible to achieve. Furthermore, the second goal, albeit achievable, in certain cases produces an artificial separation and leads to confusing code. Finally, the authors claim that an AOP language like AspectJ provides an elegant way of separating transaction mechanisms from the functional part of a program, but that this separation is strictly syntactic and should be handled with care. This work is similar to ours in its overall goal, namely, to assess the benefits of using aspects to modularize error recovery code. However, there are some fundamental differences: (i) we use exception handling as a mechanism to handle failures, instead of transactions; (ii) we substantiate our conclusions with measurements based on a metrics suite for aspect-oriented software, instead of examples; and (iii) we do not address concurrency.

In another study, Soares and his colleagues [25] employed AspectJ to separate persistence and distribution concerns from the functional code of a health care application written in Java. The authors found out that, although AspectJ presents some limitations, it helps in modularizing the transactional execution of methods in many situations that occur in real systems, thus contradicting some of the conclusions of Kienzle and Guerraoui. Furthermore, they employed aspects to modularize exception handling code for exceptions signaled by the newly introduced aspects, but did not attempt to assess the suitability of AspectJ for this task.

An early position paper by Fradet and Südolt [10] discusses the features that an aspect-oriented language for detecting errors in numeric computations should provide. It proposes pointcut designators that work as global invariants whose violations trigger the execution of recovery code (advice). This work is complementary to ours because it focuses on error detection while ours emphasizes error recovery. Both are fundamental activities in the construction of fault-tolerant systems [1],

6   Concluding Remarks

In this paper, we presented a study to assess if AOP improves the quality of the application code when employed to modularize non-trivial exception handling. We found out that, although the use of AOP to separate exception handling code and normal application code can be beneficial, aspectization can bring more harm than good if exception handling code is non-uniform, strongly context-dependent, or too complex. We believe that effective use of AOP requires some a priori planning and must be incorporated in the software development process. For exception handling, ad-hoc aspectization is beneficial only in simple scenarios.

Our most immediate future work is to derive a predictive model for using aspects to implement exception handling, based on the lessons learned from this study. With this model, developers will be able to recognize the situations in which it is advantageous to use aspects to modularize exception handling code. Moreover, we intend to document as patterns some strategies for structuring exception handling aspects. The two scenarios presented in Section 4 represent a first step towards these goals. Some initial results appear elsewhere [5].

As mentioned in Section 4.3, we have not evaluated the scalability of AspectJ for implementing exception handling. In the near future, we intend to analyze two scenarios: (i) whether aspects scale up well when the number of handlers grows; and (ii) whether it is difficult to integrate exception handling aspects with aspects implementing other concerns, such as distribution and persistence.

Acknowledgements

We would like to thank the anonymous referees, who provided several useful comments and suggestions. Fernando is supported by FAPESP/Brazil under grant 02/13996-2. Cecília is partially supported by CNPq/Brazil under grant 351592/97-0, and by FAPE-SP/Brazil, under grant 2004/10663-8. Fernando and Cecília are partially supported by FINEP/Brazil under grant 1843/04 of CompGov, which is a project for Shared Library of Components for e-Government. Alessandro is supported by European Commission grant IST-2-004349: European Network of Excellence on Aspect-Oriented Software Development (AOSD-Europe), 2004-2008.

References

1. T. Anderson and P. A. Lee. *Fault Tolerance: Principles and Practice*. Springer-Verlag, 2nd edition, 1990.
2. Nelio Cacho, Claudio Sant'Anna, Eduardo Figueiredo, Alessandro Garcia, Thais Batista, and Carlos Lucena. Composing design patterns: A scalability study of aspect-oriented programming. In *Proceedings of the ACM Conference on Aspect-Oriented Software Development (AOSD'06)*, Bonn, Germany, March 2006.
3. Roy H. Campbell and Brian Randell. Error recovery in asynchronous systems. *IEEE Transactions on Software Engineering*, SE-12(8):811–826, 1986.
4. Fernando Castor Filho, Paulo Asterio de C. Guerra, Vinicius A. Pagano, and Cecília Mary F. Rubira. A systematic approach for structuring exception handling in robust component-based software. *Journal of the Brazilian Computer Society*, 10(3):5–19, 2005.
5. Fernando Castor Filho et al. Exceptions and aspects: The devil is in the details. Technical Report IC-06-08, State University of Campinas, Brazil, 2006.
6. Fernando Castor Filho and Cecília Mary Fischer Rubira. Implementing coordinated error recovery for distributed object-oriented systems with AspectJ. *Journal of Universal Computer Science*, 10(7):843–858, July 2004.

7. S. Chidamber and C. Kemerer. A metrics suite for oo design. *IEEE Transactions on Software Engineering*, 20(6):476–493, June 1994.
8. N. Fenton and S. L. Pfleeger. *Software Metrics: A Rigorous Practical Approach*. PWS, 1997.
9. R. Filman and D. Friedman. Aspect-oriented programming is quantification and obliviousness. In *Proceedings of the Workshop on Advanced Separation of Concerns, OOPSLA'2000*, October 2000.
10. Pascal Frader and Mario Südolt. An aspect language for robust programming. In *Proceedings of the ECOOP'99 Workshop on Aspect-Oriented Programming*, Lisbon, Portugal, June 1999.
11. Erich Gamma, Richard Helm, Ralph Johnson, and John Vlissides. *Design Patterns: Elements of Reusable Software Systems*. Addison-Wesley, 1995.
12. Alessandro Garcia, Claudio Sant'Anna, Christina Chavez, Viviane Silva, Carlos Lucena, and Arndt von Staa. Separation of concerns in multi-agent systems: An empirical study. In C. Lucena et al., editors, *Software Engineering for Multi-Agent Systems II*, LNCS 2940. Springer-Verlag, February 2004.
13. Alessandro Garcia, Claudio Sant'Anna, Eduardo Figueiredo, Uira Kulesza, Carlos Lucena, and Arndt von Staa. Modularizing design patterns with aspects: A quantitative study. In *Proceedings of the 4th ACM Conference on Aspect-Oriented Software Development*, pages 3–14, Chicago, IL, USA, March 2005.
14. I. Godil and H. Jacobsen. Horizontal decomposition of prevlayer. In *Proceedings of CASCON 2005*, Richmond Hill, Canada, October 2005.
15. G. Kiczales, J. Lamping, A. Mendhekar, C. Maeda, C. V. Lopes, J-M. Loingtier, and J. Irwin. Aspect-oriented programming. In *Proceedings of the 11th European Conference on Object-Oriented Programming (ECOOP'97)*, pages 220–242. Springer Verlag LNCS 1241, 1997.
16. Jörg Kienzle and Rachid Guerraoui. Aop: Does it make sense? the case of concurrency and failures. In *Proceedings of the European Conference on Object-Oriented Programming (ECOOP'02)*, LNCS 2374, pages 37–61. Springer-Verlag, June 2002.
17. U. Kulesza, C. Sant'Anna, A. Garcia, and C. Lucena. Aspectization of persistence and distribution: Quantifying the effects of aop. In *5th ACM/IEEE International Symposium on Empirical Software Engineering*, Rio de Janeiro, Brazil, 2006.
18. R. Laddad. *AspectJ in Action*. Manning, 2003.
19. Martin Lippert and Cristina Videira Lopes. A study on exception detection and handling using aspect-oriented programming. In *Proceedings of the 22nd International Conference on Software Engineering (ICSE'2000)*, pages 418–427, Limerick, Ireland, June 2000.
20. Miguel P. Monteiro and Joao M. Fernandes. Towards a catalog of aspect-oriented refactorings. In *Proceedings of AOSD'05*, pages 111–122, March 2005.
21. G. Murphy, R. Walker, E. Baniassad, M. Robillard, and M. Kersten. Does aspect-oriented programming work? *Communications of the ACM*, 44(10):75–77, October 2001.
22. Hridesh Rajan and Kevin Sullivan. Eos: Instance-level aspects for integrated system design. In *Proceedings of Joint European Conference on Software Engineering/SIGSOFT Symposium on Foundations of Software Engineering (ESEC/FSE'2003)*, Helsinki, Finland, September 2003.
23. Claudio Sant'Anna, Alessandro Garcia, Christina Chavez, Carlos Lucena, and Arndt von Staa. On the reuse and maintenance of aspect-oriented software: An assessment framework. In *Proceedings of the 17th Brazilian Symposium on Software Engineering*, pages 19–34, October 2003.
24. Sergio Soares. *An Aspect-Oriented Implementation Method*. PhD thesis, Federal University of Pernambuco, Recife, Brazil, 2004.
25. Sergio Soares, Eduardo Laureano, and Paulo Borba. Implementing distribution and persistence aspects with aspectj. In *Proceedings of the ACM Conference on Object-Oriented Programming, Systems, Languages, and Applications (OOPSLA'02)*, pages 174–190, Seattle, USA, November 2002.

26. Kevin J. Sullivan, William G. Griswold, Yuanyuan Song, Yuanfang Cai, Macneil Shonle, Nishit Tewari, and Hridesh Rajan. Information hiding interfaces for aspect-oriented design. In *Proceedings of the 10th European Software Engineering Conference held jointly with 13th ACM SIGSOFT International Symposium on Foundations of Software Engineering*, pages 166–175, Lisbon, Portugal, September 2005.

27. Tigris. aopmetrics home page, 2005. Address: http://aopmetrics.tigris.org.

28. John Viega and Jeffrey M. Voas. Can aspect-oriented programming lead to more reliable software. *IEEE Software*, 17(6):19–21, 2000.

29. H. Zuse. History of software measurement, 2005. Address: http://irb.cs.tu-berlin.de/ zuse/-metrics/History_00.html.

Errors and Exceptions – Rights and Obligations

Johannes Siedersleben

T-Systems Enterprise Services GmbH
Dachauer Str. 651, 80995 München, Germany
`johannes.siedersleben@t-systems.com`

Abstract. This paper addresses the numerous and painful problems of improper exception handling. It explains the difference between errors and exceptions and describes a practicable way for handling errors and exceptions which neither mingles responsibilities nor discloses hidden implementation information

1 Introduction

Exception handling and the principle of information hiding are hardly compatible with each other, since information hiding means working mostly locally, i.e. within the scope of one's own component, and addressing other components only via their interfaces without any knowledge of their implementation. However, the handling of exceptions requires, firstly, some picture of the overall situation and, secondly, some knowledge of the implementation – and both is not really compatible with the principle of information hiding. Thus, it is not surprising that the handling of errors and exceptions in daily practice over and over again gives rise to discussions and misunderstandings, and sometimes results in bizarre constructional defects.

Purists reject this topic altogether; they demand the avoidance of exceptions and not their handling. Software, however, contains errors like every man-made work. Even if there was error-free software: such software also would have to run in an environment of hardware, operating system and other components, the correctness of which nobody will guarantee.

Until today there is no generally accepted definition of the term of exception. The exception mechanisms of the various programming languages basically differ to some extent. The use of exceptions differs from project to project; what is worse: many projects lack a documented concept for handling errors and exceptions, whatever these terms mean in each case. In practice we find that often the largest part of the systems deals with situations which are considered to be abnormal, exceptional or undesired, and that it is only a smaller part that is dedicated to the proper application. For this reason the handling of errors and exceptions is one of the major topics of the software architecture.

The idea of exceptions in modern programming languages consists in separating the proper application from the handling of undesired events. The use of exceptions is now popular, but here again it is only the program construct which has established itself, while the underlying ideas have been largely forgotten. So there are many open questions with the use of exceptions:

C. Dony et al. (Eds.):Exception Handling, LNCS 4119, pp. 275–287, 2006.
© Springer-Verlag Berlin Heidelberg 2006

1. Who is responsible for the handling of exceptions?
2. How are exceptions of the bottom level (e.g. database access) transformed into exceptions which are meaningful at the higher levels of control?
3. Which results of a method are delivered via exceptions, which results via normal return values?

In this paper, we answer these questions and describe a practicable way for handling errors and exceptions which neither mingles responsibilities nor discloses hidden implementation information.

2 Exceptions and Programming Languages

In the past, the result of a call was returned by a return code. Although this method worked, there were a number of problems:

1. Return codes tend to multiply their instances.
2. The caller cannot cope with the interpretation of the return codes and finally ignores them.
3. The meaning of return codes changes across the different levels: errors appearing harmless at a lower level (e.g. at the database access level) are disasters on upper levels. Contrarily, an error which is disastrous from the local database point of view may be irrelevant for the application (e.g. when writing an optional log).
4. Most programming languages permit only one return value. If the method delivers a technical result, a return code is redundant. Artificial return parameters or global variables for retrieving the system status are no satisfactory solution.

Modern languages know exceptions: every call returns either nothing or a return value or an exception. In the event of an exception the return value is undefined in all popular languages. Exceptions fulfill three functions:

1. They are an additional channel of information sent from the called component to the caller usable for any purposes. Thus, they solve the problem (d).
2. They route the control flow to that catch-block which catches the exception. This catch-block may be located at any point in the system.
3. When the control flow is routed the call stack is processed appropriately.

Exceptions are merely a construct of the programming language – just like the if statement or the while loop. Like each other construct they can be used meaningfully or be misused. Goodenough [Goodenough1975] points out that the technical issues of exception handling are well understood: exceptions are raised, walk up the call stack, and are handled by aborting, retrying or just replacing the current call by a different one. But we know little about the impact of exceptions on the application. In fact, over and over again we encounter the following problems:

1. Numerous exceptions are flying across the system. It is neither clear in which instances exceptions are thrown, nor which component is to catch them and then what to do with them.
2. Many, sometimes even all catch-blocks are empty or contain absurd code.

3. In many systems a vast number of defined different exception classes overpower the caller just like the return codes of former times and, in addition, create undesired dependencies between the caller and the called component.
4. Exceptions are misused for the return of quite normal results.
5. The throw-catch mechanism creates, if applied naively, nontransparent control structures: throw as a refined goto.
6. try-catch blocks obscure the structure of the code, especially if they are nested.

Miller and Tripathi [MillerTripathi1997] address some of the major problems of exception handling mechanisms in object-oriented languages. But our concern is the impact of exceptions on software architecture. Therefore, in the next section, we reflect upon foundations laid by Parnas and Würges [Parnas1976].

3 Exceptions and Software Architecture

The term of *exception* suggests the meanings of "happens very rarely" or "disaster". This corresponds only partially to the common use of exceptions in the daily programming practice. Exceptions in terms of programming languages may be a part of the quite normal business. In Java, the InterruptedException serves to synchronize threads – this exception is neither rare nor undesired.

Thus, the term of exception is fuzzy. Many other terms were proposed: *undesired events* [Parnas1976], *system error* [Denert1992] or *disaster* [Siedersleben2002], all of which, however, imply a valuation, and therefore nearly every project will see wearisome discussions about the question of what is less bad (error) or very bad (system error, disaster or whatsoever).

The point at issue is quite different: Each method may return two basically different types of *results*[1]: The first results – we call them *normal* – match the abstraction level of the interface and they do not contain any implementation details. They belong to the same software category. The second results belong to another category and they often disclose implementation details. We call them *abnormal*, as *abnormal* is the opposite of *normal*. What matters: Every caller is free to handle abnormal results as well, but above all the caller has the right to ignore them. Abnormal results are attended to by the direct caller only in very rare cases. Rather, they are processed by a higher-level exception handling procedure (see Section Architecture of the Exception Handling System).

This is how we also act in our daily routine; let us take the car as an example: Every driver sees the well-known, simple and well-defined interface consisting of steering wheel, accelerator pedal, brake pedal and further control elements. Cars work most of the times, which is the presumed normal case. But if the car breaks down, it is not the driver anymore who is competent, but a superior instance, in this case maybe the breakdown assistance.

We propose to regard the *exception* in terms of software architecture and the *abnormal result* as synonyms independently from the randomness of programming

---

[1] This is term without any valuation.

languages. That is: every result is either normal or abnormal; *exception* and *abnormal result* mean exactly the same. The terms of *exception handling* and *handling of abnormal results* are also synonyms. We use both terms side by side. *Errors* are normal, but undesired results of the application. The distinction between desired and undesired results is subjective and irrelevant for the following statements.

We strictly distinguish between exceptions in terms of software architecture and exceptions of the applied programming language: Every result (whether normal or abnormal) can be delivered as a return code or as an exception related to the programming language. We will extend the idea of abnormal results with three examples:

First example: The component `account` features the method `withdrawmoney`. Normal results are: `ok`, `nofunds`, `accountblocked`. RMI problems (delivered by `RemoteException`), a non-accessible database, or other database problems (delivered by `SQLException`) are abnormal, as they disclose hidden implementation information: `RemoteException` signifies that RMI is used; `SQLException` signifies that a relational database is involved. The problem in this connection is not really the disclosure of information – the callers may of course know about RMI and databases. But they should not be concerned with the handling of implementation-dependent problems for which they are not responsible.

Second example: We examine the method `connectDatabase` of an access layer. In this case normal results are `ok` and `nok` (if the database is not accessible). A RMI problem (delivered by `RemoteException`) would be abnormal, since RMI has nothing to do with databases. The non-accessibility of the database is abnormal in the first example and normal in the second example. Thus, the decision of *normal* vs. *abnormal* has to be made locally, i.e. for each interface, by the designer of the interface.

Third example: There are cases where the decision of *normal* vs. *abnormal* is not evident. In this respect we examine the authorization check: Every operation of a system may be linked to an authorization check, which will fail, if the assigned user is not authorized to perform the operation. It is left to the software designer's discretion whether to make the topic of *authorization* a dedicated software category or to regard it as a part of the category of *application*. This decision depends on the scope and complexity of the authorization checks: The more important and complicated they are, the more they will be regarded as a dedicated category.

These examples show that abnormal results are more than system errors, disasters and undesired events of other publications. Lumping normal and abnormal results together nearly inevitably results in a violation of the rules of data abstraction, since the callers would also be confronted with results for which they are not responsible and which they could handle only by violating the principle of information hiding.

When distinguishing between normal and abnormal results the following issues are important:

1. The interface defines all normal results for every method. These results are independent from the implementation. The decision normal vs. abnormal is binary. There is no happy medium.
2. In most cases there are only one or two normal results; if there is a considerably higher number, the interface should be changed. For every method all normal results are fully itemized as a part of the specifications.
3. Abnormal results mostly are implementation-dependent. Therefore it is basically not possible to specify them at the implementation-independent interface, and nobody would be capable of itemizing all conceivable abnormal results. It is like with a car: If it does *not* start up once, this may be due to numerous causes. Thus, abnormal results belong to the inside view of a component – at the interface they are irrelevant.
4. Abnormal results are rare – if they occur frequently, this is due to a faulty design and the method should be redesigned.
5. Abnormal results interrupt the normal flow and demand some special treatment. In some cases it is possible to continue afterwards; in other cases the sole option is to stop the entire system.
6. Whatever cannot be handled during the runtime is always abnormal: Syntactically incorrect SQL statements and syntactically incorrect regular expressions are always reasons for exceptions.

4 Options of the Exception Handling System

How to respond to abnormal results at all? The simplest case is just to stop the system, to release resources and to log the incident. This procedure is just as easy done as said and is applied in the test and integration stage and sometimes also in live operation. But how to design a proper exception handling? The answers, of course, depend on the system, though the following tasks are typical:

1. *Logging and continuing*. Abnormal results are not necessarily bad from the caller's view. In the best case you log the circumstances and continue the job.
2. *Logging and limiting damage*. In the event of the ultimate failure the first step is to accurately log the disaster, i.e. for the maintenance programmers who will solve the problem later on and *not* for the user on the screen. The second step is to take a number of measures for limiting the damage: Closing connections, resetting transactions and the like. Afterwards it has to be decided which part of the application to terminate: Often only one session is affected; the user has to log in again. In the worst case the entire system is shut down.
3. *Waiting and repeating*. In some cases it is wise to wait until a timeout or to execute a specific number of repeated attempts. If it does not work with the first attempt, perhaps with the second or third. The number of repetitions, which of course multiplies across different layers, has to be kept within reasonable limits. The exception handling decides about the final abort from the view of the called component.
4. *Reconfiguration*. Sometimes there are two alternative components available. A standard example is a local backup database which is used whenever the actual database is not available. In this case the appropriate exception handling performs a reconfiguration if required, i.e.: the non-accessible database is replaced with the local database.

Thus, after performing the exception handling every method will have only two possible exits:

1. *Normal result*: The method was successful, which includes results that are errors from the view of the application, such as the withdrawal rejected for lack of funds. It is not disclosed to the caller whether an exception handling was required in the form of repetitions or a reconfiguration to achieve the result – only the longer response time could be some indication.
2. *Final and safe failure*: The method has finally failed; all repair attempts were unsuccessful and all measures for limiting the damage were performed. Further repair attempts are useless; the sole remaining option for the caller is to abort.

In many systems the exception handling will remain simple and manageable during the entire service life of the system. However, in case the exceptions are numerous and complex, we recommend delegating the exception handling to various experts. This is what the next section is about.

5 Architecture of the Exception Handling System

Every serious system features an exception handling routine (ErrorHandler, ExceptionHandler), i.e. a dedicated component for handling exceptions, whatever *exception* mean in the respective system. This routine performs the typical clean-up operations: release of resources, logging and proper termination of the application, maybe re-starts as well. Usually the exception handling is located at the end of the call chain; it is virtually located in the basement; the caught exception object mostly is the sole source of information.

This approach works only to a limited degree, as it is intricate and sometimes impossible to provide the caught exception object with all information which is required for a sound decision about the further proceeding. Moreover, depending on the situation (dialog/batch mode) different exception handling strategies are required. Therefore we propose the following approach.

5.1 Security Facade

There are two possibilities for calling a component: *optimistically* or *pessimistically*. In the optimistic case the component is used as is, i.e. without any precaution against possible exceptions. This way the calling and the called component form a risk community to which all other components called optimistically belong by transitivity. There is nothing to be said against it, if you just know what you are doing.

This section deals with the pessimistic call. Here the component is shielded by a *security facade* with which it jointly forms a new, secure component. Every call has exactly two possible results: success or final and safe failure (see Section Options of the Exception Handling System).

The security facade implements the same interfaces like the component to be shielded, and it handles all exceptions that may occur within the component. For this process all the

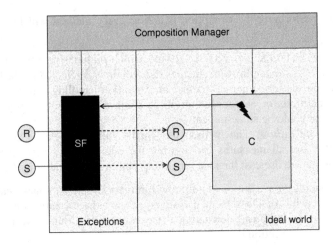

Fig. 1. Component with Security Facade

options referred to in the preceding section are available. The security facade is symmetric, as it exports and imports the same interfaces. Fig. 1 shows the Component C with Security Facade SF.

Every abnormal result of C (depicted in Fig. 1 as a flash) is routed directly to SF together with the mechanisms of the used programming language (e.g. Java exceptions). In the program it looks like this (foo and bar stand for any methods of R or S):

```
public class SecurityFacade implements R, S {
    private C x;
    public setC(C x) { this.x = x; }
    public void foo() {
        try {
            x.foo();
        }
        // Exception handling with optional access to x
        catch (ExceptionA a) { // Handling of A }
        catch (ExceptionB b) { // Handling of B  }
        catch (RuntimeException t) { // other problems }
    }

    public void bar() {
        try {
            x.bar();
        }
        catch(ExceptionA a) { .. }
        // Continue like with foo
    }
    // the remaining methods of R and S
}
```

So let us summarize how to build a security facade for an existing component:

1. Implement a new class *SF* that implements a suitable subset of the interfaces exported by the encapsulated component *C*.
2. When implementing SF call the original methods of *C* from a `try-catch` block.

Thus the caller enjoys the absence of confusing and misleading exceptions – the only remaining exception is the definite and save failure. The security facade is invisible to the caller. The security facade itself is a component of a special kind: it is symmetric, that is, it exports the same interfaces that it imports.

The separation of the handling of normal and abnormal results has three major advantages:

1. The principle of information hiding is preserved: Every component only deals with results of its own scope.
2. The Component *C* is easily re-usable, because exceptions can be handled differently depending on the situation (e.g. batch mode and dialog).
3. The development process becomes easier: At the beginning some primitive exception handling is sufficient which maybe only has the function to log the exception and to stop the system in a controlled way. Within the course of the later development the exception handling routine is becoming a dedicated, sometimes complex component.

But where is light there is shadow too: In the event of an exception, the executed method is interrupted; the control flow is routed from the place of event to the security facade. That means: After the exception handling has been performed, it is not possible just to continue at the place where the exception occurred. To be sure, the security facade may rollback a method partially executed (`rollback` within a transaction, `reset`, if a appropriate D&R interface[2] is available), it may call the method a second time or select any other option *except for one*: just resetting the call stack and continuing as if nothing had happened. Is that bad news?

Our answer is: Generally it is not, since the interruption of the control flow poses problems only in rare cases. Exceptions within the meaning of the previous section are rare by definition, and if they occur once, they must also not be noticeable. However, we cannot fully rule out that in special situations the control flow has to be continued directly after the exception handling. In such a case, the only choice is to call the exception handling method directly in the `catch` clause which brackets the critical call.

5.2 Diagnosis and Repair

Every component may provide an own interface for diagnosis and repair; we briefly call it D&R interface. It is only known to the Composition Manager and the security facade; other components do not see it. In case of application components such as

---
[2] See next Section on Diagnose & Repair.

Customer, Account, such an interface is needed only in rare cases, but with technical components (e.g. access layer) it is useful and, in addition, easily implemented. This is a proposal for the D&R interface of an access layer:

```
public interface PersistenceDR {
    boolean ok();
    boolean reset();
    boolean reconnect();
    boolean resign();
}
```

The meaning of these methods is easy to guess: ok provides information on the status; the result true means that the component is working. As for the reset method: a main problem of the exception handling consists in the fact that after an exception has occurred, the clock often has to be rolled back somewhat. In this connection the finally clause in Java is only of little use, as are the C++ destructors. What is much better is a dedicated reset method which in dependence on the status assumes all necessary resetting tasks. reconnect would be used for trying to re-establish the connection to the database; after a specific number of failures the entire component would be deactivated by calling resign.

The point here is neither the exact design of the D&R interface nor the actually selected strategy (e.g. the number of connection attempts), but the fact that with the D&R interface the security facade has all means in order to a make a diagnosis and to rectify the situation within the bounds of possibility.

D&R interfaces are not only useful in handling exceptions, but they also form the basis of any kind of system management: A control center can be used for monitoring and if required, controlling all component objects.

The Composition Manager and the security facade know the implementation of the involved components at least to some extent – which is fully consistent with the principle of information hiding, since it is exactly the Composition Manager which decides with which concrete implementation to work. For different situations (batch mode and dialog) different Composition Managers are used.

5.3 Experts for Diagnosis and Repair

Sometimes the possible exceptions are so complex that they are divided into appropriate categories, e.g. *Database* and *Connection*, maybe also *Authorization* and *EJB*. For every category there is a D&R expert; every D&R expert sees the D&R interfaces of the components for which it is responsible.

Between the components doing the actual work and the D&R experts there is, in general, a n:m relation: Every D&R expert requires the D&R interfaces of one or several components; every component offer its D&R interface – if existing – to any number of expert. The experts only see the D&R interfaces of the components which they are monitoring. Fig. 2 illustrates the interaction of the component, the security facade and the D&R experts.

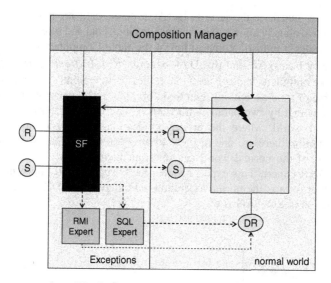

Fig. 2. Security Facade for a Component

5.4 Composition as a Risk Community

The presented architecture entails that each composition equipped with a security facade at the same time is a risk community: All composition-internal calls are optimistic;

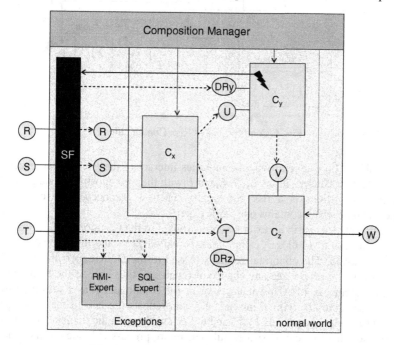

Fig. 3. Security Facade for several Components

external calls are routed via the security facade. External calls are pessimistic and thus know only the two already known exits: normal result or final and safe failure.

Fig. 3 illustrates a realistic composition of the three Components C_x, C_y, C_z with the joint security facade *SF* and two D&R experts (*RMIExpert, SQLExpert*). C_x, C_y and C_z make optimistic calls on each other; they survive jointly or die jointly.

In the course of time exceptions tend to deform any architecture whatever elegant. This tendency is met by two parallel structures: One covers the normal case, i.e. the normal or ideal world, where the proper application, the day-to-day business, is running. In addition there are one or more experts for wearisome exceptions of any kind. Programs of the normal world can interrupt their work at any time and pass control to a D&R expert. This expert handles the exception and afterwards has two options: It either restarts the normal operation via the available D&R interfaces, or it terminates the job in a controlled way.

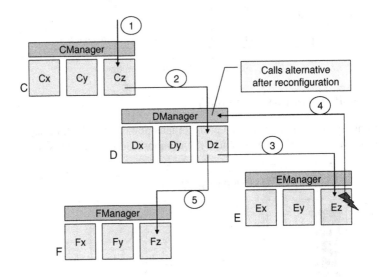

Fig. 4. Compositions as Risk Communities

Fig. 4 shows how several risk communities interact in the event of an exception. We examine four Compositions *C, D, E* and *F* with their composition managers. Each of these compositions is a risk community; each is managed by a composition manager each of which contains one D&R expert.

In the depicted scenario an external call is routed to the Component C. CManager delegates this call to C_z (1). C_z calls D_z (2), D_z calls E_z (3), and there some abnormal event is occurring. The abnormal result is passed to the D&R expert in EManager which, however, does not see any chance of repair and thus reports the final and safe failure to DManager (4). This manager owns the component *F* as a substitute for *E*. Thus it reconfigures D_z with *F* instead of *E* and repeats the call to the reconfigured component D_z which now calls F_z (5) and not E_z anymore. In the depicted scenario we have assumed that this call is successful. The entire process is hidden to the external caller; at the utmost it notices a longer response time.

6 Six Rules

Let us summarize the lessons of this paper.

6.1 Distinguish Errors and Exceptions

Errors are normal. Errors might be undesired, but are expected. For a file handling routine, EOF could be considered as an error, but it is certainly normal and expected, Exceptions are abnormal results of a call. They are unexpected. The caller has no idea how to deal with an exception and will therefore defer its handling to the next security facade.

6.2 Handle Errors Locally. Errors Are Never Propagated

Errors are normal, expected results, albeit undesired. The caller is able, prepared to and committed to react promptly.

6.3 Return Errors Via Return Values (e.g. `null`). If This Is Not Possible, Return Errors as Checked Exceptions

Handling return values is easier and more elegant than handling exceptions. Unchecked exceptions are reserved for abnormal results

6.4 Signal Exceptions as Early as Possible

In other words: program defensively. Signal abnormal events as soon as you suspect any anomaly. If not, your system will agonize and then crash hard with no hope for recovering

6.5 Security Facades Catch Exceptions and Handle Them – Nobody Else

By assigning the responsibility for catching exceptions to security facades only, there is a clear distinction between the normal world where the application code resides and the exceptional world where exceptions are handled.

6.6 Compose Components to Risk Communities

Risk communities live together or die together. They are as robust as their weakest part. A risk community is shielded by only one security facade. The design of appropriate risk communities is an important task of the software architect.

References

[Hunt 2002]   A. Hunt, D. Thomas: The Pragmatic Programmer. Addison-Wesley, 2002.
[Denert1992]   E. Denert, J. Siedersleben: Software-Engineering. Springer Verlag, 1992.

[Goodenough1975]   J. B. Goodenough: Exception Handling: Issues and Proposed Notation, Communications of the ACM 18(12), 1975, pp. 683-696

[MillerTripathi1997]   R. Miller, A. Tripathi: Issues with Exception Handling in Object-Oriented Systems. ECOOP 1997, pp.85-103

[Parnas1976]   D. L. Parnas, H. Würges: Response to Undesired Events in Software Systems. Proceedings of the Second International Conference on Software Engineering, 1976, pp. 437-447

[Siedersleben2002]   J. Siedersleben (Ed.): Software-Technik. Hanser Verlag, 2002.

Exceptions in Java and Eiffel:
Two Extremes in Exception Design and Application

Joseph R. Kiniry

School of Computer Science and Informatics
University College Dublin
Belfield, Dublin 8, Ireland
joseph.kiniry@ucd.ie

Abstract. Exceptions are frequently a controversial language feature with both language designers and programmers. Exceptions are controversial because they complicate language semantics—and thus program design, testing, and verification—and some programmers find them annoying or difficult to use properly. By examining two programming languages that have very different, even opposing, exception mechanisms, a set of exception principles is introduced that summarize the key semantic and social issues surrounding exceptions.

1 Introduction

The designers of future programming languages must decide whether to include exceptions in their new languages. If they decide exceptions are warranted, they must then consider what exceptions represent: (1) a structure for control flow, (2) a structure for handling abnormal, unpredictable situations, or (3) something in-between. Additionally, the syntax and meaning of exceptions must be considered.

The syntax of exception mechanisms is also important. Syntax impacts how program code looks and is comprehended, it influences the design and realization of algorithms, and it affects the manner in which programmers handle unusual cases and unexpected situations, and thus indirectly impacts software reliability. And, while the syntax of exception mechanisms is the aspect most programmers see, tool developers and language theoreticians must wrestle with exception semantics. In general, a small, elegant semantics is desired by all parties.

One way to consider how to design a feature like exceptions in future languages is to analyze their design in today's languages. While the analysis of exceptions in niche, historical, or research languages like Ada, Mesa, PL/I, and CLU reveals an "exceptional" gem or two[1], examining the contrary designer and user viewpoints that exist in two modern languages is more relevant to working programmers.

The programming languages Java and Eiffel offer two opposing viewpoints in the design and use of exceptions. A detailed analysis of exceptions in these two languages, as expressed through a series of *principles*: their language design, formal specification and validation, core library use, and non-technical "social" pressures, helps future language

---

[1] These three languages are frequently cited as the premier languages with innovative exception mechanisms.

C. Dony et al. (Eds.):Exception Handling, LNCS 4119, pp. 288–300, 2006.

creators design their own exception mechanisms. This analysis also informs developers, particularly those that only know one or two programming languages, of the sometimes radically different viewpoints that exist about exceptions.

While the discussions in this paper focus on two object-oriented languages, it is expected that the principles herein are not restricted to object-oriented languages. N.B. It is assumed that the reader is knowledgeable of the basic precepts of exceptions (e.g., exception nesting, handlers, etc.).

1.1 Terminology

The terminology used in this paper is the terminology used in the Java programming community.

A program is composed of a set of *threads* executing a sequence of *method calls* on a set of *objects* and *classes*. Objects are instances of classes, and classes are made up of *data fields* (or just *fields* for short) and *methods* in the Java vernacular. In the Eiffel vernacular, methods and fields are known generically as *routines*. The object calling a method is known as a *client*; the called object is known as the *supplier*.

A method's body specifies a *program behavior*. The execution behavior of a method is either *normal, abnormal,* or *divergent*. A method that terminates without an exception exhibits normal behavior; a method that terminates by a thrown exception exhibits abnormal behavior; and a method that never terminates exhibits divergent behavior.

In program code, a flow control structure is any program structure which diverts the execution of a program from the next statement. Conditional statements (e.g., an if-then-else block, a case statement, etc.) are the flow control structures typically associated with normal behavior. Exception-based program structures like try/catch blocks in Java are also flow control structures, and are typically related to abnormal behavior.

We characterize a system that behaves in an unexpected fashion as either *partial* or *total failures*. What "unexpected" means is contextual. Finding a file owned by the program disappear or not readable is an example of a typical unexpected *partial failure*, because the program can attempt to change the permissions of, or recreate, the file. An example *total failure* is discovering that a vital resource, say a physical device, is unavailable.

2 Language Design

Language design only partially influences the use of exceptions, and consequently, the manner in which one handles partial and total failures during system execution. The other major influence is examples of use, typically in core libraries and code examples in technical books, magazine articles, and online discussion forums, and in an organization's code standards. This latter "social" effect is clearly seen in the use of exceptions in Java and Eiffel and is discussed in Section 5.

Exceptions in Java are designed to be used as flow control structures. This is also true of exceptions in most other modern programming languages including Ada, C++, Modula-3, ML and OCaml, Python, and Ruby.

Eiffel exceptions, on the other hand, are designed to represent and handle abnormal, unpredictable, erroneous situations. The languages C#, Common Lisp, and Modula-2 use this interpretation for exceptions as well[2].

2.1 Exception Language Design in Java

Exceptions in Java are used to model many types of events; they are not just used for erroneous behavior. Exceptions sometimes indicate situations that should not be witnessed during a "typical" execution of a program. Most Java exceptions are meant to be dealt with at runtime—just because an exception is thrown does *not* mean that the program must exit.

Java exceptions are represented by classes that inherit from the abstract class `java.-lang.Throwable`. They are generically called *throwables* because raising an exception is Java is accomplished with the `throw` keyword.

Each Java throwable is one of two (disjoint) kinds: *unchecked exceptions* or *checked exceptions*. The former inherit from either the class `java.lang.Runtime-Exception` or the class `java.lang.Error`, the latter inherit from `java.lang.Exception` [3, Section 11.2].

Some of the most commonly witnessed runtime exceptions are `NullPointer-Exception` and `ClassCastException`. Two example errors are `Assertion-Error` and `ThreadDeath`. Examples of normal exceptions are `ClassNotFound-Exception`, `CloneNotSupportedException`, and `IOException`.

Checked Exceptions in Java. If a method can raise a checked exception, the checked exception type *must* be specified as part of the signature of a method. The `throws` keyword is used to designate such. A client of a method whose signature includes an exception E (i.e., the method signature includes "`throws E`") must either handle E with a `catch` expression or the client also must declare that it can throw E.

Thus, if a new checked exception is introduced or an existing exception is eliminated, all method signatures or method bodies involving these exceptions must change. Likewise, all methods that call these changed methods must be revised. This exception signature coupling leads to a fragile and annoying trickle-down effect that is frequently seen when programming large Java systems.

Checked exceptions are mainly used to characterize partial and total failures during method invocations, like a file not being readable or a buffer overflowing. Not all erroneous situations in Java are represented by exceptions though. Many methods return special values which indicate failure encoded as constant field of related classes. This lack of design uniformity leads to the introduction of the *Uniformity Principle*.

Principle 1 (Uniformity Principle). *Exceptions must have a uniform, consistent informal semantics for the developer.*

---

[2] Note that Modula-2 did not originally have exceptions; their addition caused a great deal of controversy through the early 1990s (i.e., compare [1] to [2]). See `http://cs.ru.ac.za/homes/cspt/sc22wg13.htm` for a historical discussion of such.

The use of exceptions in Java is contrary to the **Uniformity Principle**. While some attempt has obviously been made to use exceptions only for truly unexpected incidences, there are numerous examples of inconsistent use (e.g., `ArrayStoreException`, `FileNotFoundException`, and `NotSerializableException`). These inconsistencies are sometimes due to more serious language flaws (e.g., in Java's type system), but, for the most part, are simply inconsistencies in API design.

Unchecked Exceptions in Java. Unchecked exceptions are either runtime exceptions or errors.

Runtime exceptions can rarely (but potentially) be corrected at runtime, and thus are not errors. For example, `ArrayIndexOutOfBoundsException`, `ClassCastException`, and `NullPointerException` are common runtime exceptions of this kind.

Errors indicate serious problems that most applications cannot handle. Most errors indicate abnormal situations with either the operating environment or the program structure. Examples of errors are `AssertionError` (thrown when an assertion fails), `No-SuchMethodError` (thrown when a method that does not exist is called), `Stack-OverflowError`, and `OutOfMemoryError`. In general, if one of these errors is raised, the program exits.

Java 5. In Java 5 several new constructs were added to the Java language. Two of these constructs are parameterized classes and enumerations.

Programmers can use either of these language mechanisms to express richer exception semantics. For example, a enumeration can denote a precise set of distinct exceptions legal in a given context.

There is no evidence that the Java 1.5 team has considered either of these alternatives. There are no parameterized exception types in Java 1.5, no new exception types of note, and no use of enumerations and exceptions.

2.2   Exceptions in Eiffel

The fundamental exception principle in Eiffel is that *a routine*[3] *must either succeed or fail*: either it fulfills its contract[4] or it does not. It the latter case an exception is *always* raised [4,5]. Thus, exceptions are, by design, meant to be used in Eiffel exclusively to signal when a contract is broken.

Eiffel exceptions are not specified as part of the type signature of a routine, nor are they mentioned in routine contracts. In fact, there is no way to determine if a routine can raise an exception other than by an inspection of the routine's source code, and all the source code on which it depends.

Eiffel exceptions are represented by *INTEGER*[5] and *STRING* values—there are no exception classes[6]. Exceptions that are part of the language definition are represented

---

[3] An Eiffel *routine* is a method of a class.

[4] An Eiffel *routine contract* is a precondition/postcondition pair.

[5] Eiffel class names are always capitalized.

[6] The new ECMA standard for Eiffel introduces exception classes perhaps, in part, due to articles such as this one [6].

by *INTEGER* values, developer-defined exceptions by *STRING* values[7]. This limited and non-uniform representation of Eiffel exceptions inspires a new principle.

Principle 2 (Representation Principle). *Exceptions should have a uniform representation, and that representation should be amenable to refinement.*

Eiffel exceptions have two representations which causes design impedance when dealing with them. Additionally, because they are basic values and not objects, they have no inherent semantics beyond that which is expressed in a helper routine which necessarily cannot be foolproof because of the representation overloading in effect (e.g., one cannot differentiate two integers of the same value).

Contract Failure. Contracts are violated in several ways, all of which are considered *faults*, but only some faults are under programmer control.

Operating environment problems, such as running out of memory, are one situation in which exceptions are raised. In these cases a contract fails, but not necessarily because the client (the caller) or the supplier (the callee) did something wrong. Certainly, intentionally allocating too much memory, or otherwise using an extraordinary amount of system resources, is the fault of the program, but such situations are more malicious than typical.

Software infrastructure failures cause exceptions also. E.g., some operating system signals raise an exception. Failures in non-Eiffel libraries that are used by an Eiffel application cause these kinds of exceptions as well. For example, Eiffel programs that link with Microsoft Windows COM components witness an exception when a COM routine fails and Eiffel programs that use UNIX libraries see an exception raised when an external library fails and did not set the `errno` system variable. Additionally, a floating point exception is raised on some architectures when a division by zero is attempted.

But most exceptions used in Eiffel are not due to external factors, but instead are *assertion violations* or *developer exceptions*, both of which are used to indicate program errors.

If assertion checking is enabled during compilation, assertion violations cause an exception to be raised. These exceptions are classified according to the type of assertion that has been violated[8].

For example, the `check` instruction, which is equivalent to C or Java's `assert` statement, cause a `Check_instruction` exception to be raised. A `Loop_variant` exception is another assertion violation. This exception is raised when a loop variant does not monotonically decrease during loop execution.

Violating a contract, either by failing to fulfill a class invariant, a method precondition or postcondition, or a loop invariant, is the final kind of exception. Contract violations fall into two categories: those that are the fault of the client of a class, and those that are the fault of the supplier of a class. The classification of an exception is determined by the context of the failure during program execution.

---

[7] Earlier versions of the Eiffel language standard permitted developer-defined integer exception values, but this seems to no longer be the case. It is unclear when and why this change was made.

[8] JML uses the same assertion failure exception design [7].

If a contract is broken at the time a method is called, regardless of whether the caller is another object or the current object (in the case of a callback, or the use of the `retry` keyword, see below), then the blame lies with the caller.

Exactly one kind of exception, called `Void_call_target`, can be the blame of either the caller or the callee. If a method is invoked on an object reference with value `Void`, a `Void_call_target` is raised. If the caller set the value to `Void`, or did not check the reference prior to making the invocation attempt, then the blame lies with the caller. In situations where the reference was obtained via a routine call, either via a formal parameter or a return value, and the value is `Void`, the blame lies with the callee, as the specification of the routine is not strong enough to eliminate the possibility of the `Void` value[9].

The uniform design for signaling assertion failure with exceptions in Eiffel is contrary to that which exists in Java. Several languages exist for the formal specification of contract for Java code, and the Java Modeling Language (JML) is the de facto standard for such [8]. Unfortunately, because assertion violation semantics is so primitive in Java, there is no uniformity in exception specification across different assertion tools and specification languages. This muddle inspires the next principle.

Principle 3 (Language Specification Principle). *If exceptions are used to represent assertion failure, their design and semantics should be incorporated into the core language specification.*

Java programmers and JML specification authors have suffered because the creators of Java ignored this key point in language design, particularly because an assert statement was not introduced to Java until seven years into the evolution of the language.

2.3 Comparing Eiffel Exceptions to Unchecked Exceptions in Java

Given the above analysis, Eiffel exceptions and Java unchecked exceptions are exclusively focused on unexpected, erroneous behavior that an application should not try to handle. Thus, one might expect every Eiffel exception to map to a single Java unchecked exception. This is not the case.

Some of Eiffel's built-in exception types are equivalent to standard *checked* exceptions in Java. For example, Eiffel's `Io_exception`, `Runtime_io_exception`, and `Retrieve_exception` are similar to `IOException` and some of its children.

A number of *unchecked* exceptions are equivalent to standard Eiffel exceptions. For example, `Void_call_target` is equivalent to `NullPointerException`, and `Floating_point_exception` is equivalent to `ArithmeticException`.

Finally, some errors are equivalent to the remaining Eiffel exceptions: `Assertion-Error` is equivalent to the set of specification-centric Eiffel exceptions (`Check_-instruction`, `Class_invariant`, `Loop_invariant`, `Loop_variant`, `Postcondition`, and `Precondition`), and `No_more_memory` subsumes `Out-OfMemoryError` and `StackOverflowError`.

Missing Mappings. Several exceptions that exist in each language have no peer in the other language.

---

[9] The new ECMA standard for Eiffel introduces non-void types to deal with these issues.

`Rescue_exception` has no mapping, as Java does not perform any special handling of exceptions thrown in a `finally` clause. An extended discussion on this point is below in Section 2.3.

An equivalent for `Signal_exception` is not part of the core Java language as Java's definition focuses on multi-platform development and not all platforms have signals[10]. The original Eiffel language specification states that such system-specific exceptions should be contained in system-specific classes, but no compilers implement this suggestion [10].

An error like `Void_assigned_to_expanded` is not possible in Java as Java has no expanded types and the type system prohibits assignment of `null` to built-in types like `int` and `boolean`[11].

The Eiffel literature claims that Eiffel has no casting (cf., [11, page 194]), thus there is no equivalent to Java's `ClassCastException`. This claim is a bit disingenuous because Eiffel's assignment attempt operator '`?=`' is simply a built-in conditional downcast in the form of an operator[12].

`Routine_failure` is a generic exception in Eiffel that indicates a routine has failed for some reason. The reason is sometimes recorded (as a `STRING`) in the `meaning` associated with the exception, but this is not mandatory. This is also true of Java exceptions, each of which has an optional message associated with it obtainable via the `Throwable.getMessage()` method. Unfortunately, there is absolutely no uniformity to the use of these representations in either language, which motivates the introduction of the following principle.

Principle 4 (Meaning Principle). *When defining a new type of exception, the availability of a human **and** unambiguous machine comprehensible representations (e.g., a string value and a predicate) is mandatory.*

For the most part, exception design in both Java and Eiffel fail to fulfill the *Meaning Principle*.

None of the various Java exceptions involving out-of-bounds array access and strings exist in Eiffel because the contracts of accessor routines for these types prohibit such. Cloning-related exceptions do not exist because all objects can be cloned in Eiffel. In fact, in general numerous exception types simply do not exist in Eiffel because routine contracts prohibit the situations that must be manually dealt with in Java catch blocks. This evidence inspires a principle on contracts.

Principle 5 (Contract Principle). *Integrated contracts significantly decrease the number and complexity of exceptions.*

The *Contract Principle* is critical with regards to the development of complex modern applications and components, particularly with respect to component and system testing, verification, and evolution.

---

[10] One can catch and handle signals in Java, but internal classes like `sun.misc.Signal` and `sun.misc.SignalHandler`, or a package like that seen in [9], are needed.

[11] And, in fact, this error cannot occur with the introduction of autoboxing in Java 5.

[12] This is not the only "pragmatic circumvention" in Eiffel. Other examples include the dual semantics of routine calls (with and without an explicit "`Current`") and the semantics of the `equal` and `clone` routines of ANY.

This principle is supported by the quantitative analysis of Section 4.

The Eiffel language standard does not have several features of Java: reflection, introspection, concurrency, and sandboxing. While these features contribute significantly to the complexity of Java's exception class hierarchy it is expected that the continued application of the **Contract Principle** will see Eiffel's exception hierarchy change little with the adoption of such features[13].

Controlling Exceptions in Eiffel. Exceptions are primarily controlled in Eiffel using *rescue clauses* and the `retry` instruction. Exceptions are also indirectly controlled by the choice made in *compilation mode* during application development.

A routine may end with a rescue clause. A *rescue clause* of a routine is a block of code that will execute if any exception is raised during the execution of the routine.

The rescue clause does not discriminate between different types of exceptions. In this respect, it is functionally equivalent to the surrounding every Java method body with a `try`/`catch` block where the catch expression's type `java.lang.Throwable`. The rescue clause is *not* equivalent to Java's `finally` construct. The code enclosed in a finally block is *always* executed when a method completes, whether it completes normally or abnormally, while a rescue clause only executes when a routine fails.

The `retry` instruction in Eiffel causes a routine to restart its execution. This instruction may only be used within a rescue clause. If a rescue clause does not contain a retry instruction, then the routine fails and the current exception is raised in the immediate caller. The details of `finally` and `rescue` are discussed in the sequel.

Exceptions are manipulated in Eiffel using the EXCEPTIONS class. Using this class one can find out information about the latest raised exception (much like `errno` in C), handle certain kinds of exceptions in a special way, raise special developer-defined exceptions, and prescribe that certain exceptions must be ignored at run-time. The EXCEPTIONS class is part of the Eiffel Kernel Library, thus is available in all Eiffel compilers.

3   Exceptional Specifications and Validation

The key difference between the use of exceptions in specifications in the two languages in that exceptions are *part* of a method contract in Java and are *not* part of a routine contract in Eiffel. Thus, a fundamental notion of "Design by Contract," that of exceptions exclusively indicating contract failure, has a different interpretation in Java.

3.1   Contracts with Exceptions in Java

As mentioned previously, the Java Modeling Language is used to write formal specifications of Java components [12]. The discussion in this section is based upon experience in participating in the development and application of a denotational semantics for Java and JML and the design, specification, and verification of several Java systems [13,14,15].

---

[13] This claim is supported by the recent addition of reflection and concurrency in commercial and experimental Eiffel compilers.

The semantics of Java, and thus JML, are significantly complicated by the possibility of abrupt method termination. Verification proofs must cover three cases in Java: normal termination, abrupt termination, and divergent behavior, sometimes tripling proof size.

The default specification for a failure is simply *true*, which means that the routine guarantees nothing in particular when a failure takes place. Usually something stronger is specified and, in fact, exceptional cases are often the first part of a formal specification written.

This information, what is true of the system when an exception is thrown, helps the caller deal with the exceptional cases rather than just halting. In fact, the specification of a postcondition for abrupt termination is *mandatory* for reasoning about systems during abrupt termination. Without such assertions, class invariants can become significantly more complex because, for example, specification variables are needed to represent failure states for all of the routines of a class.

3.2   Specifications of Eiffel Exceptions

In Eiffel, the semantics of *exceptional-correct* routines is rolled into the definition of *class correctness* [11, Chapter 15 and Section 9.16].

The definition [11, Section 15.10] of *exception-correct* is:

> A routine r of a class C is exception-correct if and only if, for every branch b of its rescue block:
> 1. If b ends with a `Retry`: `{true} b {INV_C and pre_r}`
> 2. If b does not end in a `Retry`: `{true} b {INV_C}`
> where `INV_C` is the class invariant of C; `pre_r` is the precondition of routine r.

This semantics is problematic in practice because it means that an Eiffel routine must always have a rescue block that "puts everything right" (fulfills the normal precondition). But how does the routine know what went wrong and how to change the current state to fulfill the postcondition[14]?

Some programmers weaken the postcondition of retryable routines because one can barely state anything is true if the routine can either fail or succeed. Another solution is to write complex postconditions using a set of disjuncts with error-flag guarded expressions[15]. For example,

```
method_call_failed implies (F || G || H)
|| not method_call_failed implies (I || J || K)
```

This kind of specification is evident in the very few places where exceptions are handled in Eiffel code, and we speculate this is true because of the inherent complexity in such specifications.

Specifications in JML that use keywords like `exsures` and `exceptional_behavior` that are simply shorthand for these more complex expressions. E.g., an

---

[14] The new ECMA-367 standard no longer forces the restoration of the precondition.

[15] It should be noted that the new ECMA Eiffel standard changes this definition and no longer forces a restoration of the precondition.

`exsures` assertion specifies exactly what is true when a particular exception is thrown. Eiffel will benefit from such assertion expressions as well.

This semantics significantly complicates contracts and weakens their application. Neither case is surprising: either (in case 1) a rescue clause must fulfill the invariant and the precondition of the retried routine or, (in case 2) a retry does not happen so the routine has to leave the object in a legitimate state by fulfilling its invariant. What is surprising is that *nothing* is know about when or why the exception happened in the first place, since both preconditions are as weak as possible, and nothing *new* can be specified about the state of the objects when a failure takes place, since the postcondition is exactly the invariant.

JML, on the other hand, provides the ability to state a stronger postcondition in these exceptional cases, and this information is essential to verifying programs with exceptions. These observations provide evidence for a principle about exceptional postconditions.

Principle 6 (Abrupt Termination Principle). *The specification of object state when an assertion is raised, either via an exceptional postcondition or an exception predicate, is mandatory if programs are to be formally verified.*

The Java Modeling Language fulfills this principle admirably, while Eiffel fails in this regard.

4   Qualitative and Quantitative Comparisons

In the end, it is unclear how important exceptions are in the Eiffel world. This might be due to exception's perceived second-class nature in the Eiffel universe of "correct" software, as evidenced by their rare use (see below).

If exceptions in Eiffel are equivalent to unchecked exceptions in Java, and if library programmers for the two languages equally careful and capable of handling unexpected circumstances, then an analysis of exception usage in the two core code bases should yield comparable results.

The data in Table 1 is the result of such an analysis. The specific large Eiffel systems chosen for this analysis are four of the largest, highest-quality Open Source Eiffel systems available today.

In the case of the Gobo and SmartEiffel systems, all code, library and applications, was analyzed for this data. In Java 1.4.1, all source under the top-level package `java` was examined. The number of declared exceptions is determined by counting and classifying all calls to *EXCEPTIONS.raise* and *EXCEPTIONS.die*, in the case of Eiffel, and counting all descendants of `java.lang.Throwable`, in the case of Java. The number of raised exceptions is determined by a count of the number of calls to *EXCEPTIONS.raise* and *EXCEPTIONS.die*, in the case of Eiffel, and the number of `throw` statements, in the case of Java. The data on stack traces is determined by counting and analyzing all calls to routines `exception_name`, `tag_name`, `meaning`, and `developer_exception_name` of class `EXCEPTIONS`. All numbers are approximate and measured using the `wc` command.

Table 1. Use of Exceptions in Eiffel and Java

Library	Gobo 3.1	ePosix 1.0.0	ISE Eiffel 5.3	SmartEiffel 1.0	JDK 1.4.1
Number of direct/indirect mentions of EXCEPTIONS, or unchecked exceptions	18	3	17	0	525/15,000
Number of unchecked/checked exceptions declared	3/-	6/-	5/-	0/-	50/150
Number of raised unchecked/checked exceptions	66/-	87/-	13/-	0/-	3,000/2,650
Number of rescue or finally clauses	6	10	29	0	50
Number of retry commands	81	3	15	0	N/A
Number of times a stack trace is (a) checked or manipulated, or (b) printed or ignored	0/0	0/0	0/0	0/0	8/79
Total lines of code and documentation	250,000	25,000	372,000	115,000	421,000

To summarize the result of this analysis: in Java an unchecked exception is thrown for approximately every 140 lines of code, where in Eiffel one is used for every (approximately) 4,600 lines of code. This represents a difference of over thirty times in frequency. The above statistics clearly show that either or both (a) exceptions in Eiffel, either through technical issues or social pressure, have a second-class (or perhaps even ignored) status, or (b) the (built-in) existence of reasonable specification technologies inherently leads to fewer assertions being thrown. Given the preponderance of quality Eiffel software available, the latter point holds much more weight. This fact is especially highlighted in the complete lack of exception use and support in the GNU SmartEiffel system.

This data should be carefully considered by the language standardization committees for Eiffel and Java. It also provides evidence for potential avenues for language refinement, particularly with regards to the specification of abnormal behavior.

5   Exception Equivalency

Both languages have exceptions mechanisms that can be treated as equivalent. For example, a hierarchy is representable by integer or string values in a number of ways (e.g., De Bruijn indices or simple lexical encodings), so one can define an artificial type hierarchy for Eiffel exceptions if necessary.

Likewise, the minimal exception interface of Eiffel, embodied in the *EXCEPTIONS* class, is possible in Java. In fact, some Java developers advocate avoiding checked exceptions entirely, instead inheriting exclusively from RuntimeException [16]. Programming in this fashion pushes Java toward a more dynamic style, akin to programming in Objective-C.

We can find no evidence of the converse, that of Eiffel programmers using exceptions as flow control mechanisms. While Eiffel exceptions can be used in such a way, programmers simply do not use them in this way.

As any Java programmer knows, the volume of `try`/`catch` code in a typical Java application is sometimes larger than the comparable code necessary for explicit formal parameter and return value checking in other languages that do not have checked exceptions.

In fact, the general consensus among in-the-trenches Java programmers is that dealing with checked exceptions is nearly as unpleasant a task as writing documentation. Thus, many programmers report that they "resent" checked exceptions. This leads to an abundance of checked-but-ignored exceptions, as evidenced by the next to the last line of the table of the previous section.

Additionally, the presence of checked exceptions percolates through the system, as discussed in Section 2.1. As discussed by the designers of C# [17]:

> Examination of small programs leads to the conclusion that requiring exception specifications could both enhance developer productivity and enhance code quality, but experience with large software projects suggests a different result – decreased productivity and little or no increase in code quality.

This attitude guides the design of error handling in the .NET framework as well [18, see Section "Error Raising and Handling Guidelines"].

These issues lead to our last, and perhaps crucial principle.

Principle 7 (Checked Exception Principle). *Checked exceptions generally increase system fragility (because of signature refactoring), increase code size (due to explicit, localized, mandatory handling), and cause programmer angst (as evidenced by the number of empty or spiteful* `catch` *blocks in public Java code), so their inclusion in a language should be considered carefully.*

In the end, so long as an exception mechanism has a simple semantics, is consistently used, and provides a tool which programmers can understand, depend upon, and not resent, then they can be included in future languages.

Acknowledgments. This work was supported by the Netherlands Organization for Scientific Research (NWO). Thanks to the anonymous reviewers and Alexander Kogtenkov for their comments.

References

1. Sutcliffe, R.J., ed.: Modula-2 (Base Language). Number 10514-1:1996 in ISO/IEC Modula-2 Standardization. ISO/IEC (1999)
2. Wirth, N.: Programming in Modula-2. Springer–Verlag (1982)
3. Gosling, J., Joy, B., Steele, G., Bracha, G.: The Java Language Specification. third edn. Addison-Wesley Publishing Company (2005)
4. Meyer, B.: Object-Oriented Software Construction. second edn. Prentice-Hall, Inc. (1988)
5. Meyer, B.: Disciplined exceptions. Technical Report TR-EI-13/EX, Interactive Software Engineering (1988)

6. Bezault, E., Howard, M., Kogtenkov, A., Meyer, B., Stapf, E.: Eiffel analysis, design and programming language. Technical Report ECMA-367, ECMA International (2005)
7. Leavens, G.T., Poll, E., Clifton, C., Cheon, Y., Ruby, C., Cok, D., Kiniry, J.: JML Reference Manual. Department of Computer Science, Iowa State University, 226 Atanasoff Hall. Draft revision 1.94 edn. (2004)
8. Leavens, G.T., Baker, A.L., Ruby, C.: JML: A Notation for Detailed Design. In: Behavioral Specifications of Business and Systems. Kluwer Academic Publishing (1999) 175–188 Available via http://www.cs.iastate.edu/~leavens/JML.html.
9. Hester, K.: What is JavaSignals? (1999) See http://www.geeksville.com/kevinh/projects/javasignals/.
10. Meyer, B.: Eiffel the Language. third edn. Prentice-Hall, Inc. (2002)
11. Meyer, B.: Eiffel: The Language. Prentice-Hall, Inc. (1992)
12. Burdy, L., Cheon, Y., Cok, D., Ernst, M., Kiniry, J., Leavens, G.T., Leino, K., Poll, E.: An overview of JML tools and applications. International Journal on Software Tools for Technology Transfer (2005)
13. Jacobs, B., Poll, E.: A logic for the Java Modeling Language JML. In: Proceedings of Fundamental Approaches to Software Engineering (FASE). Volume 2029 of Lecture Notes in Computer Science., Springer–Verlag (2001) 284–299
14. Kiniry, J.R., Cok, D.R.: ESC/Java2: Uniting ESC/Java and JML: Progress and issues in building and using ESC/Java2 and a report on a case study involving the use of ESC/Java2 to verify portions of an Internet voting tally system. In: Construction and Analysis of Safe, Secure and Interoperable Smart Devices: International Workshop, CASSIS 2004. Volume 3362 of Lecture Notes in Computer Science., Springer–Verlag (2005)
15. Jacobs, B., Poll, E.: Java program verification at Nijmegen: Developments and perspective. In: International Symposium on Software Security (ISSS'2003). Volume 3233 of Lecture Notes in Computer Science., Springer–Verlag (2004) 134–153
16. Eckel, B.: Does Java need checked exceptions? (2003) See http://www.mindview.net/Etc/Discussions/CheckedExceptions, particularly the ensuing feedback on this issue.
17. Posted by Eric Gunnerson; original author unknown.: Why doesn't C# require exception specifications? (2000)
18. Microsoft Corporation: .NET framework general reference (2003) Documentation version 1.1.0.

Author Index

Lecture Notes in Computer Science

For information about Vols. 1–4031

please contact your bookseller or Springer